MW00774143

LOSS OF THE *SULTANA* AND REMINISCENCES OF SURVIVORS

To Charlie,

May you always remember the Sultana,

LOSS OF THE
SULTANA
AND
REMINISCENCES
OF SURVIVORS

Edited by Chester D. Berry

With a New Foreword by David Madden

Voices of the Civil War
Peter S. Carmichael, Series Editor

The University of Tennessee Press

Knoxville

The Voices of the Civil War series makes available a variety of primary source materials that illuminate issues on the battlefield, the homefront, and the western front, as well as other aspects of this historic era. The series contextualizes the personal accounts within the framework of the latest scholarship and expands established knowledge by offering new perspectives, new materials, and new voices.

Frontispiece: Detail from the *U.S.S. Sultana* memorial in Mt. Olive Cemetery in Knoxville, Tennessee. Photograph courtesy of David Madden.

This book is printed on acid-free paper.

Library of Congress Cataloging–in–Publication Data

Berry, Chester D.
Loss of the Sultana and reminiscences of survivors/edited by Chester D. Berry; with a new foreword by David Madden.— 1st ed.
    p. cm. — (Voices of the Civil War)
Originally published: Lansing, Mich. : D.D. Thorp, printer, 1892.

  ISBN 1-57233-372-3 (hardcover : alk. paper)

1. United States—History—Civil War, 1861–1865—Prisoners and prisons.
2. Prisoners of war—United States—Biography.
3. Prisoners of war—Confederate States of America—Biography.
4. United States—History—Civil War, 1861–1865—Personal narratives.
5. Sultana (Steamboat).
6. Steamboat disasters—Mississippi River—History—19th century.
7. Steam-boiler explosions—History—19th century.
I. Title.
II. Series: Voices of the Civil War Series.

E611.B53 2005
973.7'71—dc22   2004018615

CONTENTS

FOREWORD

On Loss and Forgetfulness
David Madden

THE story is deceptively simple: the worst maritime disaster in the history of this nation occurred on the Mississippi River about seven miles above Memphis at 2 a.m. on April 27, 1865, when the steamboat *Sultana*, carrying 2,222 known passengers and crew, exploded and sank.

Over 1,500 recently paroled Union prisoners of war were killed by the explosion or drowning; many of the 100 civilian men, women, and children perished. About 200 of the 586 who were saved died later of exposure or injuries in hospitals. The combined death toll was over 1,700.

They had boarded at Vicksburg, where the longest siege of the war had finally ended in Confederate surrender, ending the Vicksburg campaign, more important than any battle in the East, because control of the Mississippi River was crucial to the success of the Anaconda strategy that was to have ended the war. The boat exploded, and over 1,500 Union soldiers, homeward bound from Andersonville and Cahaba Confederate prisons, perished. All had suffered the terrors of battle, the loss of close comrades, physical and psychological wounds, the risky confinement of hospital, the humiliation of capture and surrender, escape and recapture, homesickness, boredom, the daily threat of death by starvation, disease, suicide,

robbery, injury, or death by raiding bands of fellow
prisoners. Unlike their comrades in Ohio and the
other Northern states, East Tennessee Union soldiers
had first suffered hostilities and atrocities from Rebel
neighbors and Confederate troops before enlisting.
Converging lines of force had brought them all to that
safe harbor, to that boat, that haven, with its defective boilers, its greedy or negligent officials, civilian
and military, to that explosion eighteen days after the
Confederacy had lost the war, twelve days after the
Union had lost its president to an assassin.

Even after six books on the subject, four in the last
decade, and many newspaper and magazine articles,
this unique disaster has failed to seize the imagination of American readers, even those whose fascina-
tion with the Civil War is apparently endless. The
first book was a compilation of the testimonials of 134
of approximately 500 military survivors, *Loss of the
Sultana and Reminiscences of Survivors.* In 1890,
when the survivors were old men, one lone individual
survivor, Private Chester Berry, now a reverend, set
about a humanistic venture, out of a compulsion to
remind his countrymen and to fix the disaster in their
consciousnesses, by exhorting survivors like himself
to send him their personal accounts—to help raise the
dead up into the great river of our national memory.
He published them about two years later in Lansing,
Michigan.

Personally, Chester Berry, like the Ancient Mar-
iner, wanted others to hear what he would hear over
and over again for the rest of his life: the screams of
one victim whom he watched step off toward what he
trusted to be safety from the burning, steeply slant-

ing hurricane deck to the burning wheelhouse, just as the wheelhouse broke up and mashed him, as in an iron vise, against the deck, where he flailed about and burned alive. That dreadful night, Berry, like many others, had abandoned pleading non-swimmers and kicked loose drowning men whose clutch would have pulled him down; survivor's guilt and what we understand today as post-traumatic stress syndrome may have compelled him to do the hard work of finding survivors almost three decades later, through research in military records, newspapers, but mostly by word of mouth at annual reunions, some responding when asked to tell the tale, others keeping as silent as the dead.

Some refused or neglected to respond, and some answered very briefly, even laconically. "About all I can say is that I got very wet and quite cold." A few, like E. J. Squire and C. G. Seabury, gave only basic military and civilian information, with no mention of the disaster. Brevity itself suggests post-traumatic stress syndrome. "I do not think it worth while," wrote A. Shoemaker, somewhat enigmatically, "to give my 'Sultana' experience." We might like to imagine that those who didn't respond wrote something but didn't send it, or wrote memoirs later, or wrote letters about it—that will be found someday. Hosea C. Aldrich announced he had published a book of his own privately, but mostly about Cahaba Prison life.

As far as I know, more voices spoke at Berry's urging of this major but astonishingly obscure episode than spoke of any other event of the war on any other occasion or prompting. Among other witness books of the war, compilations or single memoirs, this one is

probably unique. The 134 survivors who wrote
responses had first spoken aloud, on the deck, in the
water, later to friends and family; though some were
silent, their internal voices mingled with remembered
voices. We read here the words they wrote over a hundred years ago, but between the lines, the voices of
nearly 1,500 other soldiers and civilian men, women,
and children who died in fire and in water speak to
us. As you listen, imagine Chester Berry as having
called them forth. Think of his having quickened the
tongues of all those survivor voices as a memorial to
the 1,500 whose mouths were stopped with mud. The
voices of survivors activate the voices of the dead.

Because he wanted Americans to look upon a face
as they read each testimony, Berry provided drawings
of faces of many of them, from photographs; too few
actual photos are in his book. (More appear in later
books, as many as thirty-five in Jerry Potter's *The
Sultana Tragedy*.) "Let the names be given," we may
imagine him charging himself, "of all the victims and
the survivors." Painfully aware of his inability to
make his list fully accurate and complete, he wanted
the world to know the names of all those who died and
those who survived.

Berry wanted and wants the world to know the
cause of the explosion, so he reprints the military
court of inquiry proceedings which had been available
in the early volumes of the *Official Records of the War
of the Rebellion*, the first of which appeared in 1880.

But first Berry wants the world to see the photograph taken from the riverbank at Helena, Arkansas,
in the afternoon of the previous day. As you gaze upon
it, notice that almost to a man the freed prisoners

wanted to be in the picture, so that they who were
about to die almost sank the boat themselves. Thousands of men rushing toward the rail, toward photographer T. W. Bankes, must have stirred a sinking feeling in the pit of his stomach. We have no photograph
of the wreckage, despite the fact that for four months
it was visible, as men salvaged machinery and divers
went down searching for bodies. But let's be thankful
for the passion that went into the drawing that
emerged in *Harper's Weekly* over three weeks after
the catastrophe.

What will it take for this event, which caused such
vexation on the Father of Waters for a few hours, to
earn its rightful place as a symbolic expression,
embodying every adjective for sad loss, of the tragedy
of the Civil War for all Americans?

Snatched from behind plows in West Virginia,
Illinois, Michigan, Indiana, Ohio, Alabama, Iowa,
Nebraska, Pennsylvania, Kentucky, Missouri, Virginia, and out of the hills and mountains of Kentucky
and East Tennessee, they were thrown into the boredom of camps, the fatigue of marching, and the fire of
battle, captured, starved, teeth missing or loosened,
deprived of good water, weak, sick, in Belle Island,
Castle Thunder, Danville, Libby, Castle Morgan in
Cahaba, Alabama, recently standing waist deep in
water for five days from the rising of the Alabama River
in March, in Andersonville prison pen, hell on earth,
"den of death," digging tunnels out from abandoned
wells, wounded or killed stepping over the dead line,
mourning Lincoln, assassinated, swearing vengeance,
and then forced to march. George A. Clarkson: "a killing
march on the frozen ground, barefooted and nearly

naked," many died on the rough roads. Conveyed part
way by river and railroad, to parole at Big Black River,
a thousand miles from home for some.

Isaac Van Nuys: "The cruel war was over and their
cause triumphant." Elated, they turned their faces
homeward. A "jolly crowd" looked upon this boat,
the *Sultana*, and trusted it and its captain, J. Cass
Mason, to take them home at last. Dreamers, they
were driven on board like sheep, packed in like pigs.
Absalom N. Hatch: "I was . . . too weak to care what
became of me." Several complained the boat was overloaded, one of whom was Major William Fidler, Sixth
Kentucky Cavalry, commander of the paroled prisoners, whose death was only one of the hundreds of con-
firmations of the fear of catastrophe. Several noticed
repair of boilers going on, one of whom inspected the
four boilers himself and moved away from them to lie
down to sleep.

The traveling minstrel band, the Chicago Opera
Troupe—the number of its members not known—who
had gotten off at Memphis would remember their
good luck for the rest of their lives.

Several families were asleep in staterooms, going
north from Louisiana. But the soldiers, from bow to
stern, "we were huddled together," Isaac Van Nuys
remembered, "like sheep for the slaughter." Paroled
prisoners lay by the side of the ice box, by the rear
hatchway to the hold, on the roof right in front and
the rear of the pilot house, on the texas roof near the
steps, in front of two smokestacks, by the boilers and
furnace, by the bell; several slept on the boiler deck in
a coal bin, in the forecastle, near the jack-staff, cabin
deck in the curve of the stair banister by the state-

room door, on the main stairway, in lifeboats. "All the decks were completely covered when all of the boys laid down," almost like the old slave ships, "upon which the eye of an evil planet was resting," Murry S. Baker recalled. "I tried to get close to the boiler, but it was full there." Truman Smith still saw that "Every foot of her deck was covered with men who had fought starvation, vermin and filth." A light rain was falling, but the river was already at flood, over its banks.

Epenetus W. McIntosh, left by one steamer, had gotten on the *Sultana*. "I was sent whirling into the water." The explosion threw one boiler out of its bed. Ben G. Davis was "about to take a drink when the boiler exploded and the canteen flew out of my hand." P. L. Horn had not forgotten: "I was lost in the air . . . whirled in the air."

In the projectile breaking up of wood and metal, bones broke, noses were torn off. A spear of timber ran through William Lugenbeal's comrade's body, "killing him almost instantly." In the explosion, some died in the air, before they hit the water. The night was full of praying, laughing, lamenting, swearing, crying, and to W. G. Porter "some did not seem to know anything. Some uttering the most profane language and others commending their spirits to the Great Ruler of the Universe." William Madden and others heard the shrieks of women and children, praying, singing, singing "The Star Spangled Banner," pleading, groaning, screaming, and the awful brays of distress from mules and horses, in the "mad waters of the Mississippi." The cries of women, children, the roar of water, comrades calling to comrades, strangers to rank strangers, pleading for help,

shouting instructions for survival filled the night.
Fire, the size of the crown of a man's hat, started up
in the coal near the furnace. Madden saw a burning
hole open up, like Dante's Inferno.

A smokestack fell—broke the upper deck—and
Jospeh H. Mayes fell through to the lower deck.
Scores followed, falling from the upper to the lower
deck, into fire, burning under fallen pieces, suffocated
from the pressure and the smoke. The son of a steamboat captain—sound asleep on the larboard wheel-
house water-box on the hurricane deck—thought "if
she did not catch on fire we were all right . . . fire
burst out where the chimneys had stood. Swim or
burn." Albert Varnell: "My face was scalded so as to
put out my eye."

Nathan S. Williams: "Men were scalded and
burned, some with legs and arms blown off, and it
seemed as if some were coming out of the fire and
from under the boiler, and many of them jumping into
the river and drowning by squads." A. C. Brown: "The
chandelier in the ladies' room was burning brightly."
The crippled or maimed were trampled. Jesse Martin:
"When I came to I was down on my knees by a cow, as
though I had got there to milk her. If the cow had not
stopped me I guess I would have gone on into the
wheel house, and then I would not have survived to
write this." J. J. Zaizer was lying asleep close to the
bell. "The smoke-stack fell across it and split and one-
half of it fell over, thereby killing Sergeant Smith,
who laid by me." "We went to work to put out the fire
to keep the rest of the vessel from burning, sinking,
until the fire burned me off." Many were so scalded

when men reached to help, one man's "skin slipped off from the shoulders to the hands."

"The steam and ashes smothered us so we could scarcely breathe." James K. Brady: burning coals from the furnaces fell "all over me and my friend was trying to brush it off." Hundreds were driven off by fire into the river. A great many cried out in despair that they could not swim. Daniel Allen: "Wounded sufferers who piteously begged to be thrown overboard" were thrown into the turbid waters. At one moment near the bow, too many clustered together. Some turned and went aft, hoping to jump clear of masses of heads and flailing arms. "A large white horse fastened to the railing on the stern deck, blocked jumpers." Dead bodies clogged the *Sultana*'s broken side wheel. The surging of the crowd was like a "ram of men." Living bodies appeared crazy, dashing here and there and stopping in consternation. George F. Robinson: "The deck I had laid on was on top of me." Men were held fast under wreckage. "I had to let him burn to death."

William Lugenbeal thought of the pet alligator, chained in the wheel-house, and wanting its box, got it out of the closet and "ran the bayonet through him three times. . . . I was about as large as the alligator, seven and a half feet long."

Joshua S. Patterson: "Two elements of nature ready to devour us: fire and water—with tiger-like fury the fire rushed at us." Men above at the rails fell on men in the water. In the brilliant light of the fire, Ira B. Horner was "struggling and strangling." "I was not very well versed in the art of swimming." Naked except for diary and pictures of wife and children, Simeon D. Chelf "could not kick another lick." The flames drove the passengers off the boat, away from fallen smoke stacks, the stench of burning flesh. One man who had a fractured arm, three broken ribs, his face scalded, his body scarred and bruised all over, was frozen in the cold water to unconsciousness.

One man held to a chain at the bow of the boat. Another used hog chains to let himself down into the water; another slid down the stay rod, and swam against icy racing water at flood in the dark. "With his child in his arms, Harvey Annis jumped overboard. Ann Annis followed." Robert A. Trent: "I was knocked down on some mules that were under me."

Firelight made the screams in fire and water more ghoulish. By the glaring light of the burning wreck, the paroled prisoners used anything and everything and nothing to hold themselves up—bed slats, a plank that had been used in loading and unloading barrels, boxes, a coal box, empty candle box, beer keg—a dead mule blown off the boat saved George F. Robinson's life. Peter Roselot: "I got hold of some pieces of plank tied together with a pair of suspenders (doubtless the work of some poor fellow who had perished)." I. N. Sheaffer: "I floated down the river on a door to Memphis and was picked up by negro troops." Clinging to a trap door; to empty barrels; cracker, sugar, pork barrels; a horse trough; a jackstaff; a spar; flag staff; part of stairs, fighting over debris of the wreck, men struggled in the water. Some men threw window shutters into the river for the boys to latch on to. Some made rafts, others held on to bunk board, a bundle of clothes, a steerage pole, a trunk that contained ladies' dresses. James K.

Brady pried loose with his left foot a man's grip on his
right foot, "he taking my sock along with him, but he is
welcome to the sock; he sank out of sight and I saw him
no more." Men tackled up to the gin pole, the gangway
plank, stage plank, the wheel and the steering wheel,
rudder, decking, and used coils of rope to tie stuff
together. One man used a tent rope to tie slats, to cre-
ate "my frail bark," "my little craft." Logs drifting on
the flood, flood-wood, flotsam, roots of a big tree, a
sycamore log saved lives, but some for only a little
while longer. A woman pointed C. J. Lahue out to the
captain, saying there was "a little boy on a log, in the
brush, out on the river." Some went down in
whirlpools. They were prisoners again, under fallen
wreckage on the boat, in freezing river water. City
guards, not knowing, fired upon men who aspired to
become survivors.

Now more were dead than were alive.

Unable to see the stars for the rain, Private Wesley
Lee, clutching two boards in the river, saw the lights
of Memphis, like stars. Carried by the flood past
Memphis, some men were exposed to riflemen guarding Fort Pickering.

Did the drowning victims see their whole lives, or
just the prison ordeal, flash before their eyes? A
drowning man gripped A. C. Brown around the neck,
but Brown shook loose: "My whole life, from my childhood down to that terrible moment, passed before me
like a panorama with perfect distinctness." And did
the survivors then drown all the rest of their lives in
the memory? James A. Brady: "That sight I shall
never forget. I often see it in my sleep, and wake with
a start. . . . I can see it now as I pen these lines."

These paroled prisoners were in another battle, a battle against the hands that reached, grasped, pulled them down by the ankles, among horses and mules screaming, the sounds of fire. East Tennessee Unionist bridge burners who escaped prison to serve, and were then captured again, fought off others to hang on to burning planks. A. C. Brown: "the water seemed to be one solid mass of human beings struggling with the waves." Ben C. Davis: "You could almost walk over their heads." Alonzo A. Van Vlack: "I could place my hand upon their heads as they were going down." "While those in the water would catch hold of one another and go down in squads."

Perry S. Summerville: "Three of us from Brazil, Indiana, two were lost." Christian Ray: "They clustered together and went down." George F. Robinson: "There were three or four hundred, all in a solid mass, in the water and all trying to get on top." Commodore Smith saw them "sink to rise no more until the morning when all shall come forth." "It seemed as though we all wanted to get hold of each other." M. H. Sprinkle: "and the last I can recollect was they were trying to pry the dead man's grip loose from my leg." Water strangling, bodies falling on bodies, drowning men pulling down strong men, within minutes, "hundreds of souls were ushered into eternity": P. S. Atchley. Two hundred sank at once: "they went down in squads to rise no more," clinching each other, going down together. Some drowned with arms around a tree.

"A sea of heads." "I saw him no more," survivors often testified. The water was full of floating dead bodies. "Some to awake in the cold water and some in eternity": Samuel H. Raudebaugh. "Chilled to death," some suffered leg and stomach cramps, some spiraled down in whirlpool. Albert Norris: "My feet became entangled in my under-clothing." Wet socks dangled, got tangled, and were caught by drowning hands; some let go their shirts, some were rescued without a stitch on their backs.

Mistaking the swimmers for Confederate guerrillas raiding by water, trying to capture Fort Pickering, Negro guards fired upon them.

"Many were peppered by buffalo gnats and mosquitoes that ate them alive." Comrades kept buffalo gnats off a man whose skin had burned off.

The *Bostona II* on its maiden voyage was about to achieve the distinction of being the first rescue vessel to arrive. The ironclad USS *Essex* and the gunboat USS *Tyler*, explosives in their chambers, pulled victims of the explosion into their ready longboats and onto their clean decks. The *Lady Gay* and the *Pauline Carroll*, which had docked at Vicksburg nearby the *Sultana*, available for the transport of paroled prisoners, continued to steam upriver now without a single passenger.

P. L. Horn watched as a mule, "another floating waif of this disaster—swam along." Horses struggled in the water, wailing.

M. C. White: "A good many chilled to death" in the ice-cold water, in the water four hours, some eight. Joseph Bringman: "I feel the effects of that exposure and shaking up to this day."

Men watched the hull go by, the boat sink, leaving the survivors in "utter darkness." Hugh Kinser remembered that the "hull of the boat went down, its hot irons sending the hissing water and steam to an

immense height." "That crackling sound" of the
flames, wrote Wesley Lee, "you all remember so well."
Chester Berry heard his mother's voice, "God save my
boy's life."

George W. Stewart: The *Sultana* was to "carry us
homeward, but alas, hundreds passed on to the City
of Death, to await their loved ones."

"Horner, is that you?"

"Yes, what there is left of me."

"More dead than alive," many said.

Freed slaves reached out, pulled survivors out of
the dark flood.

"Then there was a nice large mule swam out to us
just after daylight." A snag in the river, a willow,
sycamore, cottonwood tree saved many; several spent
the night in the fork of a tree. At first, not a boat in
sight, but then boats, yawls, skiffs, picket boat, the
Jenny Lind, some men of the fire department, the
steamer *Silver Spray*, a gun boat, the *Pocahontas*,
among others, appeared. Blacks, Confederate soldiers,
and civilians worked hard to save lives. William
Bracken, colored infantry, officer of the picket guard on
Wolfe River, wanted to rescue but could find no boats.
Some were picked off the tops of trees. "I floated into
a tree top"—Ogilvie E. Hamblin—"at peep of day."
Thomas G. Love, a rescuer: "Our six messenger boys
took [a dinghy] and saved the only woman that was
saved."

Five Memphis hospitals were taking in 521 survivors, more than 200 of whom would never leave
alive. The surviving paroled prisoners were taken by
cabs and ambulances to Gayoso, Overton, Washington

hospitals. W. M. Carver survived. "But my father was among the missing ones." One of the twelve Sisters of Charity, volunteer laywomen, may have survived.

Horner was "marching along in the city with only one sock." The Soldier's Home (the name remembered variously as Soldier's Lodge or Rest or Retreat) took many in; many were attended to by Christian Association and Sanitary Commission and the Sisters of Charity, who gave them whiskey, red woolen shirts, and drawers.

They moved on to parole headquarters at Camp Chase, Ohio, and then they diverged, returning to New Sharon, Iowa; Mansfield, Ohio, a prison town; Rockford, Tennessee; Armourdale, Kansas; Medina, Michigan; Albion, Nebraska; Tulare, California; Bolivar, Missouri; Lafayette, Indiana; Buffalo, New York; Brown's Cross Road, Kentucky, and over a hundred other small towns, not only in the North, the Midwest, and the West, but the South, and to jobs, far more to farming than to the many other occupations: miner, carpenter, carriage trimmer, minister, "I am not doing much of anything," whip-stock maker, shoemaker, railway mail business, brick mason, undertaker, furniture dealer, merchant, engineer, mail carrier, "I am not able to work," stockbroker, plasterer, wood finisher, traveling salesman, medical practitioner, tile manufacturer, stock raiser, banker, telegraph operator, pattern maker, buggy dealer, blacksmith, shoe clerk, tailor, hardware merchant, fireman, real estate agent, "I am completely broken down." One survivor became a sheriff in Iowa: "Many men are now languishing within the walls of the penitentiary that surrendered only after a

desperate struggle and, overpowered by me, were compelled to give in."

Boarding the boat and as it moved up the Mississippi, many feared sabotage, and many of the survivors suspected it was the cause ("some raiding rebel
battery had thrown a shell into the boat"). P. L. Horn
believed that somebody placed a torpedo in the coal
bin; some blamed the carelessness of the captain or
the chief engineer; one man suggested that unloading
three hundred hogsheads of sugar tilted the boat,
which somehow caused one of the four boilers to
explode.

Several of those responsible perished, including
Captain Mason and some of his officers. Mason's body
was never found. Three men who might have prevented it all—Major General Napoleon Jackson
Tecumseh Dana, commander of the Department of
Mississippi; General Morgan L. Smith, commander of
the post and the District of Vicksburg; and Captain
George A. Williams, the commissary of musters at
Vicksburg—were bedded down miles away and thus
deaf to the explosion and the screams and blind to the
light of fires fitfully playing over the drowning and
struggling freed prisoners.

Prisoners of war on both sides, spending from one
to twenty months in captivity, fought some of the
most courageous battles—battles for sheer survival
on the personal level, victory on the public level as
those who were exchanged. Having survived prison,
most of the men on the *Sultana* perished, but almost
six hundred others who boarded the boat, many in
poor health or wounded, battled the dark waters of

the Mississippi above Memphis and survived. To survive war and prison and the ordeal of marching to the
boat and then to die pales the phrase "cruel irony."
But seeing the irony may make us feel absolved of
experiencing other, more complex thoughts and emotions. Irony is neat, transitory. Some died of irony. A
long list of ironies and paradoxes killed them. Ironic
that they perished in one of the most violent events of
the war in an area where there had been relatively less
war, eastern Arkansas and the vicinity of Memphis.
Our parallels and metaphors and similes fail them.

Let an account be given: 30,218 Union and 25,976
Confederate soldiers had died in prisons before the
end-of-war paroles had begun. The number of passengers known to be on board the *Sultana* was 2,222. The
three states with the highest toll were Ohio with 652,
Tennessee (mostly East Tennessee mountain area)
463, and Indiana 407, followed by Michigan 274, Kentucky 185, Virginia 18, Illinois, 2, and Missouri 1.
One thousand, seven hundred and fifty-three freed
prisoners perished in the explosion, in the river, in
hospitals. Among the civilians, in the Spikes family of
9, only 2 sons survived. Seven hundred eighty-three
were saved, but more than 200 of them died after rescue, so that more than 75 percent of the passengers
died, much higher than the *Titanic*. Seventeen hundred dead is more than twice those killed at First Bull
Run, in the Eastern Theater, and Wilson's Creek, in
the Western Theater, combined. Compare the loss
with 1,733 combat deaths in the Mexican-American
War, 385 in the Spanish-American, 148 in the Gulf
War, 35 in the Afghan war, and 145 in the Iraq war as

of the end of the major assaults. The loss of life was
over half that of our most recent war-related disaster—the World Trade Center explosions, about 2,862,
in the official exact count. The toll in the Civil War is
618,000. (Twice as many in that count died from disease as from combat. In the Mexican–American War,
disease killed ten times as many as combat.)

Newspaper coverage of the disaster throughout the
nation has been considered very slim. Why did this
horrendous story dwindle and vanish so soon? And
why did not the rest of the world take note of the kind
of event that usually shocks and arouses compassion?
Why was simple, brute curiosity not aroused? Why
were the basic *who, what, where, when, how, why*
questions not begging for answers, nationwide, world-
wide? The river, flooded over its banks that night, was
already shifting northeast. Until the Mighty Mississippi shrugged its shoulders and turned its course
away from the site where the *Sultana* sank, American
history washed over that pathetic event, already forgetting, the American people forgetting.

The flood receded, leaving bodies far downstream,
on eastern and western banks, for rats; levees, war-
wracked, let water fifty miles deep into woods, where
corpses came to rest on the ground for wild boar and
high in the trees, like Indian burial, for birds. Bodies were found as far downriver as Helena, where the
photograph had been taken, others even further
down, among the many never recovered and buried.
About one thousand bodies were never found.
Many were buried hurriedly on Hen Island, others in
Memphis ground. Unnumbered bodies remain in the

boat buried now under mud. For a while, when it was still visible as late as June, two months later, people saw bodies on the boat. So now the boat is thirty to thirty-five feet underground, in eighteen feet of water—a watery grave, covered with black dirt, good for growing soybeans. Our memory of those non-famous people on the non-famous *Sultana* is sunken.

As they who had slept in rain and mud and, in the last days of their lives, marched in mud and rain to reach a rescuing vessel remained forgotten prisoners of mud, monuments rose on ground all over the South and a lesser multitude throughout the North. The first meeting of Northern survivors was 1885 and the Southern survivors first met in 1889, in Knoxville, where they erected an impressive monument on July 4, 1916, in Mount Olive Cemetery. Mr. Keeble, one of the last survivors, who had not responded to Berry's plea, helped start that cemetery.

By contrast, in 1912, a Confederate monument was conceived, to be carved out of four-hundred-foot-high Stone Mountain, finally started in 1923, rose slowly, not finished until 1970, rising ninety feet, forty-five feet out of the stone—over twenty-five years, a visible remembrance, by contrast, to the sunken *Sultana*, but the statue is only of famous heroes, Generals Lee and Jackson, and the Confederate president, Jefferson Davis. Americans and foreigners can't miss seeing it below as our flights land at Atlanta, congested hub of the universe. As that monument rose ninety feet slowly, the recovered bodies of victims and the bodies of survivors dying one-by-one filled graves in Mansfield,

Ohio; Hillsdale, Michigan; and Memphis, among others, as the survivors were buried all over the country.

Over the years, survivors reading about the sinking of the *Maine*, the sinking of the *Titanic*, and the
sinking of the *Lusitania* must have remembered the
Sultana, their own struggle, with greater intensity. At
their meeting in 1912, in Toledo, the survivors must
have spoken of the sinking of the *Titanic*, April 14, in
which 1,523 perished. Both vessels carried about the
same total number of passengers. They must have
compared the huge, luxury *Titanic* with the *Sultana*,
big for a steam-wheeler, but small and crammed to
hellish overcrowding compared with the *Titanic*, less
crowded even than in below-decks compartments, full
of trapped Scots-Irish, like many *Sultana* victims,
among others. Only four *Sultana* survivors remained
in 1928; two in 1929; the last reunion was in 1930.
The last survivor from East Tennessee died March 4,
1931, in the month before the sixty-sixth anniversary
of the horror.

During the centennial of the Civil War, thirty years
after the last survivor died, and seventy years after
Berry's *Loss*, the second book about the *Sultana*
appeared out of the smog of forgetfulness, *Transport
to Disaster*, written by a descendant, James W.
Elliott, whose grandfather's voice speaks in *Loss* at
length, in a Victorian style even more literary than
his grandson's.

Two more decades of obscurity shrouded the victims until a Memphis lawyer, Jerry O. Potter, saw the
Sultana afire again—in a painting in a Memphis
bank. Then came Norman Shaw:

I first learned about the *Sultana* story in the
mid 1980s when I happened to come across a
1962 book entitled *Transport to Disaster* by
James W. Elliott while killing time, browsing
through the library of the McClung Collec-
tion in Knoxville, Tennessee. . . . A few years
later I was pleasantly surprised to discover
two individuals, Edgar (Si) Keeble and Mrs.
Malcolm Bloom (her father was John H.
Simpson), both in their nineties, who lived in
Knoxville [and] whose fathers, troopers in the
Third Tennessee Cavalry (U.S.), had survived
the *Sultana* explosion. It turned out that
their fathers had been close friends and, coin-
cidentally, were the last two members of the
survivors of the Third Tennessee from the
Knoxville area to pass away. . . . I decided this
little known Civil War event would make a
great topic for a presentation to the Knoxville
Civil War Roundtable. After researching and
reading what little there was on the subject
at that time, I gave a talk to the Roundtable
on March 10, 1987. . . . Shortly after . . . Fred
Brown, reporter for the *Knoxville News-
Sentinel*, wrote an article on the *Sultana*. . . .
Fred agreed to include . . . my request for all
readers who were descendants of soldiers on
the *Sultana* to meet at the *Sultana* monument in South Knoxville at 3:00 p.m. on
Sunday, April 26, 1987. . . . to my great delight about fifty people had gathered at the
monument at the designated time that same

Sunday! . . . This group of expectant descendants became the nucleus of the Association
of *Sultana* Descendants and Friends.

That first meeting took place at Mount Olive
Baptist Church, which owns Mount Olive Cemetery
where the *Sultana* monument had been erected. They
met in Knoxville for the next fourteen years, except
for two diversions, to Vicksburg and to Memphis. The
association is open to anyone interested in joining, as
descendant or friend. Even now, many of the victims'
and survivors' descendants are from Ohio and the
mountains of East Tennessee, where Rebels and
Unionists carried on a separate war. The 210 members come to Knoxville from many states. Their average age is around fifty-five, but only 133 came
to Vicksburg, where a historic plaque was dedicated in April 2002. Strangely, in 2003, only 82
showed up for the meeting in Memphis, where many
victims were buried in rows in the National Cemetery and where in Elmwood Cemetery near the
unmarked graves of three victims stands a fine monument, a salute to the "ill-fated" soldiers who perished in "terror and agony," placed by four citizens,
with the assistance of independent scholar Jerry
Potter.

Many descendants of victims and survivors have
never heard of *Loss* and of those who have, few have
ever seen the book, few have held a copy, fewer still
own one. Copies are extremely rare—only three are
now offered for sale on the Internet—and are very
expensive, ironically, at $400 to $425, although I

found the copy used for the present edition selling for $300. Now, with this publication, all the descendents and their fellow American citizens may open a copy and read.

One would expect a book on this disaster to appeal not only to people who have an ongoing interest in the Civil War but also to those who harbor an ongoing interest in disasters.

Berry's first sentence refers to the national character trait that responds only to major events. "The average American is astonished at nothing he sees or hears. . . . The idea that the most appalling marine disaster that ever occurred in the history of the world should pass by unnoticed is strange, . . . and the majority of the American people today do not know that there ever was such a vessel as the *Sultana*." What event could be more major than this one?

The usual explanation for public apathy then and now is that Lincoln's assassination happened only a week before and his train was crossing the country toward Illinois when the *Sultana* went down, that General Lee had surrendered, John Wilkes Booth had been shot, President Davis was on the run, and that, above all, people wanted now to forget violence, destruction, and death. Even so, distraction and a desire to forget are too easy, too shallow an explanation.

Perhaps today we are too sated on movies depicting disasters of every type, on television news reports of disasters, the ultimate shocks being the World Trade Center and the tsunami. Those disasters sparked international shock, in contrast to the lack of national shock when the *Sultana* exploded. We saw the twin towers disaster happen as it happened, each stage, and we watched stages of re-sponse, and reports on stages of response, and actual heroes emerged—fire-fighters, police, citizens, and stories and pictures of the dead, testimonials on TV of the survivors. Only survivors saw the *Sultana* disaster unfold, and Berry's book sold mostly to survivors.

Finally, human nature is limited; people can't imagine the loss of that many lives, as with the six million Jews, fifty years after *Loss* appeared. Our humanity needs to develop that ability—myriad-mindedness, which enables our minds to apprehend several aspects of an event simultaneously—and a compassionate imagination, a sort of tower-like omniscience by which we may comprehend this and other aspects of history. Myriadmindedness is a goal for future generations to cultivate—inner space trav-el, as we have cultivated and will continue to culti-vate outer space travel.

Through movie camera lenses, we have often visited the still-sunken luxury liner *Titanic*, and we have seen the risen Confederate submarine *Hunley* and recovered the remains of eight men. The *Monitor* became famous not because sixteen men perished when it sank in a storm, but because it was a new type of warship initiat-ing a new type of naval warfare. It is being raised. But we have not even seriously contemplated raising the *Sultana* and its passengers in the worst maritime dis-aster in American history. We make heroes today, as we see in the Iraq war, not of soldiers who die hero-ically, but of solitary prisoners who are rescued, such as

Jessica Lynch, not plausibly the most heroic soldier but implausibly the most celebrated; not such men as these freed prisoners who perished or survived the *Sultana* debacle.

Recognition will demand something that transcends the four excellent factual accounts of this preventable accident that appeared in the final decade of the last century. To turn to William O. Bryant's *Cahaba Prison and the Sultana Disaster* (1990), Jerry O. Potter's *The Sultana Tragedy: America's Greatest Maritime Disaster* (1992), and Gene Eric Salecker's *Disaster on the Mississippi* (1996) before reading Chester Berry's finger-singeing, heart-stirring assemblage of voices is very much second best. I can testify from personal struggle that no one can fault those four independent scholars who have attempted to so seize our hearts as to activate our imaginations. For twenty years, I have tried in vain, emotionally, imaginatively, and intellectually, to comprehend this simple event. Those nonprofessional historians, however, with Chester Berry, and with the living descendants of victims and survivors, but with ostensibly less compelling reason, must be counted among the few who not only know about the shameful disaster but, out of a compassionate historical imagination, have devoted many years of research to an effort to move Americans to listen to those forsaken voices. Elliott dedicated his book "to the mem-ory of my father, Green Smith Elliott, who first told me the story."

Although their ancestors were not on the *Sultana*, Potter and Salecker feel that "memory" is the note that needs to be struck all across the landscape of the American consciousness. Salecker worked on his book from 1978 to 1996, eighteen years; he is a Civil War collector, re-enactor, a campus policeman at North-eastern Illinois University in Chicago, simultaneously at work as an independent scholar. A visit to *Book Review Digest* reveals high critical praise for Elliott's book except for the outright mean-spiritedness of Lucius Beebe ("Let the names be given!" as Fighting Parson Brownlow used to say) in the San Francisco *Chronicle* directed toward the survivors themselves: "life histories of in-dividuals of small consequence have been expanded be-yond their possible deserving." No reviews are listed in *Book Review Digest* for the books by Bryant, Potter, and Salecker. Potter says his book was re-viewed with praise but general coverage was not as much as he had expected, given the star-tling uniqueness of his subject. Salecker says his book, inspired by Elliott's, got good coverage in Civil War venues and in some town papers, but not in his hometown Chicago. It has sold 2,250 copies, about 500 of which he has sold himself as he gives talks around the country. Retired, he intends now to teach American history to seventh- and eighth-graders.

Let the names of the women, nurses, the crew, the businessmen, the children be given. Berry depended only upon names given in the Memphis paper; with Potter's help, Salecker added many names, corrected spellings and regiments. These lists show the authors' desire to rescue all the names from oblivion. And their fates. "Lost. Died the next day. Probably lost. Died later on." But of the civilians, Berry includes only—but first—the voice of the engineer. The names are given in alphabetical order in Potter so that descendants may more readily look for ancestors. Because he confined his effort to soliciting the testimonials of military survivors, Berry does not tell what happened to the civilians, the women and the children, but Salecker provides this information.

Prompted by writing the preceding sentence, I checked the list of soldiers again twenty-five years after I first heard about the disaster, and I am reminded now that names from five sides of my family are listed: Carr, McArty, Merritt, Willis—all perished—and Madden, who was trapped for a while under a red hot piece of the exploded boiler, and who survived to testify for Berry. "No tongue can tell and pen is powerless to portray the agony of those moments." And only today did I realize that the William P. Madden my son unearthed in his tireless genealogical delving—my great great grandfather or uncle—I can't yet be certain—is the same William P. Madden who responded to Berry's plea with one of the longest testimonies. Elliott and Salecker chose to quote him at length, although Potter did not. All came from Ohio, however, not Unionist East Tennessee, where I was born and raised. My ignorance gives me no bliss.

Not even the fact that the explosion on the grossly overloaded steamwheeler is yet another American scandal involving greed (such as we recently suffered with Enron and WorldCom), irresponsibility (as with the Watergate scandal of the 1970s), and the conniving of civilians with military personnel can arouse by parallel our interest or even appeal to the public's insatiable hunger for such sordid conspiracies. While the immediate cause was the defective boiler, other causes include greed, neglect—and I add contingencies, fate, or bad luck—possibly sabotage, as some have argued recently, a notion rejected by Salecker and Potter in favor of greed and negligence. Greed makes a better story, symbolic of more aspects of the war, profiteering, left and right, but survivors did tell Berry of their apprehensions about espionage or guerrilla action. Negligence shifted to our national memory.

Loading on unwelcome irony, Andersonville prison, in novels, plays, movies, and historical works, including eyewitness diaries and memoirs, has consistently commanded and held the public's interest, although Cahaba is relatively obscure. And yet not even that irony serves to take us by the arm and hold us still long enough for us to grasp the impact of the *Sultana* catastrophe. Among the flood of ironies is this one: many Union survivors of Andersonville perished after all, or survived yet another descent into hell that spring night, as the assassinated president's funeral train was crossing the blood-weary land and Davis's defeated Confederates straggled home on muddy roads or fled trans-Mississippi or to South America.

It should be noted that the History Channel aired a documentary on the *Sultana* disaster in 1996 and four other documentaries are in the works.

Missing so far is a conceptual imagination that places the Sultana disaster in a "tragic" light. Only the light of an extraordinary imagination can unvex and raise this unique and complexly meaningful event from the ever-shifting muddy bottom of the Father of Waters.

If one ascribes public indifference and forgetfulness to the fickleness of the "vulgar herd" mentality, one may expect Civil War historians to explore this lesser known but important event and perhaps consider offering the *Sultana* as a major symbolic expression of the reality and meaning of the war. Its symbolic scope includes North and South, East and West.

General histories of the Civil War seldom mention the *Sultana*. Shelby Foote devotes a paragraph. One might hope that historians will awaken the interest of potential readers, many of whom are not primarily interested in the Civil War itself. As late as 1986, Foote was impressed enough to call it "the greatest marine disaster of all time" (*The Civil War: A Narrative* 3: 1026–27).

Meanwhile freelance historians and independent scholars have, as mentioned earlier, taken us by the arm. James W. Elliott was a freelance journalist, published by Holt, Rinehart and Winston, publisher of many of the best books on the war; his book, the first on the disaster and the first actual historical study, came out early in the Centennial, the events and books of which focused on battles. The most popular Civil War historians of that era—Burke Davis, Virgil Carrington, and Bruce Catton—are quoted on the jacket declaring the importance of the *Sultana*. "The sinking of the *Sultana* was one of the truly horrifying tragedies of the Civil War, and for some odd reason," Catton wrote, "it has never been properly described in the kind of detail which makes it understandable."

Between the Centennial and Potter's book stretched a wasteland of inattention. As of 1989, two articles had appeared in *Civil War Times Illustrated.* Twenty-eight years after Elliott's book, in 1990, came the work of a Middle Tennessean, an independent historian, William O. Bryant. In *Cahaba Prison and the* Sultana *Disaster*, the focus is upon prison. Another Tennessean, Jerry O. Potter, not an historian but a Memphis lawyer, is an example of how one would hope Americans would keep the memory alive. Even as a southerner, an enthusiast who is not even a descendant of a *Sultana* passenger, he seems more haunted than northern descendants. Gene Eric Salecker's book appeared from Naval Institute Press four years after Pelican, a regional press, published Potter's. Not an historian, but a campus policeman, Salecker published the definitive book on those who perished. So it was non-academic, non-professional historians who, in the decade of the 1990s, gave impetus to the strongest upsurge of interest. I reviewed Salecker's book in *BookPage*, which reaches almost a million readers in bookstores and libraries, and again in *Civil War Book Review*, the archive of which is online. Even so, his book did not seize and keep a grip on national attention. Why? It's a mystery.

But the greatest potential to arouse readers' emotions is latent in Berry's own words, in the investigation testimony concerning the greed of the owners and some of the officers, and in the account of Captain Speed's court-martial on charges of criminal negligence (he was acquitted), reported in the official records, which Berry includes in his book, and, above all, the great confluence of testimonials, long and short, in *Losses*. Even so, like Americans in 1865, both the survivors and the readers of Berry's book suffer a failure of imagination and of intellect when

trying to express adequately the reality and implications of this immediately postwar horror. But it is a
challenge deserving our effort.

In the midst of this meditation, I picked up on sale
*The Sea Shall Embrace Them: The Tragic Story of the
Steamship Arctic* that David W. Shaw felt compelled
to write because the four hundred passengers who
drowned have been forgotten. A reviewer called "the
Arctic the *Titanic* of her time"—a decade earlier than
the *Sultana* disaster, seven decades before the
Titanic—and claimed that it "like the *Titanic* holds a
special place in maritime history." Shaw, who was
inspired by Walter Lord's book about the *Titanic*, *A
Night to Remember*, does not mention the *Sultana*,
because, I would have to assume, like most people, he
has never heard of it. What has been called the
Mississippi's *Titanic* got rapidly swallowed up in a
Mississippi of Forgetfulness that has remained "over
its banks."

When one considers the current attention being
paid to the loss of eight men in the *Hunley* submarine, February 17, 1864, over a year before the sinking of the *Sultana*, it is all the more astonishing that
the worst maritime disaster in the history of the
United States has failed to seize the imagination of
Ameri-can readers, even those endlessly fascinated
by the Civil War. Recently brought up out of the mud
of Charleston Harbor—because of its status as a rev-
olutionary craft, not mainly because of a desire to
memorialize the men— the *Hunley* has taken root in
the consciousnesses of Americans. But then the loss
in a storm off Cape Hatteras, December 31, 1862, of

the USS *Monitor*, along with its sixteen men, ten months after a stand-off battle with the CSA *Virginia*, was probably not heavy on the consciousnesses of the 1,900 who were soon to die, during prison, or as they boarded the *Sultana*, or as survivors at reunions. We can, though, imagine the shifting consciousness among them and others as contexts shifted over time. If they and we remember the sinking of the USS *Maine* on January 25, 1898, with a loss of 254 seamen in Havana Harbor during the Spanish-American War today, it is mainly because of that wartime slogan "Remember the *Maine*." Some may also remember the British passenger liner RMS *Lusitania*, which sank on Friday, May 7, 1915, after being hit by a German submarine torpedo, taking about 1,200 lives.

"There is sorrow on the sea, it cannot be quiet," says Jeremiah 49:23. To drown is to drown, but drowning out at sea, with the *Titanic*'s music on deck and its lights bright even as it sank, contrasts with drowning on a river by firelight or in darkness amidst screams and prayers only a hundred feet or so from safe shore. Many of those who view *Titanic*, the blockbuster motion picture, the latest of several that bring the sinking of the ocean liner back to life, may leave the movie theater believing that the April 15, 1912, sinking of the great British liner, with the loss of 1,523 men, women, and children, was history's greatest maritime disaster.

One way to deflect our unmindful and thus remorseless guilt over our national forgetfulness is to relegate the *Sultana* to the illimitable ocean of shipwreck and drowning statistics, to reduce its magnitude by comparisons. We remember the *Maine* and the *Lusitania*, but who remembers the ill-fated souls who went down with five thousand ships in Northeastern America between 1606 and 1956?

Turning to foreign shores and greater disasters, the toll accessible by the key words "All Time Maritime Disasters" entered in the Google search engine, who can even begin to imagine such losses as one finds there? The enormity of all recorded disasters throughout history is diminished when compared with the sinkings of refugee ships—unquestionably among the great atrocities of the Second World War. The toll of the forgotten overwhelms the most compassionate imagination.

The pathos is magnified when we realize that, even when the vessel is remembered or rediscovered, even resurrected, from the bottom of the sea or a river, as was the ironclad USS *Cairo* from the Mississippi (from 1954 to 1964), it is not the passengers (there were no losses on the *Cairo*) but some uniqueness or salient historical significance that captures imagination and interest.

———⟫◆⟪———

In the spring of the new millennium, I was invited by the Association of *Sultana* Descendants and Friends to give a dramatic reading of the chapter in my Civil War novel *Sharpshooter* devoted to the sinking of the *Sultana*. That gathering of about one hundred at their thirteenth annual reunion at the Mount Olive Baptist Church just outside my hometown, Knoxville,

will forever remember what most Americans a few
days after the end of the Civil War forgot as quickly
as they could.

Growing up in the partly Unionist East Tennessee
mountains, I heard many stories but never that one.
I don't remember exactly when and where and why I
first heard about the *Sultana*, but I think it was about
1979, when I began research for *Sharpshooter*, and
that story has haunted me ever since. I may someday
write a separate novel about it, but I am glad to know
that journalist Fred Brown of Knoxville is hard at
work on one. I have struggled in vain for over twenty
years to comprehend this brief event, emotionally,
imaginatively, and intellectually, at a depth and with
a complexity commensurate with its importance. To
write *Sharpshooter*, I was moved first to tell the well-
documented, famous stories of Parson Brownlow,
rhetorically violent Unionist, later Reconstruction
governor of Tennessee, and of Dr. James G. Ramsey,
prominent Rebel and first East Tennessee historian.
But the obscure sharpshooter at Bleak House who
may have shot General William Price Sanders, took
over the novel, ignited my imagination; I imagined
that he imagined and empathized with other people,
so that he did what Berry hoped all Americans would
do. But when he is still only nineteen, returning home
to East Tennessee from a sojourn in the West after the
war, he feels that he and others who were in the war
are like the drowned freed prisoners—missing.

As a Rebel soldier, he was on the boat in disguise.
"Crossing the Mississippi River on the ferry, I had to
hold myself in to keep from falling into a panic, feeling
it all keenly again, that night when we all exploded

off the *Sultana*, maybe my kin, too, that night in the river when most of us drowned" (59).

Over the decades following, the explosion, sinking, and losses of the *Sultana* become for the sharpshooter the most painfully apt symbolic expression of the pathos of war, which all Americans missed in various ways then and have missed ever since. "I am always in the guard tower [at Andersonville Prison]. East Tennessee, South [all federals] and Ohio, North: union in death. I see all of them clearly and, suddenly, my father in a Yankee prison, Cahaba probably, even Andersonville possibly, who survived and was going home with four hundred other East Tennesseans on the *Sultana*, and I see him, and his countrymen, and all those at Andersonville, together, drown now below me. And Grandfather Mississippi Death has claimed [in 1930] most *Sultana* survivors" (139).

But I want the reader to realize at last that in his obsessed attempts to remember (imaginatively, emotionally, and intellectually) the aged sharpshooter (no older, however, than I am at seventy-one) is to some degree not missing, and that because of his personal, prolonged struggle to remember, all the other soldiers and civilians of that era are, in some sense, no longer missing. But in real life, I feel that all *Sultana* victims and survivors and descendants (now they too are dying out), and even friends alike are still missing.

I fervently recommended reprinting *Loss of the Sultana* because of a deep and abiding faith that readers will absorb into their consciousnesses the facts of the catastrophe meshed with the emotion-stirring testimony of the survivors. Oh, we all may admit the obligation. But that is as abstract as the

death and survival count. As with the incomprehen-
sible six million exterminated Jews of our own era, we
must count the dead one at a time, if we are to
retrieve and remember. We must have faith that readers of this edition of Chester Berry's battle against
forgetfulness will, in empathy and sorrow, feel the
sting of irony but go on to accept the need, the actual
desire, to imagine that night in all its strangling
humanity, and will then exert the will to retrieve and
remember.

Meanwhile, the darkness of that night still hangs,
almost 150 years deepening, over the smoke, the
screams, and the prayers of the victims and the compassionate cries of the rescuers, some of them Confederate soldiers along the bank who were also
returning home. Readers may strive to imagine the
vast, complicated canvas of folly and agony, and then
perhaps to ponder the web of implications, absorb
into their own consciousnesses the testimony of the
survivors. Hopes for a national day of mourning being
delusional, even during April, which is Civil War History Month, perhaps national recognition at least
may come sometime during the Sesquicentennial
meditation, 2011 through 2015.

Read Berry's testimonial first, then some of those
who wrote the longer narratives: Otto Bardon,
Simeon D. Chelf, J. Walter Elliott, Nathaniel
Foglesong, W. P. Madden, Samuel H. Raudebaugh,
Commodore Smith, Perry S. Summerville, Nathan S.
Williams. There is no reason to listen to these voices
in the order given, for it is merely alphabetical. Open
anywhere, gaze into the eyes of the survivor you hap-

pen upon. Read aloud, perhaps with someone who will take turns with you, listening. The repetitions from one voice to another effectively impress the facets of the event upon our minds, making a demand upon us to imagine similar torments and thoughts happening simultaneously.

Now that this book is within reach, Americans may begin to respond emotionally to the horrific sights, the screams, the smell of burning wood and flesh, the bitter taste of the flooded Mississippi, and the touch of the flailing arms of the perishing soldiers—and the civilian men, women, and children, who even Berry neglected to remember. This reissue of *Loss of the* Sultana *and Reminiscences of Survivors* becomes then our memorial to both the dead of that night and to the survivors, who are themselves now seven decades dead. Listening to their voices, we may raise *all* the dead of our Civil War from the bottom of the Father of Waters up into our streams of consciousness, tributaries to the national sea of memory.

The voices are still speaking.
They won't shut up.
We need to know that they will never stop.
Few people listened and remembered then.
  We might listen now.
Most of them are still down there.
Let us raise them up.
All 1,700—all 618,000 soldiers, all forgotten
  30,000 civilians.

LOSS OF THE *SULTANA*

AND

REMINISCENCES

OF

SURVIVORS

LOSS OF THE SULTANA

AND

REMINISCENCES

OF

SURVIVORS.

HISTORY OF A DISASTER WHERE OVER ONE THOUSAND FIVE
HUNDRED HUMAN BEINGS WERE LOST, MOST OF THEM
BEING EXCHANGED PRISONERS OF WAR ON
THEIR WAY HOME AFTER PRIVATION AND
SUFFERING FROM ONE TO TWENTY-
THREE MONTHS IN CAHABA
AND ANDERSONVILLE
PRISONS.

By REV. CHESTER D. BERRY.

INTRODUCTION.

THE average American is astonished at nothing he sees or hears. He looks for large things. Things ordinary are too tame. This, and the exciting events of April, 1865, perhaps account for the fact that the loss of the steamer " Sultana " and over 1,700 passengers, mostly exchanged prisoners of war, finds no place in American history. The idea that the most appalling marine disaster that ever occurred in the history of the world should pass by unnoticed is strange, but still such is the fact, and the majority of the American people today do not know that there ever was such a vessel as the "Sultana." And many of those who do recollect something about the occurrence cannot tell whether it occurred in the Mississippi river, the gulf of Mexico, or the Atlantic ocean; and the purpose of setting them right and instructing others, thus holding in the memory of the present generation and those yet to be the sufferings of the defenders of our country, is the object of this sketch.

The steamer "Sultana" was built at Cincinnati, Ohio, January, 1863, and was registered, as near as I can learn, at 1,719 tons. She was a regular St. Louis and New Orleans packet, and left the latter port on her fatal trip April 21, 1865, arriving at Vicksburg, Miss., with about two hundred passengers and crew on board. She remained here little more than one day; among other things repairing one of her boilers, at the same time receiving on board 1,965 federal soldiers and 35 officers just released from the rebel prisons at Cahaba, Ala., Macon and Andersonville, Ga., and belonging to the States of Ohio, Indiana, Michigan, Tennessee, Kentucky, and West Virginia. Besides these there were two companies of infantry under arms, making a grand total of 2,300 souls on board, besides a number of mules and horses, and over one hundred hogsheads of sugar, the latter being in the hold of the boat and serving as ballast. At Helena, Ark., by some unaccountable means a photograph of the boat with her mass of living freight was taken, a copy of which is in possession of L. G. Morgan of Findlay, Ohio, one of the survivors today.

Leaving Helena the boat arrived at Memphis, Tenn., about seven o'clock, P. M., of the 26th of April. Here the sugar was unloaded, many of the exchanged prisoners helping the crew, thus making a little money for themselves. Sometime in the evening, probably well towards midnight, the boat steamed across the river to the coal bins or barges and, after taking on her supply of coal, started on, up the river, for Cairo, Ill. All was quiet and peaceful, many of the soldiers, no doubt, after their long, unwilling fast in southern prisons, were dreaming of home and the good things in store for them there, but alas! those beautiful visions were dissipated by a terrific explosion, for, about two o'clock in the morning of the 27th, as the boat was passing through a group of islands known as the "Old Hen and Chickens," and while about opposite of Tagleman's Landing had burst one of her boilers and almost

immediately caught fire, for the fragments of the
boiler had cut the cabin and the hurricane deck in
two and the splintered pieces had fallen, many of
them, back upon the burning coal fires that were now
left exposed. The light, dry wood of the cabins burned
like tinder and it was but a short time ere the boat
was wrapped in flames, burning to the water's edge
and sinking. Hundreds were forced into the water
and drowned in huge squads, those who could swim
being unable to get away from those who could not and
consequently perishing with them. One thing favorable for the men was the fact that there was a little
wind, hence the bow of the boat, having no cabin
above it, would face the wind until the cabin was
burned off from the stern, then the boat gradually
swung around, the unburned part of the boat above
the water acting as a sail while that below acted as a
rudder, and finally drove the men into the water. A
part of the crowd was driven at a time, thus giving
many of those who could swim or had secured fragments of the wreck an opportunity to escape.

But there was one thing that was unfavorable, and
that was the pitchy darkness of the night. It was
raining a little, or had been, and but occasional
glimpses of timber were all that could be seen, even
when the flames were the brightest, consequently the
men did not know what direction to take, and one
man, especially, swam up stream. Another thing that
added greatly to the loss of life is the fact that the
river at this place is three miles wide, and at the time
of the accident it was very high and had overflown its
banks, and many, doubtless, perished after they reached

the timber while trying to get through the woods back to the bluffs, the flats being deeply under water. Others died from exposure in the icy-cold water after they had reached the timber, but were unable to climb a tree or crawl upon a log and thus get out of the water.

Among the passengers on board were twelve ladies, most of them belonging to the Christian commission, an association akin to that of the sanitary commission of the Army of the Potomac. One of these ladies, with more than ordinary courage, when the flames at last drove all the men from the boat, seeing them fighting like demons in the water in the mad endeavor to save their lives, actually destroying each other and themselves by their wild actions, talked to them, urging them to be men, and finally succeeded in getting them quieted down, clinging to the ropes and chains that hung over the bow of the boat. The flames now began to lap around her with their fiery tongues. The men pleaded and urged her to jump into the water and thus save herself, but she refused, saying: "I might lose my presence of mind and be the means of the death of some of you." And so, rather than run the risk of becoming the cause of the death of a single person, she folded her arms quietly over her bosom and burned, a voluntary martyr to the men she had so lately quieted.

In the official list the names seem to have been taken without reference to rank or State they were from; sometimes, apparently, a squad from one company or regiment would be taken together, but often it was the case that they were all mixed up. In other cases many were left out; for instance, a sergeant came to me and asked to see the official list. It was shown him. "Why," said he, "there are but ten of my company reported here and I know there were eighteen of us." This has been true in quite a number of cases.

On December 30, 1885, at a convention called in Fostoria, Ohio, there was a committee appointed, consisting of A. C. Brown, P. L. Horn, Wm. Fies, A. W. King, and G. N. Clinger, to prepare a suitable memorial and present the same to Congress, praying for a pension for each of the survivors of the lost "Sultana."

The Burning of the Sultana.

By Wm. H. Norton, Company C, 115th Ohio.

Midnight's dreary hour has past,
The mists of night are falling fast,
Sultana sounds her farewell blast,
    And braves the mighty stream ;
The swollen river's banks o'erflow,
The leaden clouds are hanging low
And veil the stars' bright silver glow,
    And darkness reigns supreme.

Her engine fires now brighter burn,
Her mammoth wheels now faster turn,
Her dipping paddles lightly spurn
    The river's foaming crest ;
And drowsy Memphis, lost to sight,
Now fainter shows her beacon light,
As Sultana steams in the dead of night,
    And the Union soldiers rest.

The sleeping soldiers dream of home,
To them the long-sought day had come,
No more in prison pens to moan,
    Or guarded by the gray ;
At last the changing fates of war
Had swung their prison " gates ajar,"
And " laurel wreaths " from the North afar
    Await their crowning day.

For Peace has raised her magic hand,
The Stars and Stripes wave o'er the land,
The conquered foemen now disband,
    " As melts the morning dew ;"
And mothers wear their wonted smile,
And aged sires the hours beguile,
And plighted love awaits the while
    The coming of the blue.

On sails the steamer through the gloom,
On sleep the soldiers to their doom,
And death's dark angel—oh ! so soon—
    Calls loud the muster-roll.

A—burst—a—crash—and—timbers fly,
And—flame—and—steam—leap to the sky,
And—men—awakened—but—to die—
  Commend to God their souls.

Out from the flame's encircling fold,
Like a mighty rush of warriors bold,
They leap to the river dark and cold,
  And search for the hidden shore.
In the cabins,—and—-pinioned—there,
Amid—the—smoke—and—fire—and—glare,
The—awful—wail—of—death's—despair
  Is heard above the roar.

Out on the river's rolling tide,
Out from the steamer's burning side,
Out where the circle is growing wide,
  They battle with the waves.
And drowning men each other clasp,
And writhing in death's closing grasp
They struggle bravely, but at last
  Sink to watery graves.

Oh! for the star's bright silver light!
Oh! for a moon to dispel the night!
Oh! for the hand that should guide aright
  The way to the distant land!
Clinging to driftwood and floating down,
Caught in the eddies and whirling around,
Washed to the flooded banks are found
  The survivors of that band.

Destruction of the Steamer "Sultana" in the Mississippi River, near Memphis, Tenn., April 27, 1865.

From the records of this Department it would appear that the steamer "Sultana" left Vicksburg, Miss., on April 24, 1865, and was destroyed on the Mississippi river, near Memphis, Tenn., on April 27, 1865.

A court of inquiry was thereupon ordered by Major General C. C. Washburne, commanding district of West Tennessee, to investigate the facts and circumstances of the burning of the "Sultana."

On April 30, 1865, the Secretary of War instructed Brevet Brigadier General Hoffman, commissary-general of prisoners, to inquire into the circumstances of the destruction of the steamer referred to, which officer, on May 19, 1865, made the following report :

"OFFICE OF THE COMMISSARY-GENERAL OF PRISONERS,
WASHINGTON, D. C., May 19, 1865.

"*Hon. E. M. Stanton, Secretary of War, Washington, D. C.:*

"SIR—Pursuant to your instructions of the 30th ult., I proceeded direct to Memphis, Tenn., and Vicksburg, Miss., to inquire into the circumstances of the destruction of the steamer 'Sultana' in the Mississippi river, near Memphis, on the 24th ult., by which calamity a large number of paroled prisoners, who had embarked on her at Vicksburg, lost their lives, and I have the honor to submit the following report of the result of my investigations :

"At Memphis I learned that a court of inquiry had been ordered by Major General Washburne, commanding district of West Tennessee, to investigate the facts and circumstances of the burning of the 'Sultana,' and at Vicksburg I learned that a commission had been ordered by Major General Dana, commanding department of the Mississippi, to make a similar investigation. The court and the commission were about closing their proceedings when I arrived at Vicksburg, and finding, upon a perusal of their records, that all the testimony taken would be useful to me in forming an opinion as to the merits of the case, I determined to avail myself of a copy of them, which I was permitted to do through the courtesy of the generals by whom the investigations were made.

" In addition to the above I obtained such further testimony that was within my reach, as I thought necessary to a full understanding of the matter. Upon a careful consideration of all the facts as presented in the testimony herewith submitted, I am of the opinion that the shipment of so large a number of troops (1,866), on one boat, was, under the circumstances, unnecessary, unjustifiable, and a great outrage on the troops.

" A proper order was issued by the general commanding the department for the embarkation of the paroled prisoners, and there were four officers of his staff who were responsible that this order was properly carried out, viz: Col. R. B. Hatch, captain in the quartermaster's department, chief quartermaster ; Capt. Frederic Speed, A. A. G., U. S. Volunteers, adjutant general department of Mississippi ; Capt. Geo. A. Williams, 1st U. S. Infantry, commissary of musters, and in charge of paroled prisoners, and Capt. W. F. Kernes, A. Q. M., U. S. Volunteers, and master of transportation. If there was anything deficient or unsuitable in the character of the transportation furnished, one or more of these officers should be held accountable for the neglect.

" The testimony shows that it was well understood by the four officers named that the troops in question were to embark on the "Sultana." She was provided by the master of transportation, with the approval of the chief quartermaster, upon the order of General Dana, though not upon a formal requisition, and Captain Speed and Captain Williams were to superintend the embarkation. Nothing was known positively as to the number of men that were to go on board, but it was the impression that there would be from 1,200 to 1,500 ; nor was any inspection of the boat made by either of the officers above named to determine her capacity or her condition. Neither one of them knew whether she had proper apparatus for cooking for so many men, or other necessary conveniences required for troops on transports. The troops were sent to the steamer from the camp in three parties, as is shown by the testimony

of Mr. Butler, superintendent of military railroads at Vicksburg, though Captain Speed and Captain Williams knew only
of the first and third parties ; the second party consisted of
between 300 and 400 men. As the men were being embarked
Captain Kernes seems to have been satisfied that too many
were going on one boat and he so reported to Colonel Hatch,
who agreed with him in this belief but failed to interfere himself, as it was his duty to do, or to make any report of the
matter to General Dana, because, as he states, he had had a
day or two before some difficulty with Captain Speed about
the shipment of troops.   There were two other steamers at the
landing during the day, both of which would have taken a
part of the men, and there was, therefore, no necessity for
crowding them all on one boat ; it only required an order from
Colonel Hatch, or a representation of the facts to the commanding general.

" Both Captain Speed and Captain Williams acted under the
impression that there were only about 1,400 men to be forwarded, and having also a conviction that bribery had been
attempted to induce the shipment of part of the men
on the 'Pauline Carroll' they, during the day, resisted
the proposition to divide the command between the two boats,
in the belief that in doing so they resisted an attempt at fraud.
It was not until the troops were all on board that they became
aware of the fearful load that was on the boat, and then they
seemed to think it too late to make any change, but neither of
them made any inspection of the boat to see whether there was
room enough for every man to lie down.   The testimony
shows, and by a calculation of the area of the three decks I
am satisfied, that there was scant sleeping room for all the men
when every part of the boat from the roof of the 'texas' to
the main deck was fully occupied.   At night it was impossible
to move about and it was only with much difficulty that it
could be done during the daytime.   The cooking was done
either by hot water taken from the boilers or at a small stove
on the after-part of the main deck, and owing to the limited
nature of this arrangement, the difficulty of getting about the
boat, and the want of camp kettles or mess-pans, the cooking
could not be very general.   Before the troops embarked there

were on the boat about sixty horses and mules and some hogs —one hundred or more. The great weight on the upper deck made it necessary to set up stanchions in many places in spite of which the deck perceptibly sagged.

"The impression seems to have been entertained that the paroled troops, having been so long suffering together in rebel prisons, were particularly anxious to go home together in the same boat, but there is no foundation for this belief. The men were exceedingly anxious to return to their homes and were willing to put up with many inconveniences, but they felt that they were treated with unkindness and harshness when they were crowded together in great discomfort on one boat, when another equally good was lying alongside willing to take them.

" From the foregoing, I am of opinion that the four officers above named are responsible for the embarkation of so large a number of troops on an unsuitable vessel, Colonel Hatch and Captain Speed being the most censurable. It was their duty especially to see that the service was properly performed. Captain Williams was assisting Captain Speed, and seems to have felt that there was no special responsibility resting on him ; but there was a manifest propriety in his knowing the number embarked, and if there was a deficiency of transportation he should have reported it. Captain Kernes made no inspection of the steamer to see that she was properly fitted up, but he did report her to Colonel Hatch, and also to General Smith, as being insufficient for so many troops, and his report should have been noticed. He made no report of the repairing of the boiler, which he seems to have been aware was going forward, and which it has not yet been decided positively was not the cause of the disaster. Lieut. W. H. Tillinghast, 66th United States Colored Infantry, was the only other officer connected with this service, but he had no directing control. It is shown by his own testimony that a bribe was proffered to him to induce him to use his influence in having some of the troops shipped on the 'Pauline Carrol,' which he showed a willingness to accept—at least he did not reject it—and which he failed to report until after the loss of the " Sultana." The testimony of the four officers above referred to is very

3

contradictory, and I have formed my opinion from the general tenor of the testimony and the circumstances of the embarkation.

"Brigadier General M. L. Smith, United States Volunteers, had command of the district of Vicksburg at the time, but he had nothing officially to do with the shipment of the troops; yet as it was officially reported to him by Captain Kernes that too many men were being put in the 'Sultana' it was proper that he should have satisfied himself, from good authority, whether there was sufficient grounds for the report, and if he found it so he should have interfered to have the evil remedied. Had he done so the lives of many men would have been saved.

"In reference to the immediate cause of the calamity, the testimony which I have been able to collect does not enable me to form a positive opinion. The testimony of the two engineers of the 'Sultana,' and of the inspector at St. Louis, establishes that her boilers were in good condition on her leaving that port for New Orleans, and apparently continued so until her arrival within ten hours run of Vicksburg, when a leak occurred in one of her boilers. On the arrival of the boat at Vicksburg this leak was repaired by a competent boilermaker, and was pronounced by him a good job, though he qualifies the character of the work by saying that, to have been thorough and permanent, the two sheets adjoining the leak should have been taken out, and that, in its then condition, it was not perfect. The first engineer, Mr. Wintringer, testifies that after leaving Vicksburg he watched the repaired part of the boiler, which was near the front end, just over the fire-bars, carefully, and it did not at any time show the least sign of giving way. When he was relieved from charge of the engine by the second engineer the boilers were full of water and in good condition, and on their return to Memphis, the second engineer, Mr. Clemmans, who being on watch at the time of the explosion was fatally scalded, told him before he died that the boilers were all right and full of water. I was told by another engineer at Cincinnati that he had said the same thing to another person on landing at Memphis, but this other person was not within my reach.

"There is nothing to show that there was any careening of the boat at the time of the disaster, or that she was running fast ; on the contrary, it is shown that she was running evenly and not fast.

"A piece of boiler was obtained from the wreck, by order of General Washburn, which I examined. It seemed to have been broken from the bottom of the boiler the breadth of a sheet and torn tapering to near the top of the boiler, tearing the iron like paper, at times through the rivet holes and then through the middle of the sheet. The lower or wider end seems to have been exposed to the fire without the protection of water, and if so, this doubtless was the cause of the explosion ; but this piece of iron may have been exposed to the fire of the burning vessel after the explosion, in which case some other cause must be found to account for it. The testimony of some of the most experienced engineers on the western rivers is given, to throw some light on the matter, but until the boilers can all be examined, no reliable conjecture can be made to account for the explosion. Thus far, nothing has been discovered to show that the disaster was attributable to the imperfect patching. It is the common opinion among the engineers that an explosion of steam boilers is impossible when they have the proper quantity of water in them, but the boilers may burst from an overpressure of steam when they are full of water, owing to some defective part of the iron, in which case there is generally no other harm done than giving way of the defective part and the consequent escape of steam. One engineer, who is said to be the most reliable on the river, said that even in such a case the great power of the steam having once found a yielding place tears everything before it, producing the effect of an explosion, and his view seems to be reasonable.

"What is usually understood as the explosion of a boiler is caused by the sudden development of intense steam by the water coming in contact with red-hot iron, which produces an effect like the firing of gunpowder in a mine, and the destruction of the boilers and the boat that carries them is the consequence.

"The reports and testimony show that there were 1,866 troops on board the boat, including 33 paroled officers ; one officer who had resigned, and the captain in charge of the guard. Of these, 765, including 16 officers, were saved, and 1,101, including 19 officers, were lost. There were 70 cabin passengers and 85 crew on board, of whom some 12 to 18 were saved, giving the loss of 137; making the total loss 1,238.

"I have the honor to submit herewith the following papers in support of the foregoing opinions, viz: Testimony taken before the Court of Inquiry ordered by Major-General Washburne, marked A; testimony taken before the commission ordered by Major-General Dana, marked B; testimony taken by myself, including testimony of Captain James McCown, 6th Kentucky Cavalry, taken before Colonel Badeau of General Grant's staff, marked C, and the report of Major-General Dana, commanding department of Mississippi, marked D.

"I have the honor to be, very respectfully,

"Your obedient servant,

"W. HOFFMAN,
"*Brevet Brigadier-General U. S. Army,
Commissary-General of Prisoners.*"

—————

VICKSBURG, Miss., May 7, 1865.

Will General Dana please state what officer, or officers, he considers responsible for the shipment of the paroled troops within referred to and for the proper character of the transportation.   Very respectfully,

W. HOFFMAN,
Commissary-General Prisoners.

—————

HEADQUARTERS DEPARTMENT OF MISSISSIPPI,
VICKSBURG, May 8, 1865.

Respectfully returned to Brigadier-General Hoffman. Captain Speed was entrusted with the transfer and shipment of the prisoners and assumed full and active management and control of it, and I therefore consider him fully responsible therefor. The quartermaster's department was ordered to provide the transportation, and I consider Captain Kernes,

quartermaster in charge of transportation, responsible for the character of it. N. J. T. DANA,
Major General.

The report of Major-General Dana is as follows:

" HEADQUARTERS DEPARTMENT OF MISSISSIPPI,
VICKSBURG, May 8, 1865.

"*Brigadier-General W. Hoffman, United States Army, Commissary-General of Prisoners:*

"In compliance with your verbal request this morning I have the honor to report as follows regarding the shipment of paroled federal prisoners from here:

"The commissary of musters of this department, Captain George A. Williams, 1st U. S. Infantry, was, by my order in the latter part of March, placed in charge of the duties pertaining to an assistant commissioner of exchange, with a view to transaction of business with the rebel agents then in charge of federal prisoners of war who were arriving under flag of truce.

" The rebel commissioners having positively declined to turn over any prisoners till they received an equivalent, Captain Williams was sent, first to Mobile and then to Cairo, to communicate with Major-General Canby, Lieutenant-General Grant and Brigadier-General Hoffman.

" During his absence, Captain Frederick Speed, assistant adjutant-general of this department, at his own suggestion, was assigned by me to the performance of Captain Williams' duties, and took entire charge of the receiving of prisoners from the rebel agents and of sending them to the parole camps at the north.

"During Captain Williams' absence at the north, orders were received, through me, by the rebel officials from Colonel Ould, rebel commissioner, by which they were induced to parole the prisoners; and I then ordered Captain Speed to prepare their rolls as rapidly as possible and send them north as rapidly as the rolls could be prepared, calculating, as near as circumstances would permit, about 1,000 at a load for the regular packets as they passed.

"The first load which was sent north was expected to be about 800, as that was about the number for which rolls were completed when the 'Henry Ames' was expected. She was delayed, however, and by the time she was ready to leave the rolls were ready for upwards of 1,300, and she carried them off. I had taken great interest in expediting the departure of these brave fellows to their homes and I went down to see this load start.

"The next load was by the steamboat 'Olive Branch,' which arrived so soon after the departure of the 'Ames' that rolls for only about 700 were ready for her.

"After she left Capt. Speed came to me in considerable indignation and asked for authority to place Capt. Kernes, the quartermaster of transportation at this post, in arrest. He stated that he had ordered all boats to be reported to him immediately on arrival and to await orders; that this boat had arrived in the middle of the night and had not been reported to him till eight o'clock next morning ; and that she had been unnecessarily detained after being loaded; and that he had been informed that this delay was made because she did not belong to the line which had the government contract ; and that the contract line had offered a pecuniary consideration, per capita, for the men to be kept for their boats; and the intention was to detain the 'Olive Branch' till one of the contract line came along to take the load from her. I directed him not to arrest Captain Kernes till he was satisfied, upon proper investigation, that the reports he had heard were well-founded.

"The next boat was the 'Sultana,' and she arrived so soon after the departure of the 'Olive Branch' that Captain Speed reported to me that rolls for only about 300 men could be prepared, and that, therefore, none would go by her, but they would wait for the next boat.

"Capt. Williams had arrived from the north in the night. Soon after making his first report Capt. Speed came to my office and reported that he had consulted with Capt. Williams and had decided to ship all the balance of prisoners on the 'Sultana,' as Capt. Williams had advised that they be counted and checked as they went on board and he would prepare the

rolls afterwards. I expressed satisfaction at this and asked
how many there would be, and he replied about 1,300—not to
exceed 1,400—that the exact number could not be stated owing
to discrepancies in the rebel rolls.

"About the middle of the day Capt. Williams came and
reported that the captain of the 'Sultana' said he would
leave in an hour or two and that a large proportion of the
men were still out at the parole camp, and he did not believe
that proper exertions were being made to get them off, and
that he had been informed that a pecuniary consideration had
been offered, per capita, for the detention of the men and shipment of them on the other line, and that he thought Capt.
Speed was practicing delay purposely for the detention of the
men till the 'Sultana' should leave and a boat of the other
line arrive. I then informed Capt. Williams of what Capt.
Speed had previously reported regarding Capt. Kernes and his
clerks, and stated that I thought he had the rumor wrong.
He promised to investigate it, and afterwards reported to me
that he was entirely mistaken as regarded Capt. Speed. I
also ordered a telegram to be sent to Capt. Speed informing
him that the boat would leave in an hour or two, and inquiring if any more men would go by her.

"After dark Capt. Speed reported that all the men were
in from camp.

"Up to this moment I considered that he had performed
his difficult task with great satisfaction and efficiency.

"The next morning on visiting my office I inquired of
Capt. Speed whether the boat had left and was informed she
had. I then inquired as to the exact number of men she had
taken, and was astonished to hear that there were 1,900. Having never seen the boat, I inquired as to her capacity and as to
the comfort of the men and was assured by both Capt. Speed
and Capt. Williams that the load was not large for the boat,
that the men were comfortable and not overcrowded and that
there were very few boats which had so much room for troops
as the 'Sultana.'

"I had, at first, intrusted the whole exchange business to
Capt. Williams, but he having left Capt. Speed was placed in
charge of it, in addition to his other duties, by my orders. He

assumed and managed it as I thought with ability and I never
had any report or complaint, further than is stated above,
prior to the deplorable calamity to the boat, and was not
informed of any other circumstances in the details of the
whole matter.

"I am, very respectfully, etc.,

"N. J. T. DANA,
Major-General."

The testimony referred to in General Hoffman's report is
on file in this department. It is quite voluminous, however,
and as his report was based upon that testimony and the report
of General Dana, it is believed that the foregoing will furnish
the necessary data bearing upon the destruction of the steamer
"Sultana."

Respectfully submitted,
F. C. AINSWORTH,
Captain and Assistant Surgeon, U. S. A.

Record and Pension Division.

To the HONORABLE, THE SECRETARY OF WAR.

N. WINTRINGER, Chief Engineer.

A S I was chief engineer of that ill-fated steamer at the time of her explosion I thought that my recollections of that terrible calamity would be of some interest. I believe that George Cayton, one of the pilots, and myself were the only officers of the boat that escaped with our lives. Mr. Cayton, if still living, resides in St. Louis, Missouri. I have not heard of him for some time. The "Sultana" left Cairo on that fatal trip the 15th of April, 1865, the day after the death of President Lincoln, and as all wire communications with the south were cut off at that time, the "Sultana" carried the news of his assassination and death to all points and military posts on the Mississippi river as far as New Orleans. I do not remember the exact date of our leaving New Orleans on our return trip. But on our arrival at Vicksburg, we were ordered to report to carry a load of paroled soldiers, who, I believe, were from Andersonville and Libby prisons. While at Vicksburg we repaired a boiler. Now it was claimed by some at the time that this boiler was not properly repaired, and that was the cause of the explosion. In a short time those boilers were recovered and the one that had been repaired at Vicksburg was found in good condition, whole and intact, and that it was one of the other three that caused the explosion. Now what did cause this explosion ? The explosion of the "Walker R. Carter" and "Missouri," in rapid succession, I think fully answers

that question. It was the manner of the construction
of those boilers. After these three fatal explosions
they were taken out of all steamers using them and
replaced with the old style of boiler. They were an
experiment on the lower Mississippi. They had been
used with some success on the upper Mississippi, where
the water at all times is clear and not liable to make
much sediment or scale. As I said before, those boilers were an experiment on the lower Mississippi, and
had not long been in use there, and it was the opinion
of experts that it would have been only a question of
time for all steamers using those boilers to have gone
the way that the "Carter," "Missouri," and "Sul
tana" went, had they not have been taken out and
replaced by others.

I have one word to say for the engineer who was on
duty at the time and who lost his life. It was talked
around that he was under the influence of liquor. I
can say for him, and all who were personally acquainted
with him can say the same, that he was a *total abstainer*
from anything of the kind. I went off watch on that
fatal night while the boat was lying at Memphis wharf,
at eleven o'clock in the evening of the 26th. I retired
to my berth and did not know anything until I was
aroused by the explosion, which occurred a few miles
above Memphis, said to be about two o'clock in the
morning of the 27th of April. That sight is as fresh
in my memory today as it was twenty-one years ago,
and I suppose to you, survivors, it is also. I stood
bewildered for a moment, and then saw the river perfectly alive with human beings struggling in the water,
and the cry from all quarters was "put out the fire,"

which was getting good headway by this time. But there was such a mass of confusion and such a complete wreck of the boat that nobody, apparently, could get out of the position they were in. I managed to get hold of a shutter and saw that the fire would soon force me off of the boat; I took my chances and jumped into the river. I was not in the water long until I came across a gangway plank about thirty feet long and fifteen inches wide. I abandoned my shutter for it. I was not there long until four others kept me company. There was just about enough buoyancy in the plank to keep our heads above water, and that was all. We floated in that manner for about two hours when we lodged against a snag, when one poor fellow became so benumbed with cold that he could hold no longer and sank to rise no more. In a very short time after that we were picked up by one of the relief boats that came from Memphis and were taken to the city. There was supposed to be about 2,200 people, all told, on the "Sultana" at the time, of which about one-half were lost. I would like to attend the reunion if I could make it suit at the time to do so, and hear the experiences that will be given there. Hoping you may have a pleasant meeting of old friends to talk over the perils of that terrible night, and that not one of you may ever experience such another is the wish of N. Wintringer.

[This was written April 14, 1886, and he died October 11, 1886.]

HENRY J. LYDA.

I WAS employed on board the steamer "Sultana," but left the boat about two hours before it left St. Louis for New Orleans on her fatal trip. In my estimation it was carelessness on the part of the captain and engineer that caused the disaster. The "Sultana's" boilers were not fit for duty, as that steamer stopped at Natchez and Vicksburg on the last two trips before the explosion to patch and repair her boilers. She had the tubular boilers which have been done away with since that time.

My postoffice is St. Louis, Mo. I am also a member of Frank P. Blair Post No. 1, Department of Missouri, and a pensioner of the United States; Certificate, Navy No. 1894, having served on the gunboat "Essex."

C. W. ABBADUSKA.

I WAS born in the State of Maryland, August 15, 1844, and enlisted in the service of the United States at Waldron, Mich., August 6, 1862, in Company F, 18th Regiment, Mich. Vol. Inf. I was captured at Athens, Ala., September 24, 1864, and confined in the Cahaba, Ala., prison. When the "Sultana" exploded I was asleep on one of the hatchways and jumped off into the water, supposing that we were near the shore, but when I found out that I was mistaken I got aboard the boat again and made a raft and went ashore on it. I was picked up about ten A. M.

Occupation, manufacturer. Postoffice, Waldron, Mich.

HOSEA C. ALDRICH.

I ENLISTED in the service of the United States in August, 1862, in Hillsdale county, Mich., as sergeant in Company G, of the 18th Mich. Vol. Inft. I was captured at Athens, Ala., the 24th of September, 1864, and was confined in prison at Cahaba, Ala., and released from there April 12, 1865, and sent to Vicksburg, Miss., where I went on board the boiler deck of the steamer "Sultana" with the other prisoners, like a flock of sheep, until her passengers numbered 2,141, over six times her capacity. She steamed out of Vicksburg, April 25, at one o'clock A. M., arrived at Helena, Ark., the 26th, about seven o'clock A. M., and arrived at Memphis, Tenn., the 26th of April at seven o'clock P. M. Here we stopped for a while and I went up town and got some refreshments, and I went back on the boat well fed but weary. A comrade, J. W. Dunsmore, and I bunked on the floor about midway on the cabin deck, the only place I could find as the floors of all the decks were completely covered when all of the boys laid down. We left Memphis about one o'clock A. M. April 27th. There was no danger manifested, and more than that it was not in the least anticipated only that the boat was heavily loaded. But in the darkness of that morning, between one and two o'clock opposite Zagleman (Tagleman) Landing, eight miles above Memphis, suddenly and without warning, the boiler of the steamer exploded. When it happened I was sound asleep, and the first thing that I knew or heard was a terrible crash, everything seemed to be falling. The things I had under my head, my shoes, and some other

articles and specimens that I had gathered up and had
them tied up in an old pair of drawers, they all went
down through the floor. We scrambled back. The
smoke came rushing up through the passage made by
the exit of the exploded boiler. The cry from all was,
" What is the matter ?" and the reply came, " the boat
is on fire." It was all confusion. The screams of
women and children mingled with the groans of the
wounded and dying. Brave men rushed to and fro in
the agony of fear, some uttering the most profane
language and others commending their spirits to the
Great Ruler of the Universe; the cries of the drowning
and the roaring of the flames as they leaped heaven-
ward made the scene most affecting and touching. But
it was of short duration as the glare that illuminated
the sky and made visible the awful despair of the hour
soon died away while darkness more intense than ever
settled down on the floating hulk and the victims of
the disaster. I was pushed in the water and started
for the bottom of the Mississippi, but I soon rose to the
surface and found a small piece of board, and soon had
the luck of getting a larger board, which was very
lucky for me, as I could not swim. At this time a
comrade grabbed me. I released his hold by giving
him the small board, another comrade had got hold
of the middle of the large board ; then there came an
end of a ladder in my reach, I grabbed it and pulled it
under the board, another comrade was on the other end
of it. That was the craft which we three hung to and
managed to keep away from others that were fighting
and drowning. We floated along down the river nearly
an hour I think when my limbs began to cramp; that

was the last of which I was conscious until at eight o'clock A. M. We had floated down the river six miles and lodged in the flood-wood against an island which was within two miles of Memphis, and here we were picked up by the United States picket boat, "Pocahontas." They poured whiskey down me, rolled and rubbed me, and finally brought me back to life. I was like the new born babe, not a raveling of clothing upon me, in a place surrounded by persons whom I had never seen before, but I was happy as a lark to think I was rescued and saved. They placed me on the stretchers and carried me to the Overton hospital at Memphis, gave me a shirt and drawers and placed me in a good bunk. The third day, as soon as I was able to get up, they issued a suit of Uncle Sam's blues for me and I was happy, without as much as a postage stamp, for I thought I might live so as to tell the story to friends at home, and I am glad that I have the opportunity to give this short and hasty sketch. I was discharged from the service of the United States at Jackson, Mich., July 1865. [Now deceased.]

DANIEL ALLEN.

I WAS born at Fair Garden, Tenn., on the 7th of September, 1843. I enlisted in the service of the United States in Sevier county, Tenn., a private in Company K of the 3d Tenn. Cavalry, October 3, 1863. Was captured by the rebels at Athens, Ala., September 24, 1864, and was confined in Cahaba prison until March 16, 1865, when I was paroled,—reaching parole camp near Vicksburg, March 21, and was ordered to parole headquarters at Camp Chase. But before reaching that place the sad event took place which calls for this narration. My escape and rescue from the illfated vessel were attended with much interest and excitement. The first I knew of the terrible disaster I was awakened, while in the stern of the lower deck, by the cry " she's sinking," and the shrieks and cries of the wounded and the terror stricken comrades. I pressed toward the bow, passing many wounded sufferers, who piteously begged to be thrown overboard. I saw men, while attempting to escape, pitch down through the hatchway that was full of blue curling flames, or rush wildly from the vessel to death and destruction in the turbid waters below. I clambered upon the hurricane deck and with calmness and self-possession assisted others to escape. At length, realizing that there was but little time to be lost, I divested myself of all clothing, and throwing a plank out, jumped into the water sixteen feet below. I was at once grappled by two drowning men who held on to me until I climbed into the bow of the boat to release myself from their hold. I then descended the cable and made for the Arkansas shore. I was in the water five hours, when I was picked up by a lifeboat. I was taken to the hospital at Memphis, Tenn., where I remained a day or two and then went to Camp Chase, Ohio. I was discharged from the service at Nashville, Tenn., June 10, 1865.

My occupation at present is that of a farmer and stockdealer. My present postoffice is Allensville, Tenn.

HIRAM ALLISON.

I WAS born in Franklin county, Pa., December 4, 1830, and enlisted in the service of the United States at Muncie, Ind., December 1863, in Company G, 9th Ind. Cavalry. Was captured at Sulphur Trestle, La., September 25, 1864, and confined in the Castle Morgan prison at Cahaba, Ala., until March, and then was taken to be exchanged at Big Black river, Miss. I got on the boat "Sultana" at Vicksburg. She was crowded to her utmost capacity. Arrived at Memphis April 26, in the evening, where she discharged a lot of freight. Some of the boys went up town, but I staid aboard. As near as I can tell we left about twelve or one o'clock that night. I was on the hurricane deck, close to the wheel house, lying down, and was just beginning to doze, when, all at once, I heard the crash. I jumped up the first thing, and saw a great hole torn through the hurricane deck and fire coming through. I stood a few minutes and looked at my surroundings. I concluded to take to the water. I climbed down from the hurricane deck to the cabin deck and took off all my clothes but my drawers and shirt, and then glanced around the burning wreck and saw that I would have to go, so I jumped from the cabin deck into the water. I remained there for two or three hours and then came across a horse trough with a comrade on each end of it. I took the center. When I caught up with the two comrades they were both praying. When I got on with them I said: "That was a terrible disaster." They made no reply but kept right on praying. I said no more to them and when it was light enough for me

5

to see they were gone. What became of them I never knew. I stayed on the trough till I got to some brush and logs on the Arkansas side; then I bid it good bye about five miles from the ill-fated "Sultana." I was taken to Memphis with others. I was put in the Overton hospital, remained there a few days, and then turned my face homeward. I was scalded on my legs and cut on the head.

Postoffice address is Muncie, Delaware county, Ind. Occupation, carpenter and joiner.

GEORGE ANDERSON.

I WAS born in Wayne county, Ohio, on the 20th of July, 1838. I enlisted in the service of the United States, August 6, 1862, in Wayne county, Ohio, in Company F, 102d Regiment Ohio Infantry, and never missed any duty from the time of enlistment up to the time of being captured. A small detachment of our regiment was sent to reinforce our troops at Athens, Ala., in the fight there against Forrest's command. We were taken prisoners September 25, 1864, and taken to the prison at Cahaba, where we remained until March 16, 1865, when there was an exchange of prisoners and we were sent to Vicksburg, Miss., where we went on board the steamer "Sultana" which was to take us up the river to Cairo, Ill. When we arrived at Memphis, Tenn., two of my comrades and myself got off and went up into the city, and while there, I can assure you, I did not expect to be there in the morning. Got on board the steamer again; on the hur-

ricane deck, near the pilot house, my two comrades and myself bunked for the night under one
blanket. We were asleep at the time of the explosion.
I was thrown out of reach of anybody and saw nothing
of my comrades after the explosion. I swam about in
the water for a time, and finally got a piece of railing
that was thrown from the boat and stuck to that and
floated down the river with Mr. Horn from Wooster,
and two others, (their names I have never learned,)
two miles below Memphis, making in all nine miles.
We were picked up by a gunboat and put on board a
steamer that was anchored there for that purpose.
When taken out of the water I found that I was hurt
in the left shoulder and breast, and I feel it to this
day. I was taken to Memphis where I remained a few
days and then was sent to Columbus, Ohio, where I
remained a short time and was discharged from the
service and sent home.

I now reside near Seville, Medina county, Ohio.
My present occupation is farming.

P. S. ATCHLEY.

I WAS born in Sevier county, Tenn., on the 12th of
December, 1842. Enlisted in the service of the
United States at Knoxville, Tenn., on the 5th of November, 1862, as a corporal in Company K, of the 3rd
Regiment of Tennessee Volunteers. Was on duty at the
battle of Athens, Ala., when the confederate forces,
under the command of Gen. N. B. Forrest captured that
place, and we were immediately transported to Cahaba,

Ala., as prisoners of war, and remained there, in close confinement, for about six months, when we were paroled out on the 16th of March, 1865, and sent to Vicksburg, Miss., where we went on board the ill-fated steamer "Sultana." We were highly elated with the thoughts of going home and seeing loved ones, when suddenly, as we were a few miles above Memphis, Tenn., one of her boilers exploded and hundreds of souls were ushered into eternity. My experience on that terrible morning no pen can write nor tongue can tell. I was thrown into the surging waves of that mighty river, into the jaws of death, and life depended on one grand effort, expert swimming, which I did successfully, and after swimming six or seven miles, according to statements given by citizens living on the banks of the river, landed on the Arkansas shore without any assistance whatever. There I found a confederate soldier who came to my relief, and took me to a house near by, and gave me something to eat, and I felt something like myself again, thanks to the Great Ruler of the Universe. The said confederate soldier worked hard to save the lives of the drowning men, and brought to shore in his little dugout about fifteen of them. A number of comrades got out at the point where I did. Among them were some Ohio men for whom I have great respect (but have lost their names), especially one of the 24th Ohio Regiment, that got out of the water at the same time I did. I gave him my blouse and slips as he was naked; if he is yet living I would like to hear from him. I will close by wishing God to bless every survivor.

My present occupation is farming. Present post-office address, Trotter's Store, Tenn.

MURRY S. BAKER.

I WAS born in Canton, Wayne county, Mich., and
enlisted in the service of the United States, at
Plymouth, Wayne county, Mich., 24th day of July,
1862, in Company D, 4th Michigan Cavalry. Was captured September 30, 1864, and confined in the Cahaba,
Ala., prison. In the spring of 1865 I was taken to
Big Black river and turned over to the "Yanks." I
did not keep a diary and cannot remember details.
After lying in camp awhile we were taken to Vicksburg and put on board the "Sultana." I tried to get
close to the boiler, but it was full there, so I laid
down by the stern door, beside Frank Nevins, of the
18th Regiment, Michigan Volunteers, and another
comrade of the 25th Regiment Michigan Volunteers, (he was lost). I sat up till 12 o'clock,
cooking rations, and then laid down and went
to sleep. How long I had been sleeping I do
not know. I was awakened by the explosion and
sprang to my feet and looked around ; some one said the
boat was sinking; I went out on the stern and saw that
it was not, and so went back. It was one of the worst
sights I ever witnessed. Men who were scalded and
bruised were crawling over one another to get out of
the fire. I went to the side of the boat and pulled
a board off to help me get ashore with, but a big
"Yank" grabbed it away from me. Then I got another
off from a bunk and went down to the wheelhouse and
threw it in the water, and then jumped after it. My
limbs cramped, but I kept paddling. I tried to get to
one side of the shore, but could not, then I tried the
other side, and by hard work I got on some flood-wood.

When I reached it I was about exhausted and could not speak and laid there until I was rescued. Was discharged at Detroit, 28th of June, 1865.

Occupation farming. Postoffice address, Williamston, Ingham county, Mich.

OTTO BARDON.

I WAS born in Wooster, Wayne county, Ohio, August 28, 1841, and enlisted in the service of the United States, at Wooster, Ohio, August 8, 1862, in Company H, of the 102d Ohio Volunteer Infantry, just in time to take part in protecting Cincinnati from being destroyed by Kirby Smith. Was then sent to Louisville, Ky., against Gen. Bragg and followed him through the State of Kentucky 375 miles; back to Bowling Green for winter quarters, which were cold corn-stalk camps, for we had no tents that winter of 1862 and 1863. On Christmas eve of 1862 we recaptured Clarksonville, Tenn., on the Cumberland river. In the fall of 1863 we were sent to guard the Chattanooga railroad, then back to Nashville, Tenn. In the spring of 1864 we were sent to guard the Tennessee river, and in August 1864, we were sent after Gen. Wheeler along the Chattanooga railroad and drove him across the Tennessee river. From here we went to Decatur, Ala., and

on September 24, 1864, a detail was made, at one o'clock
at night, consisting of 250 of the 102d Ohio regiment,
and 150 of the 18th Michigan regiment, to go to Athens
and see what was the matter. We got within five miles
of Athens when we met Gen. Forrest's whole brigade.
We drove him five miles and fought with him for three
hours, when we found that we were surrounded and out
of powder. In a charge we lost our best officers and
were out of ammunition. We had to surrender on the
24th of September, 1864. We were sent to Cahaba,
Ala., where we were held as prisoners until the latter
part of March, 1865, when we were taken out on
account of the high water, the Alabama river having
risen so high that we were waist deep in water for five
days. The rebels sent us to Vicksburg, where we
remained in parole camp. While here we heard of the
sad news of the assassination of President Lincoln by a
rebel. The prisoners became wild with indignation
and started for the rebel head-quarters. The rebel
major that had charge of us fled across the Big Black
river bridge for safety until we learned the particulars
of the President's death. We were put on the steamer,
"Sultana." About 2,400 men were on their way to
"God's country," as we called the North, and we all
felt happy to know that we were on our way home and
that the war was over (hallelujah, Amen). On the
morning of April 27, 1865, I was in the engine room of
of the steamer sound asleep, lying by the side of the
hatch-hole with seven others of my regiment, when the
explosion took place. First a terrific explosion, then
hot steam, smoke, pieces of brick-bats and chunks of
coal came thick and fast. I gasped for breath. A fire

broke out that lighted up the whole river. I stood at
this hatch-hole to keep comrades from falling in, for the
top was blown off by the explosion. I stood here until
the fire compelled me to leave. I helped several out of
this place. I saw Jonas Huntsberger and John Baney
go to the wheel-house, then I started in the same direction. I tried to get a large plank, but this was too
heavy, so I left it and got a small board and started to
the wheel to jump into the water. Here a young man
said to me, "you jump first, I cannot swim." This
man had all of his clothes on. I had just my shirt
and pants on. I said to him, "you must paddle your
own canoe, I can't help you." Then I jumped and
stuck to my board. I went down so far that I
let go of my board and paddled to get on top of the
water. I strangled twice before I reached the top;
then the young man caught me and he strangled me
twice. By this time I was about played out. I then
reached the wheel, and clung to it until I tore off all
of my clothes, with the intention of swimming with
one hand. I looked around and recognized Fritz
Saunders, of my regiment, by my side. I said, "Saunders, here is a door under the wheel, let us get it out."
We got it out and found it had glass panels in it.
I said, "let this go, here is a whole door." The rest
on the wheel took the first door and we started after
them with the other. We had not more than started
when a man swam up and laid across the center of our
door. I looked back and saw the wheel-house fall—it
had burned off and fell over. If we had remained there
one minute longer it would have buried us in the fire.
I said to Saunders, "let's go to the right, it is nearer

to shore." He replied, "no, there is a boat; I will paddle for it." And when we were in the center of the river the steamer was about out of sight. We met three young men clinging to a large trunk; they grasped our door for us to steer them into the timber. We had not gone far until these bore too much weight on our door; that put us all under the water. I gave the trunk a kick and raised on the door and brought it to the surface of the water. Then I said, "boys if you don't keep your weight off of the door, then you must steer the trunk yourselves." By this time I was cold and benumbed and was in a sinking condition, but having presence of mind I reached and got my board and called aloud to God for help. I rubbed my arms and got the blood in circulation again. Soon we were among the timber on the "Hen and Chickens" island, clinging to trees, but being too cold and benumbed to climb a tree. I had the good luck of finding saplings under the water. I put my foot in the fork and raised myself out of the water. I soon got warm and swam to a larger tree, and clung to it, but was not there very long until I got so cold that I fell from the tree into the water. I swam to the same tree and clung to it and called aloud to God for His assistance. I saw a man break open this trunk, it contained only ladies' dresses so it was no help to us. One of these men that had clung to the trunk was so cold that he drowned with his arms around a tree. We were on these trees until about nine o'clock A. M. It seemed as if the gnats and mosquitoes would eat us alive. We were rescued by a steamer sent in search of us from Memphis. The captain of the steamer that picked us up, ordered hot coffee

and whiskey (you bet we took it); and the Christian
commission furnished us under-clothing, and the third
day "Uncle Sam" gave us a suit of clothes, free.   On
the fourth day we took a steamer for Cairo, and were
sent from here to Camp Chase and discharged May
21, 1865.

Present occupation, carriage trimmer, and postoffice, Wooster, Ohio.

WM. BARNES.

I WAS born in the present State of West Virginia,
June 15, 1842, and enlisted in the service of the
United States in Athens county, Ohio, April 22,
1861, in Company H, 22nd Regiment Ohio Volunteers.
I was captured at Decatur, Ga., July 22, 1864, and
confined most of the time at Andersonville, Ga.   At
the time the "Sultana" blew up I was thrown from
the boiler deck and very badly hurt, but was fortunate
enough, with three unknown comrades, to get hold of
a bale of hay, upon which we floated till nearly opposite
the city of Memphis, where we were picked up by a
boat.

My present occupation is that of a miner, and my
postoffice address is Nelsonville, Ohio.

GEORGE BEMENT.

I WAS born in Mason, Cass county, Mich., November 6, 1841, and enlisted in the service of the United States at Adamsville, Mich., August 3, 1862, in Company F, 25th Regiment Michigan Volunteers, and was captured at Cedar Bluffs, on the Coosa river, Ala. October 10th. I was confined first at Selma, and afterwards at Castle Morgan, Cahaba, Ala. As to my experience on board the "Sultana," about all I can say is that I got very wet and quite cold. I reached shore somehow all right.

My present occupation is farming, and my postoffice address is Adamsville, Mich.

CHESTER D. BERRY.

CHESTER D. BERRY, born August 1, 1844, at South Creek, Bradford county, Pa. Removed, when ten years old to Michigan, thence to Minnesota, and back again to Michigan. Enlisted August 18, 1862, at Marshall, Mich., in Company I, 20th Regiment, Michigan Volunteer Infantry. Served with that organization in all its campaigns, except Fredericksburg at which time I had typhoid fever, until I was captured June 2, 1862, at Cold Harbor, Va., and taken to Pemberton building, Richmond, Va., where I was confined for a while then taken to Andersonville, Ga., arriving there June 16, 1864. Here the rations, which at first were small enough, kept diminishing, until the 1st of September, 1864, there were but two tablespoonsful of very coarse corn meal, the same of stock peas, with about two ounces of fresh beef, and wood enough to about half cook the rations. The beef first, then the peas were eaten raw and the meal made into a gruel and drank. About the last days of October, 1864, we were removed to Millen, Ga., thence to Savannah and down the railroad to Blackshear Station. Were kept here in the woods with a heavy guard around us for about two weeks, then taken to what was at the time the end of the railroad at Thomasville, Ga. Were kept here about two weeks then marched across the country sixty miles to Albany, Ga., there put on board the cars and taken back to Andersonville, entering the prison the second time on Christmas eve, 1864. Here we remained, with scarcely a ray of hope, till the 25th day of March, 1865, when we were put on board the cars, taken to Montgomery, there transferred by boat to Selma, thence by rail to Meridian. Here we were kept

over night, where my pocket diary for 1864 was stolen
from me. In it I had recorded the exact amount and
kind of rations drawn for every day while in prison.
From Meridian we were taken to Jackson, Miss., then
marched across the country to the Big Black river,
crossing it on the 1st day of April, 1865, lacking one
day of ten months that I had been in the hands of the
confederate authorities—and I could not say yet that I
was out of their hands, for we were put into a camp
called "Camp Fisk," which is four miles from Vicksburg, and were under a confederate major, but fed,
clothed, and sheltered by "Uncle Samuel." We
understood at the time, and I do still, that our government had made a proposition to the confederate authorities that if they would remove their prisoners on
to neutral ground, they might still have control of them,
but our government would feed, clothe and shelter us.
I never experienced a happier day in my life than I did
when we marched under the old Stars and Stripes at
the Big Black river railroad bridge and drew my first
cup of coffee and a single hard tack. It looked like a
stingy way for "Uncle Sam" to do business, but the
boys who served us told us that when the first squad of
prisoners arrived that they (the cooks) kicked open the
boxes of hard-tack among them, just as they had been
in the habit of doing among themselves, and the result
was that there was a number of deaths before night;
so we were happy with our meager rations, finding
more joy in looking up at the old flag, that we loved
so dearly, than in anything else, and it seemed to us
that the All-Wise Ruler had gotten up a bit of sunshine
and a small breeze in order that we might see that

glorious emblem of liberty proudly unfold itself and kiss the sunshine. I have seen many beautiful things in my life, but never anything that looked more beautiful than the flag of my country did upon that 1st day of April, 1865. We remained at "Camp Fisk" for about twenty days, then 1,965 prisoners who had been exchanged were placed on board the "Sultana," where there were already a number of passengers and thirty-five exchanged officers, the entire number of persons being a little over 2,300. You will notice that the number of prisoners, officers, and men was just 2,000. I understood at the time, and have had no reason to change my mind, that it was a contrived plan with the United States' quartermaster at Vicksburg and the captain of the boat. I will explain: At the fall of Vicksburg Gen. Grant gave many of his men furloughs to go home and recruit themselves after their unusually hard service. The officers of the steamers, knowing that the men would pay almost any price, charged exorbitant rates of fare to Cairo, Ill. The men paid what was charged, but, just before the boats started, Gen. Grant learned what had been done. He at once sent an officer to tie up the boats and ordered that all but $5 from each private and $10 from each commissioned officer be refunded. The government adopted that rule, and whenever troops were sent by private boats they were allowed $5 per man for transportation. There were a number of boats at Vicksburg at the time we (the exchanged prisoners) were to be sent north, but all demanded the $5 per man and would take but 1,000 men. Finally the quartermaster succeeded in persuading the captain of the "Sultana" to take the

entire 2,000 at $3 per head, that would give him $6,000
for the trip, whereas, if he only took 1,000 at $5 he
would only make $5,000. The report said that the
captain of the "Sultana" signed the papers for $10,-
000, and that the quartermaster cashed them on the
spot for $6,000. How true that was I cannot tell, but
I know it was believed among the men at the time.
All went gay as a marriage bell for awhile. A happier
lot of men I think I never saw than those poor fellows
were. The most of them had been a long time in
prison, some even for about two years, and the prospect of soon reaching home made them content to
endure any amount of crowding. I know that on the
lower deck we were just about as thick as we could
possibly lie all over the deck, and I understood that all
the other decks were the same. The main thought
that occupied every mind was home, the dearest spot
on earth. I well remember, as the boat lay at Memphis
unloading over one hundred hogsheads of sugar from
her hold, that my thoughts not only wended north-
ward, but I put them in practical shape. The Christian commission had given me a hymn book. At the
time I left home the song "Sweet Hour of Prayer"
was having quite a run. I found this, and before
the darkness had stopped me in the evening I had com-
mitted those words to memory and sang them for the
boys, little dreaming how soon I should have to test
the power of prayer as well as the hour when it was
held. The last that I remembered that evening was
that the boat was taking on coal, across the river from
Memphis, preparatory to going up the river. There
had been considerable talk among the boys, that it

would be a grand opportunity for guerillas. If they only knew that there was such a boat-load of prisoners coming up the river, how they could plant a battery on the shore, sink the boat, and destroy nearly if not all of the prisoners on board; consequently, when the terrific explosion took place, and I was awakened from a sound sleep by a stick of cord wood striking me on the head and fracturing my skull, the first thought I had was that, while the boat lay at Memphis, some one had gone up the river and prepared such a reception for us, and what had only been a *talk* was now a realization. I lay low for a moment, when the hot water soaking through my blanket made me think I had better move. I sprang to the bow of the boat, and turning I looked back upon one of the most terrible scenes I ever beheld. The upper decks of the boat were a complete wreck, and the dry casings of the cabins falling in upon the hot bed of coal was burning like tinder. A few pailsful of water would have put the fire out, but alas, it was ten feet to the water and there was no rope to draw with, consequently the flames swept fiercely up and back through the light wood of the upper decks.

I had often read of burning vessels and nights of horror on the deep, and almost my first thought was, "now, take in the scene," but self-preservation stood out strongest. I went back to where I had lain and found my bunk mate, Busley, scalded to death; I then secured a piece of cabin door casing, about three or four inches wide and about four feet long, then going back to the bow of the boat I came to the conclusion I did not want to take to the water just then, for it was

7

literally black with human beings, many of whom were sinking and taking others with them. Being a good swimmer, and having board enough to save me, even if I were not, I concluded to wait till the rush was over.

The horrors of that night will never be effaced from my memory—such swearing, praying, shouting and crying I had never heard ; and much of it from the same throat—imprecations followed by petitions to the Almighty, denunciations by bitter weeping. I stood still and watched for a while, then began wandering around to other parts of the boat when I came across one man who was weeping bitterly and wringing his hands as if in terrible agony, continually crying, " O dear, O dear." I supposed the poor fellow was seriously hurt. My sympathies were aroused at once. Approaching him, I took him by the shoulder and asked where he was hurt. " I'm not hurt at all," he said, " but I can't swim, I've got to drown, O dear." I bade him be quiet, then showing him my little board I said to him, " there, do you see that; now you go to that pile of broken deck and get you one like it, and when you jump into the water put it under your chin and you can't drown." " But I did get one," said he, " and some one snatched it away from me." "Well then, get another," said I. " I did," said he, "and they took that away from me." " Well, then," said I, " get another." " Why," said he, " what would be the use, they would take it from me. O dear, I tell you there is no use; I've got to drown, I can't swim." By this time I was thoroughly disgusted, and giving him a shove, I said, " drown then you fool."

I want to say to you, gentle reader, I have been sorry

all these years for that very act. There was little or no rush for the water at that time and had I given my board to that poor fellow, then conducted him to the edge of the boat and seen him safely overboard, he might, perhaps, have escaped, while, as it was, I have no doubt that he was drowned. If he was not, and should ever see this, I wish he would write me the fact. But some one may ask, "what would you have done without your board?" I could have got another from the pile of rubbish, which would have been a very easy matter, and I have not the faintest idea that anyone would have tried to take it from me, for, as the boys tell about, "I was not built that way."

After looking at the burning boat as long as I cared to, and as the waters were comparatively clear of men, I sprang overboard and struck out for some willows that I could see by the light of the burning boat, they appearing to be about one-half mile distant. I had gone but about twenty or thirty rods when, hearing a crash of breaking timbers, I looked back. The wheel-house or covering for the wheel, (it was a side-wheel steamer,) had broken away partially from the hurricane deck, and a poor fellow had been in the act of stepping from the hurricane deck onto the wheel house. I presume it was then the hurricane deck fell in. When it reached an angle of about forty-five degrees it stopped, for some unaccountable reason, till it nearly burned up. He succeeded in reaching the wheel house but got no further, for it broke and let him part way through, then held him, as in an iron vice, till he burned to death, and even now, after the lapse of years, it almost seems as though I could hear the poor fel-

low's screams, as the forked flames swept around him.
I then turned and pressed forward towards my haven
of safety, but soon became aware that I was not gaining upon it.   The fact was, I was swimming toward a
small island and was, in fact, now swimming up stream
but was not aware of the truth.   The icy water was
fast telling upon my weak system, and the moment I
became aware that I was being carried away from the
timber instead of gaining it I became completely discouraged, the only time I think in my life.

Being now quite despondent, I had about concluded
that there was no use of my trying to save myself, that I
would drown in spite of my efforts ; and that to throw my
board away and sink at once would be only to shorten
my misery.   I was just in the act of doing so when it
seemed to me that I was transported for the moment
to "the old house at home," and that I was wending
my way slowly up the path from the road gate to the
house, but, strange for me, when I reached the door,
instead of entering at once, I sat upon the step.   My
mother was an earnest devoted Christian, also my
father had been, but father was deaf and dumb consequently the family devotions fell to mother, and I
knew that in the years of my home life, that if one of
the family were away from home during the hour for
prayer, nine o'clock in the evening, that one was
especially remembered in the prayer.   As I sat upon
the step I thought it was nine o'clock in the evening,
and as plainly as I ever heard my mother's voice I
heard it that evening.   I cared but little for the prayer
until she reached that portion that referred to the ab-
sent one, when all the mother-soul seemed to go up

in earnest petition—"God save my boy." For ten long weary months she had received no tidings from her soldier boy, now she had just learned that he was on his way home and her thoughts were almost constantly upon him; and for him her earnest prayer was made. I fiercely clutched the board and hissed between my now firmly set teeth "Mother, by the help of God, your prayer shall be answered." I started out for a grand effort.

Just then I heard a glad cry from the burning boat and looking around discovered that past the boat, down the river, two or three miles as near as I could judge, was the bow light of a gun-boat. I turned and was now obliged to swim past the burning boat, for I was up the river about eighty rods above it; when nearly past the boat, which I kept a safe distance to my left, I ran into the top of a tree that had caved off from the bank and whose roots were now fast in the bed of the stream, upon which I climbed and was nearly asleep when a number of men from the boat came along and climbed upon it also. Their united weight sank it low into the water, whose icy coldness coming upon my body again awakened me. Then, to more fully arouse me, a man got hold of my board and tried to take it away from me. I remonstrated with him, but he claimed the board belonged to him and that I was trying to steal it. This fully aroused me—it was the straw that broke the camel's back. Giving the board a quick jerk I sprang backward and went swimming down the stream on my back, holding my board high least I might lose it. I soon turned over and proceeded more slowly. I began again to have an almost irresistible feeling of drowsiness. I was cold and sleepy. Just then I came across, or thought I did, a dry black ash sapling about two and one-half or three inches in diameter at the butt and six or eight feet long, that pronged in two branches about three feet from the butt end. I put this with my board and trying them found they would float. I then gave myself up to sleep and did not awake until long after sunrise. I then stood upon a large snag in the river that was pronged or forked something like I imagined the black ash sapling was in the night. I stood on the lower prong which was about a foot under water, while the upper prong was nearly two feet above the water, and, what to me was stranger than all, I had, instead of the little board four inches wide and about four feet long, a two inch plank about four inches wide and about six feet long.

I was out of my head and imagined that some terrible danger threatened me, but if I could only get that plank upon the upper prong of the snag, all would be safe. I soon came too enough to know that I was working a useless scheme; then I realized that it was worse than useless as it would take some of my strength to hold the plank on the snag while it would do me no good whatever. I then abandoned the project and began to cry with the pain of my fractured skull, but I soon stopped that also, saying to myself, crying does not ease pain. Then came the first clear thought of the morning and I realized what had happened and that I was but about five rods from the woods upon the Arkansas shore, the shore itself being under water.

Quickly shoving my plank into the water and

starting for the place where the shore ought to be,
which was the most foolish move of all, for when I
arrived there and had pulled myself up a small cotton-
wood tree I was surrounded by a perfect swarm of buffalo gnats, which made lively work for me, and
although I had firmly seated myself upon a limb of
the tree and employed both hands with bushes whipping
them off my neck and breast—the only parts that were
exposed—which were a solid blotch in less than an hour.
Had I remained on a snag in the river I would have
been free from the gnats and nearer passing steamers,
by which I hoped to be carried away. I remained in
this tree but a short time, perhaps an hour or more,
when the steamer "Pocahontas" came along, picking
up all the men they could find.

I soon attracted attention and was taken on board
the steamer, and soon after landed at Memphis and
was then taken to Washington hospital, where my
wound was poorly dressed, as I remember it, none of
the broken pieces of skull being taken out. I remained
here a little over a week, and although I gave my name,
company and regiment to a reporter, and also to the
hospital steward, yet about two or three months afterward my mother received official notice from Washington that her son was killed upon the "Sultana;"
and my name stands today upon the Michigan Adjutant General's Report for 1865 as killed by the explosion of the steamer "Sultana." Yet, when in after
years, I applied for a pension for that fractured
skull, which was so bad that the surgeon at Washington hospital told the man in the next bunk to mine
that I could never get well, I was obliged to prove

that I was upon the "Sultana" and that I was hurt or had my skull fractured at that time. Such is the ease with which pensions are procured, and such the liberality of the government officials when they have the official evidence in government reports before them.

After my brief sojourn in Memphis, I, with others, was placed on the steamer "Belle Memphis" and taken to Cairo, remaining there over night, thence via Matoon, where we were obliged to wait a few hours for cars. Here I was obliged to go hungry, or beg from the citizens, although I had a meal ticket at the eating house given me by the Christian commission, but the landlord refused to honor it. From here we were taken to Indianapolis where another halt was made, then on to Columbus, when I was sent to Tripler hospital and doctored up for about two weeks; then sent to Jackson, Mich., to be mustered out of the United States service on special telegraphic order from the War Department.

My present occupation is Minister of the Gospel. Postoffice address, Tekonsha, Mich.

WM. BOOR.

I WAS born in Cumberland county, Pa., January 20, 1825. Enlisted in the service of the United States October 5, 1864, as a private in Company D, of the 64th Regiment Ohio Volunteer Infantry, at Sandusky, Ohio. Was captured at Franklin, Tenn., November 30, 1864, and confined in prison at Meridian, Miss., Cahaba and Selma, Ala. I was finally released from prison and sent to Vicksburg, Miss., arriving there

March 19, 1865. Remained in camp until the 22nd of April, I think, when we received orders to break camp and be ready for our homeward journey. The train from Vicksburg came on time. The Ohio men were first called, and, responding promptly, were taken aboard the train and landed at Vicksburg. We were then ordered to fall into line and march aboard the steamer "Sultana." When going on board my attention was attracted by the noise and work at the boilers going on at that time. We were marched to the hurricane deck and informed that this was to be our place of abode, but I thought different. I turned to Comrade Wm. A Hulit, and, asking him to take charge of our clothing which I had at the time, I went below and looked at the boilers, which were not very favorable to my mind. I went back to the boys, told them that we had better look for some other place and that I thought that there was danger; and if the boat should blow up and we were on that deck we would go higher than a kite. We started for the deck below, taking our position at the head of the stairway. Six of us took our places here, and enjoyed ourselves the best we could considering the crowded condition of the boat, all looking ahead to the happy time when we should reach home to see our loved ones.

While thus apparently everything was moving along smoothly and safely, if not to our comfort, in the stillness of night on the morning of April 27, 1865, about two o'clock, we were awakened by the exploding of the boiler of the boat, the cracking of timbers, wailing of men and the screams and moaning from the wounded, and the frantic men rushing to and fro, not knowing

what to do, while the flames were madly rushing
through the broken kindling of the boat cabin. It soon
cleared the boat of its human freight. When the explosion occurred we all, except one, rushed out from
under the wreck. Comrade Thos. Brink was fastened in
the wreck. I commenced clearing away the broken timbers that were about him and got him out. We went
down stairs; I asked him if he could swim, he said,
"yes, I can swim," and I told him I could not swim,
but would meet him somewhere on the shore. I was
not, however, permitted to realize that happy event
but was forced to the painful thought that he had
perished, and the gallant Thos. Brink was no more.
After I parted with my friend on the bow of the boat
I went up stairs and got in under the wreck of the
cabin roof. There I dressed, and took my rubber
blanket and a spare shirt and tied them up, expecting
if the board could carry me it also could carry my
clothing, for I thought they would come good after
having been in the icy cold water for a few hours.

Now, I thought that I was prepared for any event
that might overtake me. I went down on the boiler
deck. While there I had a good view for quite a distance around the burning boat. It was a most distress-
ing scene to see hundreds of men in the water pleading
for help, clinching one another while they would hold
on to each other—going down by the dozens at a time.
At the same time I wonder how so many were saved as
were, laboring under so many disadvantages, hundreds
of them being thrown into the air as soon as the explosion took place,—scarcely having time to awake out

of sleep,—and plunged into the water which was almost
icy cold.

The time for me to escape was now at hand for the fire
was sweeping through the stairway.   I had taken a
survey of the river and made for the side which I
thought was nearest the shore.   Comrade Crawford of
the 102d Regiment, and I started for the same place. At
my saying to him we would have to leave he led the
way, and I waited until the way was clear again. While
waiting, my bundle caught fire, and, as I struck the
water, I heard a hissing noise caused by the water coming in contact with the fire.   Here I met with an accident which came near proving fatal to me. I got into
one of those whirl-pools in the water, and while there
I could not manage my board. I finally got tired out,
and then for the first time I thought I must give up
the struggle and drown as I could not get away from
there. I finally concluded to dive to the bottom and
get a good start not thinking that the water was forty
or fifty feet deep in the channel.   I went down but it
was not long before I was in need of the fresh air.
When I came near the surface of the water, as luck
would have it, I cleared the pool and got my board.   I
rested a short time and made up my mind to
get to the wheel-house of the boat and get
on it and stay there until picked up, or go
down with the burning boat, but in trying to get
there I came across a board about eight feet long.   I
put my other board under this and got on the other
end of the board which projected about a foot out of
water. I got a good start. When I came to the bow
of the boat there was a man doing his best to keep his

head above water. He called to me to know if that
board would not carry us both. I told him we had got
where every one must be for himself, and that I could
not swim and had to depend on that board to bring
me to safety. He told me that he could not swim and
pleaded for me to aid him. I could not withstand the
plea, and told him if he would get off in case the board
would not carry us both, he could get on with me. It
proved sufficient and we floated down stream and landed on the Arkansas side of the island opposite Mound
City, where a rebel captain got us out on a rail raft,
(which he had made so as to cross to the island).

When rescued I was so chilled that I had no recollection of being rescued or taken off of the board.
After getting on land I have some recollection of how
I fell over, as I could not walk or stand, but I got hold
of the fence and held on to keep up. Although it was
daylight, with me it was all darkness. The last that I
could remember was hearing some ladies tell me to go
to the fire. How long I was unconscious I know not;
but before my sight came to me I began to revive, I
could hear some of the remarks that were made, and
also could feel that someone was washing my face, but
did not understand the meaning of this. When I
awoke I found myself before a big fire in the yard. A
man handed me a bottle, I took it and was soon satisfied that I knew what it contained. I handed it back
to him and said, "I do not drink whiskey;" (this was
the first I uttered after being rescued). There were
nine of us rescued at this place, Mound City (?), and
were well treated by the two families that lived there.
A widow gave us a good meal and made us as comfort-

able as possible while we were there. The steamboat "Pocahontas" came along and took us on board for Memphis, Tenn. When we arrived there the ladies of the Christian commission supplied us with under-clothing. I took an ambulance for Overton hospital, where I changed clothes and went to bed and soon lost myself in sleep.

Those of us that were able to go North were sent out of the hospital to the Soldier's home for dinner. In the evening about two hundred or more took a boat for Cairo, Ill., where we landed on the following evening. A grand reception was given to the soldiers at Mattoon, Ill. I was discharged from the service at "Camp Chase," Ohio, May 17, 1865.

My occupation is whip-stock making. Postoffice address, Sandusky, O.

WM. BRACKEN.

I WAS second lieutenant in Company D, 88th United States Colored Infantry. At the time the "Sultana" blew up I was officer of the picket guard on the Wolf river and was close enough to hear the shrieks and groans of the wounded and drowning soldiers and crew, but was powerless to aid them for want of boats. The United States picket boat "Pocahontas" picked up all who were alive next day. On board the "Pocahontas" were a number of soldiers belonging to the 113th Regiment Illinois Volunteers (the regiment to which I had formerly belonged), and they said that the general impression among the survivors was that the boilers had

been tampered with, and that the boat was blown up
purposely to cause the destruction of the soldiers on
board.   One or more of the employes of the boat were
also of this opinion and they so expressed themselves.
I visited the hospitals in Memphis and saw the most
heart rending sight I ever witnessed.

My postoffice address is Putnam, Ill.

JAMES K. BRADY.

I WAS born near Highland, Marion county, Ohio,
September 23, 1846, and I lived on a farm until
1861 when my father and his entire family were taken
sick with typhoid fever.   My father died and I lay
seventy-eight days before I was able to leave my bed.

In the fall of 1862, the day before I was sixteen,
September 22, I enlisted in Company B, 64th Regiment Ohio Volunteer Infantry, and was in every battle
with my regiment from that time on until the last
battle of Franklin, Tenn.   In front of Atlanta, Ga., I
received a scalp wound in the back part of my head.
At Franklin, Tenn., I received a flesh wound in the
right hip, and, with five others of my company, was
taken prisoner, November 30, 1864.   Marched the next
day to Columbia, Tenn., and after being held there a
few days we were marched with about 1,800 or 1,900
other prisoners to Corinth, Miss., where we were confined for a few days in a stockade.   When we reached
this we were in a terrible condition, having marched
several hundred miles over very bad roads, in the winter
season, with our clothing worn out and nothing much

to eat, some barefooted, others sick. We were shipped from here to the place which the boys called "hell upon earth," the prison pen of Andersonville.

On March 26, 1865, I, with several hundred others, was taken out of prison and after a long journey, part of the way by rail and the rest on foot, we reached Big Black river, and went in camp near Vicksburg, Miss.

About the 23rd or 24th of April, I, with a lot of paroled prisoners, was loaded aboard the ill-fated steamer "Sultana," at Vicksburg, Miss. Our condition on this boat was more like a lot of hogs than men. With the other passengers and crew, there were about 2,100 in all, besides a freight cargo, making in all more than double the carrying capacity of the boat. We were headed up the river for Cairo, Ill. The boat landed at Memphis, Tenn., on the evening of April 26, where a part of the freight was unloaded. Some time after we steamed up the river, making a landing to take on coal. My friend, David Ettleman, and I went up to the hurricane deck and made our bed, as we were crowded too much below, and laid down. That was the last that I knew until the explosion, which occurred about two o'clock, A. M., at which time I was suddenly awakened to my senses, as the fire was all over me and my friend was trying to brush it off; it had already burned most of the hair off from the top of my head. We finally got the fire out and began looking around for some means of saving ourselves, for we could see that the boat was on fire. We could see nothing to get, so we went to the front end of the hurricane deck and took hold of some ropes and went down to the bow of the boat, and O, what a sight met our gaze ! There

were some killed in the explosion, lying in the bottom
of the boat, being trampled upon, while some were
crying and praying, many were cursing while others
were singing. That sight I shall never forget; I often
see it in my sleep, and wake with a start.

After looking for something to save ourselves with
in vain, we had about given ourselves up as lost, when
all at once we saw a crowd with something which
proved to be the gang plank. As this seemed to be
our last chance my friend and I both grabbed hold of
it, just as it was going over the side of the boat, and
we all went down together. I think not less than forty
or fifty men had hold of that plank, at least there were
as many as could crowd around it when it went into
the water, and it was very heavy. I ran beside it. It
struck the water end first, and I thought it would
never stop going down, but it finally did, and slowly
arose to the surface. I think there were about fifteen
or sixteen of us that had stuck to the plank. But now
a new danger had seized me, as some one grabbed me
by the right foot and it seemed as though it was in a
vise; try as I would, I could not shake him off. I
gripped the plank with all the strength that I had,
and then I got my left foot between his hand and my
foot and while holding on to the plank with both
hands I pried him loose with my left foot, he taking
my sock along with him, but he is welcome to the
sock; he sank out of sight and I saw him no more.

By this time the plank had been turned over and
we lost some more of our passengers. I looked back
and saw that there were two men on the plank behind
me, how many were in front of me at this time I could

not tell, but I knew that my friend was there as every little while he would call out some encouraging word to me to keep up my spirits. The two men on the plank behind me would crawl up on top of it and finally upset it again, and one of them lost his grip and went down to rise no more. Then the other fellow seemed to get crazy, for he not only climbed upon the plank be- hind me but reached over and tried to grab me by the shoulder. Just as his fingers were touching my shoul- der I dropped under the water and he went right over me into the river, like a big frog, turning the plank over with the force of his plunge, but I came up on the other side of the plank, grabbing it with my left hand. I never saw that man again.

I was now getting very tired, in my weak state, as I only weighed 96 pounds when I came out of prison. (I weighed 154 pounds the day before I was taken pris- oner.) I was almost ready to give up when I heard my friend Ettleman say, "now boys, this plank is able to carry fifteen or twenty men if properly handled, and there are but five or six of us; now I will steady the plank while the rest of you get on and lie flat, then I will get on." We all got on and laid flat down and paddled with our hands. It was not long after this that one of the men in front said that he could see a house, and for us to paddle on the left side. We did as we were told and soon had our plank along side of the building, which proved to be a log stable with an old set of harness hanging up in it. The stable was standing on the levee of the river, but as the river was all overflowed there was not much of the stable out of the water. When it got light enough to count up we

9

found there were twenty-three of us on the stable, and
as far as the eye could see, upon every old snag and
every little piece of drift big enough, you would see a
man. That sight I never will forget. I can see it now
as I pen these lines.

A little after daylight a man swam out about three
rods above us and got on some drift. The sight I hope
I may never see again for he was scalded almost to
pieces, and he said, "boys, it is going to kill me," and
he laid down and died. I don't think he lived three
minutes after he got out of the water. Then there
was a nice large mule swam out to us just after daylight.
He had a piece of railing twelve or fourteen feet long
tied to his halter strap. One of the boys got down and
unfastened it. What became of the mule I do not
know, as he was there in the water the last I saw of
him with just his back, neck and head out of water.

A little after sunrise we could see the smoke of a
steamer coming up the river, and in due time she came
up to where we were. The steamer came as close as
she dared to and sent out little boats to take us in.
I had now become so stiff that I could not move and
my friend, with some of the boat's crew, carried me
down into a little boat and took me over to the large
one, which proved to be the "Jenny Lind." There
was a doctor on board and he gave us something to
make us throw up the water, but I did not throw any
up. They carried me in the cabin, and that was the
last I knew until about four o'clock in the afternoon.
When I awoke there was one of the Sisters of Charity
trying to pour a hot sling down my throat with a
teaspoon, for I found that I was in a hospital at Mem-

phis, Tenn. After waking up it was not long until I opened my mouth, and I think there was about a gallon of water ran out of it. I wanted to go out and see if the other boys were safe. They would not allow me to go, for they said I was too weak, but the next afternoon they let me go and I found three of my companions alive—some of them badly hurt. The other two were either drowned or killed in the explosion.

The next day we took a steamer for Cairo, Ill., arriving there just after dark. Most of the boys went to the barracks as they were afraid they would get left, but I, with a few others, stopped at the Soldier's home, where we received the finest of treatment, a good supper (something we had not had for three long years), and a nice bed. It was not long before I was sound asleep, and I knew no more until I got a gentle shake from one of the attendants that awoke me, but at the same time he said don't be in any hurry you have plenty of time. I got up feeling greatly refreshed, dressed and washed myself and sat down to a breakfast that was good enough for a king. After breakfast one of the men went to the train with us, getting there just five minutes before leaving time. Then we started for Mattoon, Ill., arriving there about eleven o'clock, and O, what a sight we witnessed ! The platform at the depot was crowded, from one end to the other, with the citizens of Mattoon and surrounding country, with baskets filled to over-flowing with every thing you could think of to eat. As fast as a basket was empty it was refilled, and after we had eaten all we could it seemed as though the baskets hadn't been touched. Let me say that during my entire term of service I never received such treatment as while in the State of Illinois.

After we had finished eating the citizens wanted us to go home with them and stay until evening, for we could not get a train before that time. In the afternoon it was learned that we could not get away until one o'clock that night. The people of the town called a meeting in a new hotel, which was not completed inside yet. That evening the local speakers of the town made several patriotic speeches to us, but what was the nicest thing of all there were about forty ladies, dressed in red, white and blue, that sang several patriotic songs; among the rest they sang "Welcome home, dear brothers," and it seemed that we were. Ever since that time I have had a warm place in my heart for the people of Mattoon and surrounding country, also for the people of Cairo, Ill. But all things have an end, and so at one o'clock we started for Columbus, the capital of the great and glorious old state of Ohio. In due time we arrived; but oh, what a change, instead of being treated like lords, as we were in Illinois, we were treated more like so many dogs than human beings. Myself and a few others could not endure this kind of treatment, so we took French leave and went home. In about two weeks I received notice to come to Columbus and get discharged. We were discharged by order of special telegram from the War Department, without any descriptive list. I came home and went around to see my friends and neighbors, but when I went around it seemed as though everybody was gone or dead.

Being in so much company for three years I became

restless, packed my kit and went to Missouri. It was a little more lively there, as every man I met had a large navy revolver strapped to him. It made no difference whether he was a banker, dry goods man or a farmer; it was all the same, the revolver was there. I remained there eighteen months and was never treated better by any people anywhere, and I never carried a weapon of any kind. Then I came home, married, and went to farming. I didn't like that. Then I went into the timber business, getting out spiles and stave bolts. I finally quit that and went into the retail grocery business. I followed that for about nine years, but at the present time I am not doing much of anything.

My post office address is Morral, Ohio.

JOSEPH BRINGMAN.

I WAS born in Mansfield, Ohio, on the 16th of April, 1841. Enlisted in the service of the United States at Mansfield, Ohio, on the 6th of August, 1862, in Company D, of the 102d Regiment Ohio Volunteer Infantry. Was captured at Athens, Ala., on the 24th of September, 1864, and confined in the prison at Cahaba, Ala.

When I went on the steamer "Sultana," at Vicksburg, I was sick and very weak and all of my teeth

seemed to be loose (the result of prison life). Sometime in the evening of the 26th of April, 1865, we
stopped at Memphis, Tenn., to take on coal. After
this was done we started up the river and I laid down
outside of the balusters on the cabin floor, on the left
side of the boat. I did not sleep very soundly and my
sleep was disturbed by dreams. I had kept on my
clothing as it looked rainy. A rope was stretched
some twelve or fifteen feet above the deck, running to
the spar, with which I came in contact some way as I
afterwards found the marks of the rope on my body,
which causes me to speak of it here. It appeared to
me in my dream that I was walking leisurely on an
incline or sloping hill, and when I reached the top
there appeared to be a ledge or projecting rock over-
hanging a river; I seemed to step upon it so as to look
down into the water, and just as I took the second
step the rock seemed to burst with a report like the
shot of a distant cannon. I felt pieces of rock striking
my face and head and I seemed to be hurled out into
the river. The sensation was like striking the water
with my side and shoulders and going under with a
waving or oscillating motion. I came to the surface,
but was still not fully conscious, and started down
again with apparently the same motion but did not
seem to go down so far. I became more conscious, and
began to strangle. I now found that it was not all a
dream, and also that my clothing was an incumbrance
and at once divested myself of it. On coming to
the surface of the water I struck a scantling some four
inches square, I seized it and also managed to get some

more floating debris, and by this means I was able to keep above the water.

My thoughts were more collected now, and I could see men in the water near me and also horses struggling in the water, and one horse came near capsizing my frail float. My impression was that the boat had capsized and thrown us off. I then asked some of those that were in the water " what had happened to the boat." None of them knew. A moment later we saw a light and then we knew that the boat was on fire, and in a very short time the flames lighted up the river all around. I shall never forget that terrible ordeal. The water was icy cold and in every direction men were shivering and calling for help, while the water was carrying us swiftly down the stream. The boat did not follow and the darkness prevented us from seeing each other.

After floating some distance I heard Phillip Horne, of Company I, telling some of the others how to work to get ashore. I called to him and he asked who I was. I told him, and then he asked me what I had for a float. I answered and he said that they had part of a floor and called to me to come and get on. I worked over to them and tried to get on, but their floor seemed to sink too much and I did not venture on. I told them that I would stick to my boards and scantling. Had just let loose of their floor when it struck something and turned over. I understood that several were drowned. Floating along I several times came near the shore, but each time the current drew me back toward the middle of the stream. I could see the buildings on the bank of the river at Memphis as I floated

past and hallooed for help. The steamers along the
wharf were ringing their bells and men were out in
canoes, but I was on the opposite side of the river and
was not noticed. I was so chilled that I was powerless,
and a kind of drowsiness came over me. I felt that I
was going to sleep and I seemed as comfortable as if in
a downy bed. I soon dropped to sleep, or to unconsciousness, with the music of the bells of the steamers
ringing in my ears. The next I knew I was on a boat
at the wharf or landing at Memphis, lying on a mattress, and several men were working over me trying to
bring me to consciousness. The boat had picked me
up with others, from eight to fourteen miles below
where the explosion took place. I knew nothing about
this except what I was told. I learned that our boat,
the "Sultana," had blown up. There were twelve
of my company on board that boat and only two of us
escaped. I was taken from the boat and conveyed in
a carriage to the hospital at Memphis, and on going up
the stairway I dropped down and was unconscious till
the next day. My injuries were a fractured arm, three
broken ribs, my face somewhat scalded, scarred and
bruised all over, and frozen to unconsciousness. I was
at the hospital about four days when an order came to
discharge all that were able to go home. I got up and
walked around to show that I was able to go, but I suffered terribly before I got very far.

I was discharged at "Camp Chase," Ohio, on the
20th of May, 1865, and was soon at home but could
not do any work until cold weather that fall, and I feel
the effects of that exposure and shaking up to this day.

My present occupation is farming, postoffice address
Enon Valley, Pa.

A. C. BROWN.

I WAS born in Clermont county, Ohio, on the 24th of
November, 1838. Enlisted in the service of the
United States on the 3rd of September, 1861, in
Company I, 2nd Ohio Volunteer Infantry and served
in the first brigade of first division of the fourteenth
army corps, Army of the Cumberland.

While in command of my company at the battle of
Chickamauga, September 20, 1863, was taken prisoner ;
had already served over two years of active service.
Was taken from the battle-field to Belle Isle, which is
in the middle of the James river, opposite Richmond,
Va. ; remained on the island but a short time and was

then transferred to Smith's building, opposite Libby
prison, in Richmond. In this prison we had the best
fare while in the so-called Southern confederacy. They
gave us all the mule meat we could eat. The guards
around this prison were not unlike those that were on
duty at many others, always watching for an excuse to
kill a "Yank," and, as many of the guards had never
been to the front and were not likely to be sent there
as they were too cowardly to be trusted, their only
chance to kill a "Yank" was to take one of us that
was unarmed and shut up in a building where the
"Yank" could not even get at him with his fist. It
was only when they were sure that they were out of
harm's way that they had the bravery to shoot one of
us. Our boys had noticed that some of the guards
wanted to immortalize their name by killing one of us,
so we concluded to test their marksmanship. Late at
night, when most of the boys were asleep, we would
raise the window and present the "Yank" that was to
be sacrificed in order that the guard, who was exposed
to the dews and night fall, might get a furlough
and go home for his health. This, I believe, was the
order at all the prisons, that if one of us was shot for
breaking the rules the guard that did the shooting was
furloughed. As soon as the "Yank" would appear at
the window the boys would commence to tantalize the
guard to get him to shoot. Bang would go the gun
and the "Yank" would fall back pierced by ball and
buckshot. We did not have much trouble to stop the
blood, as the supposed "Yank" was a broom-stick
with a piece nailed across to represent arms, clothed in
blouse and cap; so the same "Yank" would immedi-

ately appear in the window and call in question the marksmanship of the guard. Of course such performances would alarm the rest of the guards and there would be a detail made to double the guard for the rest of the night. Many instances of my prison life might be referred to which were similar to that.

After two months at Richmond, by which time they had to commence eating the mule meat themselves, we were taken to Danville, Va., (where they had the riot last fall and the darkies killed so many of the white people). We were kept at Danville the balance of the winter of 1863 and 1864, and in the spring of the latter year were taken to Andersonville, Ga., where I was introduced to Capt. Wirtz, April 18th. On our arrival here I told my comrades that we were in for the war. This proved to be the fact. I was kept here until the 18th of March, 1865, which made my stay at Andersonville eleven months to a day, and a little over nineteen months a prisoner of war. The records at Washington show that over 180,000 of our soldiers were captured and imprisoned during the war, and only about twenty-five or thirty thousand are now supposed to be living.

We left Andersonville on the 18th of March, 1865, destination unknown to us. Of course, as it was on all occasions when we were being transported from one prison to another, "we were going to be exchanged." We started south and finally, after traveling by railroad, river and on foot, we came to Big Black river, twelve or fifteen ⟨eight⟩ miles from Vicksburg and were here paroled. The conditions admitted of our Sanitary Commission feeding and clothing us, but we

were to remain under control of the Confederate major
until legally exchanged.

While here I was called upon by the agent of the Southern express company at Vicksburg who informed me
that he had received a dispatch from the superintendent
of the Adams express company at Cincinnati, Ohio, re-
questing him to render me any assistance I required in
cash or otherwise.   I requested that the agent would
kindly return my thanks to those of my friends North
who had so kindly remembered me and my sufferings,
and all the favor I asked was when we were to be sent
North that cabin passage be procured for me.   It was
while here in camp that word came of the assassination
of our beloved president, Abraham Lincoln.   Our
Confederate major concluded that it was not a healthy
place for him and deserted us—so I am still on parole,
having never been exchanged.   A train was sent for us
and we were shipped to Vicksburg.   When marching
from the train to the wharf, and when near the boat,
I saw my friend, the express agent, awaiting me on the
cabin deck.   I stepped on the ill-fated steamer and was
introduced to the first clerk, when I was informed that
my fare was paid to Cairo.   The express agent, after
wishing me a safe trip, bade me good-bye and went up
town.   It was now about eleven o'clock.   I soon sat
down to dinner.   You can imagine the contrast between sitting down at a table filled with all the sub-
stantials and pastry, in the finely furnished cabin of a
steamer, compared with the surroundings and fare at
Andersonville.   After eating a very light meal of the
plainest food on the table, I helped myself to more
than some would think proper under different circum-

stances and carried out to my comrades quite an arm-
ful of victuals. I found them going for the hard tack
and "Lincoln" coffee with a relish. A happier crowd
I never saw; we all felt that a few more hours would
land us at home where anxious friends were awaiting
our return. Our names had already been forwarded
by telegraph to the press North, and many hearts were
made light by the prospect of meeting a son, a husband, brother or sweetheart. It is well, my friends,
that we cannot see into the future. Little did this
happy throng know what awaited it; that in a few
more hours some were to be roasted—yes burned to
death—while others would be struggling with the waves
only to sink, to rise no more. Many the tears I have
shed in remembrance of this doubly sad calamity.
After my comrades had faced the leaden hail, had
fallen into the hands of the enemy, passed through all
the harrowing experiences of prison life, that they
should meet such a fate when almost in the embrace of
friends at home seemed doubly sad.

We left Vicksburg in the evening after supper. The
clerk and myself had quite a chat and he seemed to take
quite an interest in having me relate some of my prison
experiences. I broke in on his questioning to find out
how many there were on board the boat. (The "Sultana" was one of the largest boats on the Mississippi
river.) The clerk replied that if we arrived safe at
Cairo it would be the greatest trip ever made on the
western waters, as there were more people on board
than were ever carried on one boat on the Mississippi
river. He stated that there were 2,400 soldiers, 100
citizen passengers, and a crew of about eighty—in all

over 2,500. We arrived at Memphis, Tenn., at about
ten o'clock at night, April 26th. I retired to my state-
room, and the last that I remember they were taking
on coal. I was wakeful, and commenced to plan what
I would do in case of an accident to the boat. There
were so many passengers on board that there would be
great excitement. I decided that in case of a fire I
would get off the boat as soon as possible. I then went
to sleep. * * *

I learned after the accident that it was about three
o'clock in the morning of the 27th of April, 1865, in dark
and misting rain, when about seven or eight miles
above Memphis and near the cluster of islands called
the "Hen and Chickens," that one of the boilers of
the boat exploded and the boat burned to the water's
edge. The first I knew after going to sleep I found
myself laying on the opposite side of the cabin from my
stateroom, about the middle of the boat. The steam
was rushing up all about me and the fire was starting.
The boat from midway forward was all torn to fragments, and this was the part of the boat that was occupied by the boys. Back of me the chandelier in the
ladies' room was burning brightly. I got up and
started to the rear of the boat through the ladies'
cabin; passed a lady who was putting a second set of
life preservers on a little child; this was the only child
on board. When I reached the railing at the rear of
the boat, after assisting a lady to throw overboard her
trunk, I laid off my heavy army shirt that I might not
be incumbered by its heavy weight in the water, and
overboard I started. Before I reached the water something was thrown over that hit me and down I went

under the water. As I came up a drowning man caught me around the neck with a death grip, and under we went—the second time for me. As we sank I strangled. I now passed through the same experience that only a drowning person or those about to drown undergo. In those few seconds of time my whole life, from my childhood down to that terrible moment, passed before me like a panorama with perfect distinctness. As we came to the surface I freed myself from his deadly grasp and struck out for myself. I now took account of stock and found all I possessed of this world's goods was a string around each ankle. As I did not want to be weighed down with the garment that was afloat and fastened to the strings, I swam with one hand at a time and with the other hand broke the strings. When about three or four hundred yards away from the boat the whole heavens seemed to be lighted up by the conflagration. Hundreds of my comrades were fastened down by the timbers of the decks and had to burn, while the water seemed to be one solid mass of human beings struggling with the waves. The light and the screams at this time cannot be described. Out of 2,500 only about 600 were rescued, and about 200 of the rescued died soon after from the injuries received at the time of the accident. Most all on board were from the middle and western States.

The adjutant general of the State of Michigan, in reporting for the last year of the war, refers to the "Sultana" explosion as being the greatest calamity of the war; a great many Michigan men were on board and lost.

I swam about four miles and came to an island covered with timber. I climbed a tree, and the water surrounding it was about ten feet deep. Now, when I hear persons talking about being hard up, I think of my condition at that time—up in a tree in the middle of the Mississippi river, a thousand miles from home, not one cent to my name, nor a pocket to put it in —and, to contrast my appearance then, with my face scratched and swollen, my weight about one hundred pounds, with my appearance today reminds me of two Irishmen who, on meeting, each thought he recognized an old acquaintance, afterwards found they were mistaken and one said to the other: " You thought it was me and I thought it was you, but bejabers it is naither of us !"

I was about to close and leave myself up a tree. After remaining in the tree about four hours, a boat came along and took me off. Was mustered out of the service on the 6th of May, 1865.

My present postoffice address is Canon City, Col.

MICHAEL BRUNNER.

I WAS born in Bavaria, Germany, on the 25th of January, 1841. 1 enlisted in the service of the United States, in September, 1861, at Georgetown, Ohio, as a private in Company C of the 59th Regiment Ohio Volunteer Infantry. I was captured on the 19th of September, 1863, at the battle of Chickamauga, Tenn., confined two days at Belle Island, then in a warehouse of Royster & Bros. in Richmond, Va., thence to Danville prison, No. 5. From Libby prison, I, with

three other comrades, escaped, but was recaptured
near the Blue Mountains, Va., and taken back again
to Libby prison, and thence transferred to Andersonville, Ga., in 1864. In December escaped from the
hospital at Andersonville with two comrades, Joseph
Pritchet of Ohio and Alex. Simpson of Indiana. We
were recaptured near Bainbridge, Ga., near the Florida
line, and returned to Andersonville in sixteen days
after escape. Remained in Andersonville until March
1865, when I was taken to Black river, Miss., near
Vicksburg, and paroled. Was placed on board the
steamer "Sultana" on the 25th of April, 1865. I
was on the outside of the cabin deck near the stairway
at the time of the explosion and jumped on a stage
plank and remained on it until it broke down, crushing
many prisoners under it. I then remained on the front
part of the boat until she was nearly burned up and
sinking, when I got hold of a piece of plank which
supported me until I floated ashore on the Arkansas
side of the river, where I was picked up by a skiff and
conveyed over to Memphis by the steamer " Bostonian."
I was discharged from the service at Columbus, Ohio,
on the 6th of May, 1865,

My present occupation is that of a shoemaker.
Postoffice address, Georgetown, Ohio.

11

WM. CARVER.

I ENLISTED in the service of the United States
November 5, 1862, in Company B of the 3rd Tennessee Cavalry, to serve three years or during the war.
Was captured at Sulphur Branch Trestle, which is
near Athens, Ala., September 25, 1864, and from there
was taken to Cahaba, Ala., where I remained until
the water had overflown the prison.   Left Cahaba
on the 6th and arrived at Vicksburg the 16th of
March, 1865, where I remained until the 24th of
April, and boarded the steamer" Sultana.''   On the
morning of the 27th of April, 1865, between two and
three o'clock, the explosion took place.   I was asleep
on the hurricane deck of the boat, behind the wheel-
house.   The report partially awoke me, and the next I
heard were the cries of the terrified people, which
words are inadequate to express.   I remained on the
boat as long as I could with safety, then went to the
lower deck and jumped overboard.   The drowning
men grabbed me and held me under the water.   As
soon as I got clear I came to the surface of the water
and swam to the wheel of the boat.   A comrade reached
down and helped me upon it.   I was very much
exhausted, and rested awhile, when I felt the wheel
giving way.   It broke loose and fell into the water and
drew me under.   I felt something strike my side.   It
was the iron rod in the wheel.   I clung to it the best I
could.   When the flames came towards me I buried
myself in the water as long as I could.   I was burned
severely on the right side of my face and shoulder.   In
some way I got on a board with a comrade, and we

floated to a drift pile on the Arkansas side of the river. I had no clothing on, and it was about daylight when we landed on the drift pile and two men came out to us in an old dugout and took five of us to the Arkansas shore. After a time the steamer "Silver Spray" came along, took us on board and landed us at Memphis, Tenn. I was placed in the hospital and well cared for, but my father was among the missing ones.

We left Memphis on the 30th of April for "Camp Chase," Columbus, Ohio, and from there to Nashville, Tenn., where I was discharged from the service June 10, 1865.

ABRAHAM CASSEL.

I WAS born in Montgomery county, Pa., and lived there until I was seventeen years of age, and then came to Ohio. Enlisted in the service of the United States at Findley, Ohio, on the 19th of January, 1861, in Company B 21st Regiment Ohio Volunteer Infantry. Was captured at Kingston, Ga., November 6, 1864, and taken to Cahaba, Ala. At the time of the explosion I swam about three miles and was rescued at 10 A. M., more dead than alive.

Not able to work. Postoffice address McComb, Ohio.

SIMEON D. CHELF.

I WAS born in Green county, Ky., on the 17th of
January, 1844. I enlisted in the service of the
United States at Liberty, Ky., on the 23rd of July,
1862, as a private in Company G of the 6th Kentucky
Cavalry. About the 1st of March, 1865, our regiment
left Nashville, Tenn., for East Port, Miss. After
letting our horses rest a few days we started on what
was known as the "Wilson raid," we supposed for
Mobile, Ala. Gen. Crookston with the first brigade,
which consisted of the 4th Kentucky Mounted Infantry,
2nd Michigan Cavalry, 6th Kentucky Cavalry and was

8th Iowa Cavalry, was en route for Tuscaloosa, Ala., and on the 31st encamped within twenty miles of Tuscaloosa. The next morning, by gray daylight, our pickets commenced firing. We were all soon mounted, and Companies C and G of the 6th Kentucky Cavalry were detailed for rear guard. Our army marched down the road and was gone about one hour when the firing increased. Then it ceased for a few minutes. Our companies were in line ready to march when the rebels commenced firing on us again. We swung into line and seeing so many blue coats we hallooed to them to cease firing which they did for a moment. Capt. Paris and Lieut. J. J. Surber ordered a charge, which was made expecting to regain our command although we encountered a larger force of rebels. We charged through the line of battle, then into a brigade that was marching by fours. At the rear of this brigade was a barricade (or a fence) built across the road. There five of us stopped and were firing down the column of another brigade, and while there we had to surrender. The rebels took us back on the road about a mile and then began to take such clothing from us as best suited them. Oh, well do I remember of a rebel who traded me a pair of shoes for a good pair of boots, and all the difference I got was: "Set down you 'Yank,' or I'll put my bayonet through you, while I pull them boots off." Of course the persuasion caused the trade. They then started to take us to prison. While marching along an old man came out to the road and said, "I guess, d—— you, you 'uns ain't out stealing horses today like you 'uns were yesterday." S. H. Davenport looked at him and said, "Yes, d—— your old soul,

you ain't hid in the woods like you were yesterday."
They marched us afoot until late in the night, and not
a bite to eat until on the 2nd of April, about 10 o'clock,
and that was dry corn dodgers.

We got to Uniontown, Ala., the 4th of April, and
while there some twenty or thirty of the 1st Mississippi
Cavalry came in.   They wanted to know " what kind
of guns you d—— ' Yanks'' got?' (We had Spencer car-
bines.) I told them that we could wind them up and
start them to shooting at sunrise and they would not
stop until sundown.   " Well, I believe it; for you 'uns
kept a solid cloud of lead over our breast-work at
Selma."

From Uniontown we went to Moberly, Ala., on Tombigbee river.   There we stopped for the night and I asked
permission to go and buy some sweet potatoes of some
"darkies."   It was granted, and a guard (we called
them our body-guard) went with me.   I got as many
potatoes as I could carry for a five-dollar confederate
bill, and on my return to where the rest of the boys
were I saw a confederate soldier peddling whiskey.
I asked him how he sold it, and he said, "five dollars a
glass."   I told him I would take three glasses.   I
drank one, gave one to my messmate and the other to
my lieutenant.

On the following morning we boarded a boat, crossed
the river and there the home guards were out, all of
them, wanting to kill a "Yank."   Then we started
from there to Meridian, Miss., where they searched
every one of us and marched us into prison.   When
the first two of our squad entered the prison the old
prisoners commenced yelling, "fresh fish."   After we

all got in they flocked around us to get the news from the outside world. Everyone was anxious to know what our army was doing. After we were in the prison awhile we drew our rations which were one pint of corn meal, ground cob and all together (this was one man's rations), and a half of a hog jowl for ten men per day, and also some pine wood with which we did our cooking. After our fires were in full blast one of the 7th Illinois Cavalry and I were talking. I said to him, "I do not want to hurt your feelings, but a body-guard is crawling on your neck." His reply was, "it does not hurt my feelings at all; if the sun shines out you will see plenty of them." (There is no use of my telling it for few will believe it.) The sun shone bright next day and you could see them crawling all over the prison, but lucky for us we did not remain there long.

We were on the road to Vicksburg, Miss., to go into parole camp. We were there when Lincoln was assassinated (one of the best men that ever sat in the presidential chair, and if he was alive today we, the rank and file, would be better treated by the law-making powers of the land). After we got into parole camp and had plenty to eat we were happy once more.

We boarded the ill-fated steamer "Sultana" April 25, 1865, and at dusk she started out with her heavy freight for Memphis, Tenn. The river was up to high-water mark (I thought it was over high-water mark when I came to try it).

We landed at Memphis, April 26, 1865, and unloaded some sugar, I don't know how much. We then pulled out to a barge of coal and took on enough to run to

Cairo, Ill. Then we started up the river, everything seeming to be safe. About two o'clock in the morning of April the 27th the boiler of the boat exploded· When this took place I was sleeping on the bow of the boat with my head against one of the cable posts. Seth H. Davenport was at my left and on his left was a man who was killed. A piece of iron glanced my head, and in the excitement I thought the rebels had fired a battery on us. My blankets were covered with ashes, cinders and fragments of timber and they were rather heavy to crawl from under. The front part of the cabin and the pilot house were blown to atoms and the stairway damaged so it could not be traveled. The boat was crowded with soldiers from boiler deck to hurricane deck. A man stood on the lower part of the stairway and hallooed, " the boat is sinking !" The men rushed to the bow of the boat and jumped overboard as fast as they could, tumbling into the river upon each other and going down into the deep by the hundreds.

After the main rush was over I had more room and could see what was going on. While gazing about I saw the fire start up in the coal that lay near the furnace. I looked for a bucket so as to get water to put it out, but couldn't find any. I went to the bow of the boat to see what had become of the man that was killed. He was still there but all of his clothing was torn off him by the men running over his body. I began to look for something to aid me in swimming. I found a board fourteen or sixteen feet long, and was watching my opportunity to jump off and to keep as far from anyone as I could, when A. M. Jacobs came to

me and asked me to save his life. He said, "you can
swim and I cannot." I replied, "I will help you all I
can, but a man cannot do much in water." He then
asked me to give him my board for his pole, as he
called it—it was a small post used in the framework
of the cabin, and was four by six inches square at each
end and the rest was worked down. I did so. We
both went to the bow of the boat to jump overboard,
but there were too many men in the water, the water
being covered with men's heads, all of them begging
for something to be thrown to them on which they
might escape. I believe I saw 150 or 200 men sink at
once near the bow of the boat.

The fire was now getting headway and sweeping
everything with which it came in contact, and I knew
I must take to the water. I looked around for the
man that was killed, but he was gone (I suppose some
one threw him overboard to keep him from being
burned up). Jacobs and I walked to the edge of the
boat and stopped and prayed, and, at the amen, we
both jumped overboard. Jacobs held to the board I
gave him, and when I came to the surface of the water
I told him to put one end of the board under his breast
and hold it there with one hand, paddle with the other
hand and to kick with both feet. After he got started
on his board I told him to do the best he could and I
started for the Arkansas shore.

The boat being now under heavy flames gave good
light so I could see the timber. When I got about half
way between the burning steamer and the shore a boat
came down the river with bales of hay, which were
dumped into the river. The waves overtaking me I

was strangled by their slapping me in the face. At length I got the run of them by diving through one and riding the next. When I was within three or four hundred yards from the timber a young man came swimming up behind me and said, "ha ! pard, haven't you something I could rest my hand on until we get to the bushes?" I stopped and looked at him and asked him if he had any clothes on. He said he had on his shirt. I told him to take it off and he could swim better. He did so, and I pushed my post back and he put his hand on one end, I on the other, and we both got the "step" and landed in the bushes together. Thinking now of having a good rest, I took hold the tops of two bushes; letting myself down full length and not finding bottom I concluded that was no place to rest and started out in the brush to find land. Coming to a leaning willow I threw my left arm and foot over it to rest. It held about half of my body out of water, but I got chilly in that position and again let down for bottom but could not find it. I then pulled out for the shore, but was unable to find it after wandering around one or two hours. (This is very much shorter than I thought it was at that time.)

I then started for the main part of the river, thinking some boat might pick me up, every now and then hallooing, "has anybody found land?" A man hallooed, "here's a good dry log you can get on." I told him to keep up a noise so I could find him (it being then the darkest hour of the night—just before daybreak). We kept up a chat until I reached the log which had a limb about three feet long. I threw my arms over the limb, but I could not kick another lick. I could not have got on the log if he had not helped me. I placed my feet on the limb and with my hands rubbed and hit myself on the breast. I got so blind I could not see. After that wore off I could stand up; then I jumped up and down to start the perspiration. After the dawn of day mosquitoes came on us by the thousands. We had it pretty lively then until we were taken on board of a vessel the name of which I do not remember. We were landed at Memphis and taken to the Soldiers' Home. All the clothing I had was a rebel hat, calico shirt, and a pair of red flannel drawers. A. Rhodes and I slept on a newspaper so as to keep our clothes clean. We remained there eight or ten days.

After we drew our clothing we were put on a boat and started for Cairo, Ill. There we stopped at the Soldier's Rest, afterward boarded a train and ran up to Mattoon, where the citizens had provided plenty for us to eat. From there we went to Terre Haute, Ind., where we were treated well by the citizens. From Terre Haute to Indianapolis, where we received a good supply of bacon and beans. Our next stopping place was Columbus, Ohio, where we stopped over night in Tod Barracks, and the following morning started for "Camp Chase" where we were discharged from the service.

While walking up the street we met a man who had a boiled shirt and he asked A. Rhodes, "What regiment is this?" He answered, "No regiment at all; just a detail of Wilson's cavalry sent down the Mississippi river to catch alligators."

My present occupation is farming. Postoffice address Lebanon, Kansas.

WILLIAM A. CHRISTINE.

I WAS born in Wooster, Ohio, September 23, 1841, and enlisted in the service of the United States at the same place, August 6, 1862, in Company H, 102d Ohio Volunteer Infantry. Was captured at Athens, Ala., 24th of September, 1864, and confined in the Cahaba, Ala., prison. At the time the "Sultana" exploded I was sleeping with my comrades on the hurricane deck. I looked around but saw nothing of them, so I went down into the cook room and found a barrel, with one end out, and threw it overboard and then jumped after it; but got into a crowd, so I let it go and got on the wheel and undressed and again jumped. Something fell on me and burned my head. On looking back I saw a plank floating toward me and grabbed hold of it. A young man who had a plank divided with me, and then we started on our trip down the river. Soon after this we were joined by comrade Elias Hines of the 18th Michigan. We noticed that the first man was not in his right mind, and on reaching one of those strong currents which carried us around, he fell off and I suppose was drowned. As he was about eight feet from either of us we could not help him, we had all we could do to hold the planks together. We floated down the stream until daylight, when, on reaching Memphis, we were picked up by some of the fire department and taken up the stream about a mile, when we crossed over and landed below the city among some barges. I received a blouse from Comrade Hines and a pair of pants from some one on the wharf, then went to the hospital and got cleaned up. The 102d Ohio Volunteer Infantry had one hundred and five (105) men on the boat and only thirty-two were saved. Out of fourteen men in Company H only three were saved.

Occupation, railway mail business. Postoffice address 319 East Spring street, Columbus, Ohio.

F. A. CLAPSADDLE.

I WAS born near Unionville, Columbus county, Ohio, July 28, 1842, and enlisted in the service of the United States, at Alliance, Ohio, August 9, 1862, in Company F, 115th Regiment Ohio Volunteer Infantry. Was captured at Block House No 1, Nashville & Chattanooga Railroad, December 4, 1863, and confined in the Meridian, Miss., and Andersonville, Ga., prisons.

The night of the explosion being a warm night I took off all my clothes but my shirt and drawers before lying down. I was on the hurricane deck, near the bell frame, fast asleep when the explosion took place Something fell and struck the frame, covering me so that I could not get out at first, but by hard pulling I crawled out under the rods or braces of it. The deck appeared to be deserted, I could not see anyone. I threw a blanket over my shoulders and jumped to the cabin deck and from there to the lower deck. I will ever remember the terrible scene I witnessed there. I got a small board, went to the west end of the boat, near the wheel, and commending myself to the care of Him who ruleth all things, I jumped into the water. I went down deep and strangled badly, but, being a good

swimmer, did not get excited. My greatest fear was
that I would get into the jam and someone would get
hold of me and pull me down under. I was within
talking distance of but one person while swimming.
I picked up two short pieces of boards while in the
water, and laid one across the other under my breast,
so that I kept above water without much trouble. I
became very cold and my limbs began to cramp. After
a while seeing a light I headed for it, and when I
reached the place some men threw a rope out to me; I
let my little bark go and grabbed hold of it, and about
daylight they pulled me ashore. I was very badly
chilled. There were fifteen of my company on the
boat and eight were lost.

Occupation, farming. Postoffice address Marlboro,
Stark county, Ohio.

GEORGE A. CLARKSON.

I WAS born in England, April 8, 1835. I enlisted
in (Capt. Motts) Company B, 1st Michigan Lan-
cers, August 5, 1861, and mustered out of the service
with regiment March 21, 1862. Re-enlisted as a
corporal in Company H (Capt. Purdy), 5th Michigan
Cavalry, August 18, 1862, at Milford, Mich. At the
battle of Trevillian Station, Va., June 11, 1864, was
taken prisoner with eighteen of my company. Was
taken to Richmond, Va., first to the Pemberton building—there stripped and searched for money, then to
Libby prison, and from there to Andersonville. Our
sufferings on the cars for the want of food and water

were great. Left Andersonville for Millen October
31st, and afterwards sent to Savannah, Blackshear, and
Thomasville. On the 20th of December, 1864, we were
started on foot for Albany—a killing march on the
frozen ground, barefooted and nearly naked—and on
December 25 were again placed in Andersonville where
we remained until March 25, 1865.

We afterwards crossed the Black river to the neutral
ground in rear of Vicksburg, Miss., on the 1st of April,
having taken an oath at Jackson, Miss., not to leave
until duly exchanged (do not know whether I was
exchanged or not). I left there for home April 25th
on the steamer "Sultana." I was suffering with diar-
rhea and scurvy, and a short time before the explosion
was to the rear of the boat. The men lay so thick that
I could not see any of the deck. All was peace and no
sign of disaster. I spoke to the engineer of how nicely
we were going and then returned to my place on the
deck, which was about twelve or fifteen feet forward of
the boilers next to the guard or railing of the boat.
Being chilly I wrapped my blanket around me, thereby
saving myself from the scalding water when the boiler
exploded. Wm. Brown of my company lay next to me
and was lost. Also one of Company M of the 5th regiment who was next to him. All of those around me
were scalded.

I remained on the boat until the fire drove the most
of us off of the bow of the boat into the water. I
threw a barrel into the river, but some one got it.
Men were thick in the river. I jumped as far as I
could, but someone caught hold of my feet and I kicked
him off. I was very weak, but an expert swimmer. I

secured a small piece of board about four inches by three feet which someone threw into the river. I had taken off all my clothes except my drawers and vest; in the latter was a diary and pictures of my wife and girls; these I saved. I did not try to swim, but floated about four miles, heading for the bank of the river. Getting into a clump of four or five small cottonwood trees I managed to get most of them bent down and stood on them up to my waist in the water. Once in awhile, losing my hold, I would get a ducking. I was on the Arkansas side of the river and the land was so overflown there was no getting to hard ground. I was rescued by the gunboat, "Pocahontas," at 9 A. M., and was so used up that I had to be lifted into the yawl by the sailors. Some ladies were on the gunboat who gave us shirts and drawers. It looked at the landing, at Memphis, as though all the vehicles in town were there to take us to the hospitals, etc. I was taken to the Washington Hospital, and after getting some new clothes was sent to " Camp Chase," Ohio, and from there I received a furlough (by order of the Secretary of War), and went home. I was mustered out of the service, July 5, 1865, at Detroit, Mich.

Since that time I have resided at Milford, Oakland county, Mich., and am completely broken-down, so that I have to live on my pension. I was a sash and door maker in factories.

GEORGE M. CLINGER.

I WAS born at Chester, now Maysville, Ky., August 4, 1844. Enlisted at Camp Kenton, Ky., in the service of the United States, October 13, 1861, as a corporal in Company E, 16th Kentucky Infantry. Was captured November 30, 1864, at Spring Hill, Tenn., near Franklin, Tenn., and taken to Cahaba, Ala., and was confined until the water rose to four feet deep in the prison; not one foot of dry ground was seen for six days. A steamer arrived from Selma, loaded with artillery for Mobile; she was ordered to halt at the prison, where we waded out and crawled on to the deck. We started down the Alabama river to Mobile as we were told, but on account of the heavy fighting we had to turn back. We then went up the Tombigbee river to Gainesville, where we were taken off and marched to Big Black river, back of Vicksburg, Miss., where we camped on neutral ground until the 24th of April, 1865. We received orders to pack up, which occupation did not take long for there was not much to pack. We were put on board the steamer "Sultana" while they were patching the boiler, and I heard the captain of the boat tell the quartermaster not to put any more on, as he had a load already.

We were driven on like so many hogs until every foot of standing room was occupied. We proceeded up the big Mississippi. As you all know, the river was out of the banks, and the levees were all overflowed. We stopped at a town called Helena, in Arkansas, where a photograph was taken of our steamer with about 2,300 souls on board. We arrived at Memphis,

13

Tenn., on the evening of the 26th of April where we unloaded some hogsheads of sugar and other freight, and about one o'clock in the morning of the 27th we left the coal bins on our journey home as we were told. All were in good spirits to think of going home to see loved ones; some of us had not seen either for more than two years.

About two or half-past two o'clock in the morning the awful explosion took place. I was sleeping with comrade Wilison of my company, next to the wheel-house, aft the boat on the Tennessee side. The wheel-house broke loose and I came near going down with it. That was the last I ever saw of Comrade Wilison. As nearly all were trying to get to the Tennessee side I did not see any chance to be saved there, so I went to the Arkansas side and jumped overboard and started away from the burning boat with George Proper, I think, and had swam until we got sight of the trees when I came across a small window shutter. I had not gone far when a man near me called for help for he was drowning. I shoved the shutter to him and by this means his life was saved. He was picked up with me by the steamer "Silver Spray." He was a captain, I believe, and belonged to the 2nd Michigan Cavalry. He made me give him my name, company, regiment and place of residence, and said he would visit me as I was the means of saving his life—that is the last I saw or heard of him.

We were taken back to Memphis, Tenn., where we were treated very kindly by the ladies of the Sanitary Commission who gave us under-clothing so as to cover our nakedness. After remaining there a few days we went on board a steamer bound for Cairo, Ill. From there we went to "Camp Chase," Ohio, thence to Louisville, Ky., where we were discharged from the service on the 17th day of June, 1865, under general order No. 77, current series, by Capt. Chas. Fletcher, 1st United States Infantry.

Am now a brick-mason and contractor. Postoffice address, Maysville, Ky.

J. S. COOK.

 I WAS born in Ireland February 15, 1842, and enlisted in the service of the United States at Cleveland, Ohio, in Company C, 115th Regiment Ohio Volunteer Infantry August 20, 1864. Was captured near Franklin, Tenn., December 5, 1864, and confined in the Andersonville prison. On the 24th of April, 1865, I with 2,400 other prisoners of war, was put on board the steamer "Sultana" at Vicksburg, Miss., on the Mississippi river, bound for Cairo, Ill., and from thence to our several homes as the war was over. Most of us died more than a dozen living deaths while in prison, and looked more like candidates for the bone-yard than for anything else. Nevertheless, when we heard the news that we were going home and back to God's country, we felt light-

hearted and merry as we thought of seeing our girls
again.

While Gen. Bangs walked down the gang-way, the
boys following him saw the old flag floating from the
jackstaff, they cried for joy and hugged each other like
school girls, but alas, our joy was of short duration.

We arrived at Memphis, Tenn., on the evening of the
26th of April, left there the same night and steamed
up the river. When about eight miles above Memphis
one of the boilers exploded while most all on board
were sleeping. What a scene of consternation! I pray
God to never let me witness anything like it again.
Men lying in all imaginable shapes, some crying, some
praying, many who, perhaps, never prayed before for
God to help them until it was too late; some with legs
broken, or arms smashed, and some scalded and
mangled in all ways. Those who were not disabled
seemed to be at a loss to know what to do. Many of
them stuck to the burning boat until the flames drove
them off and they went down in squads to rise no more.
After the survivors were picked up and placed in the
hospital at Memphis there were only six hundred, half
of whom were nearly dead. Many of these were picked
off of the tops of trees, as the river had overflown its
banks so that it was ten miles wide. I, with my bunkmate, J. C. Coak, was lying close to the bell on the
hurricane deck. The smoke-stack fell on the other
side, which crushed it down on the next deck below
and buried us up under a lot of boards so that I thought
for some time I could not extricate myself. When I
got on to my feet Coak spoke to me and I answered
him, and seeing what was the matter I turned around

to get a board to take with me to be of use in the
water. I looked around for Coak, but could not see
him and never have since. This was the saddest part
of my experience, as he was the only son of his father
and I had something to do with his enlisting. It so
affected the old man and grieved him that he died partially insane some years after.

Now my choice was between drowning and burning to
death. I chose the former and scrambled to the edge
of the boat and jumped overboard into the icy cold
water. I could not swim very much; and floated down
the stream about as fast as the boat so that I could see
everything that was going on. In my voyage I came in
contact with a large log floating down stream and got
upon it, but found that the log wanted to be on top of
the water only half of the time, so I gave up that ship
and clung to the little board until almost on the verge
of despair. The scenes of my life were passing through
my mind and I was about to give up all hope when I
saw down stream a dim light; this gave me new courage. As it approached me I saw that it was a
steamer, and as she neared me I shouted with all the
strength of a drowning man for help. When they
heard me they stopped and threw me a rope, by which
I was helped on board. After I was placed in the cabin
of the boat, a Union lady (whose name I have often
wished I knew), took off my wet clothing, put a dry
suit of "Uncle Sam's" clothes on me, got me up to
the stove and made me drink two horns of whiskey,
about fifteen minutes apart. This is the only time that
I felt that whiskey did me any good. These kind
actions were performed as a mother would perform a

duty for her child. I love to think of that woman, and
if I knew her whereabouts I would make her a visit.

WM. CRISP.

I WAS born in England, January, 1834, and enlisted
in the service of the United States at Hillsdale,
Mich., August, 1862, in Company D, 18th Regiment
Michigan Volunteers. Was captured at Athens, Ala.,
September 24, 1864, and confined in the Castle Morgan,
Cahaba, Ala., prison.

I was put on board the "Sultana" at Vicksburg.
The boiler exploded when about seven miles above
Memphis. I was badly burned and lost the use of one
arm; swam three miles and a half, and got in a tree.
I was rescued at seven A. M., April 28 (27th), 1865.

Occupation, farming. Postoffice address, Silver
Creek, Neb.

BEN G. DAVIS.

I WAS born in Brejen, Glamorganshire, South Wales,
on the 12th of May, 1827. Enlisted in Company
L, 7th Kentucky Cavalry. Was taken prisoner at La
Fayette, Ga., on the 23rd day of June, 1864, under
Col. Watkins' command, and taken to Cahaba, Ala.,
and remained there until about November, 1864. Was
then removed to Meridian, Miss. Stayed there about
four or five weeks, when I was taken back to Cahaba,
Ala., and remained there until about March 20, 1865,
when the Alabama river overflowed the country, rising

about two feet all over the prison. We had to do our cooking on rafts, and a great many men were sleeping on them. During the high water a steamboat came up the river and took about six hundred of the prisoners away, they being sent to parole camp at Vicksburg. When the boat came in sight there was a great rush for it. Everybody wanted to get out of prison. There was a sick sergeant that belonged to my regiment, his name was Morris Malaley. He was not able to travel through the water to the boat and I undertook to carry him through. When I got to the stage plank the boat had let loose and we had to go back to the prison. We remained there three days, when another boat came and I had to carry the sick man again, but this time we caught the boat and were taken to the parole camp. In about three weeks the " Sultana" came to Vicksburg and took nearly 2,300 on board to go to "Camp Chase," Ohio. A little above Memphis the boat stopped to get coal, and when everything was ready they started up the river. About two o'clock in the morning I got up to have a smoke. I went to the boilers to get a light for my pipe and going back to the hurricane deck, where I had been sleeping, I sat down for about ten minutes. When I got through with my smoke I got a canteen of water, and was about to take a drink when the boiler exploded and the canteen flew out of my hand. I never saw it again. Morris Malaley and myself, from Covington, Ky., John Andorf and Joe Moss, from Cincinnati, were sleeping under the same blankets, and when the explosion took place I thought the boat had all gone to pieces. In the conusion there was no command whatever. I remained on the boat until the side wheel was burned clear to the water; by this time it was getting too hot for me and I let myself down to the lower deck by a rope. There were so many people in the water you could almost walk over their heads. The fire was sweeping through the boat so that I could not bear to stay there longer. I got a shutter about three feet square, and at this time I found Joe Moss. He begged me to let him have the shutter as he could not swim. I threw it into the river and told him to follow it, which he did; I never saw him again. I pulled off all my clothes except my shirt and jumped into the river, making toward the Arkansas shore. I knew I had a good journey before me, but got there all the same. When I reached the Arkansas willows I could not find a safe place, so swam about forty or fifty yards down. Here I found a large log fast in the willows so I mounted it. I could hear so much groaning that I "hollered" to them to encourage them, telling them I was on shore. One man, who was pretty close to me, asked me what regiment I belonged to. I told him to the 7th Kentucky Cavalry, and he said, "here's a 4th Michigan after you." They kept on coming till there were five of us on the log. I always did believe that I was the first to land on the Arkansas shore, that morning about half-past three o'clock A. M. Between eight and nine o'clock a man in a canoe came and picked us up, taking us down to a plantation right opposite where the hulk of the "Sultana" was tied up. There I met John Andorf, one of my bunk-mates. I guess everyone that was on the "Sultana" knew something about the monstrous alligator that was on the boat. It was nine and one-half feet long. While the boat was burning the alligator troubled me almost as much as the fire.

My postoffice address is Covington, Ky.

JOHN DAVIS

WAS born near Ottawa, Putnam county, Ohio, October 26, 1840. When about one year old was moved to Ayersville, Defiance county, Ohio, which has been his home till the present. He enlisted July 30, 1862, in Company D, 100th Regiment Ohio Volunteer Infantry. Took part in the battles of Rocky Face Ridge, Resaca, Dallas, Utoy Creek, Atlanta, Columbia and Franklin. Was slightly wounded at the battle of Resaca, and was captured at the battle of Franklin on November 30, 1864. Was confined at first at Meridian, Miss., but was soon removed to Andersonville, Ga., and finally taken from there and placed on neutral ground in the rear of Vicksburg, Miss., till sent north with other exchanged prisoners on the ill-fated steamer "Sultana."

At the time of the explosion was sleeping on boiler deck within fifteen or twenty feet of the stern door. Had as bunk mates A. W. King, Wm. Wheeler, George Hill and James A. Fleming. The last named was lost, as well as Valmore Lambert who was on cabin deck over the boilers.

After the explosion he reached the stern door in a rather suffocating condition, but was not much injured by the explosion, and remained upon the boat until driven off by the flames. The river was very high and the water icy cold. Was in the water at least two or three hours, but was finally picked up by a boat sent to the rescue. When taken into the boat could not stand alone and was perfectly prostrated. Was put to bed in the cabin of the boat and carried to Memphis. Remaining in Memphis two or three days was then sent by steamer to Cairo, Ill., thence by rail to Columbus, Ohio, and there discharged by special telegraphic order from the War Department.

Postoffice address is Ayersville, Ohio.

L. A. DEERMAN.

I WAS born August 11, 1837. I enlisted in the service of the United States on the 1st of February, 1864, at Nashville, Tenn., in Company K, of the 3rd Regiment of Tennessee Cavalry. I remained at Nashville until the 18th of June, 1864, then started for Athens, Ala., and arrived at that point on the 20th of June, 1864, as well as I can remember at the present time. We went into camp and remained there until the 25th of September, 1864, when I was captured at the battle of Sulphur Branch Trestle, which is six miles above Athens.

Cahaba was the next point. It was an awful one, too, when I arrived there, but I must come back to the night before I arrived at Cahaba.. One of my friends and I made our escape by jumping from a flat car, about ten o'clock P. M., at a place about ten miles above Selma, Ala., in the swamps—the darkest and

lonesomest place that I ever saw. We stopped close
by the place where we leaped from the car until morning, then we started out, wading the water that was in
the swamp. The water kept growing deeper and
deeper until it compelled us to change our course and
we soon arrived at a large farm. It being cloudy and
foggy we soon lost our course and traveled around at
random about one hour. The sun shone out and we
found that we had been lost. We stopped to rest until
night, but in a short time our rest was disturbed by
the barking of dogs and "hollering" of men. They
soon came upon us. There were five dogs and two men.
We surrendered, of course, as we had nothing by which
we could defend ourselves. We were then carried to
Selma, Ala., and from there to Cahaba prison, arriving
there about the first of October, 1864. I remained
there until the 6th of March, 1865, but my friend
made his escape from the prison before this and succeeded in reaching Nashville, Tenn. I was taken on
board a boat bound for Vicksburg, Miss., on the 6th
of March, 1865, arriving there about the 18th or 19th
of March, 1865. To the best of my recollection I
remained there until about the 24th or 25th of April.

From Vicksburg I went aboard of the great steamer
"Sultana." Late in the evening she pulled out and
landed at Memphis, Tenn., to unload sugar, leaving
there the evening of the 26th, or morning of the 27th
of April. As I had been up all of the previous night
and had not had any rest or sleep, two or three of the
boys and myself went half way back on the deck and
made us a good bed out of our blankets and went to
bed like white people, as we had not done for some time

prior. I never knew when the boat left Memphis, nor did I know anything until about three o'clock next morning, when the noise of the explosion awoke me from my dreams. The first thing I knew I was standing on my feet looking, listening, and thinking what in the world is the matter now? I soon found out what was the matter. I turned and looked and saw one of the smoke stacks lying in front of me. I saw at once that it was torn to fragments, and such screaming and yelling was never heard. By this time nearly everybody was in the water swimming for life. I saw that I would soon have something to do. One of my messmates that went to bed with me that night came up to me with a board which was one and one-half inches by ten inches and eight feet long, and said, "Lewis, I can't swim a lick, do you think this will be of any good?" I replied, "Yes," and picked up a short board about three feet long and said to him, "Come on, I will help you all I can." I jumped into the water, holding on to my board and told Frank to put his board in and "I will hold on to it until you get on; you stay on one end of the board and kick with your feet, and don't let anyone get on with you if you can help it." He did so. I gave him a start and got him out from among the crowd. He made it all right and was the first man I saw the next morning with whom I was acquainted. I went on and on swimming for my life on my short board. It seemed to me that I was in the water about an hour and a half. While I was in the water I struck an old log; one end of it was hanging to something and the other end was floating about in the water. I caught hold of the end of it and pulled myself upon the log and here remained until eight o'clock in the morning. I could hear the boys, all up and down the river banks on logs, bushes and drift, smacking and rubbing themselves to keep warm, and crowing like chickens while many a poor boy was sinking or floating in the deep waters of the Mississippi. Oh! this was so unexpected to that crew that night.

We were carried back to Memphis and remained there ten days, and then we took a boat and started for Cairo, Ill., and from thence to "Camp Chase," Ohio. We remained at this place a few days and from here went to Nashville, Tenn., where we remained until the 10th of June, 1865, when I was discharged.

I was a farmer when I enlisted in the service and am still trying to farm. I live in St. Clair, Ala., near Steel's depot on the A. G. S. railroad.

J. W. DUNSMORE.

I ENLISTED in the service of the United States at Ionia, Ionia county, Mich., December 25, 1863, in Company I, 1st Regiment Michigan Engineers and Mechanics, and joined the regiment at Bridgeport, Tenn. Was captured at a small place called Ackworth, August 8, 1864, and taken to the Cahaba prison. In March I was taken to Vicksburg and put on board the "Sultana." Her boiler exploded when about ten miles above Memphis. At the time H. C. Aldrich and myself were lying on one of the upper decks, near the starboard wheel-house. He said, "What shall I do, I cannot swim?" I replied, "You have got to." I got two

blinds for him from a window and he went overboard.
I followed him as quickly as possible. While I was
swimming for dear life, a man called to me and asked
for a chew of tobacco. I started to swim for the timber and was caught in an eddy and nearly drowned.
When I got out of it I could see the lights of Memphis, but could not reach the dock, and finally was
pulled out by a colored guard at Fort Pickens. Was
sent from there to "Camp Chase," Ohio, and was
given a furlough. I was discharged at Detroit, June,
1865.

Occupation, farming. Postoffice address, Harrison,
Clare county, Mich.

J. WALTER ELLIOTT.

I WAS born in South Hanover, Ind., March 22, 1833,
and enlisted in the service of the United States at
La Fayette, Ind., April 18, 1861, in Company E, 10th
Regiment Indiana Volunteer Infantry, and promoted
as captain, in Company F, 44th Regiment, United
States Colored Troops, in July, 1864; was captured
near Nashville, Tenn., December 2, 1864, and confined
in the Cahaba, Ala., and Andersonville, Ga., prisons.

I have seen death's carnival in the yellow-fever and
the cholera-stricken city, on the ensanguined field, in
hospital and prison, and on the rail; I have, with wife

and children clinging in terror to my knees, wrestled with the midnight cyclone; but the most horrible of all were the sights and sounds of that hour. The prayers, shrieks and groans of strong men and helpless women and children are still ringing in my ears, and the remembrance makes me shudder. The sight of 2,000 ghostly, pallid faces upturned in the chilling waters of the Mississippi, as I looked down on them from the boat, is a picture that haunts me in my dreams. But to the narrative. Where shall I begin? Memory with faultless faithfulness, reproduces a thousand pictures of the dark days of the winter of 1864-5.

Captured and paroled in October; ordered on duty without exchange, and again captured while trying to steal through Hood's lines at Nashville on December 2, 1864, I knew full well that a recognition would be swiftly followed by a drumhead court-martial and my execution. Therefore I assumed the name and command of one Capt. David E. Elliott, of Company E, 75th Indiana, who I knew was with Sherman on his march to the sea, and never until I had shaken the dust of the confederacy from my feet did I disclose my identity to friend or foe—and the sixty autograph albums gotten up by my companions in Castle Reed will attest it.

Shall I tell of the march over ice and snow; the wading of deep streams from Nashville to Dixon, two miles below Cherokee, on the Memphis & Charleston railroad; the suffering from cold and exposure in the dead of winter, and from hunger, when I bought a bushel of corn meal for thirty-two dollars in greenbacks, and then eating not half what I craved, but dividing with my fellows; of seeing a wagon load of corn on the ear, driven into the prison-corral and thrown out to us as though we were a lot of fattening hogs; of the number of dead we left on the ground next morning, killed by eating raw corn after a four days' fast; of my confinement, without food, for a day and night in a close, crowded box-car, in which fresh horse dung was half a foot deep; of the indignities, the humiliations and cruelties heaped upon us by cowards playing Provost Marshal; of our sojourn at Cahaba, Ala.; of our removal from that purgatory to that hell of hells at Andersonville, presided over and improved upon daily by his Satanic Majesty's most loyal representative on earth, Capt. Wirz, ably assisted by his brothers of royal blood, who were kenneled, fed and guarded by one of the C. S. A.'s most trusted lieutenants, with a picked command, scarcely second to the historic Old Guard? Oh! the long and dreary winter in prison; the suffering from cold, hunger, and the petty tyranny of cowards clothed with a little brief authority; the stench of rotten meat, of which we had not half enough to eat; the bitter, bitter feeling that our country had abandoned us to our fate, refusing to exchange because it would be exchanging able-bodied soldiers for us who were starved until we could be of no service.

How day by day, through long weary weeks each of us watched his fellows slowly but surely starving to death, and already mourned as dead by fond loved ones at home. "Get ready for exchange," came the order. Oh! the joyous shout that made the castle walls ring out. How each of us laughed and cried, shook hands with and hugged his fellows, and joining hands in a

15

circle, in good old Methodist campmeeting-altar style,
as we all joined in singing "Rally Round the Flag,
Boys." The joy of that good hour more than repaid
for all past tribulations.

Sixty-five officers formed in line awaiting orders.
"Behold death on a pale horse," says that grand old
soldier, Gen. Noble, of Bridgeport, Conn., as Capt.
Wirz enters the stockade on a white pony. At
the cars we joined some 500 privates from the
stockade, and a more pitiable sight city life in its
worst phases never disclosed. All were begrimed and
blackened by exposure, without a pretense of protection
from summer's sun or winter's rain; all weak and
lean from starvation; many, too feeble to take care
of themselves, were literally encased in scales, beneath
which were myriads of living vermin eating all vitality
away. Two I saw doubled up and scarred all over,
having been literally torn in pieces by the dogs, because
they attempted to escape from the devil's domain.

We left a good many poor fellows dead along our
entire route. Thrice derailed, twice we had two cars
wrecked, crippling a good number of the boys. On
March 26 we hailed the glorious flag of our country as
it floated on the breeze. Tears flowed at sight of that
proud emblem, while Big Black river, Jordan-like,
divided the forlorn C. S. A. from our Canaan. We
crossed; we gathered at the river; we sang and danced
and rested under the shade of the trees. Out from the
gates of hell—out from the jaws of death—going home.

On our arrival at prison camp, six miles in rear of
Vicksburg, we received a glorious welcome and invitation to "take something;" that is, we were taken to

the Commissary, where barrel after barrel of pickled cabbage was rolled out and the heads knocked in, and we, marching round and round, gobbled out and ravenously devoured the cabbage and licked the vinegar from our fingers, the sweetest dainty to my bleeding gums that ever I tasted.   We feasted on pickles.

Next day we exchanged our filthy rags for clean clothing, wrote home, rested and feasted. About 2,500 embarked on the Sultana for St Louis, together with a good many passengers, crowded, jammed and packed on all the decks and guards and in the cabin. But what cared the survivors of Andersonville—the war was over and we were going home.

Nothing unusual occurred until we reached Memphis, although I had suffered much from fear of the boys crowding to one side of the boat and capsizing her. One instance in particular: While at Helena a photographer was "taking" the boat, and each soldier seemed to be bent on having his face discernible in the picture. I entreated and exhorted prudence, while I sat on the roof, my feet pendant and my hands on a float, momentarily expecting a capsizing and sinking.

Each night the cabin was filled with a row of double-deck cots. I had been fortunate in securing one of these, but on the night previous to reaching Memphis, I suddenly conceived and executed the purpose of making a stranger, whose name I never knew—our Commissary Sergeant in parole camp—occupy my cot while I spent the night in a chair.

The boat lay at the Memphis wharf discharging freight, and the cots were being placed, when my

friend of the night before came to me and asked if I
had a cot. I pointed to my hat, placed on one to hold
it. He said that one was in a hot, unpleasant and
dangerous place over the boilers, and that he had
reserved one for me in the ladies' cabin; that I had
my way the night before, and he must have his way
now.

"Give it to some poor fellow who had none last
night," I said; but a moment afterwards he came and
told me he had removed my hat to the cot selected by
him, and that I would have to take that or none. Soon
I retired to the cot, read until weary, fell asleep, was
partly aroused by the boat leaving the wharf a little
after midnight, but relapsed into sweet slumber, dream-
ng of the loved ones at home—a motherless daughter,
a noble christian mother, two devoted sisters, and my
brothers. How I reveled in the joy of the reunion.

A report as of the discharge of a park of artillery,
a shock as of a railroad collision, and I am sitting bolt
upright, straining my eyes and stretching my arms out
into the Egyptian darkness; face, throat and lungs
burning as if immersed in a boiling cauldron. Crash,
crash fall the chimneys on the roof ! Oh, that I could
shake off this horrible nightmare ! But now from all
around rise shrieks, cries, prayers and groans. Have
I awakened in the dark regions of the lost? I spring
to my feet, hastily dress, start forward, groping my
way between the state-room doors and the cots, to learn
what has happened.

Suddenly I find a yawning opening in the floor. I
pause in doubt and uncertainty for a second, when the
scene lights up from below, disclosing a picture tha

beggars all description—mangled, scalded human forms heaped and piled amid the burning debris on the lower deck. The cabin, roof and texas are cut in twain; the broken planks on either side of the break projecting downward, meeting the raging flames and lifting them to the upper decks.

Women and little children in their night clothes, brave men who have stood undaunted on many a battle field, all contribute to the confusion and horror of the scene as they suddenly see the impending death by fire, and wringing their hands, tossing their arms wildly in the air, with cries most heart-rending, they rush pell-mell over the guard into the dark, cold waters of the river; while the "old soldier" is hastily providing for himself anything that will float—tables, doors, cots, partition planks—anything, everything. What a worse than Babel of confusion of sights and sounds as each seeks his own safety, regardless of others. Where is the cot of my selection a few hours previous, and where its occupant? Ask of that holocaust below. "There is a divinity that shapes our ends."

"Captain, will you please help me?"

I turned in the direction of the voice so polite, so cool and calm amid this confusion. There, on the head of the last cot on this side of the breach, which was covered with pieces of the wreck, sat a man, bruised, cut, scalded in various places, both ankles broken and bones protruding. With his suspenders he had improvised tourniquets for both legs, to prevent bleeding to death.

"I am powerless to help you; I can't swim," I replied.

But he answered, "Throw me in the river is all I ask; I shall burn to death here."

I called Capt. Chapman of LaFayette, whom I never saw afterward, and we bore McLoyd aft and threw him overboard. I then got hold of a life-preserver for myself just as a frightened maiden in nightgown only rushed past me. I seized her as she was leaping from the guard and called the chambermaid, who put my life-preserver on the girl. I then had no chance for escape, as I thought, and death seemed inevitable.

I worked and toiled to my very utmost to assist others, until all was done that I could do. Then the thought occurred to me that it was my duty to make an effort to save myself. I saw two Kentuckians meet, each lamenting that he could not swim. "Then let us die together," said one. "Well," replied the other, and, embraced in each other's arms, they leaped, sank, and the muddy waters closed over them. I saw others, blinded by the explosion, leap into the fire and die.

I now cast about me for something I could use as a buoy, but everything available seemed to have been appropriated. I tried to improvise a life-preserver out of a stool. I threw a mattress overboard; it floated and was at once caught on to by several who were struggling in the water. I got another mattress, and slipping down a fender onto the taffrail I dropped it, but it no sooner touched the water than four men seized it, turned it over, and it went under as I jumped. Down, down I went into the chilly waters. Some poor drowning wretch was clutching at my legs, but putting my hands down to release myself and vig- orously treading water, I rose strangling to the surface, my scalded throat and lungs burning with pain. The mattress was within reach, with only one claimant. God only knows what had become of the three others. Placing my arms on the support I began a life-and-death struggle to escape from the falling wheel-house, which I barely succeeded in doing, but its waves strangled me and came near sweeping my companion off. There seemed to be acres of struggling humanity on the waters, some on debris of the wreck, some on the dead carcasses of horses, some holding to swimming live horses, some on boxes, bales of hay, drift logs, etc. Soon we parted company with the wreck and the crowd and drifted out into the darkness almost alone.

A boat—the Gen. Boynton—passed near, whistled and hove to, but finding her efforts at rescue futile, she steamed away and gave the alarm at Memphis, and the gunboats and steamers there sent out lifeboats and yawls to pick up those floating by from seven miles above. Having floated nearly five miles we struck a small drift that seemed stationary, and that I correctly thought was on the overflowed Arkansas shore. I crawled upon a large floating tree. Chilled and benumbed, I could not sit up. I had three large doses of quinine in my pocket, took them all at once, and by vigorous rubbing soon was able to stand and walk. Meantime my companion was helpless, and could not get onto my drift. I held the mattress to the drift, and with a keen switch I struck the man—who, by the way, was dressed in but one garment, and that a very brief one—and striking first one place, then another, he begging piteously all the while and rubbing where

I struck—I hope he has forgiven me that whipping—I
soon had him up, and together we pulled one young
woman and two men out of the water, who soon chilled
to death in spite of all we could do for them.

Shivering with cold, silently we paced back and
forth on that floating cypress.   Minutes seemed hours,
as we kept our lonely vigil over the lifeless form of
that beautiful girl and of the two brave men who had
passed the perils of field and prison only to die in this
way just when all danger seemed past.   There was no
sound to break the oppressive silence save the plashing
of the cruel waters and the gurgling moan of a poor
fellow who had clasped his broken, scalded arms over
a scantling and drifted, with his mouth just above the
water, and lodged near us, dying.   An occasional feeble cry of distress near by on the river side, was answered by voices up the bank.   Oh, would morning
never dawn on night so hideous?

At last the sun, as if reluctant to light the scene of
horror, slowly disclosed to my view the poor wretch
clinging in unconsciousness to the floating scantling,
who immediately expired when taken from the water.
There were also to be seen some half dozen soldiers on
the roof of a cabin above us, and here and there a chilled
half-frozen soldier clinging to the branches of a tree
or perched on a bit of floating drift; but my attention
was devoted especially to a man some forty yards from
me on the river side, clinging to a pole or upright snag,
worn smooth by the waters.   When first I made him
out his feet were above the water, and he was climbing
with all the strength he had to reach a projecting snag
to rest thereon; but failing, he stopped, then slipped

gradually, inch by inch, down the pole until his feet
were beneath the water. Again he tried to reach the
rest above, falling short of the point before reached.
So periodically climbing and falling back, each time
he sank lower and failed to climb as high as before.
At last he had to throw his head back to keep his chin
above water, and, climbing, he failed to get his waist
out of the flood.

Only a few minutes and he will make his last futile
effort and the lifeless body will be borne away on the
muddy tide. Oh, how I wish I could swim! Now
comes a Confederate soldier in a batteau, from his
camp not far inland. I hail him and send him in
haste to the rescue. With great effort, and danger to
himself, he drags the stiffened and almost lifeless body
from that pole and bears it to a place of security on
the log-cabin roof, where with vigorous rubbing the
boys soon "bring him round." Here and there goes
that batteau taking the imperiled to places of safety.

And now the Jenny Lind—a little steamer from
Memphis—comes, and "Johnny" puts his passengers
on board, taking them from cabin-roof, drifts and trees;
myself the last one in sight. At the boat Lieut. Mc-
Cord, of Bellevue, O, our "Susan" of Castle Reed—
pulls me on board, and in the joy of the meeting we
for the moment forget the loss of many of our brave
companions. If "Susan" still lives, I wonder if he
ever laughs over my giving him my red flannel drawers
and of his promenade with me through Memphis to the
Quartermaster's, barefoot and clad only in red shirt
and drawers.

Just after boarding the boat, I saw a "dugout,"

paddled by a citizen, coming out of the woods, and in the bottom there lay McLoyd. I helped lift him on board and lay him on deck and gave him a tumbler of whisky. When I left Memphis he was in the hospital there, and I know not whether he survived, but rather think he did.

But what had become of my chivalrous knight of the gray? How he dignified "the gray." Silently he had disappeared when his good work was done, with that modesty inseparable from true royalty of heart. Would that I knew his name.

Reaching Memphis I met young Safford, of North Madison, Ind., whose father had joined us at Vicksburg as a Sanitary Commissioner. The father's arms were both badly scalded, and he was otherwise injured. The son put two life preservers on his father and one on himself, and they hastily got upon a state-room door in the water. A horse leaping from the boat struck the door, knocking them off and separating them. The son was taken up unconscious opposite Memphis by the life-boat from the "Essex" and now restored he was inquiring and searching for his father. Together he and I opened more than a hundred coffins on the wharf, hoping to have the satisfaction of giving him a burial, that his body should not be lodged on some bar to become food for fishes.

Then together we visited the office of a morning paper, where I for the first time gave my real name and command. Here we met Erwin, a United States scout, who had been the senior Safford's companion and he gave the young man his father's watch, a very valuable gold one, and told us that Mr. Safford had been

discovered and rescued in an unconscious state by some
negroes on President's Island, having floated twelve
miles.

The son took the first boat for the island, where he
found his father as had been told him, and took him
to Madison some days after.

I, with a number of surviving officers, was sent to
quarters at a hospital. I was sent for that afternoon
by Mrs. Hartsock of Illinois, aunt of my deceased wife,
who had seen my name in the paper. Soon I joined
her at the fort below.

When I returned to the city the second day afterward I was hailed at every turn, "Captain, they have
left us. You must get transportation for us and take
us home." So I gathered up the boys—all who were
able to be moved, about 250—and shipped them for
Cairo. We had a dozen or more scalded men laid on
the cabin floor, and nursed them. At Cairo I placed
the well in barracks and the wounded in hospitals for
the night. I succeeded next day in getting cars, by
which we arrived at Mattoon at early dawn of the day
following. We had had nothing to eat for twenty-four
hours, and there was no way to feed the men. Citizens
crowded around to see the heroes of the great disaster,
who, at my request, took the boys to their homes and
breakfasted them.

Then came trouble about cars. If cars should be
sent thence to Indianapolis they would be kept for
debt owing by one road to the other, but on my personal pledge to return the coaches we got them, which
pledge the superintendent at Indianapolis cheerfully
redeemed.

From Mattoon I wired the mayor of Terre Haute, and also Governor Morton. Terre Haute gave us a dinner worthy of my grand old native State. At Indianapolis we found ambulances in waiting for the disabled, and a good supper prepared for all. Here I surrendered my charge, and, completely worn out by my watching and nursing on the river and rail, I stopped at the first inn I found, that of an Englishman, on Illinois street, near the Union depot, who generously tendered the hospitalities of his house to me and my companions.

My present occupation is farming and fruit-growing. Postoffice address, Arba, Ala.

WILLIAM FIES.

(Adjutant National " Sultana" Survivors' Association.)

I WAS born in Ellmendingen, Baden, Germany, October 17, 1841. My parents emigrated to the United States in the year 1847, and located in New York city, from which place we removed to Marion, Ohio, in the month of September, 1852. At the age of seventeen years I was apprenticed to learn the trade of cabinet making. On the 30th day of October, 1861, I enlisted as a private in Company B, 64th Regiment Ohio Volunteer Infantry, at Marion, Ohio; was appointed corporal November 16, 1862, and was promoted to sergeant April 1, 1864. I served with the company and regiment until January, 1864, when I re-enlisted at Blain's X Roads, East Tennessee, for three years longer, and was re-mustered January 27,

WILLIAM FIES.

1864, in Company B, 64th Regiment Ohio Volunteer
Infantry, participating in all the campaigns, battles
and skirmishes, with the company and regiment, except the battle of Chickamauga, at which time I was on
detached duty and engaged in recruiting service.

I was taken a prisoner with five others of my company at the battle of Franklin, Tenn., Nov. 30, 1864;
marched the next day to Columbia, Tenn., and after
being held there a few days, we were marched with
about 1800 other prisoners to Corinth, Miss., Selma
and Montgomery, Ala., finally reaching Meridian,
Miss., where we were confined for a few days in a stockade.   When we reached this place most of us were in a
deplorable condition, having marched several hundred
miles over bad roads, in the winter season, with scanty
clothing and scantier rations; a great many were barefooted, and a number were sick.   We were shipped
from here to Andersonville, Ga.   I will not attempt a
description of this hell on earth; nearly all have read
descriptions of it.   On March 26, 1865, I, with several
hundred others, was taken out of the prison, and
finally, after a tedious journey, partly by rail and the
rest of the distance on foot, we reached and were
encamped on the Big Black river, near Vicksburg,
Miss.   On the 23d or 24th of April, (according to the
records of the War Department) 1865, paroled union
prisoners of war, of which number I was one, were
loaded on board of the ill-fated steamboat, "Sultana,"
at Vicksburg, Miss., more like so many cattle than
men, which, together with the passengers and crew,
made in all about 2,021 souls, besides a freight cargo,
making in all a cargo of several times the carrying

capacity of the boat, and were headed up the river, our destination being Cairo, Ill.

The "Sultana" landed at Memphis, Tenn., on the evening of April 26, where a portion of her cargo of freight was discharged. Some time during that night the boat left the wharf at Memphis and steamed up the river, making a landing to take on coal. Before we left Memphis my bunk-mate, comrade A. O. Cranmer, of my company, and I fixed down our bed on the cabin deck and on the starboard side near the railing. I remember, just before I fell asleep, Captain Mason, in command of the boat, came up from below, to go to his stateroom I presume, and was compelled to crawl around on the rail, as the deck was so crowded with men lying down that he could not find room to step, and was in consequence made the subject of several jokes. After this incident I fell asleep, and did not wake up until after the explosion, which occurred about two o'clock A. M., at which time I was brought to my senses by some water which was thrown over me by some one on the hurricane deck. When I came to my senses I found myself standing on a part of the wreck, in front of and near the starboard wheel house, surrounded by wreckage, and in the midst of smoke and fire. The agonizing shrieks and groans of the injured and dying were heart rending, and the stench of burning flesh was intolerable and beyond my power of description. I was not aware at that time that the boilers had exploded, but thought the boat had caught on fire.

Judging from the injuries I received I must have been knocked senseless by the explosion, as I found the

left side of my face bruised and bleeding, my left hand
badly scalded, and my left shoulder disabled, which
afterwards proved to be a very bad dislocation.   When I
took in the situation, and saw the dangerous place I
was in, I took hold of an iron brace rod near me which
was so hot that it actually blistered my hands, and
scrambled onto the hurricane deck, where I found a
number of men trying to extinguish the fire by throwing water with buckets.   From them I first learned
that the boilers had exploded.   From there I slid down
a rope to the bow of the boat, carrying with me a small
wooden box, which I thought might become useful to
me in case I was compelled to take to the water.   I
changed my mind, however, and threw it aside.   I saw
a number of men bringing from the hold empty cracker
barrels and jumping overboard with them, but I saw
they were worse than useless in keeping the heads of
the men above water, having only one head in them
they would not balance.   Just at this time the stage
plank was lowered from its hangings and about as many
as could get a hold of it were trying to launch it, first
on one side then on the other, finally it went overboard
carrying with it a great number, but as it was heavily
bound with iron it sank, and must have carried down
with it a great many who had a hold of it and others
who were struggling in the water to keep afloat and
save themselves.

Seeing now that all other means of escape were cut
off, I began to look around for something to save
myself with, as it was now apparent the fire was fast gaining headway, and would soon burn through the slight
barrier formed by portions of the upper decks which

had fallen down, and which had up to this time kept
most of the flames from reaching those of us who were
on the bow of the boat. Just at this time I saw Robert White, a member of my regiment, standing with
one arm around the flag staff, looking on the struggling mass of humanity in the water below him. As I
knew he had followed steamboating before the war, I
thought he might be able to give me some advice. I
went to him and said, "Bob, what is to be done?" and
all he said was: "Billy, I guess we will all be drowned
or burned up." I was of the same opinion, but made
up my mind to at least make an effort for my life, in
which I was successful, while poor Bob was either
drowned or burned up as he predicted, for I never saw
him again.

After this incident I went aft a short distance to
find, if possible, something that would keep my head
above water, but all I could find was some splinters of
boards; everything else had been taken, even to a box
which had contained a live alligator. I had picked up
a piece of rope with which I tied the splinters together
into a convenient bundle. About this time the fire
had burned through the wreckage, and it became
apparent that those of us who were still on board
would either be compelled to jump overboard or burn
up. I chose the former, and went over with my
bundle and sank a few feet under water. I rose to
the surface and about this time some other fellow, who
I thought must have weighed at least 200 pounds, came
down on top of me and knocked me under again.
When I again came to the surface my bundle of splinters was gone, and I was just about gone myself as some

other fellow had taken a hold of me, but I kicked him loose. Notwithstanding my disabled condition and being at best only a poor swimmer, I managed to keep my head above water at least a part of the time, and get away from the mass of men struggling for life.

When I was just about exhausted and thought my time had come, I came to a fellow with a nice large board. He was the only occupant but I saw at once that he was very much excited and was not making any headway. I took hold of the board, throwing my disabled left arm over it, when he cried to me, "For God's sake let go, I am drowning." I said to him, "You fool, keep cool, this board is large enough to save both of us and several more if managed right," but he did not heed my advice and at once made an effort to get it away from me by whirling it over and over edgewise, he going over with it at almost every revolution. I kept very cool, occasionally putting my hands on it, thus keeping myself afloat, knowing that he must soon exhaust and perhaps drown himself, which proved to be correct, as he soon disappeared below the surface, and sank to rise no more. When I had full possession I struck out as best and as fast as I could, fearing that others might want to take passage with me, but not knowing where the strong current would land me.

After being in the water for quite a long time, which seemed to me an age, part of the time in company with others going down the river, some swimming, others floating on driftwood and all conceivable kinds of rafts, everything that would float being utilized; some were shouting for help, others praying, singing,

17

laughing, or swearing. I finally came in sight of some bushes which I took to be on the shore, but which as I afterwards learned was the larger one of a group of islands called the "Hen and Chickens." The current carried me in some distance and I brought up by a cottonwood sapling. I thought perhaps I could touch bottom here, but found the water too deep, the river at that time being very high, overflowing the islands and surrounding country. Realizing that in the condition that I was then in, being almost chilled to death, that unless I could get out of the water I would probably perish before help would reach me, I made an effort to climb the sapling, but being then almost helpless, I failed in my first attempt, and almost lost my life, for I slipped into the water over my head, but with the assistance of my board my second effort was successful, and I found myself safely perched in the sapling, where I had plenty of time to meditate upon the situation. I thought of a great many things, of home, relatives, and friends, and of my poor comrades who must have perished, but particularly of my intimate friend and comrade, A. O. Cranmer, who I knew had a wife and children at home anxiously awaiting his coming, but who I thought must surely have perished for he could not swim a stroke.

I sat on my perch trying to keep from freezing by fighting buffalo gnats, which were very annoying, until some time after daybreak when I heard a steamboat coming up the river and knew by the shouts for help of those who were similarly situated as myself, and from the frequent stops of the engines that help

was near at hand. In a few moments the boat was
near me. They saw me and sent a row boat in after
me. I was lifted by willing hands from my uncomfortable seat, placed in the boat, carried to
the steamboat and lifted upon the decks; the
first person I saw was my dear friend, A. O.
Cranmer, whom I had given up for lost, but he had
landed on the same island and was picked up just a
few moments before I was. To say it was one of the
happiest meetings of my life would hardly express it.
I was immediately given some hot stimulants and
plenty of hot coffee, and was put into a nice warm
bed. In due time the boat landed us at the wharf at
Memphis, where those of us who were injured were
given some clothing by the good ladies, and conducted
to a hospital.

When the boat landed us, I saw standing on the
wharf Major Coulter, formerly of my regiment, who
was then on his way to some southern port. He reached
out his hand, but was so overcome with grief that he
could scarcely utter a word. He had been with us the
evening before, treating and giving some of us a little
spending money, little thinking at the time that so
many would so soon find watery or fiery graves.

I was placed in a ward with quite a number who
were severely scalded, or otherwise badly injured, and
such misery and intense suffering as I witnessed while
there is beyond my power to describe. The agonizing
cries and groans of the burned and scalded were heart-
rending and almost unendurable, but in most cases the
suffering was of short duration as the most of them
were relieved by death in a few hours. I suffered

intense pain from my injuries, especially from my dislocated shoulder and scalded hand, not having had any
attention from the surgeons in charge, but I did not
murmur or complain, as I saw all around me numbers
of poor fellows whose injuries needed attention more
than mine.   A kind-hearted matron came to my cot
and washed me and wrote a few lines to my parents,
informing them of the disaster, and that I was saved.
It was then that I thought again of my good, kind
mother at home, and longed to be with her as I fancied
I could see a strong resemblance between them.   I was
finally taken to the operating room, put under the
influence of chloroform, and the dislocation reduced
and my other injuries attended to.

I did not remain long at the hospital.   I soon found
a number of my comrades, and with them, without
leave or orders, boarded a boat bound for Cairo.   As
none of us had transportation or money with which to
pay our fare the captain and clerk, after some parley-
ing, kindly consented to carry us.   In due time we
arrived at Cairo, and after getting transportation from
the quartermaster's department, were sent to Columbus, some to "Camp Chase," the injured ones to
"Treplar Hospital," where right in sight of the capitol
of our own glorious state of Ohio we were treated more
like brutes than soldiers, and were almost starved to
death by some inhuman, dishonest scoundrel, in the
employ of the government.   I had too much grit to
put up with such treatment and took "French leave"
and left for home, where I soon received notice to
return immediately to be mustered out of the service
May 30, 1865, under a special telegraphic order from

the war department, having served just three years and seven months in the army.

In all that long service, I am pleased to say, I was not at any time sick enough to go to a hospital and was only once wounded, and that only slightly, at the battle of Stone river.

About twenty members of my regiment were aboard of the "Sultana" at the time of the disaster, ten of whom were lost. I quote from the records of the War Department, a copy of which I have in my possession, the following: " The reports and testimony show that there were 1,866 troops on the 'Sultana,' including thirty-three paroled officers; one officer who had resigned, and the captain in charge of the guard; of these 765, including sixteen officers, were saved, and 1,101, including nineteen officers, were lost. There were seventy cabin passengers and eighty-five crew on board, of whom some ten to eighteen were saved, giving a loss of 137, making a total loss of 1,238." I had always estimated the loss greater, but presume the records are correct and am only too glad that the loss was not greater. It was without doubt the greatest marine disaster on record, in either ancient or modern times, and I am surprised that so little is remembered about it at this time, and especially by persons who were at that time great readers and can to this day tell all about some battle or skirmish or other disaster where the loss of life was trifling as compared to this.

Present occupation, furniture dealer and undertaker. Postoffice address, Marion, Ohio.

NATHANIEL FOGLESONG.

I WAS born at Mansfield, Richland county, Ohio, in the year 1842, and moved from there to Wright, Hillsdale county, Mich., when ten years of age, living there until the fall of 1862. I enlisted to defend my country and to stand by the old flag in Company A of the 18th Michigan Infantry. From Wright we went to Camp Woodbury, Hillsdale, Mich.

I served with my regiment in all its campaigns until captured at the battle of Athens, Ala., on the 24th of September, 1864, by Forrest's cavalry. They robbed us of our blankets, watches, and of all our valuables, and then we marched over rough roads, through rivers, and by rail to Cahaba, Ala., where we remained until the 12th of April, 1865, when we were taken to "Camp Fisk," which is four miles from Vicksburg, Miss., there to be recruited up so that we could stand a journey north. They commenced giving us one quarter rations and increased it as we starved creatures could stand it. We remained here until we received orders to board the train at five o'clock P. M., on the 24th of April, 1865, for Vicksburg.

While at Vicksburg the steamer, "Sultana" came steaming in with passengers and crew numbering 110. The steamer remained here about thirty hours, and during that time was boarded by 1,996 federal soldiers and 35 officers—just released from the prisons at Cahaba, Ala., Andersonville and Macon, Ga., and belonging to the States of Michigan, Indiana, Ohio, West Virginia, Kentucky and Tennessee. We were crowded on the boat like a flock of sheep until the whole num-

ber of passengers was 2,141, besides horses, mules and a
large number of hogsheads of sugar ; over six times her
capacity. The overloaded boat steamed out of Vicksburg at one o'clock A. M., on the 25th of April and
arrived at Helena, Ark., at seven o'clock A. M., and
left there at eight o'clock. The boat ran smoothly
and the soldiers were enjoying the thought of being
homeward bound. Yes, with joy that cannot be expressed, although many of them were suffering from
wounds received in battle, and all were sadly emaciated from starvation in the prison pens where we had
been confined. But now we were en route for home,
the cruel war was over and the long struggle closed.
Battles, sieges, marches and prison pens were things
of the past.

We arrived at Memphis at seven o'clock in the evening of the 26th. A guard was stationed at the edge of
the boat with orders not to let any of the prisoners get
off. I was not very well so I did not disturb the
guard, but a number of the boys went off the boat and
enjoyed themselves. After unloading the cargo of
sugar she took on a supply of coal, and then started
from Memphis about one o'clock in the morning of
the 27th. So far the presence of danger was not manifested nor was it in the least anticipated except that
the boat was heavily loaded, but in the darkness of
that terrible morning, between two and three o'clock,
just opposite Tagleman's Landing, eight miles above
Memphis, suddenly, and without warning, the steamer
exploded one of her boilers with terrific force, and in
a few moments the boat burned to the water's edge.

The steamer was running at the rate of nine or ten miles an hour.

Mr. Roberry, the chief mate, who had charge of the boat, and who was among the survivors, was in the pilot-house with Mr. Claton, the pilot, at the time of the explosion. At that time I was sound asleep and the first thing I knew or heard was a terrible crash and everything coming down upon us. I was lying on the lower deck near the stern of the boat. I laid still a few minutes after the explosion and my comrades said, "Thaniel, why don't you get up; the boat is all on fire?" My reply was that I could not swim, but they said, "get ready and go with us." I told them to save their own lives as I might be the cause of losing them. I went with them to the edge of the boat and there we saw that the water was full of men, horses, and mules. Several of the boys were determined to jump off into the river, but I persuaded them to wait till the water was clearer and they did so, thus saving their lives. I still remained on the boat and heard the cries of comrades for help. Some of them calling on God for help, while others took his name in vain. One poor fellow, Pat Larky, who belonged to Company E of my regiment, had secured a board, and it seemed that every time he would try it it would throw him off into the river. Pat shouted, "Come help poor Pat, he is a drowning." The poor fellow went down. By this time the flames were cracking and snapping over my head, threatening my life. I was thinking whether to burn or drown, when a woman with a little babe about two months old came to me crying for help. I told her it was every one for himself. I saw that she had on a life pereserver but it was buckled down too low. I stepped up to her and was going to unbuckle it, when she said, "Soldier, don't take that off from me." I said, "it must be up under your arms." I placed it there, and took her by the hand and she jumped into the water. She thanked me and said, "may the Lord bless you." She lost her husband, baby, father, and mother there.

When I saw my condition I went down upon my knees and asked God to be merciful to me, a sinner, and offered up the following prayer: "O Lord, if it is thy will for me to be drowned in the Mississippi all is well, or, if not, may I return home to see my father, brothers, and sisters." I then climbed up on the banisters close to the rudder; being weak and feeble I almost lost my hold, I grasped tighter and drew myself up and getting a new hold, reached out my arm so that I could just place my fingers and foot on the rudder, then bent my head and body, shoved my arm around the rudder, and as I let go dropped down on to the lower deck. While hanging to the rudder a man cried, "Get off from me." I replied, "In a minute." There were nine of us that had hold of that rudder and I being the top one kept quiet. Soon the coals from above began to fall on my head and shoulders and I began to think that I must get out of there. A part of the deck burned off and fell into the water, and I tried to get those that were under me to swim and get on to it, but all they said was: "My God, if we let go of this we shall drown." I answered, "Let us die like men, helping ourselves, for God helps those who help themselves in this case and I believe in all others." The coals came thicker and faster so that I had to brush them off my head and shoulders with one hand and hang on to the rudder with the other.

It will be seen that I had now to do something, consequently, I made up my mind, by the assistance of God and his mighty power, that I would jump into the water, and cried "Here goes for ninety days." I sank three times, and as I came up the third time I grabbed a comrade by the heel. While catching my breath he kicked me loose and down I went again. As I came up I grabbed the same comrade by the ankle with one hand and with the other grabbed a wire rope to which I hung, being nearly exhausted. Looking around I found a piece of scantling about 3x4, and I thought it would help me in getting to a piece of deck which had floated away from the boat, so I went kicking and paddling like a dog till I reached the piece of deck. As I climbed upon it I heard comrade Borns of my regiment say, "My God, is that you?" I replied, "Yes, all that is left of me." He then said, "I have two boards and you shall have one."

I then started for the center of the deck. There was a hole burned in it which I did not observe and down I went, but throwing out my arms I recovered myself before falling far. Afterwards I was more careful, moving around closer to the edge of the piece of deck, when, behold, there laid one of the deck hands and two women scalded to death. I found a door and a piece of siding. I took the piece of siding and shoved the door down to the comrades that were hanging on to the rudder, and finally they all got upon the piece of deck.

By this time the citizens had their raft made and came and took us to the shore where there was a log stable, and near it was a log heap where we warmed ourselves and dried our clothes. As Sergeant Borns was destitute of clothing, and the wind being very chilly, I took my pants and blouse and gave them to him thus leaving me with my shirt and drawers. Borns said to me, " Foglesong, let us go and pray to God, thanking Him for saving our lives and permitting us to stand upon the earth once more?" I agreed, and he made the best and most fervent prayer that I had ever heard.

Soon after this a boat came along, took us on board and carried us back to Memphis. I crawled into a bunk and soon fell asleep. The first thing I knew two Sisters of Charity came along and said, " Here is a soldier." They awoke me and I asked: " What do you want?" They said: " We want to put dry and clean clothes on you." I was so weak that I could not stand alone, but they dressed and led me to the top of the stairs where a lieutenant of an Indiana regiment took me, carried me down and placed me in a bus with those two ladies. They took me to the Overton hospital, and as I went into a ward one of my comrades of my regiment, Sergeant Nelson Voglesong, grabbed me, saying, " I never expected to see you again after I left you on the boat." He is dead now. They took me to the next ward which was quite well filled with the boys that were on the boat, some of them nearly dead and dying with the injuries received from the exposure. I remained in the hospital ten days, then went by boat to Cairo, Ill., and from there by rail to

"Camp Chase," Ohio, where I was discharged from the service on the 21st of June, 1865, and then went home to Wright, Hillsdale county, Mich., where I now reside.

_____

MARTIN FRAZEE.

I WAS born at West Farms, New York, January 1, 1841, and enlisted in the service of the United States at Milton, Indiana, April 18, 1861, in Co. C, 2d Regiment Indiana Cavalry, and was captured near Scottsville, Alabama, April 2, 1865, and confined in the stockade at Meridian, Mississippi, for about one week. I hardly think it necessary for me to give my "Sultana" experience, as I have no doubt that there will be plenty of experiences of far greater interest than mine. I will just state, however, that I was severely scalded on my body and feet and did not walk for five months after the explosion.

My present occupation is that of carpenter, and my postoffice address is 1209 New Main street, Louisville, Kentucky.

W. S. FRIESNER.

I WAS born at Logan, Ohio, August 19, 1838, and enlisted in the service of the United States October 9, 1861, in Co. K, 58th Regiment Ohio Volunteer Infantry. I was never captured. Was the officer in command of the guard in charge of the paroled prisoners. When the explosion occurred I was the last one to leave the boat. There were a few men still on the forecastle, forward of the burning debris, whom I saw after I left the boat, some of whom, I was informed, were taken off by rescuing parties. I floated off on a stateroom door. I think I was in the water for nearly two hours, and was picked up by the steamer " Bostonia."

Postoffice address, Logan, Ohio.

HENRY GAMBILL.

HENRY GAMBILL was born in Blaine, Lawrence county, Ky., December 17, 1844, and enlisted in the service of the United States, at Louisville, Ky., April 10, 1863, in Company B, 14th Regiment Kentucky Infantry. Was captured near Adairsville, Ga., August 13, 1864, and confined in the Milledgeville and Andersonville, Ga., prisons.

He says: At the time of the explosion I was asleep at the head of the stairway, in front of the cabin, with Elisha Curusitte of Company G, 14th Regiment Kentucky Infantry; he was killed and I received a severe wound in my left leg. I helped to cut down and throw overboard a stage plank and got upon it, with twenty-five other comrades. One of them caught me by the shoulders. I finally succeeded in getting him to release his hold in time to save my own life, but he was drowned. I then beseeched my comrades to get off the stage plank and rest themselves on its edges. By so doing it would not turn over, hold us all up and we would be safe, but my pleadings availed nothing. Finally they all drowned but myself and four others. We succeeded in steering it to the wall of an old stable, that was almost under water caused by the high tide of the Mississippi river. When we reached that most coveted spot I was so weak and exhausted that my comrades had to help me to a place of safety. We remained there until about sunrise, when we were rescued from our perilous condition and taken back to Memphis with joy and delight.

My present occupation is that of a merchant. Post-office address, Blaine, Ky.

DANIEL GARBER.

I WAS born in Washington county, Pa, April 8, 1828, and enlisted in the service of the United States at Belleville, Ohio, August 16, 1862, in Company E, 102d Regiment Ohio Volunteer Infantry, as a private.

The regiment was assigned to the 20th Army Corps. I engaged in the campaign in Kentucky and Tennessee in pursuit of the rebel Gen. Bragg in 1862. In all the marches and engagements of the regiment I took part, from Louisville, Ky., until I was taken prisoner at Athens, Ala., September 23, 1864. The union forces were attempting to drive Gen. Hood back. I was at the time afflicted with catarrh in my left hand and was unable for duty. I, with about forty others, was quartered in a large brick mansion which for the time served as a hospital.

The rebel cavalry, under command of Gen. N. B. Forrest, captured the town of Athens, and surrounding the hospital made prisoners of all within except a comrade who escaped by climbing up the chimney. They were then taken by the way of Cherokee to Meridian, Miss., and while passing through here a citizen asked, " Where did all those 'Yanks' come from?" The colonel in charge replied, "They are chiefly from Ohio and Indiana, and are good boys."

"They may be good boys, but they have stolen all our negroes," was the reply.

We continued our journey through Selma, Ala., to Cahaba in the same State. When we arrived here we were required to register, and received instructions as to the position of the dead line, which it was certain death to cross. I once stepped over this line, but fortunately was not seen by the guard. An escape was planned and the inside guard was overpowered and disarmed, while the guard outside ran away, but owing to the lack of decisive action on the part of the prisoners the attempt failed, and we were driven back into the prison. A cannon was planted in the door of the main building and we were called upon to surrender. Our punishment was a fast of forty-eight hours. In the meantime a guard had said he had bayonetted a prisoner, and we were compelled to undress and hold our clothes above our heads, and march between the guards, but fortunately he was not discovered.

On or about the 1st of March, 1865, the Alabama river got very high, owing to the incessant rain for the past few days, and consequently overflowed the prison to the depth of two feet, at the highest place, making it very disagreeable, for we had no place to stand up or lie down but in the water.

About the 16th or 17th of March I was taken out with the last squad for parole, and we were taken via Selma, Demopolis and Jackson, Miss. While over night at Demopolis, Sergeant D. P. Canada, of my company, died. We stopped a day at Jackson, where a few of the boys drew some clothes. From there we

19

were taken to Big Black, in the rear of Vicksburg,
where we arrived on the 21st day of March.

Our men received us under the glorious stars and
stripes on the 22d, and we went into parole camp
three or four miles in the rear of Vicksburg. Here
we remained until the 25th or 26th of April, when I,
with about 2,100 other paroled prisoners, was taken on
board the ill fated steamer "Sultana." We started up
the broad Mississippi with fond hopes of soon seeing
the dear ones at home, but how few of us had the
pleasure of realizing these hopes.

We arrived at Memphis a short time before dark
and took on coal and other matters. We left Memphis
shortly after midnight on the 27th and when seven
miles above there the steamer's boiler exploded. I was
at that time lying by the side of the pilot house with
Corporal Jacob Irons of my company, and was asleep
when it occurred. My first recollection was that I was
on my feet and enveloped in a cloud of hot steam, and
was considerably scalded in the face. After the steam
had risen I said to Corporal Irons what is the matter?
and he said the boat had blown up. He seemed to be
very much excited, and told me they thought they
could make the shore. These were the last words he
spoke to me, but as the boys kept jumping off from
the boat into the river he kept calling for them not to
for they would all be saved.

I then began to look around to devise some means
of escape. I stepped back to where some of my company's boys were untying a yawl; I thought that I
would help them get it down, and then I thought if I
did they would all jump for it and perhaps be lost,

which I learned afterward was the case.   I then got a
shutter and board from off the pilot house and tied
them together with a pair of drawers.   By that time
the flames had come through.   I then got over the
railing behind the wheel house and climbed down to
the lower deck.   By this time all was confusion and
men were jumping off into the river to get away from
the flames.   I looked around for a clear place to jump,
for I knew that if I jumped in where men were struggling they would seize my board and I would be lost,
for I could swim but very little.

I waited a short time and when there was an opening
large enough I threw my board in, jumped on and
went down under quite a way, but came up all right
and floated away from the boat.   After I had gone
four or five rods a bundle of clothing came floating
along and I took it in with my right hand and held on
to the board with my left.   I then floated with the
current.   Think I went on the south side of the island.
I saw a boat going up on the other side and could see
it by the side of the wreck as I floated down the river.
I also remember seeing the lights of Memphis as I
went past.

I was picked up four miles below Memphis by two
men in a yawl and rowed to the gunboat "Pocahontas" where I was taken in, eleven miles from the
scene of the disaster.   I wish to state here that there
were thirteen of my company on board the "Sultana,"
and but two besides myself were saved.   Their names
were William Lockhart and William Yeisley.   About
the last thing I remembered was that I was very nearly
chilled to death and could not survive much longer.

They gave me some stimulants, and I did not remember
any more until the next morning when I found myself
undressed and between two mattresses. We were given
red drawers and shirts by the Christian Sanitary Commission.   I was then taken to the "Gayoso House,"
where I think I stopped two days. After drawing
clothing we were put on the steamer "Belle of St.
Louis," our destination being Cairo, Ill. While going
there in the night I remember several incidents that
were amusing. Some of the more timid were springing up at every little noise, thinking there was going
to be another explosion. At one time we supposed
that they were having a race with another boat, and
one comrade said if he had a gun he would shoot the
captain. I wish to mention another little incident
right here.   There chanced to be a citizen on the boat,
and discovering that I was a Mason, he gave me a dollar and told me to get something I needed with it.   I
thanked him very cordially, for it was the first money
I had in my possession for a long time. I hope if he
is living now and sees this he will remember this incident and will know that I have not forgotten him.

I think we arrived at Cairo in the evening of the
second day after leaving Memphis.   We left here after
twelve o'clock that night for Mattoon, Ill., where we
arrived the next day, about two o'clock, and here the
good citizens gave us a lunch. Our next destination
was Terre Haute, Ind., which we reached at ten that
night. We remained here until the next morning.
Our next move was to Indianapolis. We stopped
there part of a day. From there we went to "Camp
Chase," Ohio, where we arrived on the 4th or 5th of

May, 1865. Here I was discharged by special telegram from the War Department on the 21st.

When I came home I worked at my old trade, on the shoe bench, for about ten years; since that time I have been farming. Have raised a family of four girls and three boys, and all are married but one boy.

My postoffice address is Butler, Ohio.

STEPHEN M. GASTON.

I WAS born January 11, 1850, at Centreville, Wayne county, Ind., and am, perhaps, the youngest ex-prisoner of war, if not the youngest soldier that was in the service. I enlisted in the service of the United States at Indianapolis, Ind., October 19, 1863, in Company K, 9th Indiana Volunteer Cavalry (121st Regiment). Was captured by Gen. Forrest's troops at Sulphur Branch Trestle, September 25, 1864, while on our way to relieve the troops stationed at Athens, Ala., and was confined as a prisoner of war until about the 10th of April, 1865, at Cahaba, Ala., when we were formally exchanged; (were sent from Cahaba to the mouth of Tombigbee river, up that river to Gainesville, thence to West Point, Meridian, and Jackson, Miss., to Black River, where the commissioners had established a camp of exchange). Comrades, it did my very soul good to see the old flag floating in the breezes once more, proclaiming to the world that it still floats and is able to shelter those who desire its protection. Many shed tears, a few shouted, but the majority were too overcome to give vent to their feelings and said: "Thank God, we are surely exchanged and will not be returned to that hell hole of misery again."

After crossing the river we were taken to parole camp, about four miles from Vicksburg, and after some little rest in camp we were ordered (that is I was along with others, for at parole camp nearly every regiment in the service was represented), on board the "Sultana," to the number (I always understood) of 2,300. Sixteen of that number belonged to Company K, 9th Indiana Cavalry. We arrived at Memphis safely and discharged some two hundred hogsheads of sugar and also some horses. I found a hogshead of sugar broken (as soldiers always do find) and my comrade, Wm. Block, and I filled everything we could find with sugar, intending to eat the sugar and hard tack while going up the river to our destination. We stored our sugar in front of the pilot house at our heads, for we had made this place our bunk and turned in for the night. Our evening dreams were sweet, for we had eaten about two pounds of sugar each, and then were we not going home to see our loved ones who had mourned for us as dead? We dreamed the soldier's dreams of home and loved ones, of camp life, of the battle and the prison, the scanty fare and the cruel guards, when, suddenly, our dreams were broken. I felt myself raised to a height and then a crash came; the smoke stack had fallen directly on the pilot house crushing it down almost on us. I felt for Block and called his name but no answer came. The cries of the wounded were heard all around me. I was a prisoner again, for a network of rubbish surrounded me. The stack above the remnant of the wheel house behind the boat was on fire, and directly below some poor fellows were wedged in at my right hand and begged for help. I was helpless and could render no assistance. They soon smothered from the heat and smoke. After trying again and again I finally extricated myself and, going to the hatchway or steps, I found my way obstructed and debris scattered everywhere.

I finally concluded to jump to the lower deck, but found I could swing down on to the breeching of the stack. I did so, and Oh! God, what a sight. I was on the bow of the boat and could not see aft, but what misery I did see was enough for me. Men were crying, praying, swearing, and begging. Wounded in every shape, some with broken legs and arms, others scalded, burnt and dying, their cries made the already dark night hideous, lighted up by the now fiercely burning boat.

My senses remained and I thought it would be best to try some mode of escape. (I was wounded and badly scraped from my exertion to get from under the smokestack.) On looking around I found an empty flour barrel, and divesting myself of clothing I jumped into the chilling waters. Taking the precaution to see that no person was near I was fortunate to get clear of the boat without encountering anyone, although two or three tried to get to me, but drowned before reaching me. I saw at least twenty drown at once. As fast as one would feel he was drowning he would clutch at the nearest, and I believe many a bold swimmer was drowned that night who could have saved himself if alone. I was finally rescued by a life-boat from the steamer "Bostonia" and taken to the cabin of that steamer in a cramped and exhausted condition, and was then taken in an ambulance to Overton hospital. After remaining there three days was sent to the Soldier's Retreat, then with some three hundred others forwarded to "Camp Chase," Ohio. I stopped at Terre Haute, my home, and followed in the evening to Indianapolis, thence to "Camp Chase," from which place I ran away and reported back to Indianapolis to Adjt. Gen. Noble, and was given transportation home and a pass for twenty days. Was discharged at Indianapolis June 28, 1865.

My occupation is that of engineer of Eagle Mills.

W. N. GOODRICH.

I WAS born in Whiteford township, Monroe county, Mich., November 21, 1842, and at the present am living in the city of Menominee, Mich. Enlisted in the service of the United States at Ridgeway, Lenawee county, Mich., on the 31st of July, 1862, in Company E of the 18th Michigan Infantry. After a short stay in camp at Hillsdale we proceeded to what we supposed was the front, but which was Kentucky. After tramping through most of this State and spending one winter at Lexington, we finally, in April or May of 1863, boarded the cars for the front, but we were again mistaken and only got as far as Nashville, Tenn., where we halted at a large building called "Zollicoffer Building." We remained there two or three days, spending most of our time in killing graybacks as they were thicker than fleas on a dog. From there we went into camp, which was very much better, and I thought if this was the front it was about as nice as could be. Soon, however, our fun began. Being on duty almost every other day it was fun for a time, but soon became a drudge. We remained there a long year, and then the glad news came for us to pack up and go to the front. This was some time in May or June. We started for the seat of war, or what we supposed to be it, arriving at Decatur, Ala., in the night and pitched our tents just outside of the city, on the hills that were covered with the filth and rubbish of the city.

On the 23d of September it was reported that a band of "Johnnies" were tearing up the track near Athens, Ala., and a detail of about 400 men was made from our brigade and boarded a train of flat cars some time in the night. Crossing the river and waiting until daylight, we then proceeded as far as we could on the cars, then going on foot for a short distance we were suddenly fired upon by the enemy. The firing was returned by us and the enemy fled. Our orders were to go to Athens, so we went on. Getting in sight of Athens, what did we see? "Johnnies" all around us. Hundreds of them in our front and rear. We fought with them the best we could and tried to get to the fort, as our dear old stars and stripes were still flying. But alas! as we had got almost there the gates swung open and out marched our boys in blue. What could we do but surrender? It was with long faces that a flag of truce was sent to the commander that we had surrendered. Soon we were surrounded by the "Johnnies," asking for something to eat. It seemed to me as though they were about starved, and we soon found that our captor was Gen. Forrest. When I heard this I thought my time had come, as the massacre at Fort Pillow was fresh in my memory.

We did not remain long at Athens but were hurried off to a Southern prison, Cahaba, Ala., where we were fed on corn meal for almost six months when the glad news came that we were to leave; some thought for Andersonville, others thought for home. It proved to be the latter. After riding in dirty box cars and then marching, we arrived at Big Black river on the 21st of March, 1865, and remained in camp, which was four miles from Vicksburg, for three or four weeks. Then the glad news came that we were to go North and be exchanged.

We marched to Vicksburg and went on board the steamer "Sultana." We were a jolly crowd, but our joy was of short duration. Everything went along smoothly until we were about eight miles above Memphis, when the explosion took place by which so many lives were lost. As for myself I had no thoughts of dying just then, so I looked around among the wreck and found a box, carried it to the side of the boat and waited until the coast was clear; then threw it overboard and jumped in after it. It seemed to me as though I was going down to the bottom, but such was not the case. Soon coming to the surface of the water I seized the box and started down the river for shore, or any place where I could get out of the water. After floating and swimming about four miles I landed safely on a small willow tree. Soon after getting nicely fixed on the branches, making myself as comfortable as possible under the circumstances, a man by the name of Williams, of the 1st Kentucky Cavalry, came floating along and caught hold of a log that was fast to the tree. After watching him a few minutes I descended from my perch and helped him upon the log, held him there for two hours, and was rewarded by seeing him come to life again, as he was as near dead as any one I have seen who was not dead.

Early in the morning of the 27th of April boats were seen coming up the river searching for the victims of the disaster. Some of the poor fellows were hanging to the trees, some were on logs, and some were found in almost every conceivable place. At about eight o'clock I was picked up, taken on board a steamer and about twelve o'clock landed at Memphis. Remaining there four days, I again started for the north, this time with fear, thinking that we might meet with the same catastrophe, but we landed safely at Cairo, Ill., there boarded the train for "Camp Chase," Ohio. Arriving there I remained two weeks and then was sent to my native State, where I was discharged from the service.

My occupation, mail carrier.

***

N. W. GREGORY.

I WAS born in Erie county, Ohio, June 8, 1845, and enlisted in the service of the United States at Norwalk, Ohio, December 28, 1861, in Company C, 55th

Regiment Ohio Volunteers, and was captured at South
Mountain, Ga., October 28, 1864, and confined in the
Andersonville, Ga., prison.

At the time of the accident was asleep on the cabin
deck. I was, of course, aroused from my slumber and
found myself mixed up with the debris of the wreck.
Had some difficulty in releasing myself from between
the two decks, but after some little time succeeded.
I found there were a great many looking for safer
quarters. The jam of men was so great that after I
slid down it seemed impossible for me to get a foot-
hold, and I came near being carried overboard by the
surging crowd, but after a long struggle got on my
feet again. By this time the fire was beginning to
drive the crowd back and I saw the time was short for
anyone to stay on the boat. Seeing a large coil of rope
at one end fast to the boat I threw it overboard, got
ready for a swim, but before jumping made a search
for pieces of boards or something that would give me
some assistance after I left the wreck, which I did not
intend to do until the fire forced me off. I managed
to get a couple of panels of a door, and by this time
the heat was more than I could bear so I let myself
down into the water with the rope which I had prepared before. The water was alive with men for some
distance from the wreck, but I was a good swimmer
and made good use of it; that is, as good as I could
after being six months at Andersonville prison and not
having strength for a very long struggle in the water.

After being in the water a short time I got on to an
old tree — there were three men on it already. After
a couple of hours I was so chilled and stiff that if I

had been forced into the water I could not have helped myself. One of the men that was on the tree chilled and drowned before he was rescued. I was taken from the water by the steamboat "Silver Spray" about eight o'clock in the morning, not far from where the explosion took place. Was taken to Memphis and placed in the hospital. Have many thanks for the people of Memphis for the good care and treatment of the survivors.

On the way north, after starting for home, there were sixty of us in the crowd that left Memphis. Was pleased when we arrived safe at Cairo, Ill., for I had a dread of steamboat travel. There was an incident on the way after leaving Cairo that is well worth mentioning. I am sorry that I cannot remember the place or the name of the family that is connected with the incident. The cars stopped at a small town just at three o'clock in the morning after riding all night from Cairo. At this place we were obliged to stay until ten, as we had to change roads. After a short stay at the depot I took a stroll upon one of the streets, and when near a large, fine looking place I was taking a view of it, when a man came out and invited me in. I readily accepted. Taking me into the sitting-room I found nine of the boys all waiting for breakfast. After the meal was over the man of the house provided himself with ten one-dollar bills and gave one to each of us. I have given him many a thought, but, like all other soldiers, I was careless at the time. I hope this will remind some of them who were there of the incident, if they are living, and in this way I may find out the name of this family.

My present occupation is mining. Postoffice address,
Lead City, South Dakota.

SAMUEL C. HAINES.

I WAS born in Burlington county, N. J., March 5,
1843, and enlisted in the service of the United
States, at LaFayette, Ind., December 10, 1861, in
Company G 40th Regiment Indiana Volunteer
Infantry, and was captured at the battle of Franklin,
Tenn., November 30, 1864, and confined in the Ander-
sonville, Ga., prison.

About the 1st of April, 1865, I, with about 600
other starved prisoners, was taken from the prison to
Vicksburg and paroled. We waited there several days
and regained much of our lost strength. While there
we heard of President Lincoln's assassination, which
caused greater grief than any defeat we had received
while on the battlefield. The remaining time his
assassination was the subject of heated conversation, and
the southern sympathizers kept well out of our way.
At last word came for us to get ready to go home.
We boarded the illfated " Sultana" in the afternoon.
Myself and two comrades, John Thompson and Chas.
May, of Company G, 40th Regiment Indiana Infantry
(both were lost), went directly to the upper deck, back
of the pilot house, and laid down to sleep. We awoke
when they stopped at Memphis, but after leaving there
we went to sleep again and knew nothing until
awakened by the explosion. About the first thing I
thought of was that some raiding rebel battery had

thrown a shell into the boat. I then heard screams of men below. Some one cried "Keep quiet! Keep quiet! We will run ashore." That made me feel good. In a few moments fire broke out, and as I could not swim I stayed on board until driven off by the heat. I helped tear off a flight of stairs from the passenger deck to the hurricane deck, intending to jump in the water with it, but quickly changed my mind. I talked a moment with Nathan D. Everman, an excellent swimmer. He promised me help, but when he saw me afterward he bid me "good bye," saying that I was all right.

After leaving the stairs and Everman I ran into the cabin, clutched a bunk with both hands and jumped into the river with it. It went down twice with me. I let loose of it after the second sinking, having swallowed some water and almost strangled. I could not keep my head out of the water, and thinking I was going to drown I began to dive, hoping to find something to cling to and reach the shore. In a few minutes I found myself near two men clinging to a board. They tried to keep me off, but I was too strong for them and succeeded in getting a firm hold on it. They afterwards told me they were good swimmers and the board would float all three of us. We floated down the river about a mile, when we drifted among five or six men who were drowning. They broke my hold of the board and I again thought I was lost, but fortunately I bobbed up by a long steerage pole. It was about twenty-five feet long. An Irishman, one of the boat hands, was on one end of it. I was carried along on it very nicely going down stream I said to him, "Let us steer for the shore, we can use our limbs and may get into a tree top." We landed on the Arkansas shore, as I afterwards learned, and remained there till about seven o'clock A. M. A steamer came up from Memphis and sent a skiff out to us, and we, almost naked, were taken to the steamer and afterwards to Memphis. Some citizens gave me a pair of shoes and five dollars in our money. They treated me as kindly as any one could. I went to the quartermaster's department and drew a dry suit of clothes. I had lost all but shirt and pants when in the water, and with what the citizens gave me I was now fitted out.

I stayed in Memphis about two weeks and met my friend Everman, who was very glad to see me. We were afraid to try the boats again and waited for the train to go North. We received word that they would not run any train for several weeks. We were too anxious to get home to wait any longer, so we again tried the water. This time we succeeded in getting to Cairo, Ill. Here I boarded a train for Indianapolis. At Terre Haute we were given a grand dinner, and I began to think I was in God's country again. We then proceeded on our way to Indianapolis and received a furlough for thirty days. When the time was up I went back and was honorably discharged June 20, 1865.

My present occupation is trader and stock buyer. Present postoffice address, Romney, Ind.

OGILVIE E. HAMBLIN.

I AM a resident of Pulaski township, Jackson county, Mich., and am now fifty years old (March, 1892). I enlisted in the United States army, at Jackson, Mich., in 1863, as a private in Company E of the 2nd Regiment Michigan Cavalry, and went from Jackson to Grand Rapids, Mich., thence to Nashville, Tenn., and there we drilled for regular service until February, 1864. Thence we went to Cleveland, Tenn., to join our regiment. We did not see much actual service until May 5, 1864, when we started with Sherman for Atlanta. We went as far as Kenesaw and Lost Mountain and then turned our horses over to Cook's command and came back to Nashville to guard the Nashville & Franklin Railroad until Atlanta was taken. We then drew horses and drilled at Franklin until Forrest came back in Sherman's rear and crossed the Tennessee river. We were then sent to drive him back again. After driving him back we were ordered to guard the river to keep Hood from crossing, our company being sent to Raccoon Ford where Hood was attempting to cross. There was a small engagement took place there when our cavalry was surrounded and all taken prisoners, I being so unfortunate as to get shot through the arm near the shoulder. This was on the 30th day of October, 1864. They took me from Raccoon Ford to Florence, Ala., and there, for practice, the young rebel doctors cut off my arm; I think it could have been saved.

They kept me in the hospital at Florence until the 1st of December, when Hood again commenced mov-

21

ing toward Nashville. Then I was sent to Columbus, Miss., to the rebel hospital, and as soon as I was able I was sent to Cahaba prison, Ala., where I remained until they sent me to Jackson, Miss.; thence to Vicksburg, where I boarded the steamer "Sultana," and then we went up to Memphis, Tenn., and while they were unloading some sugar at Memphis my chum, Frank Perkins, and I spread down our blankets, took off our top clothes all but our shirts and drawers, and were soon in the hand of slumbers, dreaming of battle fields and of all the scenes which we had passed through, when we were suddenly awakened by a terrific explosion. I sprang to my feet only to find the whole boat in a tremendous tumult and uproar. The cries of the dying and the groans of the wounded, and the loud appeals for help, were heartrending. The hold of the boat was full of comrades. They cried for the door of the hold to be opened. My chum (Frank Perkins) and I pulled the door away, when they came rushing out of the hold like bees out of a hive, followed by dense clouds of steam and smoke. I remained on board the boat until the fire and steam drove me off. I then looked the situation over calmly, and, thinking that my underclothes would be a hindrance to me while in the water, I took every stitch of my clothing off as coolly as though about to take a bath which proved to be of considerable duration. The water was already full of the seething mass of humanity. Some were swimming boldly toward the shore, others going down to rise no more. Some were clasping and dragging down to death those who could have saved themselves had they been left unencumbered. All in

all it was a terrible sight to behold and one from which
I shrink and shudder to this day, nor do I ever wish
to witness such a sight again.

Screwing my courage up to the sticking point I
prepared to take the leap into the icy waters which I
expected to be my sepulchre. I watched my chance
for a clear spot so that no one would catch onto me
and drown me at once. Into the water, and when I
arose to the surface I struck out as best I could.
Having but one arm to swim with I found I could do
nothing against the strong current, and so let myself
float down with the current. After floating for some
time I came across my old chum, Frank Perkins, again
and three other fellows on a plank. They asked me
to get on but the plank would not hold all of us up so
I put my arm on his back to rest myself and floated
along; then I struck out again, when, behold, a welcome object was in sight—some trees on an island.
I floated into a tree top and caught fast with my arm
and shouted for help. When nearly exhausted some
woodsmen heard me and came to my rescue with a
boat. They took me to their shanty. I never was as
cold in all my life; I shook until I thought I would
shake their shanty down. The steamer blew up
between one and two o'clock and I was rescued just
before daylight. I could not tell the distance we
floated down the river, nor the length of time we were
in the water, but it seemed a long time and I do not
want another bath like it. The United States steamer
"Pocahontas" came up the river and picked us up
and took us back to Memphis.

It was quite embarrassing for me when I got off the

boat onto the wharf. I was still in the same condition
as when I leaped into the water—entirely naked.
When we reached the warehouse the United States
Sanitary Commission gave me a pair of red drawers
and undershirt, when I felt comparatively happy. I
was then taken to the Soldiers' Home at Memphis, and
there fitted out with a full suit and cared for like a
human being. I remained there three days and was
then taken to Columbus, Ohio. Thence to Detroit
and from there to Jackson, the place of beginning.
As I look back over the past, mine was an experience
which I would not want to go through again. I am
now comfortably situated but am almost totally blind
and expect, ere this is published in book form, to be
shut entirely out from the light of day, which I can
trace back to poor vaccination and exposure while
undergoing the above written sufferings.

ROBERT N. HAMILTON.

I ENLISTED in the service of the United States on
the 9th day of July, 1862, at Huntsville, Scott
county, Tenn. I was a private in Company F of the
3rd Regiment of Tennessee Cavalry, and was captured
at Athens, Ala., on the the 24th of September, 1864,
and confined in Cahaba Prison, Ala., and released
from there about the 12th of March, 1865. About
two o'clock on the morning of April 27, 1865, the
explosion of the "Sultana" occurred, and every deck
was covered wlth sleeping soldiers. I was sleeping
with Corp. H. C. Jones of my company on the boiler

deck, about midway between the boilers and the stern
of the boat. The noise awoke me. I thought that I
would be crushed to death by the falling timbers; but
I soon found that the boat was on fire. I began to
make preparations for my escape. I first went toward
the stern of the boat, but everywhere was confusion.
Men and women were praying, and most of them not
thinking of trying to save their lives. They were
leaping off into the water on top of each other—
hundreds drowning together. I saw that was not the
place for me to make my escape, so I turned around
and went back to about the center of the boat and got
a thin board—about six inches wide and about ten
feet long—and went out through the wheel-house,
climbed down on the wheel, and got off into the water
without sinking.

Soon after I got into the water some one got hold
of my board. I spoke to him to let go of it, as it was
not sufficient for both of us, but I had to jerk it away
from him. I then heard Buck Leonard exclaim, "Is
that you, Bob?" I told him it was. He said, "Don't
get excited and you will get out." I thought he was
taking things rather cool, as he had on all of his
clothes, even to his hat and boots. He got out alive
and, I reckon, is living today. I still held on to my
board and swam for some time but did not seem to be
getting very far from the old wreck, which had, in a
very short time, burned down to the boiler deck. I
suppose I had been in the water something near one
hour when I saw a steamboat going down the river.
I started toward it, as I thought it would stop to pick
us up, but it kept on going. I had got back nearer the

burning wreck. Seeing several of the boys had got
back on the bow of the boat, I swam to where one of
the spars was lying with one end in the water and the
other end on the bow of the wreck. I climbed it and
got back on the bow, where I, together with about
twenty others, was taken to land by two citizens, on
the Arkansas side of the river. After getting back on
the old wreck I met Thomas Pangle of my company
and saw the bodies of three men that were burned
beyond recognition, and helped to pull a man up on the
boat; he was one of the engineers. His nose was
torn off, all except a small particle of skin, and he died
before he was taken to land. It was now about sunrise. The hull sank soon after the last load was taken
off. The two men that rescued us brought ashore the
bodies of two dead women, mother and daughter, who
were of a family of about eight persons, all of whom
were drowned except a grown son who was frantic
with grief at the sight of his dead mother and sister.
A boat soon came to our relief. Thomas Pangle and
I found Jarson M. Elliott of our company on the boat.
He was scalded all over and unable to help himself,
but was perfectly composed and bore his suffering
with great fortitude. He had his army badge which
he requested me to give to his parents. He died that
night at Gayoso Hospital, Memphis, Tenn. Next day
I met my brother John and several more of our company. My brother Henry was lost with about twenty
others of the company.

About the 29th of April we were again started north
and landed at Cairo, Ill., where we took the cars for
Mattoon, Ill. On arriving at Mattoon we were met by

the citizens of the surrounding country with wagon loads of provisions, the best that the country afforded. The vast multitude manifested their sympathy for us through speeches made by chosen orators. Never shall I forget seeing the tears shed by the stoutest hearts on that occasion. We then went to "Camp Chase," Ohio, where we remained a short time. Eventually, all the paroled prisoners were ordered to their respective States to be mustered out of the service by general order No 77. I was discharged from the service of the United States on the 10th of June, 1865, at Nashville, Tenn.

Thus ended nearly three years of hard service which I gave my country, and of which I feel proud today. All I regret is that I could not do more for my country. I try to teach my children the importance of honoring our country and its glorious old flag. God bless it, may it wave over a free country as long as time may last.

My present postoffice address, Van Alstyne, Grayson county, Texas.

ABSALOM N. HATCH.

I WAS born in Steuben county, New York, March 8, 1839. Enlisted at Saginaw, Mich., November 11, 1861, Company F, 1st Regiment Michigan Engineers and Mechanics. Was captured near Huntsville, Ala., May 5, 1864, and confined in a prison at Cahaba, Ala., also at Marion, Miss.

I was put on board the "Sultana" too weak to care

what became of me, but the air from the river, with
the sweet crackers and other dainties provided by the
ladies, seemed to put new life into me. I began to
realize that I was on my way home after a prison life
of ten and one-half months.

On the night of the disaster I did not lie down until
the boat loosed from her moorings at the coal barge
near midnight, and then found that some comrade had
occupied my place or rather the one that I had selected
on the boiler deck. There was no other way than to
find another, a task easier thought of than accom-
plished, but which I proceeded to do. I first explored
the boiler deck, then cabin and hurricane decks, but
all were full. I then went below and out in front of
the boilers, near the flagstaff on the bow, and rolled
myself up in a blanket, between coils of rope. Had
just gone to sleep when the explosion occurred. Several men ran over me and jumped into the river before
I could get on my feet. I stayed on the boat until the
wheel or covering on the left hand side began to topple
into the boat, when I jumped in the river with an oak
scantling (2x4) for company, floated within three miles
of Memphis and was finally picked up by a boat just
at peep of day.

The sight while on the boat, previous to leaving it,
brings a shudder even to this late day.

P. S.—Yours found me just attacked with erysip-
elas, wrote off what you find on this sheet; the next
morning both eyes were swollen shut, have just got
around again. Would have written more if I had been
well. Present occupation is that of farming. Postoffice address, Ellington, Tuscola county, Mich.

JACOB HELMINGER.

I WAS born in Allen county, Ohio, in 1839. Enlisted in the service of the United States, at Huston, Ohio, August 1, 1862, in Company B, 50th Ohio Infantry. Was captured at Franklin, Tenn., November 30, 1864, and confined in the Cahaba prison.

The loss of the "Sultana," on the morning of the 27th day of April, 1865, will remain fresh in the minds of the survivors as long as life lasts. I have seen men shot down in battle, treated like brutes while prisoners of war, but the explosion of the "Sultana" caused the greatest horror I ever witnessed. In giving my experience in the affair I will not attempt to give the experience of others, for each one had all he could do to look out for himself.

A few of my own company and myself were sleeping on top of the hurricane deck. In my sleep I heard a noise and felt a terrible jar of the boat. In an instant I was wide awake, and before I could realize what had happened my comrades were also on their feet. Smoke and steam had already taken possession of the boat, and we were not long in perceiving the situation of affairs. I stepped where I could see and looked at my watch, and I think it was about two o'clock. This watch I brought out with me and have it yet. We now saw that the boat was on fire. Many of the injured ones were screaming and groaning, I

told my comrades to remain there, while I went down
on the next floor to see if there was anything we could
use as a raft, and if so I would return to them and we
would at once aim to make our escape. I had great
difficulty in getting below, every body and everything
being in the way, and finally, after getting there, I
found nothing but what was already in the hands of
some one or thrown overboard with perhaps a hundred
men contesting for its possession. I then made my
way back on the hurricane deck, but found the boys
I had left there gone or scattered, and saw nothing
more of them until after daylight, finding all of them
at Memphis but one. This was G. W. Shearer
of my company. He has never been heard from
and can only be accounted for as one among the lost;
about seventeen hundred (1700) brave soldiers that
found watery graves.

I then saw that none could assist each other but
that each would have to look out for himself, and that
I would have to watch my chance and make my escape·
To jump into the water just at that time would have
been certain death, for the river looked to me like a
solid mass of men. Some appeared to be swimming
away, others trying to get back to the boat, while
others were drowning, and not only themselves but
pulling others under with them. Some were praying,
some swearing, while others appeared quite calm and
only looking for a favorable opportunity to get away.
I heard the captain of the boat giving a command.
He told us to come to order, that the hull was not
hurt and we would land. Now, if the fire could be
put out I would have thought this order very advis-

able, but I could see no possibility of stopping the flames unless they were quenched by water.

The fire had now become so great a person could see a considerable distance each way from the boat. The crowd in the water had also scattered, so I began to muster my courage and prepare to leap overboard. I had great confidence in myself as a swimmer, and hoped to make shore if I was not interfered with by drowning people or getting cramped. All the clothes I had on was my pants, shirt and socks. This had been my night dress, and I concluded to swim as I was. I was ignorant of the distance to either shore and thinking, perhaps, it was not over three or four hundred yards either way I would take the Tennessee shore, I looked for a clear spot and made a final leap. When I came to the surface I looked around to see if any one was near me, and seeing there was not all I had to contend with was the mighty waters of the Mississippi. I now put in my best efforts and pulled for the shore ; I imagined myself making great speed for a while, but finally noticed I was drifting down below the boat. I could see at once that the current of the river was against me, and thought I would try for the opposite or Arkansas side. This effort was also a defeat. Somehow the current worked against me in this direction more than in the other.

I headed down the stream and could see some lights, not knowing what and where they were, and resolved to steer for them. I had not gone far until I noticed an object of some kind in the water ahead of me. I kept my eyes on it, and after awhile heard some one talking in that direction and so called to them. They

answered and told me to come to them, so I did my
best and after awhile caught up with them.   It proved
to be a large plank capable of holding from four to six
men, while there was only two upon it.   They invited
me on board with them and of course I accepted.   My
new companions appeared quite cheerful, under the
circumstances, and one of them said the lights ahead
of us was Memphis, and on nearing them found that
our comrade was right.

It did not take long for our plank to slide down the
river, opposite the wharf.   A man came to us with a
skiff and landed us on shore.   It was now daylight and
the wharf was already crowded with people, all anxious
to know the cause of the explosion.   Of course we
could give no reason, or at least I could not, and in
fact I did not feel like talking for I was so benumbed
with cold that I felt very little interest in anything or
anyone.   I have never been a whiskey drinker, but on
this occasion drank nearly a pint at a time given me
by a ferry-boat captain.

I am a carpenter by trade.   Postoffice address, New
Sharon, Iowa.

———

WILLIAM S. HILL.

I WAS born in Blount county, Tenn., in the year
1845, and enlisted in the service of the United
States at Knoxville, Tenn., in the fall of 1863 in
Company L, 3rd Regiment Tennessee Cavalry, and
was captured at Sulphur Trestle, Ala., in the fall of
1864, and confined at Cahaba, Ala.

At the time of the explosion of the steamer "Sultana" I was blown into the river and floated about nine miles before I was picked up. My present post-office is Rockford, Tenn.

WILEY J. HODGES.

I WAS born in Sevier county, Tenn., November 4, 1835, and enlisted in the service of the United States at Knoxville, Tenn., on the 15th day of June, 1863, in Company F, 3rd Regiment Tennessee Cavalry. Was captured at a trestle in Alabama, September 25, 1864, and confined in the prison at Cahaba, Ala., until the 6th day of March, 1865, when I was taken to Vicks-burg for exchange and was sent up the river on the ill-fated steamer " Sultana." My bunk was near the boiler, and on the night of the terrible accident I lay with a blanket over me. I was awakened by the explosion and found myself covered with burning coals from the furnaces. I was not long in springing to my feet and throwing my burning blanket away and getting away from that locality. I remained on the boat until the fire became uncomfortable when I obtained a plank, and throwing it into the river followed after it. I soon found that it was not sufficient to hold me out of the water so I caught hold of a floating barrel, but after turning it over a few times concluded I did not want it and let it go. I then turned back to the boat and obtained three planks, and putting them together held them with my hands and feet and found then that I could keep my head out of water. I floated down the

river in this manner until daylight, when I saw two
men upon the bank to whom I hallooed for help.
They came to my rescue and took me to a house where
I remained till a steamer came along and carried me
back to Memphis.   I was discharged from the service
of the United States at Nashville, Tenn., on the 15th
day of June, 1865.

My occupation is that of a farmer.

P. L. HORN.

I WAS born in the city of Wooster, Wayne county,
   Ohio, October 24, 1844, and pursue the vocation of
a confectioner and baker.   I enlisted as a private in
Company I of the 102d Regiment Ohio Volunteer Infantry, at Wooster, Ohio, August 7, 1862.   Was captured at Athens, Ala., September 24, 1864.   Was held
as prisoner at Cahaba, Ala., for seven months; was
then released and sent to Vicksburg, Miss., where I got
on board the steamer "Sultana," that had sailed from
New Orleans, and upon which the eye of an evil planet
was resting.   At Vicksburg, Miss., one of the boilers
underwent a process of repairing.   We steamed up the
river, the vessel running smoothly and all going
"merry as a marriage bell."   We reached Memphis
on the evening of the 26th of April, 1865, where a
cargo of sugar was unloaded.   Departing thence at
about midnight we pressed up the river and took on
coal.   While this was going on I fell asleep.   After
that I knew but little and seemed to live a thousand
years in a minute.   My first conception or self-identi-

fication was that I was lost in the air, and true it was—I was whirled in the air.

When the explosion took place I was lying on the left side of the boat on the cabin guard at the foot of the stairs that goes up to the hurricane deck. I was either blown through the stairway or thrust out side-wise into the river, but my first consciousness was that of being in the air. When I struck the water I went down twice, when, upon rising the second time, I encountered a piece of the wreck which I seized. I think it was a part of the cabin guard which was about twenty feet in length by six to eight feet in width. Seven other comrades clung to the wreck upon which we floated down the river, passing the city of Memphis. On the way down in this life and death struggle, two of the men, through sheer exhaustion, relinquished their hold, and sinking back into the arms of the cruel river, were drowned. I do not know their names; they were strangers to me.

It was now just before daybreak and the darkness was most terrible, but nevertheless we sounded the loudest possible alarm, which was heard by men in a gunboat lying near, and we were picked up by a skiff with three men in it. There were six of us in the boat and one of them, my bunkmate, Joseph McKelvy, of my company, was scalded from head to foot in the explosion. I was the first one to get into the boat. McKelvy recognized me and said: "For God's sake, help me in." I said: "Is that you?" "It is," he replied. I asked: "Are you hurt?" He answered: "Yes, scalded from head to foot." I took him by the arm and one of the boatmen took hold of him also,

and we helped him into the skiff. The boatman
removed his coat and put it around McKelvy to prevent him from taking cold. We then started up the
river toward Memphis and when crossing the river in
the direction of the Tennessee side (we were then on
the Arkansas side), we were fired upon by some negro
guards (Union men) who thought that we were Confederates and who were guarding the river some distance below Fort Pickens.

We then headed up stream and met a steamer in
anxious search of the victims of the terrible disaster.
One of the skiffmen with a lantern signalled the
steamer and it came to a halt and we were taken on
board. McKelvy was hurt the worst and received the
most kind and tender attention. A bed was made on
the lower deck for him, his clothing removed and his
body sprinkled with flour, if possible to mitigate his
sufferings.

The dense darkness still prevailed and the steamer
continued its journey down the deep broad current on
the alert for victims till after daylight, when it returned to Memphis not having found any more of the
unfortunates. Shortly after we were taken on the
steamer a comrade (stranger to me) died, but prior to
to his death they placed him on a barrel and for a
time rolled him quite vigorously, thinking that he was
gorged with water. When we arrived at Memphis the
ladies of the Sanitary Commission were the first to
come to us with dry clothing, giving each of us a
flannel shirt and a pair of drawers. We changed our
clothing and then were driven in cabs to the hospital.
The unfortunate McKelvy was taken to a different

hospital, in some part of the city, where he died. We remained in Memphis two or three days and those who were able and well enough were transported to Cairo, Ill., and thence to Columbus, Ohio, where I was discharged from the service May 20, 1865.

At the time of the explosion McKelvy and I were lying together asleep, and it is a matter of wonder to me how I escaped when he was so seriously injured. When the explosion took place my first impression was that I was experiencing another railroad disaster, as I had just passed through an ordeal of that kind on the way to Athens, but when I collided with the water this impression was soon corrected. How far or how high I was blown into the air I do not know, but I remember that my feet first struck the water and with the exception of being slightly hurt on my left side I suffered but little from the shock. It was not a laughable matter then, but it is now, when during the night we were clinging with a death grip to the wreck, a mule—another floating waif of this disaster—swam along and dumped us all into the river, compelling us all to exert our strength to regain our hold on the wreck. The current at times would compel the men to relax their grip and with the greatest difficulty they would recover it again. It is my opinion that the explosion was caused by a torpedo having been placed in the coal by the Confederates at the last coaling station. One of the boilers of the Sultana had just been repaired at Vicksburg. Many of the men who lost their lives were soldiers who had been prisoners for many months, some even for twenty months.

23

IRA B. HORNER.

I WAS born in Ohio, in 1847. I enlisted in the service of the United States at Findlay, Ohio, October 25, 1861, as a private in Company K of the 65th Regiment Ohio Volunteer Infantry, and was promoted to corporal at Nashville, Tenn.

I passed unharmed through all the engagements of my regiment until at the battle of Stone River or Murfreesborough, December 31, 1862, where I was wounded in my left hip and thigh. At Chattanooga, Tenn., I re-enlisted in the same company and regiment, and as a corporal. During the second term I was most fortunate in escaping sickness and was leading a most charming life, but while in battle at Franklin, Tenn., November 30, 1864, my good fortune seemed to have forsaken me, and the worst of evils befell me—I was a prisoner in the hands of the Confederates. The day following our capture we were placed in a line and searched, and everything that would be of any value to them was taken from us. I had a new pair of boots which I was compelled to exchange for a pair of shoes two sizes too short for me, which had to be cut before I could wear them. I had a watch which I sold as soon as I entered the enemy's line for one hundred and fifty dollars confederate money. Also had thirty-three dollars of our money hidden under the cover of a pocket testament and as the men who were despoiling me had no use for the latter it was left in my possession and the treasure therein became the means of saving the lives of three comrades and myself. I bought one or two bushels of corn meal without which it would have been impossible for us to live.

When we were to be exchanged and were passing out of the prison grounds the monster who had presided over our prison tortures said by way of parting, "I had rather shoot every one of you than see you exchanged."

The explosion of the steamer Sultana and my escape from a watery grave at first seemed like a horrid dream, but in a short time I learned it was reality. When first awakened from my slumbers it seemed as if some poor emaciated comrade had fallen upon me.

The next I knew I was struggling and strangling in the water. I was not very well versed in the art of swimming; but fortunately for me a stick of timber came floating along. I grasped it and soon found another, and by the aid of these I thought that there would not be much danger of my drowning. While clinging to the timbers a poor fellow clutched me by the legs, and for fear that he would drown us both I pushed him off, letting one of my socks go with him. Probably well I did so, for I should not have been able to have taken him with me.

After getting through with this my attention was drawn to a brilliant light. Some comrades asked what light that was. Some said that it was the boat burning and others that it was a boat coming to our rescue. Although I felt that I would not drown at the same time I did not feel comfortable from the fact that there was an alligator seven and one-half feet long keeping me company.

While floating along on the timbers I heard a familiar voice hallooing to me, " Horner is that you?" I answered, " Yes, what there is left of me." On my asking him what he was on he replied on a piece of the hurricane deck of the boat. I asked if it would be sufficient for me to come on with him, " All right," he says, " Horner, come along." I could not see him but struck out and soon found him. The craft was only about four by six feet and two comrades were with him; less fortunate than myself they could not swim. My timber was gone, therefore I had to remain. Now there was a squad of four, two swimmers and two hangers on. One poor fellow was badly scalded as well as myself. We floated gently and peacefully along until we came to where the city guards were stationed; they fired upon us not knowing what was the matter. Soon we arrived in sight of the city lights. I was well aware if we got any help outside of our own efforts we might get it there, so I hallooed with all my strength and soon a party of two, with a small boat, came to our rescue. I felt like if I had all the world I would give it to those boatmen. They rowed us to a larger boat, the " Essex." There the attendants on board gave us something to drink from a canteen which set the blood in circulation, and also something to eat in the shape of hard tack and dried beef.

After landing we marched up to the town of Memphis, I marching along in the city with only one sock, shirt and drawers on, but we felt fortunate to be alive and free. We were placed in the Gayoso Hospital where we remained and were cared for about ten days. Before leaving we donned another suit of blue, then we went on board a boat bound for Cairo, Ill. On arriving there we felt quite relieved to know that we were off the water. The next morning we went by rail to Mattoon, Ill., where a bountiful repast was served, and also a ten dollar note was given to me which I gave a portion of to my messmates. The word had come that all Ohio soldiers that were able to be transported were to be sent to the State to be mustered out of the service as the war was over. Of course we wanted to go whether able or not, and of course I went though I went on crutches, being scalded and bruised on the left side and my left shoulder dislocated.

We arrived at Columbus at the Seminary Hospital where we remained three weeks, then we were mustered out of the service by order of the War Department May 15, 1865. I arrived home on or about the 18th of May, 1865. The people at home looked on me as one of the dead, as they had learned that I was on the boat and they did not expect to see me alive again, but they did not know that I had learned to swim since they last saw me. If I had not learned to swim I should, without any doubt, have drowned.

My present occupation is farming. My present post-office is Weston, Ohio.

JACOB HORNER.

I ENLISTED in the service of the United States on the 14th of August, 1862, for three years, at Nashville, Holmes county, Ohio, as a private in Company A, 102nd Regiment Ohio Volunteer Infantry.

I was captured in the engagement before Athens, Ala., and made a prisoner of war on the 25th of September, 1864, and taken to Cahaba, Ala., where I remained until the 14th or 15th of March, 1865, when I was paroled out and sent to Vicksburg, Miss., arriving there on the 21st of March. I remained there until the 24th of April, when I went on board the steamer "Sultana" bound for Cairo, Ill. We arrived at Memphis, Tenn., on the evening of the 26th of April. On the morning of the 27th of April, the steamer exploded one of her boilers and there were about one thousand four hundred and fifty (1,450) drowned and killed. My life was saved by swimming about two and a half miles and landing in the brush (the water had risen so high that it had overflowed its banks).

As to the cause of this disaster I never knew. The number of passengers on board (according to what I have learned) was two thousand two hundred and fifty (2,250). This disaster, of which I am writing, was the greatest accident that ever happened during the war, and neither pen nor tongue can describe it.

I was discharged from the service at Camp Chase, Ohio, on the 20th of May, 1865.

W. A. HULD.

I WAS born near Lucas, Richland County, Ohio, May 19, 1841, and enlisted at Mansfield, Ohio, October 2, 1861, in Company A, 64th Ohio Volunteer Infantry. Was captured near Franklin, Tenn., November 29, 1864, and confined in the Cahaba, Ala., prison.

When the explosion occurred I was lying near the head of the stairs on the cabin deck, and was suddenly awakened by a terrible crash and nearly smothered with hot steam.

I soon realized that a frightful disaster had occurred and heard the groans of the suffering and cries for help. Hastily making my way down the stairs to the bow of the boat, I found all was confusion. Men were shoving off gang planks, some tearing boards off on which to float, others walking through the crowded deck, seemingly crazed or wringing their hands and calling on God for deliverance. Others were crying, while many were being crowded off into the river by dozens and going down to a watery grave clasped in each others embrace. I made my way through the crowd down to the bow of the boat, picking up the hatch door on my way. I dropped it into the water and leaped after it, but unfortunately for me three other parties seized and got away with it. That gave me some room and I got out of the crowd without being hindered by anyone. I swam until my strength was about exhausted, when I saw, by the light of the burning vessel, a small cotton-wood tree floating near with a man poised in its branches. When it came near enough I caught hold of the roots and held on. As soon as the man saw this he made serious objections, saying that it would not carry two men and that he could not swim a lick. To which I replied, "I only wish to rest a minute and I will surrender the tree to you." Slipping my suspenders from my shoulders and extracting myself from my government pants, I applied all my strength to swimming again. In this way I toiled on, fighting the mad waters of the Mississippi, until to my great surprise I saw something in the darkness floating near by. I struggled towards it and laid my hand on a large plank, covered with pitch and gravel, which proved to be a part of the hurricane deck of the "Sultana." On this plank I floated for several hours, and as the day dawned on the morning of the 27th of April, 1865, I was picked up by the steamer "Bostonia" and carried to the city of Memphis, Tenn.

My present occupation is that of a plasterer. Postoffice address, Armourdale, Kansas.

JOHN H. JAMES.

I WAS born in Paris, Trumbull county, Ohio, November 13, 1844, and enlisted in the service of the United States at Limaville, Stark county, Ohio, August 11, 1862, in Company F, 115th Ohio Volunteer Infantry. Captured near Nashville, Tenn., December 4, 1864, and confined in the Meridian, Miss., and Andersonville, Ga., prisons.

The first thing I knew of the explosion I found myself under one of the fallen smoke stacks. I cannot tell how I got out. I floated and swam down the river until about sunrise. Was picked up by a gunboat yawl, more dead than alive.

Occupation, wood finisher. Postoffice address, 707 North Howard Street, Akron, Ohio.

G. J. JOHNSON.

I WAS born in Philipsburg, Alleghany county, N. Y., May 18, 1840, and enlisted in the service of the United States at Hudson, Lenawee county, Mich., August 21, 1862, in Company A, 18th Regiment Michigan Infantry, and was captured at Athens, Ala., September 24th and confined in the Cahaba, Ala., prison.

When the explosion took place I lay between the smoke stacks asleep. I remember jumping into the water, but knew no more until about sunrise, when I was picked up on the Arkansas side by the picket boat "Pocahontas."

Occupation, farming. Postoffice address, Medina, Lenawee county, Mich.

LEWIS JOHNSON.

I WAS born in Henry county, Indiana, November, 1845, and enlisted in the service of the United States at Henry county, Ind., December, 1863, in Company G, 9th Cavalry. Was captured at Sulphur Trestle, Ala., September 25, 1864, and confined in the Castle Morgan and Cahaba prisons.

When the "Sultana" exploded I was lying in front of the wheel house. I got up, and walked across the boat, pulled off my clothes and jumped into the water. I was burned very badly on my neck and shoulders. I swam out to some timbers on the Arkansas side and got on a log. There were nine of us on it. We were there until eight o'clock when we were taken in by a boat.

Occupation, farming. P. O., Muncie, Ind.

BENJAMIN F. JOHNSTON.

I ENLISTED on the 16th of August, 1862, at Almont, Lapeer county, Mich., as a private in Company A of the 5th Regiment Michigan Cavalry. Mustered in the United States service at Detroit on the 26th of August, 1862, and left Detroit for Washington, D. C., on the 6th of December, 1862, arriving there on the 9th, and went into winter quarters on East Capitol Hill. Our regiment, in the spring, joined the army of the Potomac and I was taken prisoner on the 11th of June, 1864, at Trevillian Station, Va. Taken first to Libby Prison in Richmond, Va., and from there to Andersonville, Ga., where I was confined until the 25th of March, 1865. I was paroled out and sent to Vicksburg, Miss., arriving at Black River on the 1st of April, 1865, crossed the river and went into camp, remaining there until the 24th of April, afterwards marching about four miles to Vicksburg where we went on board the steamer "Sultana."

My company being near the rear of the column

would naturally fall on the lower deck and on the bow of the boat. We arrived at Memphis, Tenn., on the evening of the 28th of April, and the steamer stopped and unloaded three hundred hogsheads of sugar which detained her until nearly eleven o'clock at night. Left there about that hour and went up the river about four miles, where we stopped and took on a supply of coal to last as far as Cairo, Ill., leaving the barges about two o'clock in the morning of the 27th, when, after steaming up the river three more miles, the explosion took place.

Taking in the whole situation at a glance I got up, put on my shoes and waited for a favorable opportunity to leave the boat, realizing that I was safe on the boat as long as the fire did not affect me. When the opportunity presented itself I took off my blouse, hat and shoes, keeping on all my underclothing, and took an ambrotype likeness of my wife and boy, out of my blouse pocket and put it in my pants pocket so that if I was lost and ever found it would be the means of identifying me. I then put my left hand on the railing of the boat and jumped into the river and commenced swimming for the shore. After being in the water a short time a piece of board, about six inches wide and from six to seven feet long, came floating along in front of me. Having secured it and placed it under my breast I had no trouble in reaching an island, but on account of high water it was overflown. After a great amount of trouble I finally succeeded in getting out of the river into the fork of a small tree and remained there until eight o'clock, when I was picked up by a steamer and taken to the

Soldiers' Home at Memphis. Left there the second day for Michigan. Was discharged from the service as a veterinary surgeon, at Detroit, July 7, 1865.

A. A. JONES.

I WAS born in Stow, Summit county, Ohio, on the 25th of April, 1843. Lived with my parents on the farm. Enlisted in the service of the United States August 11, 1862, and mustered into the service September 18, 1862, in Company C of the 115th Regiment Ohio Volunteer Infantry. Spent first year of service in the State of Ohio, mostly at Cincinnati, guarding paroled prisoners, looking after Morgan, quelling Vallandigham riots, etc. ; were ordered to Murfreesborough, Tenn., in the summer of 1863. The regiment was distributed along the Nashville & Chattanooga railroad. Fifty or sixty of my company, myself included, were stationed at Fort Lavergne, where we remained until December 5, 1864, when we were unceremoniously taken under Gen. Forrest's wing who promised us a parole in a very short time. Notwithstanding, we were moved hastily into Dixie land, across Tennessee into Mississippi, and hardly halted until we saw the inside of the filthy enclosure at Meridian, Miss., remaining there until the barefoot stragglers came up, feet bleeding and frozen, caused by the ice and snow that lay on the ground at that time. Many a poor fellow went to his long home on account of the cruel treatment of the enemy in taking away his boots and shoes. Arrangements were very soon made to remove us from here, as ''Pap'' Thomas was making it rather lively for Hood about this time, and we were moved into Alabama, thence into Georgia, where we went into winter quarters in the most dreaded of all prisons, Andersonville.

It must have been the last days of December when we arrived at this ''den of death.'' We remained there until the last of March, 1865, when some 2,500 men were sent out on exchange—arriving in camp at Black River, Miss., the fore part of April, 1865. Here it was we wrote the happy news to our parents, wives, and sweethearts that we would soon be with them at home. How our hearts leaped within us with anticipation. On the morning of April 25th the news came that transportation had been secured, and we were marched out, with light hearts, to Vicksburg where the ''Sultana'' lay awaiting us. It was not at all necessary to be invited to go on board, and as we did so we noticed the repairing of the boilers. Some 2,500 sandwiched ourselves as best we could until every available spot and place was occupied.

The repairs of the boilers, the overcrowded condition of the boat, the drunken captain, who furnished transportation—made everything blue—because the captain of the boat objected to taking on so many. These very important things were unnoticed by the comrades in their anxiety to reach home and friends once more. But the sequel proves we should have been more wary. Near the bow of the hurricane deck was the place selected by our squad who had stuck together through all our afflictions during the war.

My health was very poor while at Andersonville. The hurried march into our lines, change of climate and diet, etc., made my case no better, consequently I was most miserable when I boarded the vessel, and asked as a favor of my comrades, Martin Baird and Robert Gaylord, if they would permit me to sleep between them as we had only one blanket. They cheerfully consented, and although the nights were quite cold to us bloodless fellows, yet by being so closely packed we managed to keep three sides comparatively warm. This was the position we occupied during the night of the 26th up to the time the crash came, which must have been about 2:30 A. M. What a crash! My God! My blood curdles while I write, and words are inadequate; no tongue or writer's pen can describe it. Such hissing of steam, the crash of the different decks as they came together with the tons of living freight, the falling of the massive smoke stacks, the death-cry of strong-hearted men caught in every conceivable manner, the red-tongued flames bursting up through the mass of humanity and driving to death's door those who were fortunate enough to live through worse than a dozen deaths in that "damnable death pen" at Andersonville. We had faced death day by day while incarcerated there, but this was far more appalling than any scene through which we had passed.

Awakened with the dreamy whisper of mother, sister or other darling on our lips. But oh, what a change in one short moment! Comrades imploring each other for assistance that they might escape from the burning deck; officers giving orders for the safety of their men; women shrieking for help; horses neighing; mules kicking and making the terrible scene hideous with their awful brays of distress. These are a few of the many scenes and sounds that greeted my sight and came to my ear.

After a most desperate effort on my part I extricated myself from the section of the wreck that by the explosion had been thrown upon me. My sleeping comrades. Alas! where were they? Martin Baird that slept on my right and Robert Gaylord that slept on my left, where were they? God can answer, I can not as I never saw or heard of either of them after that. Poor fellows, they were kind to me and I trust that I may yet touch elbows with them across the river whose waters are so pure. I climbed as rapidly as my strength would permit to the railing on the edge of the boat and from there looked down on the awful scene below. The darting flames by this time lighted the whole panorama. Can I ever forget the scene? Not while my senses remain. Masses of drowning men clinging together until they were borne down by their own weight to rise no more alive. Their poor, pinched, and ghastly faces are indelibly engraved on my memory.

Life is sweet, and all those scenes of destruction did not prevent me from thinking of the dear ones at home and how I was to save my own life. I climbed to the lower deck and grasped a plank. Was sliding it over the edge of the boat when a comrade asked permission to slide down. It was granted. When he reached the water he caused me to loose my hold; then he moved off with it. This robbed me of what I first expected to save my own life on, but I bear no malice, my earnest wish being that the plank he robbed me of saved his life or that of some other comrade. I stood wondering what next to do, but as God was watching over me there was a way that soon proved to me that there was a power ruling over all stronger than man. A plank like the first floated from beneath the swell of the boat. As soon as I noticed it I sprang into the water, came up, and remained as near the boat as possible. I swam to the bow, then swam away as quickly as I could to avoid obstacles being thrown on me, as I had observed many a poor comrade pass to his watery grave in this manner. After getting a short distance from the boat on the Tennessee side there was something I took to be an island, as the flames by this time lighted far out on either side. I started, as I supposed, for the island but soon got into the current and, it being very swift and the plank large, I was swept down at a rapid rate and the water being very cold soon chilling my weak physical struc-

ture to such an extent that I gave up all hope of my
reaching shore by any exertion of my own; so I floated
with the current.

I cannot describe my feelings as I lay motionless on
the plank, my lower limbs being benumbed and
cramped so that I had no power over them.   I never
can forget the scene of horror as I looked upon it the
last time.   Those noble men who had faced battle in
all its fury; who had not flinched when the word "forward" came, even though in the face of the cannon or
screaming shell; had faced worse than death at Andersonville; standing there on the bow of that burning
boat wringing their hands, rushing to and fro begging
and imploring their comrades to assist them that their
lives might be saved to their dear ones!

I floated on out of sight and hearing of that terrible
picture until life in me was well nigh extinct.   When I
saw in the gray of the morning the street lamps at
Memphis, when I realized this fact, I was more horrified than at any time, for the thought of going beyond
that city into the wild region below, in that mad,
rushing current, was enough to curdle the blood if any
was left in my veins, which I doubt, for as I remember
the sensation that every particle of blood had been
forced to the uppermost portion of my brain by a one
hundred horse power engine and that the top of my
head would fly skyward.   Providence stepped in again in
my behalf when I so much needed assistance and hope
had well nigh given away.   I heard the dip of oars and
felt a strong hand grasping and raising me from my
faithful friend, the plank, and placing me in the bottom of a boat that was being used to patrol in front of

the city to pick up those who were floating down that far. I was taken to a wharf boat and as I was borne along by two strong men, two women (God bless them!) came forward with a blanket and wrapped it about my naked form.

Comrades, will we ever realize what force there was back of the women of our country to aid and assist us in crushing out the life of the cruel war? This country owes them much for their untiring zeal, patriotism and courage.

I was taken to the Washington Hospital as soon as I was able to sit up, where we received very kind treatment until we left for the North, two days later.

My present postoffice is Parkman, Ohio.

NICHOLAS KARNS.

I WAS born in McArthur, Ohio, on the 25th of December, 1839. I enlisted in the service of the United States August 12, 1861, at McArthur, Ohio, as a sergeant in Company B of the 18th Regiment Ohio Volunteer Infantry, and mustered into the service at Camp Wool, Athens county, Ohio, in September, 1861.

Our regiment being assigned to the Army of the Cumberland, I served under Gens. Buell and Rosecrans, and consequently was in the battles at Stone River and Chickamauga. Was captured on the second day's fight (September 20, 1863), at Chickamauga and was taken with several thousand prisoners to Richmond where we were searched and robbed of our valuables. I was assigned to the old Pemberton building where I remained about two months, and then I, in company with comrade Johnson, was taken to Libby prison where they confined us in darkness for thirty-six hours. We were then taken out and placed on Belle Isle where we remained the rest of the winter, and in the latter part of March, 1864, was taken to Andersonville, and remained there until September, when I was taken out and shipped to Millen, from there to Savannah, Blackshear, Thomasville, and was finally taken back to Andersonville, arriving there on the evening of the 24th of December, 1864. We remained there until the latter part of March, 1865, when we were taken out and sent to Vicksburg, Miss. Here I would like to relate about the many happy changes, but space will not admit, neither can words express it.

At Vicksburg we were put on the ill-fated steamer "Sultana." All went along smoothly until one of her boilers exploded on the morning of the 27th of April, 1865. I was lying on the cabin deck when the explosion took place, and with the aid of a number of comrades secured a stage plank and launched it out into the deep, rough waters.

Many were forced to let go and were drowned, but those that were fortunate stayed with the plank. We tried for some time in vain, to make to the Tennessee shore, but the current being against us we were drifted down stream until we lodged in some driftwood that had caught in an old tree top. I clambered through the drift until I reached a log where I found a Michigan comrade who divided his clothing with me, which

was the means of saving my life as I was nigh chilled
to death. When daylight came I made my way back
to the old stage plank, where all hands joined in rowing it to an old shanty and we climbed to the roof and
remained there until about nine o'clock A. M., when
the relief boat "Jenny Lind" came to our rescue.
I was then taken to Memphis and placed in the hospital,
where I remained until after I drew my clothing. Was
then taken by boat to Cairo, Ill., and from there by
rail to Columbus, Ohio, where I was discharged from
the service May 11, 1865.

My present occupation is salesman. My present
post office is Plain City, Ohio.

E. J. KENNEDY.

I WAS born in New York City, December 23, 1841,
and enlisted in the service of the United States at
Cleveland, Ohio, April 1861, in Company E, 7th
Regiment Ohio Volunteer Infantry. Was captured at
Cross Lane, West Virginia and at Franklin, Tenn.,
August 1861, and November 1864, and confined in
the following prisons: Libby, New Orleans, Salis-
bury and Andersonville.

I was sound asleep when the explosion took place,
and awoke to find myself in water. I managed to get
hold of a piece of the wreck, and in company with one
of my comrades stuck to this for nearly four hours,
when we were picked up by a gunboat.

Occupation—merchant. Postoffice address, Berea,
Ohio.

RINALDON KIMMELL

WAS born in Williams Center, Ohio, January 22, 1840 and enlisted in the service of the United States at Farmer, Ohio, September 11, 1861, in Company E, 21st Regiment Ohio Volunteer Infantry. Was captured at the battle of Chickamauga, September 20, 1863, and confined in the following prisons: Pemberton building, Richmond, Va. ; Dansville, Va. ; Andersonville, Ga ,—a prisoner for eighteen months and eleven days.

He was on board the "Sultana" when the boiler exploded, and asleep at the time. On awakening called to his partner Dunafin, who was sleeping with him, but received no reply. Could not swim, and the alternative of burning to death or drowning presented itself. He chose the latter. Securing a small board before leaving the boat, he threw it in and jumped after it, managing to get hold of it when it came to the surface; it helped him through. He was among the first to leave the boat. Floated down to Memphis, just at daybreak, and was taken from the water nearly lifeless. Was not in his right mind for several hours. Left Memphis April 29th. Dunafin was never heard from.

[R. Kimmel died March 25, 1891.]

ALBERT W. KING.

I WAS born at Eickerhofe, near Wittenberge, Germany, March 6, 1842. Came to Defiance, Ohio, March, 1849. Enlisted in Company D, 100th Regi-

ment, Ohio Volunteer Infantry, on July 17, 1862, at
Defiance, Ohio. I was with said company and regiment until I was captured at the battle of Franklin,
Tenn., November 30, 1864. In company with several
hundred others captured at the same time was taken
south. Our first experience in prison was at Meridian,
Miss. Sometime later we were transported to Andersonville, Ga., where we were exposed to all the weather
during the winter months, consequently we suffered
intensely. Our best clothes, blankets and tents had
been taken from us when captured.

Early in April, 1865, we were taken from the stockade and transported to our lines at Big Black river,
near Vicksburg, Miss., and placed in parole camp.
About the same time large squads of prisoners arrived
from Cahaba and other prisons. Here we remained
until we were furnished transportation on the steamboat "Sultana" at Vicksburg. The trip to Memphis
was very tedious, though pleasant in spite of the enor-
mous crowd on the boat. We were on our way home,
and everybody was cheered by the thought. John
Davis, George Hill, William Wheeler, Adgate Fleming
and I, all belonging to the same company, occupied a
small space on the boiler deck, about twenty feet from
the stern of the boat. We arrived at Memphis on the
evening of the 26th. While the boat lay at the wharf
sugar in hogsheads was being unloaded and we helped.
When tired we went upon the streets of Memphis, but
soon returned to the boat fearing it might leave us.
When our steamer left Memphis we started for our
lodging place. Some distance up the river the steamer
made a stop at the coal barges and a supply of coal was

taken on. When the steamer was again under headway we fell asleep. We had slept about an hour when
the crash came. Men, coal, wood and timbers from
the boat were thrown over and beyond us. The steam
and ashes smothered us so we could scarcely breathe.

Several seconds passed before I recovered sufficiently
to know what had happened. When I came to my
senses I rushed for the stern entrance, falling several
times before I reached the fresh air. My four companions were soon by my side, having also escaped any
serious injury from the explosion. Now hundreds of
men came rushing out to get breath. Jamming and
crowding commenced. Those crippled were trampled
on. The high hanging bridge plank crushed many as
it was cut down. The life boats were cut from their
fastenings; but in such an immense crowd amounted
to mere nothing. The cabins over the boilers were
shattered and torn out and soon that portion of the
boat was on fire. Men called for buckets, but none
were left on the boat, and in a few minutes later the
fire assumed great proportions. Men, women and
children in the cabins called for help. Men jumped
from the upper decks to the water below. Hundreds
had been blown into the water when the explosion
occurred. It was an exciting scene.

We could not see how any of us could be rescued.
Not a boat in sight. The Tennessee shore was a half-
mile away and the high water extended far back over
the Arkansas flats. Our little squad of five were still
on the stern deck trying to break off a large piece of siding, but, on account of a large white horse fastened to
the railing on the stern deck and directly in the way,

we did not succeed. Fleming had repeatedly asked
us for God's sake to tell him what to do, that he could
not swim. Our answer was, to avoid the big crowd
and remain close to us, but when he saw that we were
disappointed as to getting off the piece of siding he
rushed into the crowd going overboard and was never
heard of afterward. The fire was close on to us and
we must soon leave the deck. Davis, Hill and Wheeler
were now with me, but a minute later they had disappeared I looked for something that would furnish a
little support in the water but could not find anything. I climbed the stern railing and jumped far as
I could to avoid the crowd just below me. When I
reached the top of the water my head struck the boat.
I had got turned in the water by coming in contact
with drowning men.

For a short time I was obliged to fight and keep out
of the grasp of drowning men. Frequently I was
pulled under but always gained the top. I used my
best efforts to get away from the boat, and when I saw
I could get out near the stern I worked fast to get
away, when I was once more knocked under by some
person jumping upon me. As I came to the top a
lady was beside me grasping me and calling for help.
I managed to get away but on getting a hold on some
wreckage I returned and assisted her. Many others
were near and around us calling for help. We were
going toward the Arkansas side and in course of time
we left the burning boat quite a distance.

Toward morning it became so dark we could see
nothing before us. Men in different directions could
be heard calling for help. All this time my lady com-

panion was quiet except that she would occasionally say "for God's sake, tell me, do you think we will be saved ?" I said but little as I was beginning to fear that we were a long distance away from anything on which to rest, as it was quite dark and I could see nothing ahead of us. All at once, however, my feet came in contact with brush, this encouraged me, and I worked fast, fearing if it was an island under water we might accidentally pass it. I now saw that we were among small trees and brush, but my feet would not reach bottom. The current was sweeping over this island and it carried us down. Fortunately we were now within reach of a drift lodged against saplings. I soon discovered a log among the drift which I mounted. It sank partly, and I had no trouble in seating my companion. I held her with one hand grasping the little tree next to me with the other. Our weight upon the log brought it down and we were in the water to our shoulders. In a few minutes we became so chilled that we could scarcely speak. Soon it was daylight, and no one in sight who might rescue us from our dangerous position. Later in the morning two men in a river yawl came near and were passing us when someone behind us called to them to run in as a man and woman were in the drift near him. They obeyed, and in a few minutes we were lying in the bottom of the boat. This gentleman who beckoned to the boatmen to pick us up first is Comrade L. G. Morgan, of Findlay, Ohio, for whom I have ever since had much regard. I have often met him since.

We were taken to a shanty near by where quilts and blankets were thrown over us and we were placed in front of a fire. Several others were brought in soon after. George Hill of my company was among the number. He conversed with the lady, and while they were thus talking she drew a ring from her finger, handed it to me saying that all the valuables she had with her on the "Sultana" were lost excepting that ring, and it was all she could at the time offer me as a token of reward. Later in the forenoon we were put on a steamer and taken to Memphis. On arriving here we separated. I was taken out to the Soldiers' Home, and the lady was no doubt taken care of by the doctors, at least I have never seen or heard from her since.

Valmore Lambert of my company who slept in the cabins directly over the boilers was lost. John Davis, William Wheeler and George Hill of my company were rescued.

My postoffice address is Defiance, Ohio.

GEORGE A. KING

ENLISTED as a private in Co. B, 2d Regiment Tennessee Cavalry, and was enrolled on September 1, 1862, at Blount county Tenn. Was captured in Alabama while carrying a dispatch from Athens, Ala., to Gen. J. D. Morgan, near Tuscumbia, Ala., on the 10th of October, 1864. Was sent to Meridian, Miss., thence to Cahaba, Ala., and remained a prisoner until the spring of 1865.

The destruction of the "Sultana" occurred near Memphis, Tenn., April 27, 1865. I was sleeping on the top of the boat when the explosion awoke me and I thought the boat was being fired upon by the enemy, but soon found what was the matter. I then stripped myself to try the water and went to the lower deck by a rope. I then went to the bow of the boat to get off. I thought that I would rather drown trying to save myself than to burn to death on the boat. After I got into the water I was struck by a piece of timber which disabled me. I was then caught by some one but managed to get loose. The water was a mass of men, some trying to make their escape and others drowning. I went some distance from the mass and then steered for shore. I think I could not have reached it but for four men passing by me on a plank. I caught hold of the plank and rested a little, then got on. We five made for the timber, which we reached in safety. We went some three miles down the river and caught on to a tree and climbed up. Just after we got up five others landed there, though one was so weak he died in the water. We were taken on a boat about eight o'clock A. M. and were landed at Memphis. From Memphis we were taken to "Camp Chase," Ohio, thence to Nashville, Tenn. Was discharged from the United States service June 14, 1865.

Occupation, farmer. Have been deputy sheriff for the last four years for my county. Postoffice address, Tong, Blount county, Tenn.

HUGH KINSER.

I WAS born in Leesburg, Ohio, on the 4th of October, 1836. Enlisted in the service of the United States at Leesburg, Ohio, on the 16th of August, 1862, in Company E, 50th Ohio Volunteers. Was captured at the battle of Franklin, Tenn., on the 30th of November, 1864, and taken to Cahaba, Ala., where I remained until about the 15th of March, 1865, when I was sent to Vicksburg, Miss., to parole camp, where I remained about six weeks and then took passage on the steamer "Sultana" on the 24th of April, 1865. Landed at Memphis, Tenn., on the evening of the 26th, and took supper at the Soldiers' Home. The captain was very urgent that all should return soon so as not to be left. But notwithstanding his orders about two hundred failed to make their appearance and were consequently left in Memphis, which, as the sequel proved, was a lucky thing for them. About two o'clock in the morning of the 27th we pulled out of the coal yard, which is about seven miles above Memphis. The boat was very heavily laden, there being about 2,300 persons on board besides the freight. My messmate and myself occupied a position on the upper deck toward the bow of the boat, just outside of the banister. I was sleeping soundly when, suddenly, I was aroused by the noise of the explosion. I arose to my feet and saw that the smoke stacks were both down. I looked below and saw that the boat was on fire. My comrade and I passed down to the lower deck, and the scene that met our eyes and the sounds that greeted our ears are beyond all description. My messmate, Johnny Carr, seized a board and said, "I am going to try to get out of this," and then sprang into the water. I watched him as long as he was visible, but he failed to carry out his purpose and must be numbered as one of the "Sultana's" victims.

I was very weak from my long confinement in prison, but I was a very good swimmer and thought I would take my chances, so sprang into the water and swam a few yards, when my strength deserted me so fast that I saw it would be of no avail to continue and turned back. A rope had been thrown over and was hanging by the side of the boat to which two or three poor fellows were hanging. I took hold of this rope and climbed above them. Gradually the hold of each one lessened and they sank in the deep waters below. My own grasp was becoming weak, and I was sliding down the same way the others had done, when a piece of board came floating down and, with an effort, I threw myself upon it and in an instant some one jumped upon me and said "shove out of here." By much tact we managed to steer clear of others who were trying to grasp at something to save themselves. One more on the board would have meant death to us all. The current carried us down stream very swiftly and the glare from the burning boat upon the water blinded us so we could not see the timber along the banks, and in fact the water was so high at this time that the timber was overflowed. We came to a bend in the river and were out of sight of the burning vessel when we discovered there was timber about five or six hundred yards ahead of us and turned to go to it.

At this point the swift current and dead water formed an eddy and we went whirling around. As we were going around a person caught on to our board, who said that she was a woman. After going around once or twice she let go and floated down on her own board, at the same time we floated out of this swift current and swam directly to the timber. We succeeded in reaching a tree, the top of which was out of the water, and my companion climbed upon it while I swam to another one about twelve feet distant. While swimming from the eddy to the tree my fingers caught in a substance which proved to be a pair of pants with suspenders on them; this was a lucky find for me as I had divested myself of all unnecessary clothing before I jumped into the water. When I reached the tree I was too much exhausted to lift myself upon it for some time. We had floated about three miles down the river and it was now getting daylight, giving me the opportunity of seeing the board which had proved to be so instrumental in saving my life. It was a poplar board about eight feet long, one foot wide, and three-fourths of an inch thick. My companion was in great distress as soon as he got out of the water and began to realize something of his condition. He was so badly scalded that his face, hands and whole body began to blister. Whether he is living or dead I know not. I have never heard from him since the second morning when I left him in the hospital at Memphis. I do not know his name, but his regiment was the 60th

Ohio Volunteers. While we were clinging to the tree we saw in the distance the hull of the "Sultana" come floating down the river, with a dozen or more boys still clinging to the burning wreck. A mound of earth which had not been overflowed had formed a sort of island, and several of the men from the wreck had floated down and lodged on it, and as they discovered the men on the hull of the boat, as it came floating down, they quickly made a raft of logs and boards and went to their rescue. From our position in the tree we watched them go trip after trip until the last man was rescued. Before they landed the last man on their return trip the hull of the "Sultana" went down, its hot irons sending the hissing water and steam to an immense height.

There were seven boats that came up the river to pick up the unfortunate. They spied my companion and I perched in the tree and came to where we were, there being a sufficient depth of water to make safe running. We were taken back to Memphis and placed in a hospital. After a day or two of rest I resumed my journey homeward. There are *many* incidents that are deeply fixed in my memory that occurred on that eventful morning, but space forbids me to mention them, but of all my war experiences of three years, including camp, march, battle and prison, there is nothing so fearful as that morning of terrors.

My present occupation is farming. Postoffice address, Albion, Neb.

HENRY J. KLINE.

I WAS born in Blackford county, Ind., September 13, 1847, and enlisted in the service of the United States December 17, 1863, in Company G, 9th Regiment Indiana Cavalry. Was captured at Sulphur Branch Trestle, September 25, 1864, and confined in the Cahaba and Selma, Ala., prisons.

At the time of the explosion of the "Sultana" I was sleeping in front of the wheel house, between Comrades King and Downey of my company. Both were lost. Comrade Downey had sent home for money from Vicksburg. He went ashore at Memphis to see some friends, but the boat left him and he gave a man two dollars for bringing him in a skiff to the mouth of Wolf River where the boat stopped to coal. When he laid down he said: "If I had not sent home for that money I would have been left." I never heard him speak again. Comrade King sprang up at the first shock, exclaiming "Oh God, Oh mother! I am lost, I am gone." I followed him across the boat but lost sight of him. Our lieutenant, Swain, followed him in the river, still crying. Swain (a splendid swimmer) got him on a plank and told him not to cry so; that he would take him out safe. King hushed and never spoke again, the lieutenant swimming behind and pushing him on. The plank in front of him came to a drift in the woods. He pushed Charlie up against the drift and told him to climb up but he was too weak. Starvation, sickness, and the chill of the water had done their work, and as Swain swung around to get on the drift himself he saw Charlie's hands go under it.

But to go on with myself. At the time of the explosion I climbed down from the hurricane to the boiler deck, and then divested myself of all my clothing except my cap, shirt and drawers and then sprang into the water, on the lower side of the boat. It floated after me and the flames burned my neck and ears. I came very near drowning. Our company had seventeen men on board and eleven of them went down.

Occupation, tile manufacturer. Postoffice address, Mill Grove, Ind.

JOHN H. KOCHENDERFER.

I WAS born in Lebanon county, Pa., on the 29th day of July, 1841, and enlisted in the service of the United States at Mansfield, Ohio, August 11, 1862, in Company D, 102d Regiment Ohio Volunteer Infantry. Was captured at Athens, Ala., September 24, 1864, and confined in the military prison at Cahaba, Ala., till in March, 1865, when I was taken to "Camp Fiske," the United States and Confederate neutral camp where I arrived on the 16th of that month.

I, with others of my regiment, was placed on board the steamer "Sultana." Five of us took up our position outside the railing in front of the left wheel on the middle or cabin deck floor, with a blanket apiece over us and our coats for pillows. We were outside and over the four great boilers, one of which caused the great destruction of lives and untold sorrow through so many of our northern homes. When the explosion occurred it threw the boiler out of its bed, ascending and tearing its way through both cabin and hurricane decks. Those immediately over the boiler were thrown in every direction, some of them being thrown directly up and falling into the fiery chasm below, while those upon the side of the boat, like myself, were thrown directly out and away from the boat. The first I realized after the explosion I found myself about 300 feet from the boat shrouded in total darkness and in what appeared to be an ocean of water. To say that I was dumfounded would but faintly express my condition. But what was I to do; give up in despair and drown? No, never! As I arose to the surface and got full control of myself I tried to isolate myself from those around me and then took a survey of the situation.

For a few minutes total darkness prevailed, then a small fire kindled itself and there being no effort made to check this little flame in a very short time it became a fierce conflagaration and the heat was intense, driving the men back, those in the center and nearest the fire crowding those on the outer edge into the river until all were driven off. The boat burned and sank, when darkness again o'er all prevailed. But all this time, while the fire was doing its horrible work and the boat drifting with the current, I was about 100 yards ahead floating down stream backwards and in a position to see the stern and one side of the boat where hundreds were dropping off into the river, the most of them going to their death. After watching them for awhile I became quite composed and fully realized my situation, and in company with another poor fellow I started out to find shore but failed. In our desperate effort, fighting the waves and current, we became separated and I know not what became of him.

Now I was alone, cold and tired. I began to look around for some support, which I found in the shape of an empty candle box which answered the purpose very well. This box I still had in my possession when picked up by a skiff eighteen miles below where the accident took place. I was brought back to Memphis and first put on a steamboat where I took the first whiskey I drank while in the service of the United States. I was taken to Gayoso Hospital, at which place I remained some three weeks before I was able to be moved, on account of an injury to the lumbar region of my spine by being thrown against a rope at the time of the explosion.

I am a medical practitioner, residing at Galion, Ohio.

C. J. LAHUE.

I WAS born in Harrison county, Ind., March 5, 1846.
Enlisted in the service of the United States at
New Albany, Ind., November, 1863, in Company D,
13th Indiana Cavalry, and was captured at New
Market, Ala., September 30, 1864, and taken to and
confined in the following prisons, viz: Cahaba, Andersonville, Meridian Stockade and Selma, Ala., and was
paroled at Black River Bridge, Miss., and placed on
the boat "Sultana" on the morning of April 24, 1865.

This boat was destined for different points up the
Mississippi river. Myself and three other comrades

laid down to sleep in the rear of the pilot house, on the texas roof near the pilot house steps. About two o'clock A. M. the explosion occurred, killing the three comrades, (Theodore Baker of Company B, 13th Indiana Cavalry, I do not remember the names of the other two), and leaving me the only surviving one that was on the texas roof. I was thrown off the boat, but caught hold of the railing of the banister and remained in that condition until driven off by the flames of the burning boat, falling into the water on the upper side of the steamer as it swung around. The water was full of struggling and drowning people. I heard a lady crying for help, asking her husband to rescue her. She was holding to a rope attached to a mule that had got overboard. I also saw the husband, with a little child on his back, struggling in the water for a moment, then sinking. The lady cried out, " My husband and baby are gone! " A comrade who had his limb crushed in the explosion by a door blown from the boat had the lady get on this door, through which means she was rescued.

I was one of the last to leave the boat; it was burned to the water's edge. I swam down the river and when opposite Memphis swam to some brush, where I found a log to cling to. I remained there until daylight. A lady discovered me and pointed me out to the captain of a boat, saying that there was a little boy on a log, in the brush, out on the river. The lady and two of the crew came in a boat and rescued me, and placed me on board the gunboat and wrapped me in blankets. I was not conscious of what was transpiring until the following evening. Was then placed in a hospital boat at Memphis. The lady who first discovered me in the brush took me to her own house and took care of me two weeks. Myself and forty-two others were sent north to Indianapolis, Ind., and from there we went home.

My present occupation is stock-raising. Postoffice address, Great Bend, Kansas.

ADAM LEAKE.

I WAS born in Knox county, Tenn., April 15, 1842. Enlisted in the service of the United States at London, Ky., on the 15th of November, 1862, in Company B, 3d Regiment Tennessee Cavalry, and was captured at Sulphur Trestle, Ala., September, 1864, and confined in the Cahaba prison.

I boarded the steamer "Sultana" at Vicksburg. When the explosion occurred I was asleep on the cabin deck, outside the railing. Was knocked insensible by flying timbers and other missiles and knew nothing until I found myself on the boiler deck near the wheel house. Then I realized a terrible calamity had occurred by seeing a perfect sea of people floundering in the water, some drowning, some grasping at objects, human and otherwise, all desperate at what seemed certain death. A horrible scene, in the contemplation of which my own condition was forgotten. With others I reached the bow of the ill-fated vessel and was standing near the jack-staff, when the wind veered and sent the flames in a solid mass against us, sending us in a body overboard. As I went over I grasped the cables in a coil and when going down continued to pay them out until I had secured a hold on their length that kept me above water and thus saved myself, as I could not swim at all.

I remained in the water about three and one-half hours, when the hull of the destroyed "Sultana" grounded on the Arkansas side and myself and such comrades as hung on with me were rescued by means of old gunwales lashed together and extending to dry land a hundred yards away. The hull sank within five minutes after.

My postoffice address is Knoxville, Tenn.

———

ASA E. LEE.

I WAS born in Galesburg, Ill., April 14, 1847, and enlisted in the service of the United States at Clinton, Ind., June 17, 1863, in Company A, 71st Regiment Indiana Volunteers, or 6th Indiana Cavalry. I was captured at Florence, Ala., October 3, 1864, and taken to Meridian, Miss., where I was confined sixty-one days, and afterwards taken to Cahaba, Ala., where I remained one hundred and forty-days, or until about April 21, 1865, when I was taken to Vicksburg, Miss., for exchange.

I, with others, was placed on board the steamer "Sultana," and on the night of the terrible disaster was asleep on the hurricane deck, near the pilot house, with my bunk mate, John May, of Terre Haute, Ind., a member of the 137th Regiment Indiana Volunteers, when the explosion took place. I was thrown to the forecastle, striking on my back and shoulders and was severely bruised by the fall. I have never seen or heard from my bunk mate since the evening we closed our eyes in sleep just before we left Memphis, and I have met only three of the "Sultana" survivors since May 10, 1865.

I left the boat while it was wrapped in flames, and after swimming nearly two miles I succeeded in getting on a log in the river, where I remained for about five hours and was then taken up by the steamer "Silver Spray" and carried to Memphis, at which place I remained about six days and was then sent north on the steamer "Belle Memphis" to Cairo, Ill., and from there to Indianapolis. There were nine of my regiment on board the "Sultana," of which six were lost.

My present occupation is carpenter and builder, and my postoffice address Tulare, Cal.

WESLEY LEE.

I BUNKED on the front part of the cabin deck, between the two stairways, and was asleep when the explosion took place. I sprang to my feet at the noise, and in doing so struck my head against the deck above, which had been smashed down and was supported by the railing around the stairs. I then crawled to the side of the boat and looked over the deck above. Just then the flames shot up from about the center of the boat with that crackling sound you all remember so well. I looked on the river at that terrible scene—a sea of heads. Oh, what a sight it was! It is just as vivid in my mind today as it was then. The hungry fire was fast eating toward me. Then I slid down a fender to a lower deck, took off my shoes, socks, blouse and pants, tore two narrow pine boards from the center of the stairway, walked to the side of the boat and jumped off, starting for the Tennessee shore, and was making fine headway as I supposed. However, on turning on my side to swim and so rest myself in a short time the water was tumbling around me and I looked for the shore but it seemed as though it was farther away. I could just see it in the distance. Then I looked up the river and saw an island, but I was too far below to try to stem that fearful current. About this time I saw a steamboat coming down the river toward the burning wreck, but soon after I was left in darkness. A little incident happened just then. Some person who had got beyond the island came across in front of me, and in a firm and manly voice said, "Don't take hold of me."

I answered, "I will not as we have plenty of room."
I mention this for if he is living I would like to know
who he is and where he is. He passed to the rear
and was soon out of sight.

After I had been in the water a long time, and
making poor headway, I became satisfied that the current was running to the other side of the river, but
would it do to change my course? I concluded not to,
for perhaps the river would soon make a turn and then
the current would favor me. I was beginning to feel
very cold and put forth every effort to reach the shore,
keeping my boards in such a position that the current
running against them would draw towards the shore;
the voices of those in the river were in the rear
and I began to make a little headway and soon the
lamps in the city became visible. Then I worked all
the harder, but it was necessary for I was getting
colder all the time. The thought of home, however,
together with the determination of a soldier "to live
as long as he can," bore me up. When I came in front
of the wharf boat, two men came out with a lantern
and I called for help. One of them jumped in a skiff
and was soon by my side, took me in and in a short
time I was by a fire in the wharf boat, where I was
given some clothing. Then they asked me what the
matter was, and when I informed them the "Sultana"
had blown up and her crew was in the water, the telegraph operator went to his instrument and in a few
minutes a steamer was moving out and picking up
men.

By the time I was well warmed the steamer "General Boynton" came to the wharf boat and put off

some men it had just picked up. Then the telegraph
operator came to me and asked me if I cared about
being mentioned as the person who gave the information of the disaster, as it would do me no good and
the river men would get pay for it. I told him it
made no difference to me, but I see by some articles in
the *National Tribune*, that the steamer "General
Boynton," gave the news, which is not correct.

Postoffice address, Winston, Mo.

THOMAS· G. LOVE, alias THOMAS LONG.

I WAS born in Providence, Rhode Island, January
13, 1843. Enlisted in the United States navy—my
second term—at Chicago, November 4, 1864, for two
years or during the war. I was sent to the ironclad
" Essex," stationed at Memphis, Tenn. Was rated
quarlermaster and was on watch at the time the steamer
" Sultana" left the wood dock about half a mile above
the " Essex " and was near the mouth of Wolf river.

The " Sultana " left the wood dock about two o'clock
in the morning of April 27, 1865, and steamed up the
river. At twenty minutes of three she blew up at a point
seven miles above Memphis, and at twenty minutes past
three I heard the cries of drowning men calling for
help. I reported to our captain, John Atchinson, and
he jumped out of bed and ordered all hands called, all
boats manned and to be away and save all that we
could. I had charge of one of the boats, the "Sky-
lark," and helped to save seventy-six of the men from
a watery grave, and when all our boats were gone

except the market boat, called the "dingey," our six messenger boys took it and saved the only woman that was saved who was on board the "Sultana." The people of Memphis sent us a barrel of whiskey in the morning, but our First Lieutenant, Wm. Berry, broke in the head of the barrel and poured the contents on to the deck. The firemen and coalmen that were left on board caught the whiskey in buckets as it ran down the scuppers and some got quite jolly, whereas, if it had been served out to the men as was intended there would not have been any one drunk.

The men in the boats worked hard without any breakfast and then we hunted for those that had strayed off into the swamps, trying to get to the dry land. All that day we found men almost dead, hanging to the trees about two miles out into the river, and among those that I rescued was one man so badly scalded that when I took hold of his arms to help him into the boat the skin and flesh came off his arms like a cooked beet. I lost my hold on him but soon caught him again, and with help he was got into the boat and saved from a watery grave. I heard of the reunion of the survivors of the "Sultana" that was held at Adrian, April 29, 1890, and went to see if I could meet with any of those whom I saved, and had the pleasure of taking the above described man by the hand. It was with a grip that did not slip as when I went to pull him into the boat. I met another man that I picked up from a bale of hay. There were nine trying to hold to it and a piece of log. I saw twenty-one men on one log that was drifting in the

river.   I took off part of them and called another
boat that took the rest.

I was through all of the war, this being my second
term, but the horror and sufferings of that morning I
never saw approached.   Pen can not write or describe
it, tongue can not tell, and mind can not picture the
despair of 2,300 scalded and drowning men in a cold
deep river on a dark night, with the current running
twelve miles an hour, and those men just released
from prison, not half-fed nor quarter clothed.   They
did not have the strength to battle with a trial like
that.   It was the most heart-rending scene that I
ever witnessed.   I hope to never see the like again.

My present occupation is that of general merchant,
and my post office address is Clayton, Mich.

WILLIAM LUGENBEAL

ENLISTED in the service of the United States as a
private in Company F of the 135th Regiment
Ohio Volunteer Infantry, at Columbus, Ohio, May 2,
1864.   Was captured at North Mountain, West Va.,
July 3, 1864, and was taken to Andersonville, Ga.,
July 27, 1864; remained in the stockade until October
1, 1864.   I went out on parole of honor and helped
build six sheds on the south side of the prison, my
quarters were near the depot and I could go a mile
from my quarters without any guard.   When I got
out of prison I weighed only a hundred pounds, but
when I was on my homeward trip I weighed one hund-

red and sixty-six pounds—so much for stealing sweet potatoes and peanuts.

March 27, 1865, I left Andersonville and was sent to the Black River, Miss., for exchange, and thence to "Camp Fiske," which is two miles back of Vicksburg, where I remained about three weeks. While here President Lincoln was assassinated. We then went on board the steamer "Sultana," and on the evening of April 26th we landed at Memphis, Tenn. While there I laid down to sleep. They took on coal and started again for God's country. Went about seven miles when I was awakened by a terrible roar and crash. I was on the second deck, my partner's name was Joseph Test, from Dayton, Ohio. A piece of timber ran through his body, killing him almost instantly. I tried to help him but could not. Then I went down stairs and the like I never saw and hope I never will again. The boat was now on fire. Reader! Imagine you are on a burning boat with twenty-one hundred men, on a dark night, what do you think you would do? Well, I will tell you what I did.

On board the boat was a pet alligator. He was kept in the wheel-house. It was a curiosity for us to see such a large one. We would punch him with sticks to see him open his mouth, but the boatmen got tired of this and put him in the closet under the stairway. When I came down stairs every loose board, door, window and shutter was taken to swim on, and the fire was getting very hot. I thought of the box that contained the alligator, so I got it out of the closet and took him out and ran the bayonet through him three times. While I was doing this a man came to me and

29

said the box would do for he and I both to get out on.
My intention was to share it with him, but I did not
speak and I do not know what became of him. I took
off all my clothing except my drawers, drew the box to
the end of the boat, threw it overboard and jumped after
it but missed it and went down somewhere in the mighty
deep. When I came up I got hold of the box, but
slipped off and went down again. When I arose to
the surface again I got a good hold of it and drew myself into it with my feet out behind, so that I could
kick, the edges of the box coming under each arm as
it was just wide enough for my breast and my arms
coming over each edge of the box; so you see I was
about as large as an alligator.

There were hundreds of men in the water and they
would reach for anything they could see. When a man
would get close enough I would kick him off, then
turn quick as I could and kick someone else to keep
them from getting hold of me. They would call out
"don't kick, for I am drowning," but if they had got
hold of me we would both have drowned. It was
about six miles from land. While the boat was burning we could see the trees on the shore, and kept our
heads that way and swam fast as we could, but the
boat burned down, sank and left us in utter darkness.
We could not tell which way to go and it was a very
lonesome place to be in.

Now I would only try to steady my box when I
would get in those whirls as I floated down the river. I
can speak of seeing two men after I started on my
voyage; it was now very dark and I could see an object
only a few feet. The first man I met in the darkness,

that lonely night, as he was passing me said, " Here goes your old tug boat." I did not answer him, as I had tug enough of my own. The next man that came near me asked which way we were going. He asked me a third time and said that he believed that we were going right down, meaning we were floating down the river.

I was taken up three miles below Memphis by a gun boat called the " Essex," and was taken from there to the Gayoso Hospital; was put in ward A, remained there some days, drew clothing and got on board the "Belle of St. Louis," came to Cairo, Ill., and then to Columbus, Ohio.

Present address, Perryton, Licking county, Ohio.

W. P. MADDEN.

I WAS born in Galway, Ireland, on the 14th of March, 1844. Enlisted at Springfield, Ohio, on the 9th of October, 1861, in Company I, 44th Ohio Volunteer Infantry and 8th Ohio Volunteer Infantry. Was captured at Lynchburgh on the 18th of June, 1864, and confined in Andersonville prison.

On the morning of the 27th of April, 1865, at about two o'clock, I was asleep dreaming of home and loved ones, of whom I had not heard a word for about ten long months that I had spent in Andersonville prison. Suddenly I was awakened by an upheaval and crashing of timbers. I attempted to arise from my recumbent position and as I threw up my hands to explore my surroundings I got them severely burned, and was horrified to find that my efforts to extricate myself were fruitless and the heat was stifling. I could not tell where I was, but could hear the groans of the wounded and the shrieks of the women mingling with the crackling noise of the flames and the hissing of the white steam that enveloped the boat for a time. All of this took place in a few moments, but those few moments were an eternity to me. No tongue can tell and pen is powerless to portray the agony of those moments. Thoughts went rushing through my brain with lightning rapidity. I thought of all I had suffered and endured for ten months and of the joys anticipated at home, and now *so near* the goal must I give up the ghost? Not without a struggle. The rebels had failed to kill me in battle, or to starve me to death in prison. I wrapped my blanket about me in order to protect myself from further violence from my hot environments. I called in the name of my Divine Master

for some one to remove whatever hindered my escape,
and may God bless whoever he may be that removed
the obstruction—I know him not. I crawled out as
black and begrimed as a coal digger. I then discovered that I had been under a piece of boiler iron about
a half of a circle, both ends being blocked with timbers and debris thrown hither and thither by the force
of the explosion.

I had a much esteemed friend by the name of George
Menenger, a Piat Zouave. His home was in Cincinnati, Ohio. He shared my blanket, but what became
of him I have not been able to learn, nor is it to be
wondered at in the confusion that followed the explosion. This was a time when strong men, who never
faltered before the galling fire of the enemy's front,
were powerless, wringing their hands and rending the
air with their piteous cries. No one now gave the
orders, each being left to battle for himself. The
deck was broken in two, presenting a fiery chasm
between like Dante's "Inferno." Burning human
forms could be seen below until the river was obscured
by the flames which soon communicated with the
upper deck. Every available thing that would float
was hastily gathered up and with precious freight went
overboard, but often only to be submerged by the
addition of others and rise again on some distant wave
far away and unoccupied, to be again possessed by
another struggler and borne safely with the current
until rescued by friendly hands.

Almost invariably the means of escape was over-
burdened, and it was often the case that parties were
drowned that others might use their floats to a practi-

cal advantage. No doubt many a good swimmer lost his life by being made powerless by the icy waters of the northwest with which the Mississippi river is flushed at that time of the year.

All this time I was endeavoring to keep from being pushed into the river by my wild and distracted comrades who were rushing to and fro. In order to do this I had to lie down often at the risk of being trampled upon. I remained on the boat as long as the heat would permit, seeing that it would be fatal to launch myself among the floating sea of perishing humanity, grasping at everything within reach and often carrying to the bottom those that would have otherwise escaped. I was fortunate in being a very good swimmer, and with confidence in my ability to reach shore I waited until the coast was clear. I then made a running jump from the fore and upper deck, but before reaching the water I lost my balance and fell face downward knocking the breath out of me and producing an inguinal hernia, which I now carry, much to my discomfort. This hurt caused me to swallow at the time a large quantity of water, causing strangulation, so that it was with the greatest difficulty that I again reached the surface. After I got my breath I swam down stream in a diagonal direction for the east bank, but for some unknown reason I changed my mind and turned for the west side. I now began to experience a peculiarly numb sensation commencing in my great toes and extending upwards. Being thoroughly awake to the meaning of all this I bestirred myself to the most vigorous and active kicking that I ever did in my life. Now and then I would pinch my limbs but could not make them believe that it was I, and yet, as long as they kept kicking, I felt safe. They had often served me and, when a boy, they had saved me many a whipping and they did not fail me on this occasion.

Somewhere between the boat and the shore I overtook three soldiers, of whom I recognized one, a sergeant of an Illinois regiment, a fine specimen of a man in every particular and I always admired him. He, with the other two, was trying to keep above the water with the aid of a very trifling bit of board. One of the party was about exhausted. I swam to them put my hands on the board and had this man put his arm on my shoulder and his other on the sergeant and we pushed on, but it was soon evident that our load was going to overtax our strength. With no evidence at hand of the distance yet to overcome, and as he was already past helping himself, true to the first law of nature I released myself, and our friend went down to be seen no more. Could I have perceived the short distance to the shore I would have saved his life, but so dark was it that the first intimation that I had of a shore was when I struck my head against a lot of drift, upon which I dragged myself at the same time shouting back to those I had parted with my deliverance and encouraging them to persevere and soon I had the pleasure of helping them to a place of safety.

I then removed my pants and shirt, wrung the water out of them and put them on again, then went at vigorous walking, as did also my friend from Illinois, but the other we had to pull along between us until a better circulation was obtained for him, after which we got along very well considering our condition. About seven or eight o'clock in the morning we were taken on board the steamer "Bostonia" and taken to Memphis.

Here I want to digress a little to speak a word of praise in behalf of the mate, who, with the pilot, was blown into the river. It was he, with the aid of a skiff, conveyed us to the boat and although wet and chilled he did not cease his efforts in caring for others as long as there were any found needing assistance. Even on the boat, where hot coffee and fire was accessible, he looked not for his own comfort until all others were first served. This self-sacrificing and unselfish devotion to the wants of others is seldom found, and I mention this as an expression of my admiration for his conduct on that occasion.

Thanks to Gen. Washburn in a few days we left Memphis for "Camp Chase," Ohio, to be mustered out of service in obedience to telegraphic orders from the War Department. And now, glorious transition. Away from the late scenes of horror, caressed and adulated by those who long ago gave me up for dead, and providential blessings through those years that have passed, have done much to compensate for what I have suffered. But oh, how many a sad and desolate home! Who can tell of the anguish in those hearts which fondly waited for the coming of the dear one.

Let us reverently treasure up in our hearts the memory of the brave dead of the "Sultana," and let our Association devote one day of its sittings in some appropriate way to commemorate their deeds of virtue.

I am engaged in the practice of medicine at Xenia, O.

JOTHAM W. MAES.

I WAS born in Huron county, Ohio, November 15, 1842, and enlisted in the service of the United States at New Boston, Mich., June 15, 1861, in Company B, 47th Regiment Ohio Volunteer Infantry. Served with my regiment in all its campaigns till on the 22d day of July, 1864, when I was captured in front of Atlanta, Ga., and taken to Andersonville. I remained there until Sherman began his famous march to the sea, when I, with others, was removed to Millen, thence to Savannah, from there to Blackshear Station, thence to Thomasville, and at last marched sixty miles across the country and put on board the cars at Albany and taken to Andersonville again, entering that terrible prison on Christmas eve, 1864. I remained here until about the 17th day of March, 1865, when five hundred of us were taken out and sent to Jackson, Miss., and from there marched to the Big Black River, where we were received by our own men, and given a ration of hard tack and coffee, with a good suit of new clothes, a blanket and a tent.

We remained at Big Black River until exchanged and put on board the "Sultana." Myself and two comrades bunked together, just back of the left wheel house, on the middle deck. The first sensation I experienced was that of falling down through space, as probably many of you have felt when you had an attack of nightmare. I soon realized that it was no nightmare for we were immersed in the icy water of the river, about three by ten feet of the portion of the deck upon which we were sleeping having been blown with its occupants into the river. The shock of the deck striking the water threw us all off from it, but we soon found it again and others came to us until that small piece of deck saved ten lives. The way we managed was to keep evenly divided around the edge and just float along. I shall never forget the terrible scene that I beheld as I glanced back at the boat and realized what had occurred. The smokestacks of the "Sultana" were lying criss-cross, crushing whoever they struck. The boat was on fire and the flames were driving the men into the water by the hundred, and no matter how good a swimmer a man might be if he got into one of those crowds his doom was sealed and he would go down with the clutching mass.

As we came in sight of the coal bins opposite Memphis we attempted to make them but the current carried us away so that we could not, neither could we reach the Memphis shore nor make the people on either bank hear us. We floated some three or four miles below Memphis before we were picked up and were then found by a quartermaster's yawl, and when taken in were so thoroughly chilled that we could not help ourselves. As we were making for the shore at Fort Pickering the troops mistook us for guerillas from the Arkansas side of the river trying to capture the fort and fired two volleys on us before they found out their mistake. Fortunately no one was hurt. We were taken to Memphis, and soon sent to Columbus, Ohio, thence to Jackson, Mich., and soon discharged.

My present postoffice address is New Boston, Mich.

JERRY MAHONY.

I WAS born in Ireland, December 23, 1842, and
enlisted in the service of the United States September 23, 1861, at Detroit, Mich., in Company I, 2nd
Regiment Michigan Cavalry. Was captured at Florence, Ala., November 9, 1864, and was confined in the
Meridian and Cahaba, Alabama, prisons.

My capture was as follows: When Sherman marched
to the sea he sent Stanley to reinforce him, but Hood
was nearer to Nashville than Stanley. Hood had Lee,
Stewart and Cheatham. Lee crossed the Tennessee
river at Florence, Ala. Stewart and Cheatham were
still on the south side. I was sent for by Gen. Crox-
ton, who asked me if I would go at night and cut the
pontoon bridge at Florence, Ala. I could go alone or
take some comrade with me. He said there was
nothing I could ask the government for but that I
could have it. I could have a commission, a furlough
or anything else, and he would open communication
with the "rebs" at daylight and exchange us, if it
took one hundred for one. I started with five others.
We got some citizens' coats and putting them on
arrived at the bridge at two o'clock A. M., and, as the
"rebs" stated in the newspaper the next day: "While
portions of that army were on each side of the river,
a party of bold federals came down the river in skiffs
and succeeded in cutting the bridge in two or three
places. Hatchets were found in their possession. It
is one of the boldest of federal raids during the campaign." We got rid of the coats before we were taken
prisoners. That night we were kept in a vacant

store, and while the guards slept three of the comrades got away but they failed to cut the bridge. I drew the attention of the guard at the door by selling my watch that was hid in my boot leg. They (my three comrades) went up stairs and got out of the window. They were missed in three or four hours and the blood hounds were sent after them, but they had crossed the river. I had no one to help me get away, so I staid. I never saw or heard of them after that. I received a seven month's furlough, and then was paroled when the rest were.

Address, 3249 LaSalle street, Chicago, Ill.

JESSE MARTIN.

I WAS born in Louisville, Ky., February 19, 1842. I enlisted in the service of the United States at Rona, Ind., September 5, 1861, in Company D, 35th Indiana Infantry. Was captured at Kenesaw Mountain, Ga., June 19, 1864, and confined in the following prisons: Andersonville, Savannah, Millen and Blackshear.

I was sleeping in the deck room when the explosion occurred. At first it seemed to me as though some one was on my breast with his knees and choking me with his hands. When I came to I was down on my knees by a cow, as though I had got there to milk her. If the cow had not stopped me I guess I would have gone on into the wheel house, and then I would not have survived to write this. The wheel was still turning and water coming in on me which helped to bring me to. I soon found out what the matter was and began to look around to see what chance there was to escape. I started to see if I could find some of my regiment but could not get to where I had left them. I then went aft to see how things were. All was confusion. Some were praying, others crying or swearing, and some jumping overboard. I found one man who seemed to be taking things coolly. I went to him and asked him if he would help me throw things to those in the water to swim on. We went to work throwing over anything we could find that would float excepting a large plank. This we saved for ourselves. We stayed on the boat until the fire drove us off. We then threw the plank in and jumped in after it but lost it. I never saw the man after that. I started to swim ashore and happened to find a small piece of plank which helped me along. I landed on an island and was picked up by the steamer "Pocahontas."

Occupation, farming; Mount Pleasant, Ohio.

JOSEPH H. MAYES.

I WAS born in Parke county, Ind., August 31, 1846. Enlisted in the service of the United States at Waveland, Montgomery county, Ind., on the 12th of November, 1861, in Company C, 40th Regiment Indiana Volunteers, and was captured at Franklin, Tenn., November 30th, 1864, and confined in the Cahaba prison in Alabama.

I was on the cabin deck of the "Sultana" when the boiler exploded. One of the smoke stacks about six feet from me fell and broke the deck in and I went through onto the lower deck. I noticed that every man had to take care of himself. I could not swim, so I got four slats one inch thick, three inches wide and about ten feet long, and took my tent rope and tied them together—then I was ready. I picked up the slats and jumped into the river and started to "paddle my own canoe." I got along finely until a drowning man caught me by my ankle. I kicked him loose and then tried to pull for the shore. Sometimes I would get within fifty yards of the shore and the current would carry me toward the other side of the river and then I would try for that side, but it would strike me again; so I just kept floating back and forth across the river. I came across a man from a Michigan regiment. I said, "hullo, comrade, advance and give the countersign." I asked him if he could swim. He said no. Then I asked him what kind of a plank he had; he replied, "one about two feet wide and ten feet long." We two got together and tried to reach the shore, but the current would carry us back and forth across the river as before, and by this time we were getting cold and somewhat discouraged.

The man from Michigan said he would have to let go and drown. I told him that would never do, and urged him to hold on. By this time we were so cold that we stopped trying to get out. We could not move hand or foot, and the Michigan man swore that he could not hold on any longer. I looked down the river and saw the headlight of a boat coming, and encouraged my comrade to hold on by saying it would probably take us in. This was about one hour before daylight. We became unconscious and did not remember when we were picked up. We came to about nine o'clock that day.

My present occupation is farming. Postoffice address, Lebanon, Boone county, Ind.

GEORGE B. McCORD.

I WAS born in Erie county, Ohio, April 8, 1844. My childhood days were spent in Erie and Sandusky counties, Ohio. I attended school in Bellevue, Clyde and Fremont, Ohio, and after the war in Cornell College, Mount Vernon, Iowa. Enlisted in the service of the United States at Sandusky county, Ohio, as a private in Company G, 111th Regiment Ohio Volunteer Infantry, in August, 1862, and mustered into service at Camp Toledo by Capt. Howard, United States Army. Received the appointment of orderly sergeant, and afterwards promoted to first lieutenant and placed in command of Company F.

31

Passed through many spirited and exciting battles and experienced many long and fatiguing marches through Ohio, Kentucky, Tennessee, Georgia and Alabama. Was in the siege of Knoxville and battles in that vicinity, Atlanta campaign and battles along the line. I was captured at Cedar Bluff, Ala., in October, 1864, made my escape and was hunted down by blood hounds and returned to the prison at Cahaba, Ala. From there was sent to Andersonville, Ga. After remaining there about six months was taken to Vicksburg, Miss., where we were comfortably clothed and properly fed. We remained there about thirty days and then boarded the ill-fated steamer "Sultana." Everything moved along quietly and pleasantly until we passed Memphis, Tenn.

I was quietly sleeping on a cot in the cabin at the time of the explosion. Was wounded, and today carry scars caused thereby. Some of my companions who were sleeping near me were instantly killed. I jumped into the water. First swimming back and taking hold of the side wheel I held on to it long enough to remove some of my clothing so that I could swim easier. I then struck out with a determination to save my life, and was only out of reach when that immense wheel that I had been holding to fell over into the water, taking with it quite a number of persons to their watery grave. After swimming some distance and making several hair-breadth escapes from drowning men and horses I came across a stage plank floating as a life preserver for ten or more persons, one of whom was an engineer of said boat and who appeared to have control of the plank. An invitation from the engineer to catch on was quickly accepted and I peacefully floated along with them. We remained in the water until after daylight when we were picked up by the steamer "Jennie Lind" and were landed in safety at Memphis, Tenn. One man was lost from the plank but ten lives were saved by it. Their names I am unable to give. Capt. Taggart and myself, by permission of Gen. Washburn, boarded the next steamer for Cairo, Ill., and from there by rail to Indianapolis, thence to Columbus, Ohio, where, a few weeks later, we were honorably discharged from the service. After visiting friends and relations in different parts of Ohio I went to Iowa, being at one time sheriff of Marshall county. Have had the usual experience of a western sheriff of shooting and being shot. Many men are now languishing within the walls of the penitentiary that surrendered only after a desperate struggle and, overpowered by me, were compelled to give in. Have been badly wounded and at one time my wounds were considered fatal, but have nearly recovered and am now in reasonably good health.

I am at present employed in the bank of Hanford. My present postoffice address, Hanford, California.

L. W. McCRORY.

I WAS born in Wayne county, Ohio, November 5, 1835, and enlisted in the service of the United States at Portage, Ohio, June 9, 1862, in Company A, 100th Regiment Ohio Volunteer Infantry. Was captured at Limestone Station, East Tenn., September 8,

1863, and confined in rebel prisons at Lynchburg, Belle Isle, Libby and Andersonville, spending in all twenty-two months in those horrible dens—one year and seven days in Andersonville.

With others I was placed on the steamer "Sultana." I took up my place on the cabin deck in the curve of the stair banister. According to the best of my calculation the boat must have blown up about one o'clock in the morning. The night was very dark and cloudy. When the boiler burst it tore its way up through the hurricane deck, which came crashing down, and in all probability would have crushed me had it not been for the stair banister which held it up and saved me. I soon crawled out of that and worked my way out on the small gang plank which was tackled up to what I think they called the gin pole. I took care to bring my valise and pocket-book along with me. The former contained a good suit of citizen's clothes, and the latter over a hundred dollars. I remained upon the plank until driven off by the fire. While here I saw the big gang plank shoved off. According to my remembrance this plank was about forty feet long and six feet wide and was heavily iron bound. I believe it was the cause of the death of at least 300 of the boys, for they were just as thick as they could cling around it and I never heard of one that was saved by it.

When the fire finally drove me to the water, fearful lest I should need one hand, I put my pocket book, which was an old fashioned iron bound one between my teeth and hung on to my valise with one hand. It seemed to me that I never would come to the surface again for I had jumped down at least eighteen feet to reach the water, and to add to my discomfort my pocketbook kept my mouth partially open so that I took in some water, but still I managed to get along pretty well and as the boys say "did not lose my head." Comrade John Cornwell of my company and regiment and myself swam together, but he was easily discouraged. After awhile he called out to me that he could hold out no longer, but I cheered him up, urging him to try a little longer, telling him that I knew he was just as able to get out as I and that I was not going to give up. He tried awhile longer and then cried out again that it was no use, he must sink. I urged him to hold on, but after we had gone about two miles he called a third time and sank immediately, and I saw him no more. This startled me a little, I had hung on to my valise all this time, changing it from one hand to the other as either arm grew tired, but when Comrade Cornwell went down I threw the valise away but hung to my pocket book which, all this time, after I came up from my dive, I had gripped in my right hand with my little finger and and the one next to it.

Now what seems strange to me is that in a very short time after throwing away my valise both arms became entirely helpless and I was obliged to turn over on my back and float in order to rest them. After floating awhile I swam a short distance when my arms gave out again, and I was forced to float once more but soon was able to swim again; I then experienced no more trouble with my arms. I soon came in contact with a log upon which I crawled, and where I remained until about nine o'clock the next day, when

I was taken off by the steamer "Pocahontas." While upon this log I saw a man reach an island who was pulled out by two of his comrades. I do not believe there was a particle of skin upon his entire body. He had been badly scalded and it had all come off. His comrades were doing their best to keep the buffalo gnats off him. What ever became of the poor fellow I never knew, but presume that he died in a short time.

About the first man I came across on the "Pocahontas" was a big darkey who was dishing out hot sling unsparingly to the boys. I took a big drink but it was not enough, so I went up to the bar of the boat and called for brandy. The bartender set down a bottle and a small glass, but I called for a large one. He then set down a big beer tumbler. I filled this brimming full and drank it, then offered to pay for it, but he refused to take pay, saying "it is free to 'Sultana' survivors." I told him that when he disposed of it by wholesale he ought to charge something. I was taken to the Soldiers' Home and soon sent north on the steamer "Silver Spray."

At the time of my capture I had one bullet put through my canteen, three through my haversack, and my clothes were literally filled full of holes, but I did not get even a scratch of the skin. On the trip from Andersonville, Ga., to Columbus, Ohio, I was wrecked six times on the cars and once on a steamboat, but was not injured a particle except a slightly sprained ankle received by jumping from the top of a box car about thirty feet down an embankment while the train was at full speed, the train breaking in two, part of it going down the embankment one way while I went down the other way.

My present occupation is farming, and my postoffice address Mungen, Ohio.

WM. A. McFARLAND.

I ENLISTED during the first call for volunteers in 1861, in Company A, 42nd Indiana Infantry, at the age of 16 years. My first duty was to act in the capacity of "marker" boy, but had not been out three months when I was carrying a gun with the other soldiers. I saw constant service until the 20th day of September 1863, when I was captured by Longstreet's command, at the battle of Chickamauga, in the second day's fight of that battle. We were skirmishing and were cut off from our command some time before we knew it. Our captors took us to Libby prison, where we were kept for four months. Our rations at first consisted of about half of an ordinary loaf of bread and a small piece of beef, each, for a day's ration, but the meat soon disappeared and we were left with nothing but the bread. I was taken with about 12,000 other prisoners from Libby to the Danville, Va., prison, where we were kept about three months and then taken to the famous Andersonville prison, where we remained for eleven months more, to suffer indescribable horrors. The cover we had overhead was the blue canopy of heaven, while we were surrounded on the four sides by a high wall and a strong armed guard. When sleeping we were obliged to huddle together to keep warm in the winter. Our food was of the very poorest kind, consisting principally of corn meal. We were allowed to cook any articles we might buy, but were made to buy the wood to do the cooking with. One Irish potato would bring from 75 cents to $1.25— a tablespoonful of coarse salt 20 to 40 cents and a handful of wood 25 cents, and in good United States money, too. Some of the prisoners had money and often bought such articles, but if they got much at a time they would be raided by their comrades.

After the war had come to a close the federal prisoners were taken from Andersonville and other prisons by the rebels, under a flag of truce, to Big Black river, twelve miles in the rear of Vicksburg, and turned over to the federal forces, after which we marched into Vicksburg. The government had chartered the steamer "Sultana" to convey 400 prisoners north. The "Sultana" was a packet plying between New Orleans and St. Louis, and was chartered on (or about) April 23, 1865.

The boat was loaded with 2,300 Union prisoners who were to be taken north to "Camp Chase," Ohio. Before the boat had cleared the landing at Memphis a number of the boys made their escape and went up town and got whiskey. They were in no fit state to drink it—being in such a wretched condition from the treatment in the prisons—and a guard was sent out to bring them back. The last to put in an appearance was a soldier hailing from Tennessee. He was a thin seven-footer, and he came down to the boat, shouting and cursing, at the point of bayonets, so drunk he could hardly walk. He was brought up to the hurricane deck, where he caused considerable disturbance.

I was quite young at that time, and it pleased me very much to tease this fellow. He tried to get at me, but the men were so thick he had to run over a number in trying to get to me, and received a number of hard licks for his trouble. When the " Sultana " was chartered there were several families on board who were on their way from Louisiana to the north and they were permitted to retain their state rooms.

After we left Memphis it began raining and continued to do so all that night. When eight miles above Memphis, between two and three o'clock in the morning, the boilers of the boat exploded. I seemed to be dreaming and could hear some one saying, " there isn't any skin left on their bodies." I awoke with a start and the next moment the boat was on fire and all was as light as day. The wildest confusion followed. Some sprang into the river at once, others were killed, and I could hear the groans of the dying above the roar of the flames. As before stated, I was on the hurricane deck, clear aft. This part of the boat was jammed with men. I saw the pilot house and hundreds of them sink through the roof into the flames, at which juncture I sprang overboard into the river. As I came to the surface of the water I saw a woman rush out of a state room in her night clothes with a little child in her arms. In a moment she had fastened a life preserver about its waist and then threw it overboard. The preserver had evidently been fastened on too low, for when the little one hit the water it turned wrong end up. The mother rushed into the state room an instant and was then out and sprang into the water and grabbed the child—all of which occurred in the space of a couple of minutes.

The next thing that occupied my attention was seeing the seven-foot Tennesseean, whom I had been teasing on the trip, close at my side. "A guilty conscience needs no accuser," and I supposed he would drown me if he caught me. I began swimming away from him. I swam seven miles down the river and into a drift, where I caught onto a log and awaited assistance. As day dawned I found that hundreds had followed my example, and although it was a serious situation I could not help laughing at the comical appearance that all made. Imagine my surprise when I observed that woman, whom I had witnessed plunge into the river after her baby, sitting a-straddle of a log about twenty feet in front of me with the little one before her. We were both picked up by a yawl sent out by the steamer "Silver Spray." The next person the yawl approached was my long Tennessee friend, who was comfortably seated on a log. He asked how far it was to Memphis, and when told only a mile, he said to the crew, "Go to hell with your boat; if you couldn't come to help me before now you had better have stayed away," and with that he slid from his log and began swimming down the river.

When the survivors arrived at Memphis that morning all the hacks and omnibusses in the city were at the wharf to convey us to the Overton Hospital—now the Overton Hotel. There were enough conveyances for all and none were compelled to walk. The seven-foot Tennesseean had arrived at the landing by the time the "Silver Spray" did, but it was found that he was still under the influence of liquor, after all the excitement of the night, and when he began to get into the conveyance he refused to ride.   They tried to force him into a hack, but in the scuffle two or three soldiers were knocked down.   A guard was detailed to march him through the streets to the hospital.   On the way up we passed through a street inhabited mostly by Jews, who kept second-hand clothing establishments, etc., and as the hack in which I was riding was slowly passing along the street I could see that long Tennesseean pulling off boots, shoes, hats, caps and other articles from the signs hanging in front, and by the time he reached the hospital he had about a dozen Jews at his heels clamoring for their wares. "Dot ish my goat," said one, and "dose vas my shoes," said another, while a third would yell, "gif me pack my bants."   The Tennesseean turned, and, glaring at the crowd, threw the lot at his feet, saying, "There, help yourselves," and as they rushed forward and stooped over the pile he began to knock them right and left.

It was afterwards learned that out of 2,300 prisoners on the "Sultana" 1,500 were either blown to pieces or drowned.   The boat was totally destroyed.   At the place where the wreck occurred the river was miles wide, making escape almost impossible.

After being at the hospital a few days, and not being injured, I made my escape, determining to reach home as soon as possible.   The first boat that came along was the "St. Patrick," a handsome steamer plying between Cincinnati and Memphis.   Like a burnt child dreading the fire, I dreaded getting on a steamboat for fear of another explosion. Adopting what I supposed was the safest plan, I crawled into the yawl hanging over the stern of the boat (as all sidewheel packets have) and never left my quarters until I arrived at the wharf at Evansville. It rained most all the way up, but I stuck it through. Every time the boat would escape steam or blow the whistle I prepared to jump, supposing an explosion was about to take place.

EPENETUS W. McINTOSH.

(Late private of Company E and A, 14th Illinois Infantry.)

I EMBARKED on the steamer "Henry Aims" at Vicksburg, with about 2,100 soldiers on board returning from rebel prisons. I remained on said steamer until we arrived at Memphis, where we landed. I, supposing she would remain some time, went into town to look around and buy some articles I needed, and while gone she moved off and left me. Along in the evening the steamer "Sultana" landed loaded with another lot of prisoners, so I embarked intending to go to Benton Barracks and join the comrades I had left on the "Henry Aims."

When some miles from the city (I cannot state the exact distance) she blew up, and I was sent whirling into the water, which I reached without any trouble from the steam, although many were scalded to death before reaching it. As I struck the water I heard groans and screams of agony on every side. O, the scene! It is impossible to describe. I knew that im-

mediate action was necessary. I decided to keep back
from the crowd, but found it was not an easy matter,
as the drowning were making for any who could swim,
and catching at a straw. It was hard work to keep
clear and save one's own life. I made for the shore,
but it looked so far away in the mist of night that my
courage almost failed me.

After eight or ten hours I touched sand on the
Arkansas shore. My strength was so near gone that I
even then came near having a watery grave. It was
with much difficulty and suffering that I was enabled
to walk or crawl onto dry land where a colored man
saw me and came to my assistance. I needed such
assistance very much as I was destitute of clothing,
having stripped myself as I swam along to lighten the
load. In twenty minutes after reaching land I was
bloated so much that I could scarcely see, and believe
that if I had not been cared for at once I would have
died. I remained there until the next day, when a
boat came across the river picking up the boys and
they took me to Memphis, Overton Hospital, where
I remained two days. I was then put on a boat called
the "Belle of Memphis" and taken to Benton Barracks
and remained there until I got a furlough.

During my prison life I suffered agonies untold.
Tongue cannot tell it all, but this awful struggle for
life in the waters was above all else I ever endured.
Owing to the necessity of constant motion, without
rest to any part of the body, being reduced to a mere
skeleton through being confined in rebel prisons was
in my favor, as I could never have survived that awful
disaster had I weighed as much as I did before my

prison experience.   My weight now was eighty pounds.

I was captured at Ackworth, Ga., about the 4th of
October, 1864, and exchanged at Vicksburg, April 15,
1865.   Was in Andersonville most of the time.   When
I was captured I weighed 175 pounds.   I will never go
back on the old flag.   Although somewhat palsied and
greatly maimed I can give three hearty cheers for the
red, white and blue, and set a rebel back if he comes
to the front almost as quickly as I could when in
possession of all my powers.

Postoffice address, Decatur, Ill.

————

DANIEL McLEOD.

I WAS a member of Company F, 18th Regiment Illinois Volunteer Infantry, and at the battle of Pitts-
burgh Landing, April 6, 1862, was shot in the right
knee with round musket ball, which caused a com-
pound fracture of the knee joint.   This wound was
examined on the battle ground by Asst. Surg. Ormsby
of the 18th regiment (afterwards surgeon of the 45th
Illinois), who stated that the leg would have to be cut
off above the knee, but that he was too busy at that
time to attend to it.   I have the affidavits of two
comrades who heard Dr. Ormsby make the assertion.
I was taken from the battle-field on the steamer " War
Eagle " to Cincinnati, Ohio, and was put in the Fourth
Street Hospital, and there treated by Dr. F. Schmidt,
who cut the ball out of the knee joint and removed
part of the fractured bones.   Drs. Norton and J. B.
Smith were consulted in the case by Dr. Schmidt.   Dr.

Norton said that the only way to treat such a case was to cut the boy's leg off, that in case he did recover what end would it serve as the limb would be of no use. From the Fourth Street Hospital I was removed to the Washington Park Hospital. While I was there I was examined by the medical purveyor of the department, Dr. Carpenter, in the presence of Drs. J. B. Smith and Norton. Dr. Norton then explained the nature and character of the wound and also stated what he, Norton, had recommended. Dr. Carpenter said "that was the course that should be taken in cases of a like character always."

On June 7, 1863, I was removed to "Camp Dennison," Ohio; August 7, to Quincy, Ill., receiving my final United States discharge from there in June, 1864. I was then examined by the United States Pension Surgeon at Springfield, Ill., and granted $8 per month pension—the full pension at that time for entire disability. I was never able to make any use of that leg.

I was a passenger on the steamer "Sultana," en route from New Orleans to St. Louis. When the steamer reached Vicksburg one of the boilers was leaking and was patched by Klien's foundry men before the soldiers were put on board. There was no necessity of loading the "Sultana" so heavily, as the steamers "Pauline Carroll" and "Lady Gay" were at the landing coming up light, but the clerk and captain of the "Sultana" were part owners of the boat, and I understood at the time that they put up money to get the transportation of the soldiers, which the officers of the other boats, having no interest, would not do.

The hold of the "Sultana" was full of sugar, and nearly every state room was taken in the cabin, besides a number of deck passengers. According to my remembrance there were taken on at Vicksburg 1,940 enlisted men, 40 officers, and a company of the 54th Regiment Ohio Volunteer Infantry, as guards. The night of the explosion, being tired from the long trip, I sat up reading at a table in the center of the cabin, and when the explosion took place I was blown over the table being, as it were, on the outer edge of the crater. All nearer the bow went up and down in the chasm made by the explosion. Both my legs were broken at the ankle. When the boat began to burn, which it did at once, every one that was able rushed to the guards. While I was dragging myself out the captain of the 54th Ohio came and pulled me out to the guards. I at once climbed down on the hog chains to where they had been broken off and let myself drop into the water, which was full of the wreck and men trying to escape, but not so many as there were shortly afterward when the flames forced them to take to the water. I had been brought up near the water and was a good swimmer, so I floated down the river about two miles and lodged in the brush on Cheek's Island, above Memphis. In the morning I was picked up and taken to Memphis and placed in Adam's Hospital in charge of Surgeon J. M. Studley who, after examining my fractures, told me that it was no use trying to save my right leg as it was in such a condition from the previous wound that it would be practically impossible to save it and that he would have to cut it off above the old wound. This he did and set the broken bones of the other leg, and soon both were healed.

My present postoffice address is 818 Market street, St. Louis, Mo.

L. G. MORGAN.

I WAS born in Perry county, Ohio, September 14, 1837, and enlisted in the service of the United States at Findlay, Ohio, September 19, 1861, in Company D, 121st Regiment Ohio Volunteer Infantry. I, with others, was captured near Kingston, Ga., and taken to Cahaba, Ala. Our rations consisted of a pint of corn meal and five ounces of beef daily, and in addition to this we would get a few beans or negro peas—about two or three spoonsful to the man. We were divided into companies of 100 men each, and one man appointed as orderly sergeant for each company to draw and divide rations. We planned a way of escape, but failed in doing so. The guards tried to persuade us to tell who the leaders of the conspiracy were, but we refused to do so. They then read an order that all rations would be stopped unless we did, but still we refused. The most of us made up our minds that we would rather starve than betray our comrades. After going through various forms of punishment some one finally told, and the conspirators were severely punished. After that things moved along quietly, nothing of importance happening, only the usual tunneling and getting caught at it. Finally the time came for us to be exchanged, and after sign-

33

ing a parole of honor, pledging the "rebs" that we would not try to escape, we took a boat and went to Selma, Ala., where we remained over night. In the morning we walked about two miles to take the train, one of the men dying on the way from overeating the night before. We got along all right until we reached Jackson, Miss. Here we went into camp and baked enough corn bread to last us through to Vicksburg. We reached Black River, where we remained over night. The next morning we were exchanged and marched across the river into God's country once more. To say that we were glad would be putting it in a very mild form.

We remained in camp for about six weeks and at last the time came for us to go north, so we marched to Vicksburg—a distance of about four miles—and were put on board the steamer "Sultana." When about half of us were on board the captain of the boat stopped us and said that he had enough, for he did not consider the boat safe enough to take so many as he had just had the boiler patched a few days before. The quartermaster, however, who had charge of us, swore that he was loading the boat and would put as many men on as he pleased. We were so crowded that it was difficult to find a place to lie down to sleep. The boiler, cabin and hurricane decks were all full. There were 2,000 soldiers and 200 passengers, besides some 700 hogsheads of sugar and I think about 30 or 40 mules and other freight. When we reached Memphis we unloaded sugar and took on coal. I think it was about one or two o'clock A. M. when we started up the river again, and when about seven miles above Memphis the boiler exploded.

I was sleeping in front of the smoke stacks on the cabin deck. I got up and looked around. It would be impossible for me to describe the scene. My first thought was to get some buckets and put the fire out, but not seeing any and being afraid to venture over the wreck I jumped off and swam to the stern of the boat, then got on again, but could not find any. Then some one asked me to help throw off the dead men, for it looked hard to see them burn. We threw off five or six. One poor fellow was pinned down by the wreck and begged some one to help him out. I tried to but the timbers were so heavy that I could not get him loose and so I had to let him burn to death. A man by the name of Henry Spaffar, who belonged to the 102d Regiment Ohio Volunteer Infantry, came to me and said, "Morgan, what am I going to do, I cannot swim?" I told him to get a plank, but he said he could not find any. I found a good one, threw it into the water and made him jump in after it. I then thought it time to get o : myself as the fire was getting pretty hot. I watched my chance and finally started. Being a good swimmer I did not take anything to help me along with. My only fear was that some one would get hold of me and pull me down and I would drown. I must have swam very rapidly for I passed a number of fellows in the water. I swam along till I got close to the timber, but it was right at a bend in the river and the current was so strong that before I could reach it I was carried below it into the river again.

I went along for awhile seeing no one, but after a

short time some one called out, "Hello, Morgan, is that you?" I replied, "yes." It was Spaffar who hailed me. I was nearly used up, for my legs were badly cramped. Spaffar floated a board to me and that helped me along. We swam down the river together and finally landed on some drift wood. Soon after sunrise we were picked up by the steamer "Rocket." The barkeeper on the boat sent a boy around with a pitcher full of whiskey and we each had a large glassful. When we reached Memphis the women of the Christian Commission gave us some shirts and drawers and took us to a place called a soldier's home, but they had no blankets for us to sleep on. After we had something to eat I started to go through the city bare headed and bare footed, and while passing a store owned by a Jew the proprietor came out and asked me if I had been on the boat. I answered in the affirmative and he gave me a hat, one of the clerks giving me a pair of shoes. A little further up the street I met an artilleryman and he said if I would come with him to his quarters he would give me a pair of pants. I accompanied him, and while there another artillery boy gave me a blouse. I got my supper with them and then went to a hospital where I was provided with a cot to sleep upon. In the morning as I was going down the street I saw a sign on a building and it said "Soldier's Lodge." That was kept by the Christian Commission and the "Soldier's Home" was kept by the Sanitary Commission. I went in and they said that I could stay. I was there for five or six days, when we took a boat for Cairo, Ill. From there we took the cars and went to Mattoon, thence via Indianapolis, Ind., to Columbus, Ohio, remaining there for six weeks. We then received our discharge and went home, I think about the last of May or first of June.

Post-office address, Findlay, Ohio.

A. J. MOURNING.

I WAS a member of company D, 11th Regiment Illinois Cavalry, and was stationed at Memphis at the time the explosion took place on the morning of the 27th of April, 1865. A detail of us was sent to the wharf very early to unload hay. We were immediately put into a yawl and succeeded in rescuing a number of the poor fellows from the "Sultana." We worked at it till about two o'clock in the afternoon.

My postoffice address is Toledo, Ohio.

A. NIHART.

I WAS born in Hocking county, Ohio, June 11, 1842, and enlisted in the service of the United States at Logan, Hocking county, Ohio, June, 1862, in company G, 90th Regiment Ohio Infantry. Was captured at Spring Hills, Tenn., November, 1864, and confined in the Andersonville, Ga., prison.

Occupation, farming. Postoffice, Bolivar, Mo.

C. M. NISLEY.

I WAS born in Harrisburgh, Pa., on the 19th of May, 1838.

Enlisted in Company D of the 40th Regiment Indiana Infantry, on the 29th of October, 1861, at LaFay ette, Ind., and took part in all the engagements that the regiment participated in until taken prisoner at the battle of Franklin, Tenn., on the 30th of November, 1864. I was captured about eight o'clock in the evening, with 1,900 others, and hurried to Columbia, Tenn., and held there until a few days before the second battle of Nashville under "Pap" Thomas, when we were removed to Meridian, Miss., and from thence to Cahaba, Ala., where we were confined in a prison called "Castle Morgan." This place was on the Alabama river, twenty-seven miles from Selma, and where the Cahaba river empties into the Alabama. We were kept here until in the spring of 1865, when the river arose till the water was from eighteen inches to three feet deep in our prison, and we were forced to stand in the water as we could not lie down for three days. We were then put upon the steamer "Henry J. King" and taken down the river to the Tombigbee, and up that river to Gainesville, Ala., then back by way of Meridian, Miss., to Jackson, and from there to the Big Black river, and then were taken to the neutral camp near Vicksburg, Miss., where we rested and cleaned up for about ten days. We were next taken over to Vicksburg, and went on board the steamer "Sultana." Starting up the river we arrived at Memphis, Tenn., on the evening of the 26th of April,

1865. The steamer crossed the river to the coal barges and took on a supply of coal and, shortly after midnight or virtually on the morning of the 27th of April, started up the river again and had run about seven miles when the explosion took place.

At the time of the explosion I was lying on the fore-part of the passenger deck. The smoke-stack fell through the hurricane deck, instantly killing John Howard of Company H, 40th Indiana Infantry, and pinned me fast to the deck, but after a few moments of struggling I succeeded in extricating myself. I then started to help put out the fire, but I fell through the decks hurting my back seriously besides getting badly burned and scalded. I immediately set about helping to extricate those who were caught fast by pieces of the boat. After this in company with Capt. Mason, of the "Sultana," I threw over broken pieces of the boat and other materials for those already in the water, but after a little time the fire became so hot that I was obliged to take to the water. A great many had sunk to rise no more, and there were but few floating and swimming about that would be liable to drag me down. Capt. Mason was the last man I talked with while on board the boat, and he was still on the boat when I left. I managed to get hold of a piece of studding about ten feet long, and with its assistance swam and floated about five miles down the river, when I caught on to a small cotton-wood tree on the Arkansas shore and hung there till about ten o'clock when I was picked up by the steamer, " Bostonia" and taken to a hospital at Memphis where I remained a few days. Was then sent to Cairo, and thence to Indianapolis.

Here I received a ten days' furlough to go to my home, La Fayette. When this expired, I, having received a commission as first lieutenant, started to join my regiment, which was at Lavaca, Texas, but was taken with typhoid fever and came near dying, so at last took my discharge and returned to my home hoping to hear the sound of war no more.

I am now over fifty years of age, but should my country ever need my services I am as ready and willing as before to give them.

Capt. Hazellaige, of Company K, 40th Indiana Infantry, was quartermaster of the troops on the boat and I was his assistant, helping to issue the rations. As near as I can remember there were 1,966 enlisted men and 36 commissioned officers on board the boat. I was afterward a witness before the court of inquiry that investigated the cause of the explosion, and I will say now, as I did then, that in my opinion the boilers were defective, the boat over-loaded, and the pumps not working properly which led to the explosion. I do not believe in the torpedo story. It does not look reasonable to me.

My present post office address is 36 Elizabeth street, La Fayette, Ind. My occupation is traveling salesman, but for the past year have not been able to do much.

JOHN W. NORCUTT.

I WAS born in Litchfield, Hillsdale county, Mich., on the 1st day of July, 1838, and enlisted at Allen, Mich., December 17, 1863, in company D, 18th Regiment Michigan Infantry. I was captured at Athens, Ala., September 22, 1864, and confined in the rebel prison at Cahaba, Ala.

With others of my regiment I was on board the ill-fated steamer "Sultana," and when the boat took fire I sprang into the river. I succeeded in securing two pieces of cabin flooring, and placing one of these under each arm I floated down the river till I came to an island that was overflowed. Here I caught hold of some small trees and held on till rescued by a steamer and taken to Memphis. I think I was in the water about four hours. I was in the hospital after this fourteen days before I could stand alone.

My present occupation is mail carrier, and my post-office address, Campbell, Mich.

ALBERT NORRIS.

I WAS born in Muskingum, county, Ohio, on the 17th of March, 1842. Enlisted in the service of the United States at Newark, Ohio, on the 18th of February, 1864, in Company A, 76th Ohio Volunteer Infantry as a private. Was taken prisoner at Little River, Ga., on the 26th of October, 1864, by the 51st Alabama Regiment (confederate), while on detail made by the Colonel to forage. Was taken to Cahaba, Ala., where I remained until I was paroled out on the 18th of March, 1865, and sent to Vicksburg, Miss., and remained in camp at Big Black river until the 24th of April, when I took passage on the cabin deck of the steamer "Sultana" for Cairo, Ill.

At half past one on the morning of the 27th of April, 1865, I was lying asleep on the cabin deck of the boat, just in front and nearly over the furnace, when one of her boilers exploded, blowing the center part of the boat into the river. I fell to the boiler deck upon the hot irons of the furnace, burning my left arm and shoulder to a crisp. The men on the hurricane deck fell upon me, and it was some time before I became conscious of my surroundings. After the men got off me, getting my right arm loose, I removed the boards that held me down and got on my feet.

Securing a cracker barrel that had one head in, I jumped over the high railing, around the center of the boat, into the deep water. Comrade Stone of Newark, Ohio, got a coal box and threw it and the barrel into the river. I caught both of them and gave him the box and kept the barrel for my own use. We started out for the Tennessee shore and he floated down stream about seven miles below where the explosion took place, or to Memphis, Tenn., where he was picked up. My feet became entangled in my under-clothing, and in trying to loosen them I came near drowning. I swam about a mile when I saw the steamer "Bostonia" anchoring within two hundred yards above the burning wreck. I swam close to her, when three men in a small boat took me in and carried me to the rescuing steamer. This boat carried one hundred of us to Memphis, Tenn. I remained in the Washington and Gayoso hospitals under the physician's care for three weeks when Dr. Shipley, of Nashport, and my brother, Wm. A. Norris, came to Memphis for me. I returned home to Frazeysburgh, and then reported to "Camp Chase," Ohio, and was discharged from the service on the 30th of June, 1865. My recollections are that there were 2,200 on board the "Sultana," and 1,600 were lost. I saw one man going down the river on a large slab hallooing: "Here goes your schooner for Memphis." Some prayed, some swore and some sang. It was worse than any battle I was ever in.

Since my discharge I have been agent and telegraph operator for the P. H. R. R. Co. sixteen years, and am now engaged in the mercantile business at Union Station, Ohio.

JOSEPH B. NORRIS.

I WAS born in Salem township, Tuscarawas county, Ohio, November 25, 1841, and enlisted in the service of the United States September 9, 1861, in Company C, 51st Regiment Ohio Volunteer Infantry. Was taken prisoner at Chickamauga, September 20, 1863, and confined in the Pemberton building at Richmond, Va., for two months, at Dansville, Va., six months, and Andersonville, Ga., ten months. Was exchanged at Vicksburg, Miss., March 25, 1865, making in all eighteen months and five days a prisoner of war.

On April 25th we received orders for all of the paroled prisoners belonging to the States of Ohio, Indiana, Michigan, and Kentucky to take the train to Vicksburg, our camp being four miles in the rear of the city, as we were to take a steamer that evening to go north. We were placed on board the steamer " Sultana." I think the list of prisoners numbered 1,964, with one company of the 58th Ohio and two pieces of artillery as guard, besides cabin passengers and boat's crew.

We steamed out of Vicksburg between four and five o'clock P M, of the 24th, and reached Memphis a little before sundown of the 26th, where we tied up and unloaded quite a number of hogsheads of sugar. The " Sultana " also took on coal at this point. I think it was about half past twelve or one o'clock in the morning of the 27th that the boat left Memphis. That was the last that I knew until after the explosion. I had gone to sleep, and was on the hurricane deck at the time. I did not hear the report, but was awakened by the cries of my comrades who were running to and fro. Some were screaming, some were praying, and others were shouting and telling the boys to keep cool. I tell you it was a hard place to keep cool, with the flames sweeping all around. I first went to the Arkansas side to jump overboard, but there were too many there in the water for me. I then went to the Tennessee side and found the same trouble. I started for the boat's stern, tearing off my drawers and shirt as I went. Finding things no better there, I thought I would wait until the boat would float down from among the men who were drowning in the water. Just then a strong breeze drove the flames so close as to make it unpleasant, and thinking it about as easy to drown as to burn, I started for the bottom of the Mississippi. I did not get quite there, but coming to the surface I started for shore.

After swimming for a long time, and being almost chilled to death, I landed in the top of some brush, to which I held till daylight, when I saw a good sized sycamore log that had lodged in the brush about thirty feet from where I then was. I pulled myself from bush to bush, as I was past swimming, and my legs were entirely benumbed with cold. I reached the log after some fifteen or twenty minutes hard work and pulled myself upon it. All the time I was holding on to the brush in the water I could hear the boys that had got into trees, as it began to get daylight, crowing like roosters, and crying "here's your mule!" It was about seven o'clock before I was able to crow. I was picked up by the United States picket-boat "Pocahontas" about ten o'clock A. M. April 27, without a stitch of clothing on my back, and pretty well tired out as well as peppered by the bites of buffalo gnats. After donning a shirt (given to me by a couple of "Sanitary" ladies) and a pair of overalls from one of the firemen, and drinking a couple of glasses of something that did not look or taste altogether like spring water, I was ready for breakfast, which was on the kitchen table of the "Pocahontas." I had not eaten at a table for nearly four years and was rather awkward, but got there just the same. Postoffice address is Randolph, Neb.

J. E. NORTON.

I ENLISTED at Pontiac, Mich., in August 1862, as a sergeant in Company A, of the 5th Michigan Cavalry. I was captured the last time at Trevillian Station, Va., with 500 of our brigade (Custer) June 11, 1864, and imprisoned in Libby ten days, Pemberton building a few days and then shipped by cars to Andersonville, Ga., where I remained until removed to Millen prison in September following. Was in the latter prison but a short time when Kilpatrick, trying to capture us with a scouting detachment from Sherman's army, drove us out and the rebels took us to Savannah, there put us on the Gulf road and run us down, finally, to Blackshear, thence to Thomasville, and from there across the country to Americus, Ga. Taking the road again we came back to Andersonville sometime in December, where we remained during the winter. Early in the spring of 1865 we were ordered to be sent to Vicksburg, where on arriving we went on board the steamer "Sultana." We were placed on this steamer by that careless officer, Gen Dana, who had charge of shipping all the soldiers at that point. May he never be forgotten as a type of first class don't care——for the boys who were returning to their long looked for home and loved ones.

On the morning of the 27th of April, 1865, I found myself waking from a stupor or unconsciousness, produced by a blow which I received at the time of the explosion upon the head just back of the center part of the brain. I was pinned or held down by the timbers or materials of some sort and felt a smarting sensation on my face; tried to raise my hand but was so pinned down that I could not. I struggled and finally loosened myself only to find I was in darkness. I did not apprehend at all what was the matter, nor was I in the least cognizant of my surroundings, for everything was all right when I went to sleep (just as we pushed off from the dock at Memphis a few hours before). My quarters upon the fated boat were in the center of the upper deck and ten feet in front of the smoke stack, the boilers being back of the smoke stack prevented my being thrown into the water. I remember distinctly of hearing a noise caused by the explosion, and can only describe the noise by measurement (being a mechanic I can do no other way). It appeared to be about one and one-half inch long, and then all was blank until I awoke one-half hour afterward. Not a sound could I hear but the splashing of water. Could see nothing and was in a great wonderment of mind as to the trouble I felt I was surrounded by. Presently I heard voices on the end of the boat crying, " Put out that fire, put out that fire !" I looked and discovered a fire breaking out above the deck about the size of the crown of a hat. It grew rapidly and soon illuminated the awful scene. The thoughts that came rushing upon me were simply appalling and too terrible for my description. I looked for something that was loose on which I could float but could find nothing. I crawled down to the lower deck (the only one which was not broken up) and, as I was so doing, a hand reached up from below me and caught my ankles and I heard some one saying, " Help me out." A timber prevented them from getting out

and I tried to raise it but could not quite. A comrade
came crawling along, bent upon reaching the lower
deck, and helped me to raise the timber from off three
or four men and thus saved them from being burned
to death.

When I reached the deck I found a box which I
made use of in floating although I was a good swimmer. Thinking that I must be in the water for a
long time before relief might come, I remained on
board the boat until the fire drove me off and then
jumped into the water. While I was swimming away
from the burning wreck a man attacked me and
wanted my box. I moved the box sideways enough
for him to miss his clutch upon it, but he caught me
by the hip and we both went down under water
farther than I ever went before or since. I finally
came to the surface of the water but so weak from
having taken water into my lungs that I could scarcely
keep up, and if it had not been for the box I think I
would have drowned. About fifteen feet away from
me I saw a bale of hay with a soldier boy lying across
it, which I made the greatest physical effort to
reach. I finally made it and putting my arm upon one
corner, and with the box under the other arm, I was
soon able to disgorge some of the water from my
lungs. As soon as I could speak I assured the soldier
boy that I would not sink his bale of hay. He was
piteously begging me not to as he could not swim. I
told him to keep a look out and not let any one get
on with us. I found by careful observation that it
would support both of us with the use of my box
under one arm.

The water was cold and chilly and but for my care the boy would have fallen off and drowned. I kept him using his limbs so as to keep the blood in cir-culation and thus prevent chilling so much. We floated down the river opposite to Memphis where we were picked up by the steamer "Bostonia," which was on her trip to the wreck, and we were afterwards landed at Memphis. I remained about a month at Memphis and then came north to Columbus, Ohio, thence to Jackson, Mich, where I was discharged from the service in June, 1865.

My present occupation is model and pattern making. Postoffice address 62 Duffield street, Detroit, Mich.

35

WM. H. NORTON.

I WAS born in Northampton township, Summit county, Ohio, February 17, 1841. I enlisted in the service of the United States in Northampton, the 11th day of August, 1862, in Company C, 115th Ohio Volunteer Infantry.

I am forty-five years of age (October 25, 1886) and my residence at the present time is Hudson, Ohio. My occupation is farming.

Was a corporal at the time of my discharge from the service, which discharge I received at "Camp Chase," Ohio, May 25, 1865. I was captured at La

Vergne, Tenn., December 5, 1864, by Gen. Forrest's command at the time of Hood's raid on Nashville, Tenn. We were started on a forced march to the Tennessee river. At a place near Florence, we boarded the cars for Meridian, Miss. I remained there in prison about ten weeks and was then sent to Cahaba, Ala., where I remained until the first of March, 1865. The river rose very high and the prison was overflowed (the water in the prison was two or three feet deep), and I was sent to Selma, from there to " Camp Fisk," near Vicksburg, Miss. I went on board the steamer " Sultana " April 25, 1865.

At the time of the explosion I was sleeping on the forward part of the upper deck and was awakened by the explosion and cries of the wounded. Men were rushing to and fro, trampling over each other in their endeavors to escape. All was confusion. Soon the flames came leaping up and I now realized that the boat was on fire. I stood for a few minutes and list- ened to that awful wail of hundreds of human beings burning alive in the cabin and under the fallen timbers. I tried to get down to the lower deck; found it impossible to go down by the stairway on account of the fire but, fortunately, discovered a rope, and by the aid of that landed on the lower deck. There the men were jumping into the river by the hundreds. The river was full of men struggling with each other and grasping at everything that offered any means of sup- port. The boat was fast burning up and the flames had reached within a few feet of me and I now knew that there was but one way of escape—the deep, dark waters of the Mississippi. I took off my shoes and clothing, except under-clothing, and jumped overboard.

As I arose to the surface several men from the boat jumped upon me and we all went down together. Others leaping on us forced us down until I despaired of ever reaching the surface again but, by a desperate struggle, I succeeded in getting out from under them and reached the surface. I tried to swim through the crowd of men but could not. One man caught hold of me but I managed to get away from him, and not knowing what to do or which way to go I instinctively turned toward the burning boat. Reaching that and swimming alongside I found the ring which is used in tying up the boat. I had no sooner caught hold of it than a drowning man clasped his arms around me in a death grip. I told him he must let go, but it was of no use; he never said a word, but all the while I could feel his arms tightening around me. Hanging on to the ring with one hand I tried to free myself from him with the other but could not. The situation was becoming terrible. To let go the ring was death to both of us. The strain on my arm was such that I could not hold out but a few minutes longer. Another man now got hold of the ring and still another grasped him by the throat and a desperate struggle was going on between them.

The wheel house had now burned loose and fell over with a crash. It seemed to me that the boat was going to pieces. With all the strength I had I made another effort to free myself from the drowning man and was successful and once more struck out into the river. This time I had no difficulty in getting through, as the men had become more scattered. A few rods ahead of me was a small box, ten by sixteen inches square, which I soon overtook and placing it under my arm I found it to be quite a help, but it would not support me. Looking off some distance in the dark. ness I saw a light and, supposing it must be a boat out picking up the men, I now made an effort to reach it, but it grew dimmer and dimmer and finally disappeared altogether. (I think it must have been the deck hands with the yawl boat.) I turned in another direction hoping that I could reach the shore, but the darkness was so intense, except towards the burning boat, that no trace of the shore could be seen.

Suffering with a cramp in my stomach, benumbed with the cold, it seemed as if I could go no farther, but if I stopped swimming I found myself sinking, and again would try to keep afloat. In this way I kept along. I could hear the cries of those that were burned and scalded screaming with pain at every breath, and men all along the river were calling for help. Away in the distance, floating down the river, was the burning boat with a few brave men fighting the fire with buckets of water. Looking to my left I thought I could see the trees through the darkness. This gave me new courage and I turned in that direction and soon some brush struck me in the face. A little farther on I was washed up against a log which had caught in the young cotton wood trees. About nine o'clock in the morning of April 27, a man in a canoe rowed me over to the Arkansas shore. I had landed on an island which was overflowed with water. Was told by the man that had rescued me that I had landed between two or three miles below where the "Sultana" exploded.

STEWART OXLEY.

I WAS born in Coshocton county, Ohio, on the 20th day of May 1842. Enlisted in the service of the United States, November 18, 1861, in Company I of the 51st Regiment Ohio Volunteer Infantry, which was organized at "Camp Meigs," in Tuscarawas county, and was assigned to the Army of the Cumberland. Was taken prisoner near Dallas, Ga., May 26, 1864, and confined at Selma and Cahaba, Ala., and Meridian, Miss., until about the 10th of March, 1865, when we came into God's country at the Big Black river bridge, near Vicksburg, Miss. In dividing off into companies at Vicksburg, I was tented with some of the 50th Regiment Ohio Volunteer Infantry boys, and one, Albert Hunter, of the 10th Ohio Cavalry, and I were bunk-mates, and when we went aboard the steamer "Sultana" we took our places on the cabin stoop on the left or west side, just to the rear and next to the cabin door. One or the other of us was there all the time. I was sick at the time and was seldom away from our place of abode. On the afternoon of April 26th we arrived at Memphis, Tenn. Just about the time we started from Memphis we spread our blankets and lay down to rest and sleep. I went to sleep very soon as I have no remembrance of anything after that until I was strangling in the water. I never felt or heard the explosion, or anything that transpired at the time of the wreck (which occurred about two o'clock on the morning of the 27th of April, about seven or eight miles above Memphis), farther than my striking on a piece of the wreck. In my struggle I got hold of the piece of wrecking and started on my lonely voyage of seven or eight miles with the current as a moving power.   Soon after I became aware there was a man on the other end of my craft.   Up to this time I could not imagine what had happened that I should be in the water.   My companion told me that the boat was on fire.   I did not remember anything after this until we came opposite to Memphis, and while passing near the gunboat anchored in the river, I think one or the other of us must have shouted and given the alarm. About four o'clock in the morning some of the boat's crew overtook us and we were taken out of the water.

In all this time I did not suffer in mind or body nor was I sensible of my danger or surroundings.   I don't think I made any effort to save myself at all.   After I was taken into the boat (I don't remember as they picked up any more before we got to the gunboat or not, but think they did not), they started back for the gunboat.   As we were put on to the deck the surgeon poured a glass of whiskey down each one and the men of the crew took off our wet clothing, cut down their hammocks for us to lie on, and did everything possible for our comfort.   The gunboat soon got under way and after doing all that could be done they came to and landed us at Memphis.   I was carried on a stretcher to the Overton Hospital where I remained four weeks, less one day.   My ribs on one side were cracked and broken, my back was badly injured, and the right side of my face and head scalded.

In the list of those saved I could never find the name of Hunter who was sleeping on the same blanket with me, and I never learned the name of the comrade that was on the piece of wreckage with me.

Of my suffering and good nursing and kind treatment by the good Sisters while in the hospital and my journey home, for want of space, I must pass over. I arrived at "Camp Chase," Ohio, May 28, 1865, and was discharged from the service the next day.

Engaged in farming and mechanical labor; my post-office address, Burr Oak, Iowa.

THOMAS PANGLE.

I WAS born in Madisonville, Monroe county, Tenn., on the 18th day of September, 1845. My parents are E. S. and H. J. Pangle, and are still living in McMinn county, Tenn. I was raised on a farm and enlisted in the service of the United States at the age of eighteen years. I still have my order of discharge, and by reference to it I see a few items of interest. I was enrolled at Nashville, Tenn., January 12, 1864, to serve three years or until the war was over, in Company "K" Captain John N. Morton, 3d Regiment Tennessee Cavalry, and was discharged June 10, 1865, at Nashville, Tenn. I was engaged in no regular battle during my service, spending most of my time with my comrades on skirmish duty. I surrendered under Colonel Campbell, at Athens, Ala., September 24, 1864, and was incarcerated in prison at Cahaba, Ala., until March 7, 1865, and returned to our lines March 16, at "Camp Fisk," Miss.

I went on board the ill-fated "Sultana" at Vicksburg, Miss., April 24 or 25, 1865, with about 2,000 other ex-prisoners. All survivors of the terrible explosion well remember the morning of April 27, 1865, when a few miles above Memphis so many true and loyal lives were suddenly hurled into eternity. It was most heart-rending to witness and the recollections of the terrible sufferings of my unfortunate comrades and their heroic efforts to swim to the shore, and so many not succeeding who sank to the bottom of the river, is most pitiable to think of. It was an affair in the history of the rebellion, that should be immortalized and all survivors should praise their Maker for their escape.

I remember well that eventful morning. I was sleeping with Rob Reed, Billy Milton and Jim Esters, and we were bunking about fifteen feet from the boiler when the explosion occurred. We supposed at first that we were being fired at from the shore, but soon realized our mistake. I was very much crippled up with rheumatism and could scarcely use my limbs, but being an expert swimmer, I concluded to go ashore. I seized a board and plunged into the water, but so cold was the water that I soon became powerless to swim, and determined to climb up on the deck of the steamer, where there were many throwing water on the burning coal, etc. We succeeded in remaining on the deck until eight or nine o'clock, when we were rescued by parties from the Arkansas shore and, finally, was taken aboard the steamer " Pocahontas" and taken to Memphis. Among those of the passengers on the "Sultana" I remember John Hamilton, Robert Hamilton, Dewitt Harris, George W. Maxwell, Solomon Bogard and Harlan Jones.

JOSHUA S. PATTERSON.

I AM a resident of Franklin township, Columbiana county, Ohio. Served in the army as a private in Company F, 104th Ohio Volunteer Infantry. Enlisted in the service near Bethel Church, on the 1st of September, 1862. I was captured at the battle of Franklin, Tenn., November 30, 1864, and taken to Andersonville prison, where I remained until I was liberated April 20, 1865; discharged from the service May 20, 1865, at "Camp Chase," Columbus, Ohio. Farming is my present occupation.

The following is a brief account of my experience in making my escape from the steamer "Sultana:" I was awakened from my slumbers about three o'clock on the morning of the 27th of April, 1865, by a terrible crash, I knew not what, but afterwards found it to be the result of the explosion. As I arose from my bed, which was at the head of the first flight of stairs, I received a blow on the top of my head which caused a severe wound, the mark of which I carry to this day. This wound was inflicted, I think, by a piece of timber, it being so dark I could not ascertain how it did occur. Realizing my danger and perceiving the unusual position of the boat, I jumped down on the lower deck and there observed more fully the horrors of our situation. I had nothing to hope from human aid, only from the mercy of the Almighty. Dejection filled my mind, the consternation became general, nothing but sighs and groans were heard—even the animals that were on board uttered the most dreadful cries. Every one began to raise his heart and hands toward heaven; and in the certainty of a speedy death each was occupied only with the melancholy alternative between the two elements of nature ready to devour us. The fire broke out in the vicinity of the boilers, which caused the soldiers to rush with tiger-like fury to the opposite extremity of the boat, or to that part farthest from the flames, without regard to rank, position or life, using the vain prerogative, "Men jump into the water."

Thus many poor hapless beings were pushed overboard by the pressure of the horrified and strickened mass of humanity. The confusion was extreme. Some seemed to anticipate death by jumping into the river. Others, by swimming, gained the fragments of the boat, while the ropes along the side were being covered by the men who were suspending from them, as if hesitating between two extremes equally imminent and equally terrible.

Being one of the number who were pushed overboard, and not versed in the art of swimming, and unable to battle with the billowy waves, which rushed to and fro bounding like so many mad men, I realized that life would soon be extinct, and that it did not seem uncertain for what fate Providence intended me. Fortunately, as I arose from the bosom of the deep, I grasped a spar of timber which projected from the hull of the boat, and having hung there until my physical powers were nearly exhausted, in the meantime disengaging myself from two or three of my drowning companions, who came up and caught hold of my clothing. At this critical moment I observed a large piece of timber floating near me, and by a special effort secured it, which I used to good advantage, being able to keep myself above water. Having floated around to the other side of the boat I observed men drawing their fellow victims out of the water by means of ropes. Availing myself of this opportunity, I grasped one of these with a death-like grip, but feeling my utter exhaustion, I put my arms through the noose of the rope and was thus drawn up into the portion of the boat which had not yet sunk. In the meantime a man and his son had come to the rescue with their raft, and by this means I was transferred from the burning boat to land a few moments before the vessel went down. My first care, upon setting foot on shore, was to thank the Almighty for my deliverance from the jaws of death, and give the homage of my gratitude to Him to whom I was so evidently indebted for my preservation.

WILLIAM H. PEACOCK.

I WAS born in Tyler county, Va., May 28, 1845.
Enlisted in the service of the United States at
Muncie, Ind., on the 15th day of December, 1863, in
the 9th Regiment Indiana Cavalry. Was captured at
Sulphur Trestle, nine miles north of Athens, Ala., on
the Nashville & Decatur Railroad, September 25, 1864,
and confined in the Cahaba prison, Alabama.

I was put on board the " Sultana" with eighteen
others of my company. The boat was so crowded that
there was not room for all of us on the second deck, so
five of us went up on the texas roof right in front of
the pilot house. I was the only one of the five that
escaped. The first recollection I had of the accident,
I was falling, and had a cut on my shoulder, bruise on

my back and my right side and hip were scalded.   This
happened seven miles above Memphis.

I worked my way out from under the rubbish, and
helped get a good many of the boys out who were
pinned down by it, until the fire got so hot that I had
to stop and look out for myself.   I saw boys start out
to swim with all their clothes on, even their overcoats
and shoes, but they did not go far before they sank.
The only clothes I had on was a pair of drawers, a sack,
a handkerchief (which one of the boys gave to me at
Vicksburg before he died), and a hat that I picked up
about a mile from the boat.

I swam back to Memphis and was rescued by the
gunboat boys and taken to Fort Pickens, seven and
one-half miles below where the steamer's boiler
exploded.   I, with the rest, had just got out of prison,
and only weighed ninety-one pounds.   At the time of
my capture I weighed one hundred and ninety-seven
(197) pounds and had not been sick a day.

My present postoffice address is Cowan, Ind.

———

W. C. PORTER.

I WAS born in Fairfield, Lenawee county, Mich., on
the 19th of October, 1839.   Enlisted in the service
of the United States at Adrian, Mich., on the 2nd of
August, 1862, in Company C, of the 18th Michigan
Infantry.   Was captured at Athens, Ala., on the 24th
of September, 1864, and confined in Cahaba, Ala., or
Castle Morgan as it is sometimes called.

The first night, April 25, 1865, on the boat several

of us slept on the boiler deck in a coalbin as the other decks were so crowded. The next day we had a very pleasant ride. All were joyous and happy with the anticipation of seeing home and friends. The moment the boat touched the wharf at Memphis, Tenn., the boys began to jump off. I went with the rest and roamed about town until ten o'clock in the evening of the 26th of April when we went back to the boat and as they were going to take on coal enough for the rest of our journey we had to find new sleeping quarters. After roaming around on the cabin deck as best I could among the sleepers, I found a place between the smoke stacks, and spread down my blanket and was about to lie down, when one of the men near by said that he was holding that place for another man. I took up my blanket and found another vacant place large enough to lie down, but before I laid down was informed that it was being held for another man.

I made my way back to the stairs and found room enough by sticking my feet over the steps, laid down and was soon lost in sleep. I slept peacefully and quietly until awakened by the noise of the explosion. The first thought was that the hurricane deck had fallen in from being overloaded, but soon found out different. It was not long before it was all confusion, some singing, some praying, some lamenting, some swearing, some crying, and some did not seem to know anything. I soon made my way down stairs. In a short time everything available on the bow of the boat was thrown overboard. There were several bales of cotton and also some bales of hay but there were generally enough men that went over with them to load them down. When the gangway board was shoved over into the water there were a great many that went over with it. It was but a short time before the fire shot up and burned the boat to the water's edge. As the boat was crowded, the flames whipped down on them and those nearest the fire could not stand it and crowded back so that a great many near the edge of the boat were pushed overboard, as the railing that went around the boat had been torn off. I remained on the boat until the largest part or nearly all had gotten off. I took off my clothing, placed it between two sticks and tied them together with a pair of suspenders, with the intention of using them to aid me in floating or swimming, as I was not much of a swimmer. When I jumped off the boat into the water I lost them, I do not know how it happened.

The most that I was afraid of was that some drowning man would catch hold of me. While making for shore I passed four men astride of something, using their hands for oars, and one of them gave the orders so that they would work together. When I got to land, or where the land is most of the time, I found that it was covered with water. The trees were quite dense, and out in the woods a few rods I found a large tree that was floating in the water, climbed upon it and called to some others that were trying to find a place to get out of the water. Some came and got on the log with me, and several got another log near by. I had to rub myself considerably to keep warm, as I did not have any clothing on. Remained there about four or five hours, when a boat came along and picked

us up. When I got on to the boat they gave me a
sheet to wrap around me. When we arrived at Memphis some of the Christian Commission came on board
and distributed some clothing (shirts and drawers) to
those that were needy. I was taken to the Soldiers'
Home, where in due time received a suit of clothes.

Of the company to which I belonged there were
fifteen on board and only three of them survived;
William Thayer, Fairfield; Michael Daley, Palmyra,
now deceased, and myself. There were fifteen on
board belonging to Company K, and only three were
lost. Other companies of the 18th Michigan Infantry
lost heavily, but I cannot give the numbers.

My present occupation is farming. My postoffice
Weston, Mich.

37

SAMUEL H. RAUDEBAUGH.

I WAS born near Lancaster, Fairfield county, Ohio, September 29, 1842. With my parents moved to Hancock county, Ohio, the 5th of June, 1848. I became a Christian by the mercy of God in August, 1853, and united with the church of the United Brethren in Christ in December, 1853. I want to say, to the praise of God, that He has helped me so to live that the church has not been necessitated to remove my name from its records from that day until now. I enlisted in Company K of the 65th Regiment Ohio Infantry, September 5, 1862. The regiment was a part of the renowned Sherman's brigade. It's first colonel was that brilliant young officer, Gen. Harker. He never commanded the regiment much but commanded the brigade until he was made Brigadier General, and then he commanded a division much of the time until his death at the battle of Kenesaw Mountain, Ga. I was married the 2d of October, 1862. Was detained in Ohio, one place and another, until some time in December, 1862, when about thirty of us recruits, in charge of Col. Castle, joined our command in a camp near Nashville, Tenn. Here, for twelve or fifteen days, we recruits had the pleasure of all the division, brigade, regiment, company and also that *famous, wonderful,* and *enjoyable squad drill.* All those days of drill came in good play in the near future, for from the 30th of December, 1862, to January 2d, 1863, we played a conspicuous part in the battle of Stone River, Tenn. Here, along with ten of my company, I was taken prisoner, but I played dead and got away from the "Johnnies," while the other nine comrades went on a journey to Libby.

I was in sixteen of the hard battles of the war, and

in the summer of 1864 on the Atlanta campaign I was
under fire more or less almost daily from the 8th of
May at Rocky Face Ridge to the 2d of September at
Atlanta, Ga. On the 30th of November, 1864, at the
memorable battle of Franklin, Tenn., I was again
taken prisoner and this time took a trip to Andersonville, that indescribable den of suffering, sorrow and
death. I want to say of Andersonville prison that
human tongue has never told, nor pen ever written and never will tell or write the horrors, suffering
and cruelty inflicted on the prisoners at Andersonville
by Werz and his guards, and I firmly believe that they
but executed the will of Jeff Davis and his allies.

I will give some death rates that I gathered from
official records as follows: Of 12,400 persons taken
to the hospital 76 per cent. died.

In May, 1864, of 18,454 prisoners, 701 died; 23
per day.

In June, 1864, of 26,364 prisoners, 1,202 died; 40
per day.

In July, 1864, of 31,678 prisoners, 1,742 died; 56
per day.

In August, 1864, of 31,693 prisoners, 3,076 died; 99
per day.

On the 23rd of August, 1864, was the greatest mor-
tality; 127 died, one for every eleven minutes. You
will allow me to say that I call that treatment wholesale murder and that of the most cruel kind known
to history.

As stated above I was taken prisoner on the 30th
of November, 1864, and hence was in Andersonville during the winter of 1864 and 1865. I, with

eleven others, bought out of Andersonville in March,
1865, and arrived in "God's country," at Big Black
river, on the 31st of March, 1865. While here along
with thousands of paroled prisoners, Lee and Johnson
surrendered, and President Lincoln was assassinated.
All of us thought that the wicked slave holders' rebellion was about bursted up.

On the evening of the 25th of April, 1865, at Vicksburg, Miss., about 2,300 of us, nearly all paroled prisoners from Andersonville and Cahaba dens, were
crowded on board the steamer " Sultana." She arrived
at Memphis, Tenn., on the evening of the 26th of
April, 1865, with her load of human beings and about
one hundred tons of sugar. She remained there until
the sugar was unloaded. I helped unload the sugar
and received seventy-five cents an hour for the time I
worked. At about ten o'clock P. M. of the 26th of
April she went to a coal barge and took on a supply of
coal. About midnight I asked one of the deck hands,
"How soon do you expect to start up the river?" and
he replied, "At one o'clock." That would be the
morning of the 27th.

Now, remember, kind reader, we were on our way
home from the cruel war, it being virtually over. We
were on our way home from those horrid dens of
cruelty and *starvation.* Yes, we had lived through it
all, and hoped, yes expected soon, to see loved ones and
home and enjoy at least some of the peace we had
fought to restore. Home! Yes, *home* under the
stars and *stripes,* once more. While thus pleasantly
meditating, all of a sudden, about half-past one o'clock
A M. one of the boilers exploded and the greater part of

that human load was blown into the river, while sound asleep—some to awake in the cold water and some in eternity. Those that were not blown off at the time of the explosion were soon compelled to jump into the river so as to escape burning to death, for the boat quickly caught fire and burned to the water's edge. About 1,750 of that homeward-bound company perished then and there, and several hundred more poor fellows died in the next ten days from wounds, burns and scalds. I say, fearless of truthful contradiction, that the explosion of the "Sultana" was the greatest calamity of the war against the slave-holding rebels, and it was the greatest steamboat disaster known to history.

You will naturally ask two questions, first, "How did you escape?" and second, "How did the calamity occur?" To the latter question I can but give you my opinion, and that has never changed since I got ashore and took time to think. I believe that some enemy of our Union had a hand in crowding so many of us on the boat, and that he knew when that southern sugar was taken off that the rest of the cargo and the boat would meet the fate that followed. I believe that some ally of Jeff. Davis put a torpedo in the coal, while we were at Memphis, where it would go into the furnace for the first fire that would be built after leaving Memphis, with the intent to destroy the boat and its mass of human heroes on their way home. I can say that in May, 1888, a man in the south, William C. Streeter, St. Louis, Mo., said that he knew the man, Charles Dale, who said he chiseled a hole in a large chunk of coal, put the torpedo therein which did the deadly work, carried it with his own hands and laid it where it must soon go into the furnace.

I will say one thing more and that is, if I were in authority I would arrest and hang the man who knew so high handed and bloody a murderer and did not try to have him brought to justice for so gigantic a crime.

Now, as to my escape. I was lying by the side of the ice-box under the same blanket with J. B. Horner of Co. K of the 65th Ohio, and J. W. Vanscoyce of Co. A of the 64th Ohio, sound asleep when the explosion took place. I was blown off the boat into the water and was under the water when I awoke. When I came to the surface I tried for a moment to get on the ice-box, for it was in the water as well as myself, but so many were trying to get onto it that it would do none of us any good, so I swam away to a spot in the river where there were no human beings, and there concluded that the boat had sank and knew no better until I saw the boat on fire. I soon got on a large rail and remained on it for some time. I lost consciousness and when I came to know again I had lost my rail. Then, as soon as I could I got a piece of the bannister of the wrecked boat, both rails together about four feet long, and on this little raft I remained and suffered with the cold and cramps until daylight, when I was picked up by a few boatmen of the gunboat "Essex," about two miles below Memphis, having floated with the current about ten miles, and had been in the water from about 1:30 in the morning until daylight on the 27th of April. I was taken to the Gayoso Hospital at Memphis and treated for injuries in my breast and groin.

I am and have for the last twenty years been a regular minister of the gospel of Jesus Christ in the church of my early choice. I want all of the readers to remember that it costs something to preserve this government's interest. I want to ask you to kindly remember the old soldiers, and especially the surviving prisoners of the late war against the most wanton rebellion and in support of the best government on earth. I wish hereby to thank God for preserving my life and permitting me to enjoy so much of the peace I suffered to hand down to future generations.

Residence and postoffice address, Lindsey, Ohio.

CHRISTIAN RAY.

I WAS born near Centerville, Ind., January 1, 1829. Enlisted at New Westville, Preble county, on or about the 20th of August, 1862, in Company C, 50th Regiment Ohio Volunteer Infantry. Was captured at Franklin, Tenn., November 30, 1864, and was confined in the Cahaba prison, Ala.

Was put on board the "Sultana" and started for Columbus to be discharged. When we arrived at Memphis they were unloading sugar and hogs. I think that a rebel fixed a torpedo in the coal. After leaving Memphis, having gone about seven miles above, the torpedo was shoveled into the fire, which caused the explosion between one and two o'clock in the morning.

It blew the pilot house and everything off within three feet of where my partner and I lay. The rubbish fell down on us and pinned us there for a

while. Finally we worked ourselves out and slid
down the stayrod. The steam was so dense that we
could not see our way, but we got down on the lower
deck amidst the crowd. Some were praying and some
cursing; all kinds of talk was going on. As we passed
along we came across a stage plank about six feet long,
three feet wide and two inches thick. My partner
knew I could not swim. We then carried the plank
to the edge of the boat and threw it off. My partner
said to me, "This is all that I can do for you, jump
on it." I never exchanged a word, but jumped on the
plank, struck one edge of the board and it turned over
with me two or three times. Finally I got my breast
fixed on one end of it and held on with one hand and
worked away with the other. The current being strong
I was carried away before the main body commenced
jumping out. Good swimmers were fighting and
kicking to keep off those unfortunates who could not
swim, but all in vain. They clustered together and
went down. When I saw this I worked harder to get
away.

In a short time I was out of sight, so that was good
bye to the burning "Sultana." I then looked up and
thought I saw a boat coming, so I turned my board up
the stream and worked hard for a little while but
found it was useless. I was going down stream all the
time, so I turned my board and let it float. I floated
back to Memphis and lodged on a pile of drift wood.
There were five other men screaming for life. After
a while some "good samaritans" ran in with a skiff
and took us out. I was nearly chilled to death, and
was carried up to the barracks. Here I was placed in

front of a roaring hot fire and given enough alcohol
to kill three men in a common condition before they
could get a reaction to take place. I was taken to the
hospital that night, which was the 27th of April. The
next morning we started for Columbus where I was
discharged and sent home. I have not done anything
for seven years. I am totally disabled and crippled up,
and have rheumatism, heart disease and dropsy.

Present post office address, Greenville, Ohio.

GEORGE F. ROBINSON.

I WAS born in Girard, Erie county, Penn., in the
year 1845, and enlisted at Charlotte, Mich., August
1, 1861, in Company I, 6th Regiment Michigan
Volunteer Infantry. Re-enlisted August 2, 1863.
Enlisted again August 3d, 1864, in Company C, 2d
Regiment Michigan Cavalry. I was taken prisoner
November 5, 1864, at Shoal Creek, Ala , by rebel Gen.
Hood. Was taken across the river, and the first night
camped at Tuscumbia. The next morning we started
for Corinth, arriving there in the evening about eight
o'clock. The next morning following we were put on
the train and taken to Meridian, Miss., reaching there
at five o'clock P. M. The first thing that greeted my
ears on arriving at the prison was "fresh fish." I had
a few rations and was told to look out or some one
would steal them. I was much surprised to think
that they would try to steal rations from a soldier
who had put over three years in the service; so I took
two pieces of rail and laid them down, took my hat,

put my haversack in it and put them both between the rails, and I then laid down on all and said to myself, "you will fool an old soldier, will you?" I slept good all night, and on awaking in the morning reached for my rations, but found none. Some one had dug a hole under the rails and stolen them. I tell you I was the most beat man you ever saw. Experience No. 1 as a prisoner.

About the 20th of November a party of eight of us commenced digging a tunnel. It was slow work for we had to look out for the guards, and they kept very close watch but we succeeded at last. Six of us got out, but when about sixty miles away were recaptured by an old woman and fifteen dogs and brought back to Meridian the worst looking lot of men you ever saw. We were covered with clay from head to foot by going through the tunnel, which was half full of water at the time of our escape. Everything went along quietly for about a month and then we started for Cahaba, Ala., the prison known as "Castle Morgan." At this time my clothing consisted of shirt, drawers and one shoe. About six miles from Demopolis, John Corliss and myself made our escape by jumping out of the car window. I did not stop immediately but rolled along after the train quite a distance. I tell you I was badly mangled and had a big hole cut in my head, but I thought it was all right for I was free once more—that is, I was in my mind, for it was not but a short time before I heard the dogs and we had to go, but we kept away from them for five days and five nights when we were recaptured. We were almost starved and nearly frozen. Had nothing to eat but raw corn

and no fire, and wallowing through the swamp in the
month of December.   If it *was* down south the weather
was awful cold, for it would freeze icicles on the trees
from three to four inches in length.

We were taken back to Meridian and then transferred
to Cahaba.   When we got there it was the same old
story, "fresh fish."   I was in prison about one month,
and then succeeded in getting out again by cutting a
hole through the wall next to the river.   John Corliss
and myself got out but were caught before we had
hardly got a start.   We were north of Selma when recaptured and were put in a large hall about eighteen
feet from the ground.   We managed to get a hole
through the brick wall, doing our work with an old
knife and a piece of round iron—I think a piece of
a poker.   We got out all right, but did not get out of
the city and were recaptured and taken back to Cahaba.
In March, 1865, the water from the river flooded the
prison to the depth of three or four feet, in consequence
of which we were ordered for exchange.

The next move was to place us on a stern wheel
steamer with four large cannons on the bow, but
before we reached our destination the boys had all the
four guns spiked with old files they found on the boat.
At last we arrived at camp, four miles from Vicksburg,
and were there when President Lincoln was assassinated.   In a day or two after this we were taken to
Vicksburg and put on board the steam boat
"Sultana."   Everything went smoothly until we
reached Memphis, Tenn., where they unloaded a large
quantity of sugar that was in the hold of the boat.   I,
for one, helped.

Now, if my memory serves me right, there were about 2,300 people on board the "Sultana." We left Memphis in the evening, went across the river to a coaling station and took on a large quantity of coal. I was asleep when we left and was lying on the promenade deck between the smoke stacks. I did not hear the explosion. I think I was stunned, for the first I recollected I heard some one calling "for God's sake, cut the deck, I am burning to death." Then I tried to find out where I was and when I did I found I was in the coal in front of the arches. The deck I had laid on was on top of me. My arms were scalded and the hot steam was so thick I could hardly breathe, and in fact I gave up. My partner, John Corliss, was lying across my legs and was dead, killed by the deck falling on him. I then heard someone say, "Jack, you can get out this way." It was some comrade helping his bunkmate out. This is the last I can recollect until some one put his hand on my shoulder and said, "What will I do? I cannot swim." I looked around, and my God, what a sight! There were three or four hundred, all in a solid mass, in the water and all trying to get on top. I guess that nearly all were drowned, but that was not the worst sight. The most horrid of all was to see the men fast in the wreck and burning to death. Such screaming and yelling I never heard before or since. It makes me shiver to think of it. At this time I was sitting on the bow of the boat with my arm around the flag staff, facing the Tennessee shore. At length the flames burned it down and I was forced to take to the water. I turned around and got in the water on the Arkansas side. There were some

amusing things transpired. For instance one man
was on a beer keg, and he would crawl up on it and pray.
He got up a little too far and over he went still hanging to it. He came up on the other side of it and the
first thing I heard him say was "d—n this thing, it
will drown me yet." I drifted away from him, and
could hear some poor soul say, " My God, I cannot hold
out any longer," and down he would go. All this
time I kept up good courage and was sure I could get
out all right. I got close to the islands but could not
make the trees. The islands were all overflowed and
some of the boys got in the tree tops. I could hear
someone calling "Morgan, here is your mule." It was
a mule that saved my life and a dead one at that. I
was almost a goner, when I saw a dark object in the
water and made for it, and it was a dead mule, one
that was blown off the boat. He was dead but not
quite cold. I crawled up on him and was there when
I was picked up at Fort Pickens three miles below
Memphis. I was unconscious at the time, being chilled
through, having been in the water about four hours.
I was put in an ambulance and taken to Memphis to a
hotel and remained there for six or seven days. Was
then sent to " Camp Chase," Columbus, Ohio, and
from there to Jackson, Mich. From Jackson to Charlotte, my home. Three months after I was weighed
and my weight was 109 pounds.

My present occupation is shoe clerk, and my postoffice address 720 Corunna ave., Owosso, Mich.

PETER ROSELOT.

I WAS born in France, October 28, 1849, and enlisted
in the service of the United States October 6, 1862,
at Mowrytown, Highland county, Ohio, in Company
E, 50th Ohio Volunteer Infantry, and took to the
field almost as soon as we reached " Camp Denison,"
Ohio, and participated in all the marches and
battles of the regiment, including Perryville, and the
Atlanta campaign.   At Atlanta was sent back to take
care of Hood, and fell back until we reached Franklin,
Tenn.   There I was captured on that bloody battle
field, November 30, 1864, and taken in the front line,
together with seven others of my company and sixty-
two of the regiment.   I was then taken back to
Columbia, Tenn, and guarded in the stone fort, where
I almost froze to death.   We eight had to lie under
one blanket, having lost all we had in the fight.   It
was very cold.   About the time that the rebels got
whipped at Nashville they made us get out of the old
stone fort in a hurry and marched us through mud,
water and rain, to the Tennessee river, where they
ferried us across in pontoon boats, then put us on
the cars, and we went to Corinth and then to Meridian,
Miss.   They kept us there until after New Year's and
then we went to Selma, Ala., where they put us in
prison over night and gave us hard tack for rations,
the last we had until we reached our lines a few months
later.   The following morning we marched to Cahaba,
Ala., where they searched every one of us and turned
us into the prison.   There we stayed two days before

we received any rations, and when we did get them there was not much, being a pint of corn meal and a taste of meat.

About this time I had to go out on the skirmish line every day, so as to keep our little friends from getting too numerous, else they would have carried us away. I refer to the faithful "gray back." So it went on until the "mutiny," but I had no hand in that. Had to do without rations for three days and pass inspection entirely naked before the rebels, on account of it. Then all was well till the prison overflowed. I think it was on March 1 when we had to hunt a dry place to lie down in. I succeeded the first and second night, but after that none was to be found. The rebels now took pity on us by taking us down town to get cordwood and fix up a scaffold out of the water. That evening we were taken out again, put on board a steamboat, carried down the river some miles, loaded a boat full of cord wood, got extra rations, then returned to Cahaba and unloaded part of the wood. We then made ready to go back in the prison, but the order was countermanded. We slept on the boat that night and got some more extra rations. They tasted good on that dry boat. The morning following we started for Selma, Ala. They put us in a dry prison and the next week we were under parole of honor, and when everything was in readiness marched us out of prison on board a train of cars and started us for Meridian and Jackson, Miss. From here we marched on foot to Big Black river, where we beheld the glorious stars and stripes once again. We cheered and shouted until hoarse, then we had a square meal of " Uncle Sam's" gruel and then marched across the bridge and bid farewell to rebeldom forever. We were then marched within about five miles of Vicksburg, Miss., where we bunked in the parole camp. This was on March 19, 1865.

We were kept in parole camp till about April 25th, on which date we were taken aboard the ill-fated " Sultana," and on the second night after embarking we arrived at Memphis, Tenn. After unloading a cargo of sugar we took on coal, then started, and when about eight miles up the river the disaster took place. I was lying with two comrades on the cabin floor forward, between the stairway and the fore part of the boat. Was sound asleep, but was suddenly awakened by the explosion. After I had recovered from the first shock I climbed down on the lower deck, by means of ropes and spikes, to the front part of the boat, for the stairway was blockaded and the upper deck or floor had fallen on it. Imagine, if you can, the scene that followed. No pen or tongue can portray it. Imagine yourself in the midst of about two thousand souls, all crowded on a steamboat torn to pieces by the explosion of her boiler, in the dead of the night. If I remember right all the after part of the deck was blown overboard and the forward part of the deck fell in. How many were killed, I cannot tell. Then in a few minutes, the fire broke out, and the boat was all ablaze. I saw many men mangled—some with arms and legs broken, others scalded and screaming in their agony, while others would be fighting over a piece of timber or plank, and some crying or praying, some jumping

39

in the water to escape from the fire and drowning.   It was a scene I never care to witness again.

There were seven of our company on the boat, and five of them perished. If it had not been for the grace of God we too would have perished. After I had got down on the lower deck I waited for a favorable opportunity to save myself. After a large number of the men had made their escape or were drowned I watched for a clear space in the river, for I was afraid some one would catch hold of me and I would share the fate of the others. I jumped off into the river, and swam away as fast as I could for a short distance. Then I took it slow, for I had a mile or two to go. I got hold of some pieces of plank tied together with a pair of suspenders (doubtless the work of some poor fellow who had perished). I put them under my left arm and steered with my right, until I reached the timber where I expected to find dry land but was disappointed, for the water was so deep that we could not touch the bottom with rails and poles (I say we because there were others within speaking distance of me). So we had to climb a sapling tree and roost there. I was almost chilled to death. If I had not held on to the sapling with one hand and rubbed myself briskly with the other I could not have survived.

After some time, however, I got warmed up and did the best I could to keep the mosquitoes from eating me up. When the sun came up it warmed me and I waited patiently for help, which did not come till about ten o'clock that morning. When the first steamboat made its appearance it cheered up the poor boys and we shouted, but it stopped way below us, so did the second, third and fourth, but the fifth one, the little picket boat, came boldly up to where we were and sent out its boats and picked us all up. We then started for Memphis where I was taken to the "Soldiers' Home." Others were taken to private dwellings, and some to the hospital where I was taken later. As luck would have it here I met my comrade, the only other one of the seven. The others were all lost. This was about April 27, 1865. In a day or two we got some new cothing and blankets and then were taken aboard the "Belle of St. Louis" and steamed up to Cairo, Ill., where we landed the next day late in the afternoon. I could not repress a shout of joy, when I again set my foot on land, for I was afraid of boats and water. From there I went to "Camp Chase," Ohio, and was discharged on May 20, 1865.

Occupation, farming. Postoffice address, Mowrystown, Ohio.

ROBERT RULE.

I ENLISTED in the service of the United States, as a private, at Nashville, Tenn., June 10, 1863, in Company A, 3rd Regiment Tennessee Cavalry, and was captured at Sulphur Trestle, Ala., in September, 1864, and coufined in the Cahaba prison.

At the time of the explosion I, with several others, was on top of the boat, and we climbed down by a rope to the deck. One of my company and myself threw a trough in the river and jumped in. I did not catch hold of the trough, but got onto a plank

with six others. We floated down the river two miles
and came to some bushes. We all grabbed onto them,
but one of my comrades lost his hold of the plank and
was drowned. The next morning we were picked up
by a boat and taken to Memphis.

Occupation, farming. Postoffice address, Rockford,
Blount county, Tenn.

O. C. RUSSELL.

I ENLISTED at Somerset, Ky., June 1863, as
a private in Company C, 3rd Tennessee Cavalry, and was captured at Sulphur Branch Trestle,
Ala., I think in September, 1864, and confined in
the Cahaba prison. Was released about one month
previous to the explosion. I took the boat at Vicksburg, about the 26th of April. We stopped at
Memphis and unloaded hogsheads of sugar. I
was asleep when we left there, but was awakened
when the explosion took place. A party of us
threw a staging overboard, got upon it, and were
rescued at Memphis and taken to a hospital. From
there we went to Cairo, Ill., then to Indianapolis, Ind.,
and on to Columbus, Ohio. Was discharged from the
service in June, 1865.

Occupation, farming. Postoffice, Morgantown, Tenn.

S. F. SANDERS.

I WAS born in Farmington, Ill., April 16, 1845, and enlisted in the service of the United States at Bushnell, Ill., May 12, 1864, in Company I, 137th Regiment Illinois Volunteers. Was captured at Memphis, Tenn., August 21, 1864, and confined in the Cahaba, Ala., prison.

The western boys were sent to Springfield, Ill., several days before the "Sultana" was loaded. I was nursing the sick in the barracks and did not leave Vicksburg until the last boat load, and so far as I have ever known I was the only Illinois boy on the boat. I had charge of sixteen sick comrades, who were sleeping in front of the cabin. I had just laid down when the explosion took place. About daylight I was pushed off from the stern of the boat into the water. I climbed on the rudder and remained there for some time with eleven others until it got too hot for us. Fortunately for us we made our way to a platform on one side of the boat and were rescued by rebels on a raft.

Occupation, physician; postoffice address, Holdrege, Neb.

———

G. S. SCHMUTZ.

I WAS born in Congress, Ohio, on the 22d of July, 1846. Enlisted in the service of the United States at Congress, Ohio, on the 2d of August, 1862, in Company I, 102d Ohio Volunteer Infantry. Was captured at Athens, Ala., on the 24th of September, 1864, and confined in Cahaba until the 24th of March, 1865, when I was released and sent to Vicksburg, Mississippi.

My experience in regard to the explosion of the ill-fated "Sultana" is as follows: In the afternoon of April 26, 1865, we arrived at the city of Memphis, Tenn., where was unloaded a number of hogsheads of sugar, which I think was one of the causes of the explosion. There were about 2,300 persons on board. A great many of the soldiers were on the upper decks, and as the boat came round a bend of the river it would careen, the water rushing to one side of the boilers, the others would become heated, and as the boat righted the water would rush to the heated boilers, thus causing the explosion.

Before leaving the wharf at Memphis I went asleep, but I remember being awakened by the boat coaling up, some distance up the river. I soon went asleep again, and the next I knew I felt a burning and falling sensation and remember calling "What's the matter?" Being a good swimmer I had no fear. My first impression was that I had been thrown into the river and I tried to swim to the boat. I soon found many in the river like myself. That the boiler had exploded never entered my mind. Presently I saw flames and knew then that the boat was on fire. In the meantime I came across some wreckage of the boat, among which was a piece of a cracker box. It was sufficient to support me. I also found out that I was scalded about the face, and every now and then plunged my face into the water to cool it off. I made no effort to swim ashore, as I knew the river had overflowed its banks, and I did not relish the idea of climbing a tree to get out of the water when I had nothing on but my shirt. That would be very unpleasant.

I took my chance going down the river, as I knew we could not be far above Memphis. I had for companion awhile a man who was moon-eyed and could not see at night. He was floating on a long board and generously offered to share his board with me, but I had all the support I needed. After I had been in the water about two hours, I heard some one rowing a boat and I called for help. The reply was "Here's one." Then I saw the boatmen row towards me and they pulled me in the boat. I now found I was badly scalded on my left side and back. After picking out of the river a few more of my unfortunate comrades the boat rowed for the shore and we were landed and taken to a convalescent camp, where I continued to suffer the most excruciating pain. I ran up and down in the cool air to relieve the pain. I felt easy going against the wind, but returning it was excruciating. I was urged to lie down, but for a time refused ; finally I yielded after putting on a pair of cotton drawers and shirt. I laid down on a cot that had been prepared for me. Soon afterwards an ambulance came and took me to Gayoso Hospital where I lay for ten days, during which time I fully recovered and, getting transportation, I was sent to Columbus, Ohio, where I was discharged from the service.

My present occupation is clerk. Postoffice address, Wooster, Ohio.

C. C. SEABURY.

I WAS born in Verona, Oneida county, N. Y., in 1844, and enlisted at Quincy, Mich., November 17, 1862, in Company B, 8th Michigan Cavalry. Was captured near Mt. Pleasant, Tenn., November 20, 1864, and confined in the Meridian, Miss., and Cahaba, Ala., prisons.

Postoffice, Coloma, Mich.

W. R. SHAUL.

I WAS born in Clark county, Ohio, February 27, 1836, and enlisted in the service of the United States at Cable, Ohio, July 16, 1862, in Company E, 95th Regiment Ohio Volunteer Infantry. Was captured at Guntown, Miss., June 12, 1864, and confined in five prisons, namely: Andersonville, Millen, Savannah, Blackshear and Thomasville.

I swam from the burning wreck to the Tennessee shore securing a window shutter to help me; got into the woods, caught hold of a limb of a bush, and held on until daylight. Then I swam to a log about twenty-five yards distant, and got upon it. I was picked up by the steamer "Silver Spray."

Occupation, dealer in general merchandise. Address, Cable, Ohio.

I. N. SHEAFFER.

BORN in Lancaster, Pa., December 5, 1833, and enlisted in the service of the United States at Canton, Ohio, September 5, 1862, in Company E, 115th Ohio Volunteer Infantry. Was captured at Nashville, Tenn., Dec. 4, 1863, and confined in the Meridian, Andersonville and Cahaba prisons.

I floated down the river on a door to Memphis and was picked up by negro troops.

Occupation, tailor. Postoffice address, Canton, Ohio.

PAYTON SHIELDS.

I ENLISTED in Company D, 31st Regiment Ohio Volunteer Infantry. When the explosion of the "Sultana" took place on the morning of the 27th of April, 1865, on the Mississippi river, I was on the hurricane deck attending to a sick comrade, and, at his request, had just lain down with him only a few minutes when the explosion occurred. I was slightly scalded but remained on deck until the flames became so hot that I could remain no longer. I then jumped from the wheel house into the water, a distance of perhaps thirty-five feet. I struck on my feet and at once began swimming. After going a distance of about three miles I caught hold of a piece of weather-beaten board about six feet long which proved to be a great help to me. I continued swimming and floating with the current until I was seven miles below the wreck, when I was picked up, more dead than alive, by

a yawl from the gunboat " Essex," and have never seen
one well hour since.

As soon as I was able to travel I left Memphis and
went on board a steamer for Cairo, Ill., remaining
there one night, then took the train for Mattoon, Ill.,
where we were met at the depot by the citizens with
hot coffee and a bountiful supper. I then proceeded
to Indianapolis, from there to "Camp Chase," Ohio,
reported to Col. Richardson and was discharged
from the service.

A. SHOEMAKER.

I WAS born in Canal Winchester, Ohio, March 3,
1845, and enlisted in the service of the United
States at Elmore, Ohio, November 29, 1861, in Company E, 72d Regiment Ohio Volunteer Infantry, and
was captured at Guntown, Miss., June 10, 1864, and
confined in Andersonville, Savannah and Lawton
prisons.

I do not think it worth while to give my "Sultana"
experience.

My postoffice address is Carroll, Ohio.

W. T. SHUMMARD.

I WAS born in Clermont county, Ohio, July 25,
1835, and enlisted in the service of the United
States at "Camp Clay," Ohio, September 11, 1862, in
Company A, 7th Regiment Ohio Volunteer Cavalry,

and was captured between Nashville and Columbia, Tenn., November 27, 1864, and confined in the Meridian, Miss., and Cahaba, Ala., prisons. After being a prisoner five months, on the 23d of April, 1865, I, with about 2,000 prisoners of war, was driven like so many sheep on board the "Sultana" at Vicksburg. We went to Memphis and stopped and unloaded some freight, then to the coal docks and took on some coal. We then proceeded up the river about eight miles, when her boilers exploded (this was about the 27th of April, 1865) about two o'clock A. M. I and twelve comrades lay side by side asleep, just in front of the boilers, on the lower deck. The first that I knew, I was holding to a chain at the bow of the boat; had a bump on the back of my head, was badly scalded on the side of my head and face, and my feet also. I tried to climb up several times on the boat not knowing what had happened. At length a man caught and pulled me up, then I saw what had happened. Of the twelve men who laid beside me, there was but one saved beside myself, this was John Bell of the same company and regiment. I staid on the boat until 8 A. M., as I could not swim, then with thirteen comrades left the boat on a small raft, and was taken back to Memphis, and soon after went to "Camp Chase," Ohio, my native State. On Saturday, the 20th of May, was discharged and went home.

Occupation, farming. Postoffice address, Brazilton, Kansas.

316 LOSS OF THE SULTANA.

J. L. SLICK.

I WAS born in Monroe county, Michigan, 1844, and enlisted in the service of the United States at Detroit, February 22, 1864, in Company A, 18th Regiment Michigan Infantry, and was captured at Athens, September 24, 1864, and confined in the Cahaba, Ala., prison.

When the explosion occurred I was thrown against the wheel house and knocked insensible. When I came to I helped a comrade on a board six inches wide and four feet long, and as he was no swimmer I took charge of the craft. We landed on a log at seven o'clock A. M., and while there I drew a comrade out of the water who had his leg scalded so badly that the flesh dropped off.

Occupation, merchant. Postoffice address Lambertsville, Mich.

COMMODORE SMITH.

I WAS born in Holmes township, Crawford county,
State of Ohio, on the 18th day of January, 1842.
Removed with my father's family to Hillsdale county,
State of Michigan, in the fall of 1854.

My great-great-grandfather and my grandfather
were soldiers in their day, and my father, Isaac Smith,
with his three sons and son-in-law participated in the
late war for the union of the States in America. Father
was a member of Company C of the 1st Michigan Volunteer Infantry. He was born of Scotch and English
parentage in the year A. D. 1809, in eastern Virginia,
being at the time of his enlistment (in October, 1861,)
fifty-two years of age. He received a wound in the
head and was taken a prisoner of war on the third day
of the notorious seven days battle before Richmond,

Va., under the command of Gen. Geo. B. McClellan. Was taken to Richmond, and confined in that h——l commonly called "Libby prison" for a period of about three months. He was soon afterwards paroled and sent to exchange camp, near Alexandria, Va., where after eight days (from exposure, starvation and disease contracted while a prisoner) he died. "Peace be to his ashes," whilst his blood crieth aloud for vengeance and just retribution against the rebel hordes that caused his suffering and death.

My eldest brother, Columbus Smith, was a member of Company I, 18th Regiment Michigan Volunteer Infantry, and enlisted August 11, 1862, and died at Lexington, Ky., of typhoid pneumonia, December 28, 1862.

My youngest brother, James Henry Smith, was a member of Company K, 27th Regiment Michigan Volunteer Infantry. He served to the close of the war and was discharged with his regiment. He died at Cambria, Hillsdale county, Mich., from the effects of la grippe, December 31, 1891.

My eldest sister's husband, Andrew A. Ewing, was a member of Company —, 2d Regiment Michigan Volunteer Infantry. He served to the close of the war and was discharged with his regiment, and is still living at this date, April 10, 1892, in Hillsdale county, State of Michigan, and long may he live to enjoy reunions with his old comrades.

I, myself, was a member of Company F, 18th Michigan Volunteer Infantry. I enlisted August 11, 1862, at Hillsdale, Hillsdale county, State of Michigan. Was captured September 24, 1864, by consolidated bands of guerillas, at Athens, Ala., the notorious rebel General N. B. Forrest being in chief command. I was taken to Cahaba, Ala., and there confined in prison for a period of nearly six months, and was reduced to a mere skeleton. My weight when captured was 175 pounds, and when I reached our lines at Vicksburg, Miss., March 16, 1865, my weight was 94 pounds, although I had not been sick a day while in prison.

We remained at Vicksburg until April 25th or 26th, when we, to the number of 2,333 souls, all prisoners, were taken on board the ill-fated "Sultana." At the time her boilers exploded I was lying sound asleep on the lower deck, just back of the rear hatchway to the hold. I was not long in waking up, for I was nearly buried with dead and wounded comrades, legs, arms, heads, and all parts of human bodies, and fragments of the wrecked upper decks. I struggled to my feet and tried to go forward on the boat, but could not on account of the wreckage and carnage of human freight which now covered the lower deck. The surface of the river for rods about the boat was covered with the same kind of wreckage. I remained on board the hull of the boat for perhaps twenty or thirty minutes, throwing overboard all the loose boards and timbers and everything that would float to assist those in the water and save them from drowning if possible.

And now occurred the hardest task of my life. The boat was on fire and the wounded begged us to throw them overboard, choosing to drown instead of being roasted to death. While our hearts went out in sympathy for our suffering and dying comrades we performed our sad but solemn duty. I say we because there were others besides myself who were fortunate enough not to be hurt or blown overboard by the explosion, and they too were doing all they could to alleviate the sufferings of their unfortunate comrades. We waited hoping, but in vain, to be rescued from the burning wreck. When at length the last shadow of hope had expired, and we were forced to leave the burning boat and try our luck in the seething, foaming, cold and turbulent waters of the mighty Mississippi, and this too at about two o'clock in the morning and almost total darkness prevailing, except the light from the burning wreck, we proceeded to perform carefully, but hurriedly, the most heart rending task that human beings could be called upon to perform—that of throwing overboard into the jaws of certain death by drowning those comrades who were unable on account of broken bones and limbs to help themselves. Some were so badly scalded by the hot water and steam from the exploded boiler that the flesh was falling from their bones. Those comrades who were doubly endeared to us through mutual suffering and starvation while we were penned up in the rebel h——s, or so called confederate prisons, and who instead of throwing them thus overboard, we were wanting to render every kindness to, dress their wounds and soothe their sufferings. But, alas! this was impossible, the only alternative was to toss them overboard.

Reader of this narrative, do you not think that this was a hard task for us to perform? If not, just hearken to this a moment; listen to the heartfelt prayers of those suffering and wounded comrades and hear their dying requests as they commended their wives, children, fathers, mothers, sisters and brothers to God's kind care and keeping, and hear them thanking us for our kindness to them, notwithstanding the pain they were suffering. They fully realized the fact that their last day, hour and even last minute to live had come; and then to hear the gurgling sounds, the dying groans and see them writhing in the water, and finally see them sink to rise no more until the morning when all shall come forth. Was this not heart rending to us? My heart, even now, after twenty-seven years, nearly stands still while I write this sad story. After we had thus cared for the helpless ones, I leaped over the burning wreck into the mighty waters and headed for Memphis, Tenn., which, from this point, was about seven miles down the river. I was a good swimmer, and after encountering several whirlpools and being carried around and around in them, each time being carried back into the center of the river, by hard struggling, keeping a cool head and using my dexterity as a swimmer I finally reached a point half a mile above the city of Memphis where I lodged in a tree out in the flats of the river. The water at this point was about twenty feet deep. I remained in the tree until a boat came, just at dawn, and picked me up together with twenty-seven others. Was afterwards taken to the city where the Christian Commission cared for us until we were able to resume our journey homeward to "God's country," as we called it, there to meet our loved ones from whom we had long been parted, and once more to enjoy the blessings of a free and united country, which we had so dearly bought, the price being "blood." Occupation hardware merchant. Postoffice address, Remus, Mich.

TRUMAN SMITH.

I WAS born in New Castle, Pa., February 6, 1848, and enlisted in the service of the United States at Gun Plains, Allegan county, Mich., August 4, 1864, in Company B, 8th Regiment Michigan Cavalry. On the 24th of November we met the enemy near Henryville, Tenn. There was but a handful of us against the army of Hood and Forrest. As the firing grew sharp orders came for us to mount and retreat to the barricade, but my horse was gone.

I made my escape into the woods with the rebel cavalry in close pursuit. Fortune favored me. There was a small marsh just ahead and I went through the mire and came out on the opposite side. The rebel cavalry tried to follow me but the horses mired. I thought I would try and find my regiment. I stayed at the house of a Union man all night and then started next morning for Columbia, Tenn. On my way I came across a wagon train which I supposed was our own, but it proved to be a rebel train. I rode two miles, and under the pretense of joining a rebel army that was passing, got off. I then went to the house of a Union man who gave me a blanket and some provisions and conducted me to a cave, saying it would not be safe for me to stay at the house as there were so many rebels around. I remained there two days and then started for the woods, but was met, not ten feet

away, by some rebels. Of course I had to surrender.
They took my arms and robbed me of everything.
Then I was taken to their camp. The night was very
dark and I slipped past the guard and made my escape,
but was soon captured again by a squad of rebel cavalry.
They hurried us on until we reached Columbia, where
they put us in Fort Misner. There were about 1,700
Union prisoners there. The rebels were on one side of
Duck river and the Union forces on the other. We
remained here several days until Hood was defeated at
Nashville. Our rations consisted of corn on the cob
from once to twice a day. We left in December for
the Tennessee river. The ground was covered with
ice and some of the boys had no shoes on—you could
track them by the blood from their feet. We forded
streams and camped where night overtook us. We
crossed the Tennessee, river and here about 400 escaped.
The rebels pricked us with bayonets and drove us like
cattle to Corinth, where we stayed a day or two and then
started for Meridian arriving there on the 25th of December. There were two stockades, one for Union
prisoners and one for rebel deserters. A squad of us
were put in the latter place. A day or two later we
started for Cahaba, reaching there about the 1st of
January. We were put in prison with about 3,000
others. Our rations here consisted of about a pint of
meal (ground cob and all), and that mouldy; once in
ten days we would receive about two ounces of meat to
the man. This we cut up in bits, and made porridge
with our meal.

There was one attempt made to liberate the prisoners worthy of note. The author of the scheme was

Capt. Hanchett. His idea was to overpower the guards, take their guns and fight our way out. About one o'clock A. M. when everything was still and the guards had made their rounds, we heard a cry for help. They had succeeded in capturing the interior guard, but as they made for the door the bar was dropped in place and we were securely trapped. A long struggle ensued before the guards found out the leader of the revolt. They furnished neither rations nor allowed us to build a fire until our leader should be produced. For three days we had nothing to eat and no fire, and then Capt. Hanchett gave himself up, saying it was better that he should die than should hundreds, who would surely perish in their famished condition. They took him out, tried him by court martial and sentenced him to be shot. He never gave away those who were associated with him in the plot to liberate the prisoners.

We remained at Meridian until March. One day an order came for 300 men to load a boat with wood. We went down the Alabama river about seven miles, when the boat went ashore and we were taken off to load wood. We carried steadily until we had some 200 cords aboard. This occupied the whole day and we then started back to Cahaba. We were permitted to stay on the boat that night. In the morning we were taken to Selma and put in the stockade, we remaining there but a few days, when the other prisoners from Cahaba were sent there. We crossed the river the same night and then took the train for Meridian, Miss., arriving there just at dark and found ourselves back in the old stockade once more. The following morning we took the train for Jackson, reaching there about night. Now we were nearing our lines and learned that our troops were near the Black river—less than forty miles. We were several days making the march. What a glorious sight met our eyes when we got there! On the opposite side floated the stars and stripes. Orders were to go into camp for the night, but I stole away and swam across the river and was once more under the old flag.

Everything was excitement here. News came of the fall of Richmond and the surrender of Lee. Everybody was wild with joy and the thought of a speedy return to our homes. Salutes were fired from all the forts. Our joy, however, was of short duration, for on the 14th of April, as we got up in the morning, we found the colors at half mast. It was sometime before we knew the cause and then we learned that President Lincoln had been assassinated. All thought of home was banished for the time being and every man swore revenge. Everything was gloomy till about the 24th of April, when word came to get ready to go home. Everybody *was* ready.

It was a short march to Vicksburg where, lashed to the wharf, was the ill-fated steamer "Sultana," on which a still greater horror was in store for the boys. We numbered about 2,200 from Castle Morgan and Andersonville, the greater part from Castle Morgan. When we boarded the "Sultana" every foot of her deck was covered with men who had fought starvation, vermin and filth. Memphis was reached without accident and we got off the boat and went to the "Soldiers' Rest," where I got something to eat. It was about midnight when the boat again got started up the river, and just after everybody had got settled down to sleep, except those in charge of the boat, there was a crash and all at once confusion. Some one cried out that the rebels had fired onto us. I thought a shell had exploded near me, but found it was hot steam. I jumped up, threw off the blankets and found that the boat was wrecked. The boilers had exploded and the boat was on fire. I started around to see what the chances were for getting ashore. The fire was burning fast and furious, and men who were buried beneath the wreck were crying for help. When the fire lit up the water men could be seen in every direction and also pieces of the wreck.

The first one of our company that I met after the explosion was Henry Norton. He had lost a bundle of clothes and swore that he would shoot the man who stole them. I told him he had better let the clothes go and make up his mind to swim ashore. He said not until he found his clothes. He was an excellent swimmer and thought he could swim ashore in a few minutes. I left him there and went to look around. I saw that the pilot house was gone and that one stack lay across the deck. The fire was making great headway and men were begging, for God's sake, to have some one help them. It was getting so hot that I concluded to leave the boat. I looked around for something to hold me up in the water, but could find nothing as we were on the hurricane deck and had slept on the wheel house. The only thing that I could see was an empty pork barrel, and thinking, perhaps, that would hold me, threw it into the water and jumped in after it. At this time I had all my clothes on. My barrel was worthless and sank. I started to swim but found that some one had hold of me and I could not get loose. We had a struggle in the water and I freed myself by giving him my blouse. The night was dark and I could not see which way to go. I swam but a few feet when I found myself with four or five others. It seemed as though we all wanted to get hold of each other. I succeeded in getting the rest of my clothes off and got rid of my company. It was only a few minutes before some one had hold of me again. This time I came near drowning. I kept getting away from the boat and about an hour after it blew up I heard some one calling for help. I had a piece of four foot wood that would keep me up nicely. I swam towards the comrade and found it was Henry Norton. I gave him the piece of wood and swam away. He must have been chilled through for he was found clinging to the piece of wood. I swam on trying to make shore. There was a large tree floating down the river and on the roots were three or four men. They were singing the " Star Spangled Banner." As I swam away I heard some one coughing and swam toward him. As I came near he kept swimming away. I called him and asked what regiment he belonged to. He asked what I wanted to know for. I told him I would write to his people in case he drowned and I should get out. He said I must not come any closer, and we made a bargain that if one should die and the other get ashore the survivor should write the parents and let them know. We kept swimming till near daylight, when some one cried "Halt!" We swam toward shore and as we came closer the command to "Halt," was repeated. I replied that we could not as we were in the water. Finally we got to shore and we were told to get out, but my limbs were so benumbed that I could not. The man came to the water's edge, took me by the arm and pulled me ashore, but I could not stand on my feet. He called his comrade who was in the tent and they together picked me up and put me in their bed, and then went back and rescued my comrade. They built a fire and rubbed us and gave us some clothes.

After a while we saw a boat coming up the river and we hailed it. It had started to pick up the survivors of the wreck. I was the first and my comrade next. The first thing after we got on the boat they brought me a tin cup of whiskey which I drank. I had got so that I could walk by this time. We kept going up the river, picking up men and making them comfortable as possible. We picked up about one hundred and started for Memphis, reaching there about eight o'clock. The dock was covered with ladies belonging to the Christian and Sanitary Commissions, who gave us each a pair of drawers and a shirt. I started up town, but at the first block I came to there was a great crowd and they wanted to know if I was on the boat. I said yes, and they gave me a suit of clothes and thirteen dollars in money. From there I went to the "Soldiers' Rest" and was afterwards sent to the hospital. I called for paper and wrote a letter home, giving a detailed account of the disaster. Then I became sick and was unconscious. What became of the clothes and money

I never knew. I was taken care of by Comrade White. My journey to Columbus must have been a tedious one. Here we met several of our regiment and among them was Chas. Seabury, he having his hands and face badly burned from the fire on the boat. We also met Ezra Spencer.

Present occupation, Captain No. 5 steamer, Grand Rapids fire department. Postoffice address, No. 5 Engine House, Grand Rapids, Mich.

EDWARD SORGEN.

I WAS born in Switzerland, in 1842, and enlisted in the service of the United States at Kenton, Ohio, April 16, 1861, in Company G, 4th R giment Ohio Volunteer Infantry, and was captured at Gettysburg, July 2, 1863, and confined in the following prisons: Belle Isle, Andersonville, Millen, Savannah, and Blackshear Station.

At the time of the explosion of the boiler of the "Sultana" I was knocked overboard and swam and floated down the river to a little below Memphis, where I was picked up by three men in a skiff and put on board one of our gunboats. This was about break of day; in the morning I was sent to a hospital and remained there only a short time, when I was sent to Columbus, Ohio.

Occupation, manufacturer and dealer in furniture. Postoffice address, Kenton, Ohio.

M. H. SPRINKLE.

I WAS born in Richland county, Ohio, September 15, 1841. Enlisted in the service of the United States at Ashland, Ohio, on the 15th day of April, 1861, in Company B, 16th Regiment Ohio Volunteer Infantry.

We were taken from the battle field at Athens, Ala., September 24, 1864, where 350 of us, under Lieutenant Col. Elliot, held our own for six hours against 15,000 under Forrest. Our ammunition giving out we were obliged to surrender, became prisoners of war, and taken to Cahaba prison. To give a correct impression of one's sufferings would be impossible, except to those who have endured the hardships of such a place. I, like all the others, had to give up my watch, chain and money—what I had not succeeded in hiding in my waistband. An officer came in and exchanged my new hat for his old one, and detecting that I had on two pairs of pants pointed his revolver at me and demanded the new pair which I had been fortunate enough to secure only the day before.

Our food consisted of a pint of corn chop once a day, providing the guard did not forget us, which he did sometimes. The longest time he forgot me was four days. We had nothing but the hard earth or boards on which to sleep. Thinking I could make a better place than this for my head, I cut off my pants legs and filled one with the siftings of my corn chop, giving the other one to a comrade for a like purpose.

We stayed in this prison until the first of April, 1865. A call was then made for 800 men to form in line. I was one of the first to fall in, for I did not care where we were going. It seemed that nothing worse could be given us than what we were receiving; but our feelings can better be imagined than expressed when, after lying two weeks in parole camp at Vicksburg, we heard that a boat was waiting at the river for us. The report turned out to be true. The boat was the ill-fated steamer "Sultana" and she was headed for Cairo.

Eighteen of my company were upon the hurricane deck at the extreme stern of the boat. Of that number I know of but four that escaped the terrible accident of the morning of April 27th. On that morning, about two o'clock, one of the boilers exploded. The boat soon took fire, and Billy Lockhart and myself threw at least fifty of those who had been wounded in the explosion overboard, thinking it better that they should take their chances of drowning than be left to burn up, which they would do if left on the boat. Finally we were compelled to go as the deck was about to fall in. I then noticed Charley Ogden, of my company, who appeared to be standing in a dazed condition. I spoke to him, telling him he must go or he would burn, but he appeared to take no notice of what I said. I felt the deck tottering and ran and sprang into the river. As I came to the surface the deck had fallen in and I have no doubt Charley perished in the flames as he had not made a move when I left him. I swam over to the west side of the river, but the banks were too steep for me, so the only alternative I had was to float down the stream, which I could easily do, or drown. I chose the former, but was nearly exhausted. On my way down the stream I came in contact with two men who were clinging to a trapdoor about three feet square ; neither of them could swim and as I was floating so easily along they begged me to help them get out. I steadied their raft for them and pushed it along down stream. We were going along fairly well when a drowning man seized my left leg. I tried to kick him loose but failing I let go the raft and tried to force him off but could not, and was obliged to drag that dead weight until we reached Memphis. We were helped out of the water just above the wharf by citizens, and the last I can recollect was they were trying to pry the dead man's grip loose from my leg. The next I knew I was on the boat and having a very hard chill. The captain gave me some brandy and I think I must have drank at least a pint before I began to feel the effects, then I began to sweat profusely. The citizens afterwards took me home with them and gave me a suit of clothes. I stayed with them about nine days, finally starting up the river on the steamer "Belle Memphis," and reaching home on the 21st day of May, 1865.

My present occupation is that of a mason. My postoffice address, Eaton Rapids, Mich.

E. J. SQUIRE.

I WAS born in Norwalk, Ohio, January 8, 1839, and enlisted in the service of the United States at Monroeville, Ohio, August 9, 1862, in Company D, 101st Ohio Volunteer Infantry. I was captured near Huntsville, Ala., January 17, 1865, and confined in the Selma and Cahaba, Ala., prisons.

Occupation, dry goods and boot and shoe dealer, Monroeville, Huron county, Ohio.

JOSEPH STEVENS.

I WAS born in Yorkshire, England, in 1842, and came to this country when a boy with my father, mother and one sister. My brother Thomas was born in Hillsdale, and mother died when he was a baby. Soon after her death father went back to England to attend to some business and died there. I, but a mere lad, took care of myself, sister and baby brother by doing anything I could get to do.

June 20, 1861, when but nineteen years old, I enlisted in Company E, Capt. W. Lombard's company, at Hillsdale, Mich., and was mustered into the 4th Michigan Infantry, in command of Col. D. A. Woodbury, at Adrian, Mich. The regiment left its rendezvous for Washington, June 25, arrived during the night of July 2, and went into camp near Georgetown, where we joined the Army of the Potomac. We remained here in camp but a few days and then were ordered to Bull Run, but were halted at Fairfax Court House, nine miles this side, until further orders. A message came from Washington to be delivered to Gen. McDowell commanding the Union forces at Bull Run. I was detailed to deliver it, and was told to take the first horse I came across. I captured a fine bay stallion from a rebel planter living near by. I mounted him and delivered my message. When I arrived there I found the army retreating towards Washington, and we camped near there all winter. In the following spring we went with Gen. McClellan's army down in front of Richmond. We were engaged in the battle of Yorktown, defeated the "rebs," and then marched on towards Richmond. At New Bridge, seven miles this side, our regiment was ordered to the front, where we

met the "Louisiana Tigers" and killed and captured
half their number with but a small loss on our side.
In the seven days' fight in front of Richmond I was
captured and sent to Libby prison. I was there but a
short time when I was exchanged on account of sickness, and was sent to Philadelphia hospital, remaining there until I received my discharge, when I went
home.

I was home only one week, for, as they were organiz-
ing a company in Hillsdale, I re-enlisted in the 1st
Michigan sharpshooters and encamped at Kalamazoo.
I was made Sergeant of Company B, and being a
veteran was appointed drill master. Shortly after this
we were mustered into the regiment under command
of Col. C. V. DeLand.

We assisted in driving Morgan out of Ohio and Indiana, and then returned to Dearborn, Mich., and
proceeded under orders to "Camp Douglass," Chicago,
where we were placed on duty guarding a camp of
rebel prisoners. We remained in Chicago nearly six
months and then were ordered to Annapolis, Md., to
join the Army of the Potomac. We arrived there in
due time, and proceeded to Warrenton Junction. A
few days later we marched across the Rapidan river,
and the following two days were engaged in the battle
of the Wilderness, we sustaining a very small loss.
Marching with the army to Spottsylvania Court
House we participated in a three days' fight, suffering
very severely. From there we marched on to Cold
Harbor, where we were engaged again, but being in
the supporting line suffered but little. We arrived
in front of Petersburg June 16, 1864, and on the fol-

lowing day happened one of the most prominent events in the history of this regiment. At night, while charging into the "rebs," I had a rooster tied to my belt that I had just captured, intending to have a feast for supper, but I was captured in that action, still holding onto the rooster, and it was eaten by the "Johnnies." The 14th New York Heavy Artillery was on our extreme left, and when the rebels came rushing out of the woods, charging upon us with a terrible yell, the New York regiment, like a flock of sheep, ran and left us. This left our extreme left without any support, and the "rebs" came upon us with a furious charge, but we met them with cold steel and had a fierce struggle until we were overpowered and obliged to surrender, leaving most of our regiment killed wounded and captured.

I was then taken to Petersburg to the provost marshal's office to be searched. I had two twenty dollar greenbacks hid on my person where they could not find them. There I was put in a tobacco house which was used as a temporary prison. The next day a squad of us were detailed to go after some rations. I was one of the first who volunteered to go, thinking I would have a chance to escape, but they had us guarded too strong. On our way a party of women that were standing before a mansion spit in our faces. I then said to the guard: "We wouldn't allow you men to be treated so in the north." He replied, "keep still you d——n yank, or I'll shoot you." They kept us here a few days under Grant's fire. One of his shells struck the roof of the tobacco house, but injured no one. From here we were loaded into box cars and sent to

Andersonville prison. We were eight days on the road, and on arriving my money was all gone—I had spent it for food.

We were then taken to the stockade in which were imprisoned at that time thirty thousand Union men. Here I met a number of my old comrades who were in my company (4th Michigan), captured the preceding year. My friends warned me of a gang of raiders, men who had become desperate. When new prisoners came these men would rob the poor fellows and some times cut their throats. We formed a company to capture the leaders of this notorious gang. We captured six of them and turned them over to the rebels for safe keeping until we could send word to Gen. Sherman to ask what we could do with them. His answer was, "court martial them, and do what you think best." They were then "court martialed" and sentenced to be hung, and the balance of the raiders to run the gauntlet. We had a scaffold erected inside the stockade, and then the rebels delivered them over to us. We stood them in a row each with a rope around his neck. Our minister then offered a prayer for them, and when he finished the trap fell, but the rope broke and let one of them loose. He ran through the crowd but was soon brought back and seeing the rest hanging pleaded for mercy, but the cry was, "string him up." He was put upon the scaffold the second time and hung there with the others until sun down, so everyone could have an opportunity of seeing them, as a warning for the rest of the gang. They were taken down and buried all in one grave.

The food they gave us was corn cobs, all ground up

and made into mush, and there wasn't near enough
of that to keep the boys alive any length of time.
Those that lived had to speculate by trading their
brass buttons, boots, etc., with the guards. There
were from one hundred to one hundred and
fifty boys dying every day. A large wagon, drawn by
four mules, was used in drawing out the dead. They
were laid in as we pile cord wood and taken to the
burying ground, generally putting fifty in a grave, and
returning would bring mush in the same wagon, where
worms that came from the dead could be seen crawling all over it; but we were starving, therefore we
fought for it like hungry hogs.

The squad that I was in was quartered on the north
side of the creek which ran through the prison. The
boys would dig wells in the day time and at night
would dig tunnels and attempt to escape. Very few,
however, ever succeeded, for the "rebs" would set
the blood hounds on the track. The hounds would
tree them and wait for their masters to come to shoot
the poor fellows down, but SOMETIMES would bring
them back unharmed. One day there was a call for a
detail of men to go to the hospital to help take care of
the sick. A friend, by the name of William Smith,
was quartermaster of the hospital. He had been captured a year before and was a comrade of mine out of
Company E, 4th Michigan. By the aid of friend
Smith I was put on the detail list, and was made ward-
master of one of the wards. The first day I was in
there the rebel doctors left prescriptions to give the
sick. I killed seven boys that evening from the effects
of that medicine. I told Smith I couldn't do that

work any longer, and the next day I played off sick so
as to get off duty, and the doctors left me medicine to
take, but I wasn't prepared to die and so did not
take any. I then commenced to make a kind of beer
which is good for dysentery. It was made of corn
meal, molasses and water. I would let it ferment and
sour over night in a barrel, and then deal it out to the
boys, a cupful only to each. This was much better
than the rebels' medicine. It was the means of saving
the lives of a good many boys. I would trade this
beer off for brass buttons and postage stamps and then
would take these and trade with the guards for sweet
potatoes. For doing this, I was taken before Werz,
the captain in command of the prison, and a villain
who would shoot our men down in cold blood. I expected to be dealt with the same, but fortunately some
of my friends (Union men) were clerking for him, and
when he was about to shoot me, after taking an oath,
with his revolver, the boys talked to him and begged
him not to. I was then searched and ordered back to
the hog pen, where I remained for ten long months.

About the middle of April, 1865, there came an
order for an exchange of prisoners. Although my
name was not called for exchange, I stole away, secreted
myself in a box car and was carried through to Vicksburg, Miss., with the others. I think where our exchange took place was at Black river bridge near Vicksburg. We then crossed the pontoon bridge into our
lines and proceeded to get clothing and recruit up.
We remained there about ten days. I met my brother-
in-law, Wm. Finch, here. He had just been exchanged from Cahaba prison in Alabama.

On April 25th, 1865, about 2,000 of us, just released from rebel prisons,were put aboard the ill-fated steamer "Sultana" and started for home. We stopped at Memphis, Tenn., to take in coal and unload 300 hogsheads of sugar. While there I and my brother-in-law took a walk up town to get something good to eat which we had not tasted for many a long day. When we returned we took our blankets and laid down on the hurricane deck next to the wheel house to sleep and dream of our dear ones at home, and believing that in a few more hours we would be in their embrace. I at once fell asleep and did not awake until the boiler blew up, six or seven miles above Memphis. The boat was soon in flames and the screaming and moaning from those that were injured was something terrible. Hundreds of them would jump into the water together, clinch each other and go down in one body. My brother-in-law commenced fretting and crying because he couldn't swim. I could not swim either and begged him not to get discouraged and give up for there was some hope yet of being saved. He started for one of the life boats and I warned him to keep away from them, for those in first were knocking everybody in the head that tried to get in. That was probably where he lost his life. I remained on the boat praying until the fire burned me off. On falling into the river I sank, never expecting to arise again, but by some means I came to the surface again and saw the captain tearing off window shutters and throwing them into the river for the boys.

I now commenced swimming dog-fashion, but my strength soon gave out and I began to strangle. I

yelled for help, and comrade Charles Taber, one whose
life I had saved while in prison, heard and knew my
voice, and swam away from the bale of hay on which
he was floating, caught me by the hair and with the
aid of the other men who were on the bale, pulled me
on top, and thus in turn saving my life. I was chilled
and lost consciousness, and when I came to I asked
if it had been raining for I was wet through. We
hung onto the bale and floated down six or eight miles
below Memphis, where we were picked up by a gunboat that was out for the purpose of rescuing survivors
of the wreck. The Sisters of Charity were there ready
to take care of us. We were then taken to the
hospital in Memphis, where I remained about two
weeks. I can well remember seeing the captain putting life preservers on his wife and little girl and
letting them overboard. The girl's life preserver
slipped too far down for she was found (drowned)
floating with her feet upwards. His wife was saved
and the captain lost his life in trying to save others.
We had a number of mules aboard the boat and some
of the boys hung on to their tails while they swam to
shore. Others would get out by means of planks and
barrels.

This was one of the most terrible steamboat disasters
that history has ever recorded, over 1,500 perishing.
I was taken to "Camp Chase," Ohio, where I received
my discharge, and then started for Hillsdale to meet
my brother and sister. I have left a great deal out
which I would like to have mentioned, but thinking I
am taking more space than is my share in your
book I will close.

Am now living in East Buffalo, N. Y., in live stock commission business, under the firm name of Dunning & Stevens.

———

GEORGE W. STEWART.

I ENLISTED in the service of the United States, on the 6th of January, 1862, as a private in Company D of the 40th Regiment Indiana Veteran Volunteers. Was on duty in the Army of the Cumberland until the battle of Franklin, Tenn., which took place on the 30th day of November, 1864, where I was taken prisoner. I was captured at the time of the charge of the rebels under Gen. Pat. Cleburne, and sent to the rear as a prisoner of war. I had $200 and a silver watch worth $50 taken from me. From the battle field I was taken to Columbus, Tenn., and kept there until the last of December, then marched to Corinth, Miss., from there by rail to Meridian, thence to Selma, Ala., and finally to prison at Cahaba, Ala. In this prison there were about 2,500 prisoners, and we were all on short rations, the customary treatment of prisoners by the Confederate States. I cannot tell the date when I left the prison, but think it was the last of February, 1865. I was with the first detachment that was sent to Vicksburg, Miss., and a hard time we had of it. We did a great deal of forced marching to get there. I never can forgive the quartermaster for not giving us rations on the night we arrived at Black river. He held the rations on one side of the river and us on the other side fourteen hours without anything to eat. We lay in camp until we were placed on board the "Sultana." I had a jolly trip to Memphis. Being the son of a steamboat captain I was at home on the river. At Memphis I was in town till midnight, and was awake when the boat was at the coal yards. At the time of the explosion I was sound asleep on the larboard wheelhouse water-box on the hurricane deck. When I awoke I was standing about ten feet from the box in a thick steam. While there my comrade, George A. Kent, came to me from the roof of the texas and asked me what was up. I told him that the boat had blown up, and if she did not catch on fire we were all right. Just at that moment the fire burst out where the chimneys had stood. I then told him we would have to swim or burn. I urged him to go with me to the texas to see if we could obtain anything to swim upon. We started together and that is the last I saw of him. I got two bed slats and went aft of the wheelhouse on the hurricane deck, and witnessed the drowning of hundreds of men. I saw the stage plank go overboard loaded with men and go under with them. When it arose there were only two or three clinging to it. I kept my post aft of the wheelhouse until the fire forced me to jump.

I at once swam away from the boat and would not let anyone come near me. By the light of the burning wreck I could see timber on the south or east bank, up the stream from me, and I believed that I held my own against the current for over one hour, when I discovered the boat was drifting and I was not going to the timber. I then changed my route and went with the current, and landed on an island three miles above Memphis, just at daylight, and fought mosquitoes until half past ten o'clock when I was taken on board a steamer to Memphis. The next day I went down to the river and met Capt. Carmer and with him to New Albany, thence to see my parents in Kentucky. Was discharged on the 29th of May, 1865, at Indianapolis.

Occupation, farming. Postoffice address, Wellington. Kan.

SAMUEL STUBBERFIELD.

I WAS born in McCane county, Pa., September 9, 1843. When I was about two years of age my parents moved to Ottawa county, Ohio, from there to Williams county, Ohio, and in 1854 I, with my parents, moved to Wright township, in Hillsdale county, Mich., where I lived at the breaking out of the rebellion. I enlisted in the service of the United States on the 26th of July, 1862, in Company F, 18th Michigan Infantry, for three years or during the war unless sooner discharged. I left the State September 4, for Cincinnati, Ohio, where we took up our line of march through Kentucky. Reaching Lexington I spent most of the winter in the hospital and convalescent camp, and about the first of April, 1863, left the State with my regiment for Nashville, Tenn., where I remained about fourteen months. I then left for Decatur, Ala., and was one of the detail that routed the rebels at Pond Spring on the 29th of June, 1864, capturing nine wagons and two ambulances that the rebels had taken from an Indiana regiment some time before this, and also one of their wagons and two of their ambulances. Was also one of the detail that helped to rout the rebels at Courtland, Ala., on the 27th of July, 1864, losing only one man from my company.

On the 24th of September I was in the detachment ordered to reinforce the fort at Athens, Ala. When we got within a mile of the place we were attacked by an overwhelming force of rebels at about six o'clock in the morning and we had to fight our way until twelve o'clock. As we neared the fort that we were to re-inforce we received grape, canister, and shell from the fort, its commander having surrendered it, and our little band with it, without our knowledge, but our small force (four hundred), fought the rebel Gen. Forrest's force six long hours before surrendering, when we were completely surrounded and were finally compelled to give in.

We afterwards took up our line of march for that miserable prison, Cahaba, Ala., at which place we arrived October 6, 1864, and remained there until the 4th of March, 1865. When I left the prison the water was from six inches to four and one-half feet deep all over the entire enclosure, had been so for seven days, and had been six inches deeper. I slept two nights on a sixteen inch wall which was fifteen feet above the water, and some of the boys did their cooking among the braces of the roof. On the date before stated (March 4), I got aboard a steamer and steamed down the Alabama river, up the Tombigbee river as far as navigable, and then by rail to Meridian. From thence we were sent to Jackson, Miss., and from there we marched to Vicksburg, where we went into parole camp March 16, 1865.

On the 25th of April, 1865, was placed on board the steamer "Sultana," which was to carry us homeward to friends and loved ones; but alas, hundreds passed on to the "City of Death" to await mothers, fathers, sisters, brothers and lovers, whom they had expected to meet in a few days, but were destined to pass over the river whence no parting ever comes. We reached Memphis on the 26th of April, and while unloading sugar there the staging parted, one-half turning over catching my right foot and leg to the knee, and bruising my foot badly. It soon swelled as full as the skin could hold and pained me badly. When the explosion took place at two o'clock A. M., April 27, I could not bear any weight on my foot, but was compelled to leave the boat, being forced off by the flames. I picked up a 4x4 scantling, which some one had discarded, and went to the rear part of the boat, jumped off into the river and sank for a moment in that chilling ice-cold water.

On coming to the surface again I struck out in the same direction that most of the others did, but thinking I had not acted wisely I turned around to go in the opposite direction when some one caught hold of my frail bark. Not feeling like parting company with my little craft so soon I clutched it with all my might and eventually succeeded in releasing it. I then struck out in the direction of some trees, reaching the little cottonwoods just at daylight. The little trees were so frail, however, and the water so deep, that my little craft with what trees I could get hold of would not keep me out of the water, and I |was compelled to remain here until about eleven o'clock in the morning of April 27th, when I was picked up by the steamer "Silver Spray" and taken to the hospital at Memphis, Tenn. I remained in the hospital until about the middle of May when I was sent to the Soldiers' Home where I was discharged the service and reached my home on the 19th of May, 1865.

My occupation is farming.

PERRY S. SUMMERVILLE.

I WAS born in Clay county, Ind., on the 4th of March, 1846. Enlisted on the 5th of December, 1861, in Company K, 2nd Indiana Cavalry.

I was captured at Stilesborough, Ga., September 13, 1864, while out with the forage train. When we were attacked by the enemy I jumped from the wagon and fell between the wheels, the hind wheels passed over my right leg, breaking it. I was put on a mule and rode till noon, then I was put in a wagon and hauled two days in it. When we got to Jacksonville, Ala., I was left at the hospital for a few days before sending me on. The man that kept the hospital gave me a fine comb, which was the means of catching at least

fifty thousand inmates of the prison, and his lady gave
me a ten dollar bill. I was then taken to Talladega,
Ala., and placed in a cell about fourteen feet square.
There were about twelve rebels in with me. I was
there a few days and was sent to Selma, Ala., and was
again put in jail, but this time in a larger and cleaner
one. I was kept there a few days when I was sent to
Cahaba. The last of September I was put in the
prison with some Tennesseans. As I entered the
prison the boys hallooed, " Fresh fish," an article I was
standing in need of at that time. I put in a part of
the day taking in my situation and looking for the
old man Brown who was taken prisoner with me.
Night came on and I had no place to lie down only on
the ground and without blankets. The only article I
had in the shape of a bed was my crutches, which I
used for a pillow. The nights were very cold. Next
morning my clothes looked more like pepper and salt
goods than blue. I had amusement for a few hours in
using my thumb nails.

I hadn't been in this prison long before my leg was
so bad that I was taken out to the hospital; but to see
the dead carried out every morning was too much for
me and I went back to the stockade. I made me a
knife out of a piece of hoop iron while out; so Brown
and I were in very good shape as he had a railroad
spike to split wood with and I had a knife to eat mush
with. We were better fixed than the average of the
prisoners. Wood as well as provisions was scarce.
We would split our wood up very fine so to make a
quick fire to make our mush or gruel. Wood being
so scarce I worked up one of my crutches to cook with

before I was able to do without it. I next burned a part of the other one, and one night I failed to lie on my cane and some fellow stole it with which to cook his breakfast. That left me in a bad fix. Our prison was furnished with river water. The water passed through the city in pipes to a hydrant outside the prison where the stock came to drink. The people would wash there and then the water would pass down through the prison for us to drink and cook with, but still it was one of the purest articles we got.

I was standing near a comrade one day who happened to get his foot on the dead line, the guard above shot at his foot, barely missing it, and the ball glanced back striking the roof. I saw a number of men shot and one man killed by having a bayonet run through him. He suffered the most before he died of any man I ever saw. Some time in February the boys undertook to break out. They were successful in capturing the inside guards, but the rebels ran their artillery up to the prison gate and said, "they would rake the prison in five minutes if we didn't lie down." One of the guards reported that he had wounded one of the boys and the next morning the officers ordered us to give up the leaders of the mutiny; that being denied they then called for the wounded man and said if refused they would strip us and have him at all events. Being again refused, they proceeded to examine us, making us strip off naked, pass out through the gangway between two officers with our clothing rolled in a bundle and held on our heads, turn once around and then pass out in plain view of the city. The man was wounded in the hand, so they didn't get him. Their next re-

sort was to starve us. They stopped our meal for three
or four days but found that would not do, and when
we got our meal and beef we did not take time to cook
it, the beef was sour in the bargain.

Some time in March the Alabama river arose and
flooded the city and our prison. The water was from
two to five feet deep all over the prison. They took
out about 700 prisoners and sent them up to Selma,
Ala. The rest remained in the prison. The boys
floated in wood and made bunks to sit on, four or five
sitting on one bunk. The water became so filthy that
we would wade out to the stockade and hold our cups
to catch the clean water as it came through the cracks.
They allowed us to go on the dead line for that purpose. The officers of the prison would come into the
prison in canoes.

The river was still up when I waded out for
exchange. I, with the rest of the prisoners, was taken
by the way of Jackson, Miss., and remained in parole
camp four miles out from Vicksburg for a few weeks,
when we were exchanged and put on the steamer
"Sultana" at Vicksburg. My quarters were on the
cabin deck on the guard on the left hand side over
and opposite the boilers. We arrived at Memphis
early in the evening of April 26th. There she
unloaded a large amount of sugar, after which she
ran up to the coal barge to take on coal, and that was
the last I knew till 1 was in the river. When she
blew up I was thrown at least one hundred feet. The
first thought that struck me was that she was running
close to the shore and that I was dragged off by the
limb of a tree. I was very much excited for a few

minutes and commenced to swim towards the boat
calling for help, but I had not gone far when I saw
there was something the matter on board. I could see
steam and fire and hear the screams of those on board,
so I commenced to swim down stream. I had not
gone far before the boat was all in flames. I managed
to get hold of a rail which proved of much assistance
to me, and I could see by the light from the burning
boat as many as twenty go into the river at once.

As I was passing the islands I could see the timber
on my right and left but I could not make to the
shore. Some two miles above Memphis I got a large
plank which I drew across the end of my rail in front
of me and held the rail with my feet and the plank
with my hands. I lay so near the top of the water
that I was almost freezing, and when taken out of the
water couldn't stand. I was hurt in the breast and
scalded on the back, and spit blood for some time from
the effects of the injury in my breast. Was rescued
at Memphis by a colored man who picked me up in a
canoe and took me to a boat to get warm. After I
had been there a few minutes a young man was
brought in who was so badly scalded that his skin
slipped off from the shoulders to the hands. They
wrapped him up in oil and he walked the floor until a
a few minutes before his death. There was a lady
brought in also who had a husband and some children
on board. She was almost crazy. I don't think she
ever heard of them after that terrible morning.

As I was floating down the river I met a gunboat,
but it didn't stop to pick me up. Also I saw a horse
floating down the stream with six or eight men

45

hanging on to him. When I heard him coming I tried to get to him, but when I saw his load I kept clear for fear some of the boys would get all I had at that time in the world—my rail and plank. There was a man by the name of Jerry Perker, of the 2nd Michigan Cavalry, swimming near me. All knew Jerry, and the boys as far as they could hear him would ask what he thought of our case. He would cheer the boys by telling them to hold out and we would get out. I saw him after we got out. He floated on a barrel. I had on a pair of socks that bothered me more than anything else. They worked partly off my feet and would catch on my rail which caused me to almost sink. My companion's name was Kibbs; what became of him I have never learned. He was cheerful except when talking about his little girl. There were three of us from Brazil, Ind., two were lost, I being the only one of them saved. I was taken to the hospital. After remaining there two or three days we started for "Camp Chase," Ohio, but when we arrived at Indianapolis Gov. Morton, the war governor, stopped us Indiana soldiers.

My postoffice address is Brazil, Ind. My occupation is farming.

WM. THAYER.

I WAS born in Watertown, N. Y., October 25, 1845, and enlisted in the service of the United States at Adrian, Mich., August 7, 1862, in Company C, 18th Regiment Michigan Volunteer Infantry. Was captured at Athens, Ala., September 24, 1864, and confined in the Cahaba, Ala., prison. I was lying in the alley way of the second deck when the boat blew up. I stayed on the boat until I saw two scantlings tied together with a pair of suspenders. I thought they would help me along and they did, for I floated down the river for about six miles and then neared the shore. I climbed a tree and tied myself there with my shirt, and about two o'clock P. M. I was picked up and taken to the hospital at Memphis.

Occupation, farming. Postoffice address, Fairfield, Mich.

MARIAN THOMAS.

I WAS born in Monroe county, June 17, 1832, and enlisted in the service of the United States at Kentucky, February 1, 1863, in Company E, Third Tennessee Cavalry, and was captured at Athens, Ala., on the 23rd of September, 1864, and confined in the Cahaba prison.

After the "Sultana" exploded I was in the water four hours. Was taken on board a gun boat, more dead than alive.

Occupation, farming. Postoffice address, Maryville, Blount county, Tenn.

SAMUEL J. THRASHER.

I WAS born in Hawkins county, East Tenn., on the 19th of November, 1839. Enlisted at Louisville, Ky., February 8, 1863, in Company G, 6th Regiment Kentucky Cavalry Volunteers. Was captured near Tuscaloosa, Ala., March 31, 1865, and confined in a prison at Marion, Ala.

On the evening of the 25th of April, 1865, at Vicksburg, Miss., I was put on board the ill-fated "Sultana," which steamed up the great "Father of Waters," until it reached Memphis, Tenn., where it landed and put off some freight, then went up the river to the coal yard, coaled for Cairo, Ill., and then after proceeding about seven miles the boiler of the boat exploded. This occurred on the 27th of April, 1865, at about half-past two A. M., there being on board at the time 1,966 paroled soldiers, a part of whom were killed by the explosion and others crippled or maimed.

When the steamer caught fire almost every one on board became frightened. The writer could not swim and thought his chance for life was slim, and stood holding to a small rope to keep the men from crowding him overboard. A comrade, Abraham Rhodes, here said if we would not get excited we could save ourselves. After the crowd quit surging so there was no danger of being knocked overboard, we got the cable rope and made it fast in the rings on the bow of the boat and threw it over into the water. We then made a large chain fast in the same way and threw it over. When the heat became so intense we could not stay on the boat any longer we went down into the water, under the bow of the boat, holding to the rope and chain until the cabin burned down. There were several swimming around and when they saw the chain and rope they laid hold of it. After the cabin had burned down, those who had got into the river prepared to swim, having on only shirt and drawers, climbed back on the boat and threw down a rope which we put under our arms and they drew us up to the hull of the burning steamer. After all were back on the hull we went to work and put out the fire, so that it would not sink so quickly.

As we were drifting down the river we struck a grove of saplings. We had made a small raft out of the timbers of the boat and ran out a line, made fast to a sapling and stopped the boat or hull. Some of my unfortunate companions went out to a house that was surrounded by water, got a large hewed log and fastened it to the raft, brought it in and took out as many as twelve at a time by lying flat across the log. The raft made some three or four trips before all were taken off. The writer and one of the 3rd Tennessee Cavalry were the last to leave the boat, and had not been off the hull but a short time when it went down. After a while a picket boat came up and took us back to Memphis where we were cared for in the hospital. From there we went by boat to Cairo, Ill., and then to Louisville, Ky., then to Nashville, where I was mustered out on the 23rd day of July, 1865.

Present postoffice address, Brown's Cross Roads, Ky.

CASWELL C. TIPTON.

I WAS born in the year of our Lord, 1844. Enlisted in the service of the United States on the 21st of September, 1862, at Blount county, Tenn., as a private in Company B, 3rd Regiment Tennessee Cavalry. Was taken a prisoner at the battle of Sulphur Branch Trestle, Ala., on the 25th of September, 1864, and confined in Cahaba prison, Ala.

With others I was brought to Vicksburg, Miss., and sent north on the steamer "Sultana." After the explosion of her boiler I remained on the boat but a short time. In company with six or seven other soldiers I made my escape on a plank that had been used in loading and unloading barrels. We were in the water until about daylight when we were rescued by parties in a small boat opposite Memphis, Tenn. I was afterwards sent to "Camp Chase," Ohio, and from that place to Nashville, Tenn, where I was discharged from the service on the 10th of June, 1865.

My present postoffice address is Trundle's Cross Roads, Sevier county, Tenn.

WILSON S. TRACEY.

I WAS born in Holmes county, Ohio, April 1, 1842, and enlisted in the service of the United States at Wooster, Ohio, August 7, 1862, in Company H, 102d Ohio Volunteer Infantry. Was captured at Athens, Ala., September 14, 1864, and confined in the Cahaba prison.

Occupation farming. Postoffice, Fredericksburg, Wayne county, Ohio.

ROBERT A. TRENT.

I WAS born in the year 1840, and enlisted in the service of the United States at Flatlick, Ky., on the 11th of March, 1862, as 4th Sergeant and Company Clerk of Company B, 1st Regiment Tennessee Cavalry Volunteers. I was captured at Shoal Creek, Ala., while in action, on the 5th day of November, 1864. Was taken to prison at Meridian, Miss., remaining there about two months, thence sent to Cahaba, Ala., where I was detained until about the 1st of April, 1865, and then sent to Vicksburg, Miss.

About the 25th of April, 1865, I was placed on board the steamer "Sultana," my destination being "Camp Chase," Ohio. I, with many others, landed for a short time at Memphis, Tenn., on the evening of the 26th of April. We started up the river about two o'clock in the morning of the 27th, and when we were about nine miles above Memphis the boiler of the boat exploded.

At the time of the explosion I was very weak from

sickness and could scarcely walk across the boat. I
had laid on some plank under the cabin, which was
back of the wheelhouse, and soon fell asleep. I was
struck on the left side of the head with something
which cut a gash about two inches in diameter to the
skull, and I was knocked down on some mules that
were under me. The lights were all out and it was
pitch dark. I saw what was the trouble in an instant.
The people all seemed excited and hundreds of them
were jumping into the river.

I remained on the boat as long as possible, knowing
that it would be sure death for me among the crowd
that was in the water, for they were fighting and
clinging to one another and making all sorts of noise.
When they got out of the the way I jumped into the
water on the Tennessee side of the boat, and swam
about seven miles, when I got hold of some brush.
This is the last that I remember until late in the evening when I awoke and found myself in the hospital
at Memphis where I remained several days unable to
get out, but, by the help of God and kind physicians
I recovered. I am very sorry that I do not know their
names so I can thank them for their kindness
toward me.

I was discharged from the service in May, 1865, at
Nashville, Tenn.

ISAAC VAN NUYS.

I WAS born in Wayne county, Ind., January 8, 1838.
I enlisted in the service of the United States on
the 23rd of April, 1861, at Richmond, Ind., as a

private in Company D, 57th Indiana Veteran Volunteer Infantry, for three years. Re-enlisted as Veteran Volunteer Infantry, January 1, 1864, in the same company and regiment. I was captured at Franklin, Tenn., November 30, 1864, and exchanged April 1, 1865, at Black river, near Vicksburg, Miss. Was confined at Meridian, Miss., most of the time while a prisoner.

After lying in "parole camp" at Vicksburg for a few weeks was sent north on the ill-fated steamer "Sultana," April 25,1865. We, to the number of about 2,300 prisoners, were marched from the camp and loaded on the "Sultana" at Vicksburg. When we were crowded on the vessel, I think it was six times its capacity, we were huddled together like sheep for the slaughter, many as yet suffering from battle wounds and most of them emaciated from starvation in prison pens, as all conversant with Andersonville can testify. Now, however, they were en route for home, the cruel war was over and their cause triumphant. The visions of loved ones greeting their return, and of dear familiar scenes and the quiet peaceful life were again theirs to pursue. All this filled their hearts with joy, making their bearing and conversation a study in human nature, rare even in those stirring days. Memphis was reached on the 26th of April. After coaling the steamer proceeded. So far the presence of danger was not manifested, nor was it in any sense anticipated. That very night, however, at two o'clock A. M., just as we had made eight miles above Memphis, suddenly and without any warning the boiler of the steamer exploded with terriffic force, and in a few minutes the boat burned to the water's edge.

No adequate cause for the explosion has ever been ascertained. The steamer was running at her proper speed (nine or ten miles an hour). No peril seemed imminent and the event remains yet a mystery. The scene that followed the explosion was simply horrible beyond words to depict, but it was of short duration as the glare of the burning steamer that illuminated the sky and made visible the awful despair of the hour soon died away, while darkness, all the more intense, settled down on the floating hulk and the 2,300 victims of the explosion, who, maimed or scalded, in addition to battle wounds, were borne down by the unpitying flood whose rapid current was strewn with the bodies of the dead and the dying and but few, in fact, but what were injured. This casualty transpired in time of intense excitement and never had the attention it ought to have had, following closely as it did the assassination of President Lincoln and the close of the war. Death and destruction had been in the land for four years, and nearly 400,000 had already given up their lives in defense of the national flag, that it might wave over a free country.

I had been in prison and witnessed the awful scenes there and on many a battle field. I thought I had seen all the horrors of war, but this disaster was the most heart-rending of any I had seen in my four years, service. I was on the hurricane deck in rear of the pilot house, asleep, when the explosion occurred. I was so shocked that I couldn't tell what had happened, for a moment, but soon found that the boat had been

blown to pieces in front of the pilot house and those
that could work were fighting the fire to keep the rest
of the vessel from burning, but it was soon given up
to the flames. I couldn't swim, and was trying to
make up my mind whether it would be better to stay
on the boat and burn or to drown in the deep water
below. After reflection I came to the conclusion I
would stand on the deck, and saw by the light of the
burning vessel that the water was full of drowning
men and floating dead bodies.

As the flames commenced bursting around me, however, and began heating me up I changed my mind,
and thought I would try the water as most of them
had gone down. With this resolve I went to the pilot
house and pulling off a loose board put it under my
arm and went to the edge of the deck. Here I found
that the side wheel had burned off and fallen into the
water and some timbers from above had drifted there.
I concluded to make the jump for the water holding
onto my board, and if I failed with it I would have a
chance on the wheel house. I jumped into the river
and went down (it seemed to me a half of a mile in
the water), and when I came to the surface again my
board was gone but I managed to catch on to the
wheel and thu ssaved myself from drowning this time.
I was so close to the burning boat that I had to let
myself down in the water to keep from being burned.
While thus situated I managed to get two pieces of
timber together by tying them with my suspenders
around one end and nailing a board across the other
end with a chunk of wood; all the time lowering

myself into the water every few minutes to keep from
being burned.

When I had completed my little raft I jumped
astride it, pushed off from the burning boat and
floated down the stream. I had a board which served
as an oar to guide my bark after it floated out of
the main current. I landed on the Arkansas side of
the river about five miles from the burning hulk.
Soon after I left the hull burned through and went
down, taking everything in its reach. As I was
among the last that left the boat I saw 1,600 go down
to a watery grave. Most of them made a rush for the
water, some thinking that they could swim, and in
that way attempted their escape, but many of them
would catch on to each other and they went down by
the hundreds. Under all circumstances you will find
men ready to joke and to receive them. As I was floating down the stream I came near a man floating on a
small piece of timber, who said: " Say, Pard, give me
a chew of tobacco, I feel like if I had a chew I could
make to the shore all right." I told him I was going
down to Memphis for a load and would give him some
on my return, but the poor fellow never got home. I
was picked up about eight o'clock A. M. and taken to
the hospital at Memphis for treatment, as I was exhausted and scalded. I remained there about two
weeks and then was sent north to our capital, where I
was furloughed home for a few days to see my loved
ones.

There was a general order from the War Department
to muster out all paroled prisoners and we were soon
called to answer to the last red tape roll call after

almost four years of service. The history of the regiment was our history. We had participated in its hardships, its labors, its duties and its countless privations. In the charge on many a battlefield we had borne our part. This closed our active service and prison-life and we could say that we had performed the duty that we owed to our country.

I was discharged from the service on the 16th day of June, 1865, at Indianapolis, Ind., as captain of my company.

I have for the last three years been unable to follow my trade, and am still unable to do any business.

J. W. VANSCOYVE.

I WAS born in Richland county, Ohio, June 27, 1836. I enlisted in the service of the United States in Company A, 64th Regiment Ohio Volunteer Infantry, at Camp Buckingham, November 30, 1861. I was captured at the battle of Franklin, Tenn., on the 30th of November, 1864, in the rear of Hood's Army. The next day we were searched and robbed of everything of value that was not taken when we were first captured. I had my knapsack, overcoat, two good blankets, and haversack taken from me. We were then marched back to the old fort at Columbia that we had destroyed. We marched from there to Chero-kee Station on the Memphis and Charleston Railroad. From there were shipped to Corinth, Miss., marching through to Meridian, and from there were taken to Andersonville prison.

I was one of the boys that S. H. Raudebaugh bought
out of Andersonville. I was to give a German comrade ten dollars. He was lost on the "Sultana." I
was laying on the cabin deck, which is over the boilers,
asleep at the time of the explosion. Part of the cabin
and deck kitchen were blown off into the river and
Hugh Bratton, Jo. Wagonner and myself and, I think,
Kennedy, were blown into the river. I was stunned
so that I did not realize anything. When I came to
I was under the water. I swam around until I found
a board about four feet long and about one-half foot
wide, and floated down within four hundred yards of
Memphis when I was picked up by some parties in a
skiff. I was scarcely out of the water until I was
entirely helpless, the parties who picked me up said
they never expected I would revive. I had no clothing on except shirt and drawers when rescued. At
the time of the explosion I was jammed in my breast,
which caused me to spit blood for several days. I
was taken to the Gayoso Hospital, where I remained but
a few days and was then sent to "Camp Chase,"
Ohio, to be discharged from the service.

My occupation is that of a real estate agent.

ALONZO A. VAN VLACK.

I WAS born in Reading, Mich., on the 8th of October, 1843. I enlisted in the service of the United States on August 5, 1862, at Woodbridge, in Company F of the 18th Michigan Volunteer Infantry. I was taken prisoner near Athens, Ala., on the 24th of September, 1864, by Gen. Forrest's cavalry, and was sent from Athens to Cahaba prison, where I suffered everything but death. My legs were one raw sore from my knees down to my feet, with scurvy.

In March we left for Vicksburg, Miss., and after remaining there until the 25th of April, 1865, we were placed on board the steamer "Sultana." We were all

happy with the thought of soon seeing our loved ones
at home; but at the dead hour of midnight, when all
or nearly all were soundly sleeping on her broad decks,
one of her boilers exploded. (Nearly 1,700 were lost.)
I was sleeping on the hurricane deck just forward of
the wheelhouse and was knocked senseless by a piece
of the deck falling on me.

After I came to, a terrible sight met my eyes. The
boat was all in flames and the water was covered with
men. My first thought was to get a door out of the
cabin. I looked down into the cabin and there saw
women and children running to and fro and screaming
for help. I shouted to them that they would try and
run the boat on shore but there was so much confusion
that they could not hear me. At last I got a barrel
but soon threw it away as I thought that would be a
poor thing to use in the water. I then slid down on
one of the posts back of the wheel, stood on the
lattice work and took off my clothes except shirt,
drawers and stockings. Then I watched my chance to
jump into the river. When all looked clear I leaped
in and soon came to the surface and struck out for the
Tennessee shore. I saw some drown so close to me
that I could place my hand upon their heads as they
were going down.

While in the water I found a bale of hay with three
or four men hanging on to it. As I made up to them
they fought me off, but I clinched on and rested for a
moment and then left them. I had gone about one-
half of a mile from the boat when I found a small
board (painted white on one side) which helped me to
get to the shore. I got quite near the Tennessee shore

but a strong current set in and took me farther from the shore. I got tangled in some grape vines that were floating in the river and came near sinking. I managed to get out of the vines, then the current carried me nearer the Arkansas shore. I could look back and see that the boat was in flames and see the fire drive those left on board off by the hundreds. When it was getting daylight I struck a snag about ten rods from the timber and flood-wood. I rested a little then swam for the flood-wood. The water came near drawing me under I was so weak. I crawled up on the logs nearly dead. I then looked back and saw men drowning and calling for help.

After daylight steamers came up the river and picked us up. I was taken to the hospital at Memphis, where I was doctored and clothed, and when able to travel was sent with others to "Camp Chase," Ohio. The Michigan men were then sent to Jackson, Mich., and from there we went home on furlough. Was afterwards ordered to Detroit, where I was discharged from the service on the 1st of July, 1865, as a private.

My present occupation is farming. Postoffice address, Cambria, Mich.

ALBERT VARNELL.

I WAS born at Knoxville, Tenn., on the 5th of March, 1839. I enlisted in the service of the United States at Nashville, Tenn., September 25, 1863, as a corporal in Company I, 3rd Regiment Tennessee Cavalry. I was taken prisoner at the battle of Sulphur

47

Branch Trestle, Ala., on the 25th of September, 1864, and taken to Cahaba prison, where I was held as a prisoner for six months and seven days. While here I had to stand in water up to my waist for seven days and nights. From here we were taken to Big Black river where we were exchanged. I remained some time at this place.

I boarded the "Sultana" at Vicksburg, Miss., with about 2,350 other soldiers who were on their way to Cairo, Ill. The boat blew up about eight miles above Memphis, Tenn. The boiler burst about three o'clock in the morning of the 27th of April, 1865. The scene was horrible to look upon. I was slumbering on the deck when a terrible shock awoke me and I found myself in the hull of the boat. I then crawled out and saw such great excitement that it seemed to me there was no hope of escape for me, but I made up my mind to save myself if I could. I then got hold of a piece of plank and looked for some chance to get through the drowning mass. At length I saw the way open and struck out for the Arkansas shore. I swam something near seven miles before I could find timber of any kind on which I might rest. Finally I found a log about a mile above Memphis and crawling upon it remained there until daylight, when I was taken off by a boat to the Soldiers' Home at Memphis. While there I was unconscious two or three days, and when I came to myself I found that the left side of my face was scalded so as to put out my eye, or nearly so. From here I was taken to "Camp Chase," Ohio, and thence to Nashville, Tenn., where I was discharged from the service of the United States.

LOSS OF THE SULTANA.

G. W. WATTS.

I WAS born in Coshocton county, Ohio, July 19, 1841, and enlisted in the service of the United States at Adamsville, on the 5th of August, 1862, in Company E., 97th Ohio Volunteer Infantry. Was captured at Franklin, Tenn., November 30, 1864, and confined in the Selma, Ala., and Andersonville prisons.

When the explosion occurred I was blown into the water and got hold of a bale of hay and floated down the river. I was in the water a long time, and was finally picked up by a gunboat. Occupation, blacksmith. Reside in Muskingum county, Ohio.

WILLIAM WENDT.

I WAS born in Prussia, Germany, March 11, 1844, and enlisted in the service of the United States, at Romeo, Mich., May 25, 1863, in Company L, 8th Regiment Michigan Cavalry, and was captured at Knoxville, Tenn., November 15, 1863, and confined in the Pemberton Hospital and Libby, Andersonville, Millen and Blackshear, Ga., prisons.

At the time of the explosion I was on the hurricane deck, next to the stairway leading up from the cabin deck. There was just room for four of us. There were John P. Day, Company L, 8th Regiment Michigan Cavalry, Geo. Meade, 21st Regiment Michigan Infantry, John Kiney, 8th Regiment Michigan Cavalry, and myself. I was awakened on the 27th of April, 1865, by the water splashing over my head. Thinking

that the boys were throwing water, I jumped up to see
who it was, when I heard the cry of fire. Then I spoke
to my mates and told them to get up for the boat was
on fire, at the same time getting my clothes ready, still
being half asleep. John Kiney got up and stepped
backwards and fell into the river, Geo. Meade did like-
wise, and I have never seen them since. I did not
see John P. Day until we met in Memphis, after we
were picked up. When I got wide awake, the boat
was burning quite fast. I took in the situation at once.
I was not able to swim. I started to go down to the
cabin deck, but the stairs were gone, so I walked down
on the wreckage towards the water's edge. There were
some that had pieces of the deck and I tried to get on
with them, but they were already crowded; I got a blind
from one of the cabin doors and went back. It seemed
to me as though the boat was lying on its side. Just
as I was going to let myself into the water I came in
contact with something that seemed to be a scantling,
and for fear the blind would be insufficient to hold me
up, I took that also. Now came the difficulty to get
out of the crowd, for it was very densely crowded on
that side of the boat. I had no sooner got onto my
blind than some one jumped onto my back, taking me
down under the water and losing my hat, but I stuck to
the blind and scantling; finally got out of the crowd
and drifted down with the current, for it was very
strong. I had not been drifting long when I saw a
light from a boat that was going down the river. Some
of the boys were hailing it. I don't know whether
any of them got on or not. I kept floating on down
the stream until I came in contact with some limbs of

trees. I grasped one of them and it happened to be
very lucky for me, for the water was deep there and
my blind and scantling shot away from me. It was
just beginning to get light and I began to look around
me. Many of the boys had landed here, some on drift
wood, some on trees, and some on a little log hut close
by me. About ten o'clock A. M. a steamer came up
the river and picked us up. I was so benumbed that
it rendered me helpless for awhile. They took me on
board and carried me back to a hospital in Memphis.

Occupation farming. Postoffice address, Capac,
Mich.

M. C. WHITE.

I WAS born in Cattaraugus county, N. Y., August 8,
1846. I enlisted in the service of the United
States in Company B, 8th Michigan Cavalry, Dec 2,
1862, at Quincy, Branch county, Mich., and served
until the close of the war as a private. I was sixteen
years of age when I enlisted. I served in the East
Tennessee campaign under Gen. Burnside, was wounded
November 18, 1863, at the siege of Knoxville.

Was with Gen. Sherman on the Atlanta campaign
until September when we were ordered to Nicholas-
ville, Ky., to recruit and get remounted. In October we were ordered to Nashville, Tenn. My regiment was in the advance and met Hood in his advance
on Nashville. I was taken prisoner by Forrest's Cavalry November 24, 1864, near Mount Pleasant, Tenn.,
and was confined in a stone fort at Columbia, Tenn.,

for two or three weeks until Hood commenced his retreat, when we were taken south. We landed at Meridian, Miss., on Christmas day, and remained there a few days when we were sent to Cahaba, Ala., and confined in Castle Morgan until March, when we were paroled and sent to Vicksburg, Miss. I was with the last squad that left Cahaba prison and reached Vicksburg March 24, 1865.

I remained at Vicksburg in the parole camp until I took passage on the ill-fated steamer "Sultana." When her boilers exploded I was asleep on the hurricane deck, aft of the wheel-house, on the Arkansas side, and was not injured by the explosion. I thought at first a rebel battery had fired on us and that a shell had exploded on board. I heard the officers give orders that we should remain quiet for the boat was going ashore, but I soon saw that it was every man for himself. I dressed and went below. The scenes were heart-rending. The wounded and dying were begging for help, some were praying, others were taking God's name in vain, while those in the water would catch hold of one another and go down in squads. The fire was getting so hot that I saw I must soon be making my escape into the water. I was quite expert in the art of swimming and thought if I could get away from the crowd I might save myself, although I was quite weak through having been sick a great deal of the time while in prison.

As I stopped to take a hurried glance around me I heard some one near me exclaim, "For God's sake some one help me get this man out." I turned and saw a lieutenant of a Kentucky regiment. He was a

very large man and was called "Big Kentuck." He
had found a man that was held fast by both feet, a
large piece of the wreck having fallen across them. I
took hold and helped the lieutenant but we could not
release him and he was soon roasted by the intense
heat. I then went to the edge of the boat, removed
my shoes and pulled my cap down, and then gave a
plunge into the water with my clothes on as they
would keep me warmer. I was very fortunate in
making my escape through the crowd without any one
catching hold of me and also in finding a plank, but I
did not go far with it when a comrade grabbed it
away from me. He was about half drowned and
apparently crazy. The plank would have answered
for us both if he had remained at one end. I tried
to reason with him, but on hearing my voice he would
keep coming for me, grabbing and yelling. He got
almost within reach of me and I was afraid to have
him get hold of my clothes for fear he would drown
us both, so I left him with the plank and struck out
without any support. It was very dark and all I could
see was the burning steamer. I could not tell which
way to make for land so I just floated on the water
and let the current take me.

When it came daylight I was going around a bend
in the river and the current carried me towards the
shore. I could see trees but no land, as the water had
risen very high and overflowed its banks. I thought
my only chance was to get to those trees. I was very
cold and nearly exhausted. When I got there the first
tree I came to the water was up to the branches. I
threw my arms over a limb and had just strength

enough to hang on to it. It was some time before I could climb up out of the water. I found that I had gone down the river six miles and landed on the Arkansas side. As it grew light I could see comrades all around me, some in trees, some in drift-wood and most all were destitute of any clothing, and to make it still worse the gnats were so thick that they nearly ate us up. Then I was glad that I kept on my clothes, for a good many chilled to death after getting out of the water before they were picked up by any of the boats. I was picked up by the steamer "Silver Spray," after remaining in the tree about three hours. We were treated kindly on the boat, bed clothing being taken from the state rooms and given to the boys to wrap around them. We soon landed at Memphis, at which place the excitement was intense, and it seemed to me as if every one in the city was down to the wharf and nearly every hack, in charge of a soldier, backed down to the wharf-boat ready to take us to the hospital as fast as we were landed.

As we stepped from the gang plank into the wharf-boat the first to greet us were the Sisters of Charity (women of the Christian Commission). God bless them! They handed each of us a red woolen shirt and drawers, and as fast as we donned our red suits we stepped into a carriage and were driven rapidly to the hospital, where all was done for us that could be to make us comfortable.

After remaining in Memphis a short time I was taken to "Camp Chase," Ohio, where I remained about two weeks. From there I went to Jackson, Mich., where I received a furlough and went home on the 9th of June, 1865. I reported at Detroit and received an honorable discharge.

There were four of us that slept together on the boat that night: Henry Narton, Charles Seabury, Truman Smith, and myself, all of my company. We all escaped but Narton (poor boy). He was lost. He had been my companion and bunkmate all through our service for the United States and I felt his loss next to that of a brother.

My occupation is farming.

NATHAN S. WILLIAMS.

I ENLISTED in the service of the United States in the State of Indiana, in Company B of the 5th Indiana Cavalry (the 90th Regiment).

I was captured near Macon, Ga., the 31st of July, 1864, together with about 500 of the command. We were taken to Andersonville prison. We arrived there on the 2nd day of August, 1864, and remained there until the spring of 1865, when I was sent to Vicksburg, Miss.

I remained at Vicksburg until sent on board the steamer "Sultana," April 25, 1865. We started up the river and got along without any trouble as far as Memphis, Tenn. There we went ashore for a few hours and got some refreshments. At the ringing of the bell we all went on board the boat again. The boat moved up the river a short distance to some coal barges so as to take on some coal. At this place I laid down and soon fell asleep and did not [awake

until the explosion took place. I received no injuries from the explosion although the upper deck fell
upon me. I got out from under it safe.

I went forward and caught hold of one of the ropes
which was fastened to the bow of the boat; there I beheld a sight that I never want to be a witness of again.
Men were scalded and burned, some with legs
and arms off, and it seemed as if some were coming
out of the fire and from under the boiler, and many
of them jumping into the river and drowning by
squads. I helped throw out the large stage plank and
intended to get on it myself, but so many men jumped
on it I saw that it would not do for me to jump off
then. I helped throw off everything that was loose,
letting the men go as fast as they wanted to, for many
would not listen to reason.

In a short time the way was made clear. All the
fear I had was that some drowning man would grab me
and drown us both, and also the danger of my limbs
cramping and letting me down. But it was not long
until I knew I must go, for the fire was getting headway and the boat was swinging around which would
bring the heat from the fire near me. I succeeded in
getting a plank eight feet long and eight inches wide.
I held it a short time thinking what was best to do. I
soon made up my mind that I could swim better with
my clothes off, so off they came. Then I threw the
plank into the water and jumped in after it and
struck out for what I thought was the timber on the
Tennessee shore, but the current took me down faster
than I could go up stream, and what I had thought
was the main land was the island. The main land

looked so far off when I looked back, and from the
light of the burning boat I could see land nearer on
the opposite shore, so I turned and took down stream
never trying to swim fast only when I would get near
some men who would try to get my plank.   When
these men would come near me I would tell them that
two could not be saved on a plank the size of the one
I had and for them to keep the one they had and follow me and we would get out safely; but no one got
out where I did, some landing above and some below.

I reached the shore about daylight but could not
wade, the water being over my head at that place, but
I found a log as I was swimming among the timbers
that was fastened to a stump. I crawled up on it and
sat there rubbing myself until I was dry and warmer
and had got the blood to circulate more rapidly.   At
sunrise a man came to me in a small dugout or canoe
and took me to a steamboat that was picking up men
below and some that were in the river.   Those on the
boat were very kind to me, assisting me onto the boat
and giving me a place near the fire and a long tailed coat
to put on. The boat soon rounded and we came to
the wharf at Memphis. The sight there was most terrible. The bodies of the dying, wounded and scalded
were to be seen on every hand. A lady gave me a shirt
and a pair of drawers.   After I put them on my
strength was exhausted and I was carried to an ambulance and taken to the Soldiers' Home. Resting there
a short time, and getting some coffee to drink, I got up
and went down stairs and wrote a letter home. I then
started out in the street for the hospital to see how
many of my company I could find. (I must have made

a fine show with nothing on but a shirt and drawers, bare headed and bare footed.)   I did not go very far in this manner before a clothier called me in and gave me a fair suit of clothes.   I then went on but did not find many of my company; most of them were lost in the deep waters of the Mississippi or had been consumed by the flames.

As I have before said I received no injuries from the explosion, but resting so long on the plank caused a double hernia, thus making it necessary that I should wear a double truss.   I have been trying since 1881 to get a pension for this and other troubles but as yet have not succeeded.

WILLIAM H. WILLIAMS.

I WAS born in Moscow, Mich., December 4, 1842, and enlisted in the service of the United States at Moscow, August 15, 1862, in Company F, 18th Regiment Michigan Volunteer Infantry.   Was captured at Athens, Ala., September 24, 1864, hustled across the country to Cherokee Station, there put on board some cattle cars and taken to Corinth, Miss.   From there was taken to Meridian, thence to Selma, Ala., and then down the river to Cahaba.   Was kept there until about the 10th of April on corn meal, ground cob and all.   We were robbed of everything we had that was good for anything.   From Cahaba we were taken to Meridian and from there to Jackson, Miss., and so on through Big Black river, in the rear of Vicksburg.

I think it was about the 25th of April, 1865, that we

crowded aboard the ill-fated "Sultana" and started up the river for "home, sweet home," but through some carelessness or devilishness many poor comrades were destined never to see their homes On the 28th (27th) the boat exploded one of her boilers, caught fire and about 1,800 poor souls were launched into eternity and many a comrade's hopes were blasted. I for one was lucky and landed in the top of a cottonwood tree. At daybreak some "Johnnies" came and got me in a dugout, took me to the Arkansas side and cared for me the best they could.

My present occupation is buggy-dealer; postoffice, Jonesville, Mich.

GEORGE N. YOUNG.

I WAS born at Columbus, Ohio, February 12, 1844, and enlisted in the service of the United States at that place August 2, 1862, in Company A, 95th Regiment Ohio Volunteer Infantry, and was captured at Guntown, Miss., June 10, 1864. I was confined in the prisons at Andersonville, Macon, Millen, Savannah, in the swamp at Blackshear, and Thomasville. I was on board the "Sultana," but as I have already written my experience in a book published by Dr. J. Howes I do not wish to give it again.

My present occupation is a merchant and my post-office address, Evans, Col.

J. P. ZAIZER.

I WAS born in Limaville, Stark county, Ohio, October 30, 1843, and enlisted in the service of the United States at my native place, August 12, 1862, in Company F, 115th Ohio Volunteer Infantry. Was captured at Block House No. 1, North Carolina Railroad, December 6, 1864, and confined in the Andersonville prison.

At the time of the explosion I was lying asleep on the upper deck, close to the bell. The smoke-stack fell across it and split and one-half of it fell over, thereby killing Sergt. Smith, who laid by me. I jumped overboard and swam ashore.

Occupation, contractor and builder; postoffice, Canton, Ohio.

OFFICIAL LIST OF EXCHANGED PRISONERS ON THE BOAT.

McCutcheon, W., private .... company C, 2d Indiana cavalry
Phillips, Wm., private .... company C, 2d Indiana cavalry
Young, J., private .... company C, 2d Indiana cavalry
Hardin, L. D., private ....company D, 2d Indiana cavalry
Lidd, L. D., private....................... company D, 2d Indiana cavalry
Stevens, W., private .... company D, 2d Indiana cavalry
Brown, J.. private .... company G, 2d Indiana cavalry
Summerville, P. S., private ....company K, 2d Indiana cavalry
Dillander, J., private................... ..company C, 3d Indiana cavalry
Keorney, M., private..................... company C, 3d Indiana cavalry
Congers, Wm., private.................. company D, 3d Indiana cavalry
Noorier, J., private...................... company F, 3d Indiana cavalry
Raina, Wm., private..................... company C, 4th Indiana cavalry
Simpkins, C. E., private............... company C, 4th Indiana cavalry
Franklin, B., sergeant................. company F, 4th Indiana cavalry
Trumball, A., sergeant................ company F, 4th Indiana cavalry
Evermore, N. D., private...... ....company F, 4th Indiana cavalry
Grubbs, Isaac, private.................. company A, 5th Indiana cavalry
Williams, N. S., private................. company B, 5th Indiana cavalry
Dean, J. D., sergeant.................... company C, 5th Indiana cavalry
Milott, R. A., corporal.. ....company D, 5th Indiana cavalry
Thevin, A., corporal .... company E, 5th Indiana cavalry
McCullough, S A., private............ company H, 5th Indiana cavalry
Evans, D. W., private... ....company L, 5th Indiana cavalry
McBride, G., private...................... company L, 5th Indiana cavalry
Mullen, J., private....................... company L, 5th Indiana cavalry
Richardson, A., private................ company L, 5th Indiana cavalry
Scott, L., private......................... company L, 5th Indiana cavalry
Applegate, J. S , private............... company C, 6th Indiana cavalry
Porterfield, W., private .... company C, 6th Indiana cavalry
O'Brien, P., private...................... company D, 6th Indiana cavalry
Scole, R., private.......................... company D, 6th Indiana cavalry
Lee, E. C., private...................... company E, 6th Indiana cavalry
Hobi, A. P., sergeant................... company F, 6th Indiana cavalry
Shal, F., private........................... company G, 6th Indiana cavalry

NOTE.—There may be some errors in the spelling of a few names, but these are according to the official record. The same is true with regard to company and regiment.

Davis, J. W., private....................company I, 6th Indiana cavalry
Roon, J., private.......................company K, 6th Indiana cavalry
Clearly, C. D., sergeant................company L, 6th Indiana cavalry
Gathman, J. H., private.................company C, 7th Indiana cavalry
Hall, J. F., private....................company C, 7th Indiana cavalry
Nemier, Jas., private...................company C, 7th Indiana cavalry
Rowe, D. B., private....................company C, 7th Indiana cavalry
Sholey, P., private.....................company C, 7th Indiana cavalry
Farrell, Jno., private..................company D, 7th Indiana cavalry
Frederick, G., private..................company D, 7th Indiana cavalry
Ames, S. P., private....................company E, 7th Indiana cavalry
Brocklon, J., private...................company E, 7th Indiana cavalry
Dany, B., private.......................company E, 7th Indiana cavalry
Hachsell, J. L., private................company E, 7th Indiana cavalry
Porter, C., private.....................company E, 7th Indiana cavalry
Corlin, W. S., private..................company G, 7th Indiana cavalry
Nichols, C., private....................company G, 7th Indiana cavalry
Armstroug, B. B., private...............company I, 7th Indiana cavalry
Barrack, W., private....................company I, 7th Indiana cavalry
Swords, E., private.....................company I, 7th Indiana cavalry
Elkin, F. M., private...................company K, 7th Indiana cavalry
Gard, W., private.......................company K, 7th Indiana cavalry
Scott, private..........................company K, 7th Indiana cavalry
Smith, J., private......................company K, 7th Indiana cavalry
Johnson, H., private....................company M, 7th Indiana cavalry
McKann, A., private.....................company M, 7th Indiana cavalry
Thompson, private.......................company M, 7th Indiana cavalry
Berry, W................................company B, 8th Indiana cavalry
Markabee, W., private...................company B, 8th Indiana cavalry
Millhen, E., private....................company C, 8th Indiana cavalry
Stiles, J. W., corporal.................company F, 8th Indiana cavalry
Fry, A., private........................company F, 8th Indiana cavalry
Talbrook, R., private...................company H, 8th Indiana cavalry
Madduy, private.........................company H, 8th Indiana cavalry
Demise, Thos., private..................company I, 8th Indiana cavalry
Smith, C., private......................company M, 8th Indiana cavalry
Curtis, Daniel, sergeant................company A, 9th Indiana cavalry
Spades, Jacob, sergeant.................company A, 9th Indiana cavalry
Day, E. R., corporal....................company A, 9th Indiana cavalry
Day, Pat, private.......................company A, 9th Indiana cavalry
Evans, Chas., private...................company A, 9th Indiana
Paul, A. H., private....................company A, 9th Indiana
Riley, Wm., private.....................company A, 9th Indiana
Talkington, Robt., private..............company A, 9th Indiana
Blessing, F., corporal..................company B, 9th Indiana
Mooney, Jno., private...................company B, 9th Indiana
Parmer, E. B., private..................company B, 9th Indiana
Reed, W. P., private....................company B, 9th Indiana

Sears, C. H., private------------------company B, 9th Indiana
Scott, Robt., private------ ------------company B, 9th Indiana
Stewart, Jno., private-----------------company B, 9th Indiana
Waller, P. J., private-----------------company B, 9th Indiana
Warner, W. C., private----------------company B, 9th Indiana
Hawkins, A. W., corporal--------------company C, 9th Indiana
Kammer, Thos., private----------------company C, 9th Indiana
Collins, W. J., corporal---------------company D, 9th Indiana
Church, C. C., private----------------company E, 9th Indiana
Gilberth, Robt., private---------------company E, 9th Indiana
Lasboytox, T., private----------------company E, 9th Indiana
McCormack, A., private---------------company E, 9th Indiana
Wood, E., private---------------------company E, 9th Indiana
Penson, Anderson, private-------------company F, 9th Indiana
Graves, W. H., sergeant---------------company G, 9th Indiana
Rodfinch, N. Z., sergeant-------------company G, 9th Indiana
Abbison, H., corporal-----------------company G, 9th Indiana
Nation, E. K., corporal---------------company G, 9th Indiana
Peacock, W. H., corporal--------------company G, 9th Indiana
Allom, J. C., private-----------------company G, 9th Indiana
Clivinger, C. W., private-------------company G, 9th Indiana
Downing, Geo., * private--------------company G, 9th Indiana
Hoober, M. C., private----------------company G, 9th Indiana
Hooman, W. H., private---------------company G, 9th Indiana
Johnson, L., private------------------company G, 9th Indiana
King, C., * private-------------------company G, 9th Indiana
Maynard, J. M., private--------------company G, 9th Indiana
Reasoner, J. R., private--------------company G, 9th Indiana
Swain, E. H., lieutenant--------------company G, 9th Indiana
Thornbury, N., lieutenant------------company G, 9th Indiana
Marity, W. J., sergeant---------------company H, 9th Indiana
Ballenger, F., private----------------company H, 9th Indiana
Bell, Jas., private--------------------company H, 9th Indiana
Blake, Geo. W., private--------------company H, 9th Indiana
Block, Wm., private------------------company H, 9th Indiana
Brown, Wm., private------------------company H, 9th Indiana
Chana, W. H., private----------------company H, 9th Indiana
Delano, G. W., private---------------company H, 9th Indiana
Dunham, A., private------------------company H, 9th Indiana
McGinnis, S. S., private--------------company H, 9th Indiana
Harden, W. H., private---------------company H, 9th Indiana
Pratt, J., private---------------------company H, 9th Indiana
Shul, Jno., private-------------------company H, 9th Indiana
Stoops, H., private-------------------company H, 9th Indiana
Hawthorn, D. F., sergeant------------company I, 9th Indiana
Foldermar, B., corporal---------------company K, 9th Indiana
Bailey, H., private-------------------company K, 9th Indiana

* Lost.

49

Emmons, J. W., private...............company K, 9th Indiana
Fisher, G. S., private.................company K, 9th Indiana
Gaston, S. M., private................company K, 9th Indiana
Green, Seth J., private...............company K, 9th Indiana
Heard, J., private....................company K, 9th Indiana
Laughton, T. P., private..............company K, 9th Indiana
Lewis, Jno. B., private.... ....company K, 9th Indiana
Masler, P., private...................company K, 9th Indiana
Newton, H. O., private................company K, 9th Indiana
Rea, W. T., private...................company K, 9th Indiana
Sawant, J., private...................company K, 9th Indiana
Shenler, T. D., private...............company K, 9th Indiana
Shockly, G. H., private...............company K, 9th Indiana
Stevens, D., private..................company K, 9th Indiana
Stocker, Jas., private................company K, 9th Indiana
Winterhost, J., private...............company K, 9th Indiana
Zix, M., private......................company K, 9th Indiana
Boner, Jno., sergeant.................company L, 9th Indiana
Woorhouse, R. A., sergeant............company L, 9th Indiana
Grevell, N. E., corporal..............company L, 9th Indiana
Alexander, J. D., private.............company L, 9th Indiana
McCartney, L., private................company L, 9th Indiana
Christian, J. L., private.............company L, 9th Indiana
Doggy, G. W., private.................company L, 9th Indiana
Isentredge, J. M., private............company L, 9th Indiana
Johnston, J. F., private..............company L, 9th Indiana
Johnston, W. F., private..............company L, 9th Indiana
Kelly, S., private....................company L, 9th Indiana
Miller, Elias, private.............. .company L, 9th Indiana
Molway, C., private...................company L, 9th Indiana
Ring, S., private.....................company L, 9th Indiana
Smith, L., private....................company L, 9th Indiana
Spacy, O. F., private.................company L, 9th Indiana
Windser, W. H., private...............company L, 9th Indiana
Gaskill, David, sergeant..............company M, 9th Indiana
Armstrong, J., corporal...............company M, 9th Indiana
Bragg, W., corporal...................company M, 9th Indiana
Hoffman, W. H,, private...............company M, 9th Indiana
Ridley, F., private...................company M, 9th Indiana
Watson, J., private...................company M, 9th Indiana
Baker, O., private....................company M, 9th Indiana
Jolly, B. B., sergeant major..........10th Indiana cavalry
Crawford, E. T., hospital steward......10th Indiana cavalry
Dixon, W. F., lieutenant..............company A, 10th Indiana cavalry
Bedman, J., corporal..................company A, 10th Indiana cavalry
Barlow, J., private...................company A, 10th Indiana cavalry
Reives, Thos. B., lieutenant..........company C. 10th Indiana cavalry
Smith, W. B., corporal................company C, 10th Indiana cavalry

Farrell, M., sergeant.................company D, 10th Indiana cavalry
Graham, J., private..................company G, 10th Indiana
McKenzie, J., private...............company G, 10th Indiana
McLelland, J., private..............company G, 10th Indiana
Kelly, G. W., private..................company H, 10th Indiana
Sanford, G. W., private..............company H, 10th Indiana
Bindle, R., private............. ....company H, 10th Indiana
Twigg, A. G., lieutenant.............company K, 10th Indiana cavalry
Mills, C. W., sergeant..................company K, 10th Indiana cavalry
Jones, J. T., private....................company K, 10th Indiana cavalry
Gaffney, M., captain.................company L, 10th Indiana cavalry
Crawler, Jacob, private..............company L, 10th Indiana cavalry
Long, Henry M., private..............company E, 11th Indiana
Morgan, F., private...................company F, 11th Indiana
Keeler, L. L., sergeant...............company H, 11th Indiana
Clansville, G., private................company F, 12th Indiana
Kline, Henry, private................company G, 12th Indiana
Mitchell, J., private...................company A, 13th Indiana cavalry
Sutton, W., private....................company A, 13th Indiana cavalry
Baker, M. T., * private...............company B, 13th Indiana cavalry
Brother, H., private...................company G, 13th Indiana cavalry
Holmes, W., private..................company G, 13th Indiana cavalry
Owens, M. J., sergeant..............company I, 13th Indiana cavalry
Whitesoll, J., private.................company K, 13th Indiana cavalry
Johnson, T. B., private..............company D, 13th Indiana cavalry
Lahue, C. J., private.................company D, 13th Indiana cavalry
Wadford, W., private................company M, 13th Indiana cavalry
Lewis, Wm , private..................company E, 16th Indiana
Thahbonger, J. W., private..........company A, 17th Indiana
Stockman, B., private................company G, 17th Indiana
Evens, G., private....................company G, 17th Indiana
Sampson, B. H., corporal............company I, 17th Indiana
Fantinger, J. H., private..............company I, 17th Indiana
Caup, M. V., private..................company H, 20th Indiana
Ashley, Y. K.............................20th Indiana
Patrick, M., private...................company H, 22d Indiana
Smith, E. J., private..................company D, 23d Indiana
Conner, Wm., private................24th Indiana
Vesser, Sam., private.................company K, 26th Indiana
Hershe, W. B., private...............company A, 29th Indiana
Brown, J., sergeant...................company C, 29th Indiana
Aldfant, S. M., private...............company D, 30th Indiana infantry
Morris, S., private....................company D, 30th Indiana infantry
Dawson, G. W., private.............company G, 30th Indiana infantry
Beard, O. S., private.................company I, 31st Indiana infantry
Huber, E., private....................company A, 32d Indiana infantry
Shoemaker, P., private..............company B, 32d Indiana infantry

* Killed.

Shemire, L., private .... company K, 32d Indiana infantry
Rass, C. P., private .... company A, 34th Indiana infantry
Tanam, M. O., sergeant .... company B, 35th Indiana infantry
Linch, Thos., private .... company B, 35th Indiana infantry
Donald, E. O., private .... company D, 35th Indiana infantry
Mulvany, P., private .... company D, 35th Indiana infantry
Crum, A. H., private .... company G, 35th Indiana infantry
McQuire, M., private .... company G, 35th Indiana infantry
Martin, J., corporal .... company K, 35th Indiana infantry
Beal, W., private .... company B, 36th Indiana infantry
Janey, J. R., private .... company B, 36th Indiana infantry
Pike, L., sergeant .... company G, 37th Indiana infantry
Taylor, S. A., corporal .... company G, 37th Indiana infantry
Cleveland, N., private .... company A, 38th Indiana infantry
Kelum, Martin, private .... company D, 38th Indiana infantry
Nash, Thos., private .... company H, 38th Indiana infantry
Slatting, J. W. H., private .... company H, 38th Indiana infantry
Monsort, R., corporal .... company A, 40th Indiana infantry
Thorn, T. J., private .... company A, 40th Indiana infantry
Howard, Jno., * private .... company C, 40th Indiana infantry
Westh, Jno., private .... company C, 40th Indiana infantry
Kent, G. A., sergeant .... company D, 40th Indiana
Nisley, C. M., sergeant .... company D, 40th Indiana
Coleman, W. L., private .... company D, 40th Indiana
Guear, Stephen, private .... company F, 40th Indiana
Hiner, S. C., corporal .... company G, 40th Indiana
Carr, J. M., private .... company G, 40th Indiana
May, Chas., † private .... company G, 40th Indiana
Thompson, Jno., † private .... company G, 40th Indiana
Cook, W. A., private .... company H, 40th Indiana
Jackson, Jas. H., private .... company H, 40th Indiana
Meyer, J., private .... company H, 40th Indiana
Ellenberger, J. M., private .... company I, 40th Indiana
Sloan, D. W., private .... company I, 40th Indiana
Hall, H., private .... company K, 40th Indiana
Haspilk, H. L., private .... company K, 40th Indiana
Smith, J., corporal .... company A, 42d Indiana
McFarland, W., private .... company A, 42d Indiana
Crabs, J., private .... company C, 47th Indiana
Goers, W., private .... company C, 47th Indiana
Marim, Wm., private .... company C, 47th Indiana
Stendevant, T., private .... company D, 53d Indiana
Versey, J., private .... company D, 53d Indiana
Fletcher, J. M., corporal .... company A, 57th Indiana
Yekk, J. A., private .... company B, 57th Indiana
Bealer, G. W., private .... company C, 57th Indiana
Lamb, M., private .... company C. 57th Indiana

* Killed.   † Lost.

May, J. T., private................company C, 57th Indiana
Newbern, E., private................company C, 57th Indiana
Smith, A., private................company C, 57th Indiana
Kibbee, J. H., private................company D, 57th Indiana
Van Magg, I., private................company D, 57th Indiana
Ginn, J. J., private................company F, 57th Indiana
Morrell, O. O., private................company H, 57th Indiana
Smith, F. J., private................company H, 57th Indiana
Hackinsberg, A., private................company I, 57th Indiana
Norris, Daniel, private................company I, 57th Indiana
Gardner, J. W., private................company B, infantry
Dickey, J. K., private................company K, infantry
Mulligan, T. W., sergeant................company G, 72d Indiana
Elliott, D, private................company E, 75th Indiana
Medsher, private................company A, 79th Indiana
Winkless, S., private................company B, 79th Indiana
Chapel, Isaac, private................company C, 79th Indiana
West, E., private................company E, 79th Indiana
Dixon, G., private................company C, 80th Indiana
Hashawe, A, private................company C, 80th Indiana
Rawley, Jno., private................company C, 80th Indiana
Reynolds, M., private................company C, 80th Indiana
Runkle, M., private................company C, 80th Indiana
Summerson, L. V., private................company C, 80th Indiana
Naler, T. H,, private................company K, 84th Indiana
Hogrlin, Jas., sergeant................company C, 84th Indiana
Lawrence, H. K., corporal................company H, 88th Indiana
Phince, corporal................company A, 89th Indiana
Habbler, H., private................company G, 91st Indiana
Williard, C., private................company E, 92d Indiana
Lindy, Sam., private................company A, 93d Indiana
Peterson, Mat., private................company A, 93d Indiana
Penster, J., corporal................company B, 93d Indiana
Franklin, M. S., private................company C, 93d Indiana infantry
Garnett, J., private................company C, 93d Indiana infantry
Pettrits, D., private................company C, 93d Indiana
Grove, Jas., private................company D, 93d Indiana
Buchanan, Wm., private................company D, 93d Indiana
McGinnis, Jno., private................company E, 93d Indiana
Stockdale, L., private................company E, 93d Indiana infantry
Alton, R., private................company F, 93d Indiana infantry
Gass, N. J., sergeant................company H, 93d Indiana
Young, J., private................company L, 93d Indiana
Alexander, J. C., private................company C, 98th Indiana
Gilmore, J., private................
Higgins, E. S., private................
Cass, J. W., private................company B, 99th Indiana
Van Over, J., private................company C, 99th Indiana

Rodgers, T., private................company G, 99th Indiana
York, A. J., private................company G, 99th Indiana
Lindlay, H. C., private..............company I, 99th Indiana
Moreh, H. O., sergeant..............company K, 99th Indiana
Noss, J. A., private................company B, 101st Indiana
Morter, J. A., private..............company C, 124th Indiana
Pain, J., private...................company C, 124th Indiana
Thompson, J. W., private............company C, 124th Indiana
Brown, Jas., private................company C, 124th Indiana
Bryant, C., private.:...............company C, 124th Indiana
Johan, Jas, private.................company C, 124th Indiana
Shinnyfield, S., private............company C, 124th Indiana
White, T. A., private...............company C, 124th Indiana
Elliott, Jas., private..............company I, 124th Indiana
Kimperlain, J. H., sergeant.........company K, 124th Indiana
Herrington, P., private.............company K, 124th Indiana
Palmer, R., private.................company K, 124th Indiana
Beardon, D. S., corporal.............124th Indiana
Esby, J. M., corporal................124th Indiana
Hickerson, J. A., corporal...........124th Indiana
Raymond, W. H., corporal.............124th Indiana
Wright, J. C., corporal..............124th Indiana
Dowhar, L., private..................124th Indiana
Meher, D., musician.................company I, 124th Indiana
Cox, W. H., private.................company B, 1st Kentucky cavalry
Cummings, C., private...............company I, 1st Kentucky cavalry
Marshall, J. T., private............company C, 2d Kentucky cavalry
Cook, W. H. H., corporal............company E, 2d Kentucky cavalry
Hall, R. T., private................company K, 2d Kentucky cavalry
Banks, J. N., private...............company A, 3d Kentucky cavalry
Marslin, F., private................company B, 3d Kentucky cavalry
Ballard, J. P., private.............company F, 3d Kentucky cavalry
Winhasher, J., private..............company G, 3d Kentucky cavalry
Gray, S., private...................company A, 4th Kentucky cavalry
Johnson, W., private................company A, 4th Kentucky cavalry
Royalty, D. B., private.............company A, 4th Kentucky cavalry
Berde, N., private..................company B, 4th Kentucky cavalry
Breckett, B., private...............company B, 4th Kentucky cavalry
Foods, A. H., private...............company B, 4th Kentucky cavalry
Marcum, N., private.................company B, 4th Kentucky cavalry
Carey, J., sergeant.................company C, 4th Kentucky cavalry
Spencer, A., sergeant...............company C, 4th Kentucky cavalry
Bowland, Abner, private.............company C, 4th Kentucky cavalry
Higdon, E. T., private..............company C, 4th Kentucky cavalry
McQueen, A., private................company D, 4th Kentucky cavalry
Gallagher, J., private..............company D, 4th Kentucky cavalry
Papers, J., private.................company E, 4th Kentucky cavalry
Bower, M., private..................company F, 4th Kentucky cavalry

Harper, E., private................. company G, 4th Kentucky cavalry
Jackson, G., private.................company G. 4th Kentucky cavalry
Hogan, M., private.................company ., 4th Kentucky cavalry
Holley, J. W., private.............. company H, 4th Kentucky cavalry
Vincent, H., private................company H, 4th Kentucky cavalry
Redman, W., private................company H, 4th Kentucky cavalry
Curry, M., private..................company I, 4th Kentucky cavalry
Galiner, James, private............company I, 4th Kentucky cavalry
Regney, James, private.............company I, 4th Kentucky cavalry
Csulter, M., private................company K, 4th Kentucky cavalry
Edwards, W. H., private............company K, 4th Kentucky cavalry
Fabrow, M. B., private.............company K, 4th Kentucky cavalry
Merrell, F., private................company K, 4th Kentucky cavalry
Williams, W. T., private...........company K, 4th Kentucky cavalry
Wolum, Jno., private...............company K, 4th Kentucky cavalry
Collins, Wm., private..............company L, 4th Kentucky cavalry
Patterson, Thos., private..........company L, 4th Kentucky cavalry
Fiddler, W. N., major................................ 5th Kentucky cavalry
Faber, J. H., private...............company A, 5th Kentucky cavalry
Wheatleigh, L., sergeant...........company A, 6th Kentucky cavalry
Bankhead, Henry, private..........company A, 6th Kentucky cavalry
Hammond, Jno., private............company A, 6th Kentucky cavalry
Beam, L., private...................company A, 6th Kentucky cavalry
Haup, Benj., private...............company A, 6th Kentucky cavalry
McKrunney, R., private............company A, 6th Kentucky cavalry
Hartman, L., private...............company B, 6th Kentucky cavalry
Lebel, G., private ....company B, 6th Kentucky cavalry
Stewart, P. A., private............company B, 6th Kentucky cavalry
Parish, C. H., captain.............company C, 6th Kentucky cavalry
Fluke, A. W., sergeant.............company C, 6th Kentucky cavalry
Root, E., sergeant.................company C, 6th Kentucky cavalry
Firey, J., bugler..................company C, 6th Kentucky cavalry
Buckley, Jas., private.............company C, 6th Kentucky cavalry
Bartlett, C. M., private...........company C, 6th Kentucky cavalry
Coleman, E., private...............company C, 6th Kentucky cavalry
Elliott, W., private...............company C, 6th Kentucky cavalry
Merrit, B., private................company C, 6th Kentucky cavalry
Moprin, T., private................company C, 6th Kentucky cavalry
Paller, W., private................company C, 6th Kentucky cavalry
Pierce, W., private................company C, 6th Kentucky cavalry
Watt, S. J., private...............company C, 6th Kentucky cavalry
Vanor, W. D., private..............company C, 6th Kentucky cavalry
Allison, R. C., private............company D, 6th Kentucky cavalry
Cuney, C. E., private..............company D, 6th Kentucky cavalry
Evansberry, H., private............company E, 6th Kentucky cavalry
Calvin, J., private................company F, 6th Kentucky cavalry
Calvin, W. L., private.............company F, 6th Kentucky cavalry
Carmarch, J., private..............company F, 6th Kentucky cavalry

Cheatham, G. H., private............company F, 6th Kentucky cavalry
Saber, J. J., first lieutenant.........company G, 6th Kentucky cavalry
Chelf, S. D , corporal................company G, 6th Kentucky cavalry
Stherher, T. J., artificer.............company G, 6th Kentucky cavalry
Brown, P. M., private.................company G, 6th Kentucky cavalry
Davenport, Seth H., private.........company G, 6th Kentucky cavalry
Jacobs, A. M., private................company G, 6th Kentucky cavalry
Jacobs, J. A., private................company G, 6th Kentucky cavalry
Hobbs, L., private....................company G, 6th Kentucky cavalry
Lay, G. W., private...................company G, 6th Kentucky cavalry
Monday, W. H., private...............company G, 6th Kentucky cavalry
Noe, H. H., private...................company G, 6th Kentucky cavalry
Saddler, M , private..................company G, 6th Kentucky cavalry
Stephens, T. N., private.............company G, 6th Kentucky cavalry
Winstead, Jno., private..............company G, 6th Kentucky cavalry
Daugherty, Thos., private...........company H, 6th Kentucky cavalry
Hoglyn, J. B., private ....company H, 6th Kentucky cavalry
Thompson, J. B., private............company H, 6th Kentucky cavalry
Carter, T. A., private................company A, 17th Kentucky cavalry
Wade, Jas., private...................company B, 27th Kentucky cavalry
Smith, Jas., private..................company D, 27th Kentucky cavalry
Clark, M. C., sergeant...............company B, 28th Kentucky cavalry
Foley, P. W., corporal...............company B, 28th Kentucky cavalry
Cook, J., private.....................company A,   1st Kentucky artillery
Lewis, W., corporal..................company H,   1st Kentucky artillery
Phelps, J. W , private...............company G, 4th Kentucky mt'd. inf
Arnold, W. F., corporal..............company B,   1st Kentucky infantry
Miller, R., private...................company K,   1st Kentucky infantry
Johnson, A. W., private.............company H,   2d Kentucky infantry
Penticuff, Jno., private.............company A,   3d Kentucky infantry
Barrow, G. E., private...............company D,   3d Kentucky infantry
Wallace, F., private.................company D,   3d Kentucky infantry
Elmor, R., private...................company G,   3d Kentucky infantry
Raysor, W., private.................company H,   3d Kentucky infantry
Hope, F. W., private................company A, 4th Kentucky infantry
Gillman, H., private................company C, 4th Kentucky infantry
Humphreys, B., private........ .....company H, 4th Kentucky infantry
Webster, P., private................company E, 4th Kentucky infantry
Kennedy, E. R., private....... ......company K, 4th Kentucky infantry
Baxon, Jno., private................company B, 5th Kentucky infantry
Hagart, W., private.................company A, 7th Kentucky cavalry
Coyton, W. A., private..............company B, 7th Kentucky cavalry
Davis, B. G , private. ....company L, 7th Kentucky cavalry
Smith, J., private....................company G, 11th Kentucky infantry
Clinger, C., corporal................company E, 16th Kentucky infantry
Wilson, H. B., corporal.............company E, 16th Kentucky infantry
Emerick, J., private.................company L, 18th Kentucky infantry
Smith, C., private....................company D, 27th Kentucky infantry

Neller, Peter, private................company C, 28th Kentucky infantry
Colwell, H. C., private...............company D, 37th Kentucky infantry
Free, M. C., private..................company M, 1st Michigan cavalry
Watson, J. H., private...............company M, 1st Michigan cavalry
Paelps, F., private...................company M, 1st Michigan cavalry
Dickerson, Simeon, lieutenant..................... 2d Michigan cavalry
Maxon, M., sergeant.................company A, 2d Michigan cavalry
Alfred, Z., private...................company A, 2d Michigan cavalry
Johnson, B., private.................company A, 2d Michigan cavalry
Tubbs, Hiram, private...............company B, 2d Michigan cavalry
Brooks, L., sergeant.................company C, 2d Michigan cavalry
Robinson, J. L., private............company C, 2d Michigan cavalry
Corliss, J. L., private................company C, 2d Michigan cavalry
Dillard, James, private..............company C, 2d Michigan cavalry
Gleason, G. G., private..............company D, 2d Michigan cavalry
Johnson, J., private..................company D, 2d Michigan cavalry
Hill, Daniel, private.................company D, 2d Michigan cavalry
Dickens, L. F., lieutenant...........company E, 2d Michigan cavalry
Perkins, F. M., sergeant............company E, 2d Michigan cavalry
Petitt, M., corporal..................company E, 2d Michigan cavalry
Warren, D., private.................company E, 2d Michigan cavalry
Nolen, D., private...................company E, 2d Michigan cavalry
Munroe, F., private.................company E, 2d Michigan cavalry
Scadding, J., private................company E. 2d Michigan cavalry
Alney, John, private.................company E, 2d Michigan cavalry
Draiman, McKenzie, private.......company E, 2d Michigan cavalry
Thomas, J. P., private...............company E, 2d Michigan cavalry
Kendric, J., private.................company E, 2d Michigan cavalry
Langley, W., private.................company E, 2d Michigan cavalry
Lindsay, W. L., private.............company E, 2d Michigan cavalry
Byron, Joseph, private..............company E, 2d Michigan cavalry
Rix, A., private ....company G, 2d Michigan cavalry
Worden, D. C., bugler...............company H, 2d Michigan cavalry
Holler, R., private...................company H, 2d Michigan cavalry
Mahony, J., corporal................company I, 2d Michigan cavalry
Gage, G., private.....................company I, 2d Michigan cavalry
Barker, F., private...................company K, 2d Michigan cavalry
Stranton, L., private................company K, 2d Michigan cavalry
Cormstead, —, private..............company K, 2d Michigan cavalry
Laybarker, P., corporal.............company L, 2d Michigan cavalry
Ranks, F., private....................company D, 3d Michigan cavalry
Thompson, M., private..............company I, 3d Michigan cavalry
Baker, M. S., corporal...............company D, 4th Michigan cavalry
Blakely, J., private...................company E, 4th Michigan cavalry
Eslich, N. A., private................company G, 4th Michigan cavalry
Davenhaff, J. C., private............company I, 4th Michigan cavalry
Fordend, L. D., private..............company I, 4th Michigan cavalry
Norton, J. E., private................company A, 5th Michigan cavalry

Finch, Wm., private................company D, 5th Michigan cavalry
Warren, H., sergeant................company G, 5th Michigan cavalry
Russell, A., private................company G, 5th Michigan cavalry
Cehart, J. L., sergeant................company H, 5th Michigan cavalry
Brown, J. W., private................company H, 5th Michigan cavalry
Bussley, * L., private................company M, 5th Michigan cavalry
Barnes, A. M., private................company D, 6th Michigan cavalry
Pick, C., private................company E, 6th Michigan cavalry
Morse, V. H., private................company E, 6th Michigan cavalry
Hart, T., private................company I, 6th Michigan cavalry
Hulett, J , private................company K, 6th Michigan cavalry
McNeal, B., private................company H, 7th Michigan cavalry
Zachary, A. K., sergeant................company K, 7th Michigan cavalry
Noble, John, private................company B, 8th Michigan cavalry
Lebrey, C. J.. private................company B, 8th Michigan cavalry
Fast, L. R., private................company B, 8th Michigan cavalry
Glum, T. P. sergeant................company C, 8th Michigan cavalry
Fitzgerald, ,W., private................company C, 8th Michigan cavalry
Snyder, H., private................company C, 8th Michigan cavalry
Vent, W., private................company C, 8th Michigan cavalry
Duberry, A., private................company D, 8th Michigan cavalry
Wells, H. C., sergeant................company E, 8th Michigan cavalry
Geer, C. B., private................company F, 8th Michigan cavalry
Warls, B., private................company G, 8th Michigan cavalry
Lubustacker, private................company G, 8th Michigan cavalry
Meeker, Clark, private................ company H, 8th Michigan cavalry
Smith, Freeman, private................company H, 8th Michigan cavalry
Snider, T., private................company H, 8th Michigan cavalry
Spencer, E., private ....company H, 8th Michigan cavalry
Burlingham, E. J., private................company I, 8th Michigan cavalry
Carey, O., private................company I, 8th Michigan cavalry
Cartwright, private................company I, 8th Michigan cavalry
Farrer, John, private................company K, 8th Michigan cavalry
Day, J. P., corporal................company L, 8th Michigan cavalry
Broadshaw, D., private................ company M, 8th Michigan cavalry
Zacharia, M., private................company M, 8th Michigan cavalry
Patterson, W. J., 1st lieutenant....company E, 9th Michigan cavalry
Wells, D. A., private................company E, 1st Michigan S. S.
Green, A., private................company K, 1st Michigan S. S.
Royal, L. S., private................company K, 1st Michigan S. S.
Hatch, A. W., corporal................company F, 1st Michigan E. & M.
Bremer, J. L., sergeant................company L, 1st Michigan E. & M.
Earl, J., lieutenant................company L, 1st Michigan E. & M.
Johnson, H., private................company L, 1st Michigan E. & M.
Decker, J. R., private................company L, 1st Michigan E. & M.
Stephens, J. A., sergeant................company B, 1st Michigan infantry
Shephard S., private................company D, 1st Michigan infantry

* Scalded to death by my side.—C. D. B.

Ives, E. H., private. ....company D, 1st Michigan infantry
Barr, G., private..... ....company G, 11th Michigan infantry
Butler, J. E., private................company A, 15th Michigan infantry
Wads, A., private...................company A, 15th Michigan infantry
Ducatt, T. A., corporal..............company E, 15th Michigan infantry
Wright, H., private..................company F, 15th Michigan infantry
Wells, W., private...................company H, 15th Michigan infantry
Doane, F. R., private................company B, 17th Michigan infantry
Pechham, T. J., corporal.............company F, 17th Michigan infantry
Waterbury, A. N., sergeant..........company H, 17th Michigan infantry
Briggs, J. C., sergeant...............company K, 17th Michigan infantry
Spring,* J., corporal.................company A, 18th Michigan infantry
Knapp,* A. J., corporal..............company A, 18th Michigan infantry
Bradish,* J., corporal................company A, 18th Michigan infantry
Johnson, G. J., private...............company A, 18th Michigan infantry
Prosser, G. W., private..............company A, 18th Michigan infantry
Doney, N., private...................company A, 18th Michigan infantry
Foglesong, N., private...............company A, 18th Michigan infantry
Koon, H., private......... ... .company A, 18th Michigan infantry
Myers, J. L., private ....company A, 18th Michigan infantry
Robbins,* J., private.................company A, 18th Michigan infantry
Rowley,* O. B., private..............company A, 18th Michigan infantry
Slick, J. L., private..................company A, 18th Michigan infantry
Ludlum* E. F., private...............company A, 18th Michigan infantry
Hale, O. P., private..................company A, 18th Michigan infantry
Rowley,* W., private ....company A, 18th Michigan infantry
Cornell, A. W., corporal............company B, 18th Michigan infantry
Aldrich, A. D., private...............company B, 18th Michigan infantry
Darrow, S. M., private...............company B, 18th Michigan infantry
Wright, F., sergeant.................company B, 18th Michigan infantry
Ainsworth, J. S., private.............company B, 18th Michigan infantry
Sprague, F., private.................company B, 18th Michigan infantry
Horton,* C. E., sergeant............company C, 18th Michigan infantry
Greenfield,* L., sergeant............company C, 18th Michigan infantry
Baker,* J. D., 1st sergeant...........company C, 18th Michigan infantry
Moore,* J., corporal ....company C, 18th Michigan infantry
Thayer, Wm., private...............company C, 18th Michigan infantry
Oakley,* E. J., private..............company C, 18th Michigan infantry
Zidler,* F., private..................company C, 18th Michigan infantry
Deline,* O., private.................company C, 18th Michigan infantry
Daly, M., private....................company C, 18th Michigan infantry
Southwick,* E., private.............company C, 18th Michigan infantry
Hayck, G. P., private...............company C, 18th Michigan infantry
Parker,* J., private.................company C, 18th Michigan infantry
Potter,* J. B., private...............company C, 18th Michigan infantry
Finch, W. H., sergeant..............company D, 18th Michigan infantry
Lawrence,* Albert W., sergeant....company D, 18th Michigan infantry

* Killed.

Wood, H. C., corporal............company D, 18th Michigan infantry
Ford,* E., corporal...............company D, 18th Michigan infantry
Young,* W., musician.............company D, 18th Michigan infantry
Mann, W., private................company D, 18th Michigan infantry
Nelson, L., private..............company D, 18th Michigan infantry
Crisp, Wm., private..............company D, 18th Michigan infantry
Norcutt, J. W., private..........company D, 18th Michigan infantry
Duesler, Geo., private...........company D, 18th Michigan infantry
Vancourt, J., private............company D, 18th Michigan infantry
Walkins, J., private.............company D, 18th Michigan infantry
Wright, N. D., private...........company D, 18th Michigan infantry
Eddy, W., private................company D, 18th Michigan infantry
Bird,* John, private.............company D, 18th Michigan infantry
Robins,* Jonathan, private.......company D, 18th Michigan infantry
Brewer, G. H., corporal..........company E, 18th Michigan infantry
Jones, S. W., private............company E, 18th Michigan infantry
Brangan, P., private.............company E, 18th Michigan infantry
Millspaugh, D., private..........company E, 18th Michigan infantry
Barnum, J. P., private...........company E, 18th Michigan infantry
Randall, A., private.............company E, 18th Michigan infantry
Smith, Thos., private............company E, 18th Michigan infantry
Mason, G. R., * private..........company E, 18th Michigan infantry
Goodrich, U. N., private.........company E, 18th Michigan infantry
Voglesong, A. N., † sergeant.....company F, 18th Michigan infantry
Cole, O. M., corporal............company F, 18th Michigan infantry
Stubberfield, W., private........company F, 18th Michigan infantry
Harris, W. H., private...........company F, 18th Michigan infantry
Holmes, N. L., * private.........company F, 18th Michigan infantry
Vangorder, D. W., private........company F, 18th Michigan infantry
Smith, C., private...............company F, 18th Michigan infantry
Abbadusky, C., private...........company F, 18th Michigan infantry
Gale, A. (Orris), * private......company F, 18th Michigan infantry
Vanvlack, A., private............company F, 18th Michigan infantry
Fuller, A., private..............company F, 18th Michigan infantry
Hines, T. F., * private..........company K, 18th Michigan infantry
Hampton, F., private.............company G, 18th Michigan infantry
Williams, W. H., private.........company F, 18th Michigan infantry
Nevins, J. F., private...........company F, 18th Michigan infantry
Lachler, Geo.,* private..........company F, 18th Michigan infantry
Palmer, G. N., * corporal........company G, 18th Michigan infantry
Faurot, W. L., corporal.........company G, 18th Michigan infntry
Lackey, P., private..............company G, 18th Michigan infantry
Hampton, P., private.............company G, 18th Michigan infantry
Burns, E., private...............company G, 18th Michigan infantry
Burns, M., private...............company G, 18th Michigan infantry
Merrifield, E. C., private.......company G, 18th Michigan infantry
Colwell, James, * private........company G, 18th Michigan infantry

* Killed,   † Since died,

Seely, F. D.,* private..................company G, 18th Michigan infantry
Plank, H. D., corporal..............company H, 18th Michigan infantry
Countryman, G. A., musician......company K, 18th Michigan infantry
Haight, G. C., musician.............company H, 18th Michigan infantry
Mallison, S., private.................company H, 18th Michigan infantry
Fink, M. L., private...................company H, 18th Michigan infantry
Snyder, D. L., private................company H, 18th Michigan infantry
Shaffer, B. B., private................company I, 18th Michigan infantry
Main, S. H., private..................company I, 18th Michigan infantry
Patterson, R., private................company I, 18th Michigan infantry
Upton, W. S., private................company I, 18th Michigan infantry
Wiechard, A. B., private.............company K, 18th Michigan infantry
Sulier, L. C., private.................company K, 18th Michigan infantry
Shetterson, Jno., private............company K, 18th Michigan infantry
McEldowney, A. J., * private.......company K, 18th Michigan infantry
Berry, C. D., private.................company I, 20th Michigan infantry
Mead, J., † private...................company F, 21st Michigan infantry
Seward, R. W., private...............company F, 21st Michigan infantry
Love, J. H., private...................company C, 22d Michigan infantry
Smith, A. B., sergeant...............company K, 22d Michigan infantry
Boyce, E., private....................company K, 22d Michigan infantry
Cole, David, private.................company B, 23d Michigan infantry
Freeland, G., private.................company E, 23d Michigan infantry
Ludlow, A. E., private...............company E, 23d Michigan infantry
Westhorpe, Geo., private...........company E, 23d Michigan infantry
Vancover, A., private................company E, 23d Michigan infantry
Harris, Israel, private..............company H, 24th Michigan infantry
Luchane, D., † private..............company F, 25th Michigan infantry
Bement, Geo., sergeant.............company F, 25th Michigan infantry
Richardson, T. W., private.........company A, 1st Ohio infantry
Banner, Thos. H., private..........company B, 1st Ohio infantry
Anderson, James, private..........company D, 1st Ohio infantry
Eavens, E., private..................company D, 1st Ohio infantry
Hawk, M., private...................company D, 3d Ohio infantry
Sorger, G., private..................company G, 4th Ohio infantry
Edwards, Jacob, private............company I, 4th Ohio infantry
Lentimore, J. B., private...........company M, 4th Ohio infantry
Madden, W. P., private.............company I, 8th Ohio infantry
Miller, D. S., private................company D, 13th Ohio infantry
Longshon, J., private...............company I, 13th Ohio infantry
McCordy, J., private................company K, 13th Ohio infantry
Nelson, N., private..................company K, 13th Ohio infantry
Van Fleet, H., private..............company I, 14th Ohio infantry
Carter, F. M., private...............company D, 15th Ohio infantry
Ezzle, M., private...................company F, 15th Ohio infantry
Myers, C. W., private...............company G, 15th Ohio infantry
Carnes, N., sergeant................company B, 18th Ohio infantry

* Killed.   † Lost.

Lampsell, H., private------------------------------11th Ohio infantry
White, W. A., private-------------company H, 19th Ohio infantry
Shirley, W. H., sergeant-----------company B, 21st Ohio infantry
Casbell, A., private----------------company B, 21st Ohio infantry
Markford, P., private--------------company B, 21st Ohio infantry
Morgan, Levi J., private------------company B, 21st Ohio infantry
Usher, A., private------------------company B, 21st Ohio infantry
Engal, J., private-------------------company D, 21st Ohio infantry
Donaphin, A., sergeant-------------company E, 21st Ohio infantry
Kendals, R., private----------------company E, 21st Ohio infantry
Forest, F., private------------------company K, 21st Ohio infantry
Davidson, John, private-------------company A, 22d Ohio infantry
Mershen, G., private---------------company E, 22d Ohio infantry
Field, G. G., corporal---------------company D, 23d Ohio infantry
Gray, William, private-------------company I, 23d Ohio infantry
Badcock, John, private-------------company K, 24th Ohio infantry
Kelly, J., private---------- ---------company K, 25th Ohio infantry
Miller, J. R., corporal-------------company D, 26th Ohio infantry
McClutock, W. G., private---------company H, 26th Ohio infantry
Shields, P., private--- -------------company D, 31st Ohio infantry
Long, J. B., private----------------company I, 33d Ohio infantry
Lyman, R. J., private--------------company I, 33d Ohio infantry
Sheppard, W., private-------------company E, 34th Ohio infantry
Whyler, L., private-----------------company D, 35th Ohio infantry
Sharp, E., private------------------company E, 35th Ohio infantry
Brown, A., private-----------------company A, 37th Ohio infantry
Wertermier, J. D , private---------company B, 37th Ohio infantry
Anderback, G., private------------company C, 37th Ohio infantry
Webler, John, private-------------company C, 37th Ohio infantry
Cealer, C., private-----------------company D, 37th Ohio infantry
Hysenger, J., private--------------company D, 37th Ohio infantry
Hiss, John, private----------------company E, 37th Ohio infantry
Mathews, O., private--------------company D, 41st Ohio infantry
Clearley, J. R., private------------company F, 41st Ohio infantry
Shacher, J., private --------------company E, 42d Ohio infantry
Thacker, J., private----------------company E, 46th Ohio infantry
Klutter, L. R., private------------company K, 46th Ohio infantry
Mass, J. W., private---------------company B, 47th Ohio infantry
Buckleyhower, A., private------ ---company H, 47th Ohio infantry
Hesser, L., private----------------company K, 47th Ohio infantry
Gay, Asa, corporal-----------------company A, 49th Ohio infantry
Huffey, J, private----------------company B, 49th Ohio infantry
Fox, John, corporal---------------company A, 50th Ohio infantry
Rice, M. L., private---------------company A, 50th Ohio infantry
Roberts, Jno., private-------------company A, 50th Ohio infantry
Hellinger, J., sergeant------------company B, 50th Ohio infantry
Humphrey, W. C., private---------company B, 50th Ohio infantry
Merron, William, private---------company B, 50th Ohio infantry

Sheare, W. G., private*..............company B, 50th Ohio infantry
Walker, J., private...................company B, 50th Ohio infantry
Huston, D., corporal.................company C, 50th Ohio infantry
Ray, Christian, private..............company C, 50th Ohio infantry
Picket, E., corporal.................company D, 50th Ohio infantry
McClarey, private....................company D, 50th Ohio infantry
Holmes, S., private..................company D, 50th Ohio infantry
Richmond, W., private................company D, 50th Ohio infantry
Shulton, William, private...........company D, 50th Ohio infantry
White, G. W., private................company D, 50th Ohio infantry
Lee, William H., sergeant...........company E, 50th Ohio infantry
Ruslant, Peter, corporal.............company E, 50th Ohio infantry
Vananda, R., corporal................company E, 50th Ohio infantry
Carr, John, private †...............company E, 50th Ohio infantry
Krinzer, H., private.................company E, 50th Ohio infantry
Meaker, F., private..................company E, 50th Ohio infantry
Pettyjohn, S., private...............company E, 50th Ohio infantry
Moore, T., corporal..................company F, 50th Ohio infantry
Green, W., sergeant..................company G, 50th Ohio infantry
Cruse, C. F., corporal-..............company G, 50th Ohio infantry
Bacan, Nornear, private..............company G, 50th Ohio infantry
Badgley, B. B., private..............company G, 50th Ohio infantry
Boyd, George W., private.............company G, 50th Ohio infantry
Cotton, W. S., private...............company G, 50th Ohio infantry
Lehman, N., private..................company G, 50th Ohio infantry
Station, G. W., private..............company G, 50th Ohio infantry
Gilmore, S. D., private..............company H, 50th Ohio infantry
Griffin, J. O., private..............company H, 50th Ohio infantry
Jordan, H., private......... ....company H, 50th Ohio infantry
Matter, F., private..................company H, 50th Ohio infantry
Murphy, C. C., private...............company H, 50th Ohio infantry
Winters, E., corporal................company K, 50th Ohio infantry
Shellard, P., private................company K, 50th Ohio infantry
Culp, A. J., private.................company K, 50th Ohio infantry
Phillips, W., private................company B, 51st Ohio infantry
Norris, J. B., private............... company C, 51st Ohio infantry
DeMoss, J., private..................company D, 51st Ohio infantty
Smith, W., private...................company D, 51st Ohio infantry
Altof, E. W., private................company E, 51st Ohio infantry
Belnap, C. M., private...............company F, 51st Ohio infantry
Lahr, J., private....................company F, 51st Ohio infantry
Sayer, S. R., sergeant...............company H, 51st Ohio infantry
Hleg, L., corporal...................company I, 51st Ohio infantry
Miller, J., private..................company E, 52d Ohio infantry
Gregary, W., private.................company C, 53d Ohio infantry
Scan, W., private....................company C, 54th Ohio infantry
Patte, W. S., private................company G, 54th Ohio infantry

* Lost.   † Killed.

Wiles, A. G., private......................company C, 55th Ohio infantry
Githorn, L., private......................company F, 56th Ohio infantry
Blaire, P. Q., sergeant major......................... 59th Ohio infantry
Brumer, M., private......................company C, 59th Ohio infantry
Brudgeman, A. A., private......................company F, 63d Ohio infantry
Whoyle, L., sergeant......................company G, 63d Ohio infantry
Barnes, W, private......................company H, 63d Ohio infantry
Hult, W. A., corporal......................company A, 64th Ohio infantry
Van Scoyte, G. W., corporal......................company A, 64th Ohio infantry
Brinke, Thos., private*......................company A, 64th Ohio infantry
Fise, W., sergeant......................company B, 64th Ohio infantry
Cramer, A. O., sergeant......................company B, 64th Ohio infantry
Barr, W., private......................company B, 64th Ohio infantry
Brady, J., private......................company B, 64th Ohio infantry
King, B., private......................company B, 64th Ohio infantry
Zumner, C., private......................company B, 64th Ohio infantry
Zimmer, C., private......................company B, 64th Ohio infantry
Brenton, H. W., sergeant......................company D, 64th Ohio infantry
Landon, S., corporal......................company D, 64th Ohio infantry
Carnock, T. J., corporal......................company E, 64th Ohio infantry
White, R., sergeant......................company I, 64th Ohio infantry
Eddermon, D., corporal......................company I, 64th Ohio infantry
McKinley, D., private......................company I, 64th Ohio infantry
Stickney, J., private......................company I, 64th Ohio infantry
Kennedy, Ed., private......................company K, 64th Ohio infantry
Ryan, J., private......................company K, 64th Ohio infantry
Gregory, E., sergeant......................company C, 65th Ohio infantry
Nickerson, Chas., private......................company E, 65th Ohio infantry
Grebaugh, D., private......................company G, 65th Ohio infantry
Mathias, E., sergeant......................company K, 65th Ohio infantry
Horner, Ira B., corporal......................company K, 65th Ohio infantry
Bishler, Jno., private......................company K, 65th Ohio infantry
Emerlin, Eli, private......................company K, 65th Ohio infantry
Fairchild, O. W., private......................company K, 65th Ohio infantry
Roddybaugh, S. H., private......................company K, 65th Ohio infantry
Shoemaker, J., private......................company C, 70th Ohio infantry
Black, J. C., private......................company K, 70th Ohio infantry
Davis, J. W., lieutenant......................company B, 71st Ohio infantry
Brant, F., private......................company A, 72d Ohio infantry
McIntyre, B., private......................company B, 72d Ohio infantry
Shoe, E., private......................company C, 72d Ohio infantry
Duke, Wm., sergeant......................company D, 72d Ohio infantry
Stalley, M., sergeant......................company D, 72d Ohio infantry
Shoemaker, A., private......................company E, 72d Ohio infantry
Shoemaker, W., private......................company E, 72d Ohio infantry
Trimmer, Wm., private......................company E, 72d Ohio infantry
Flint, Thos., corporal......................company F, 72d Ohio infantry

* Lost.

Crane, J., private .... company F, 72d Ohio infantry
Hague, S., private .... company F, 72d Ohio infantry
Kirk, W. H., p·ivate .... company F, 72d Ohio infantry
Aubrey, M., private .... company H, 72d Ohio infantry
Holendesk, J., private .... company K, 72d Ohio infantry
Andrews, W., sergeant .... company A, 75th Ohio infantry
Barnes, Ed., private .... company F, 75th Ohio infantry
Waltz, M., private .... company H, 75th Ohio infantry
Thompson, J., private .... company A, 76th Ohio infantry
Yeisley, E. H., private .... company A, 76th Ohio infantry
McCarty, Jas., private .... company D, 76th Ohio infantry
Stone, Jas., private .... company D, 76th Ohio infantry
Thomas, Thos., private .... company H, 76th Ohio infantry
White, Jas., private .... company E, 78th Ohio infantry
Clepner, J., private .... company H, 78th Ohio infantry
Marks, Chas., private .... company F, 79th Ohio infantry
Rammel, A. W., private .... company E, 80th Ohio infantry
Shaw, C. M., private .... company B, 81st Ohio infantry
Cord, A., private .... company F, 90th Ohio infantry
Nihart, A., private .... company G, 90th Ohio infantry
Bady, J., sergeant .... company A, 93d Ohio infantry
Sharits, Z., private .... company E, 93d Ohio infantry
Young, G. H., private .... company A, 95th Ohio infantry
Reed, Oliver H., private .... company A, 95th Ohio infantry
McMillan, D. E., private .... company B, 95th Ohio infantry
McMillan, D. M., private .... company B, 95th Ohio infantry
Miller, P., private .... company E, 95th Ohio infantry
Owen, W., private .... company E, 95th Ohio infantry
Poycell, H. W., private .... company E, 95th Ohio infantry
Poycell, W. W., private .... company E, 95th Ohio infantry
Rollins, G. H., private .... company E, 95th Ohio infantry
Shaul, W. R., private .... company E, 95th Ohio infantry
Little, J. W., sergeant .... company F, 95th Ohio infantry
Vanhorn, B., private .... company F, 95th Ohio infantry
Jackson, T., corporal .... company G, 95th Ohio infantry
Parker, J A., private .... company G, 95th Ohio infantry
Lease, J. W., corporal .... company I, 95th Ohio infantry
Wilcox, M., private .... company I, 95th Ohio infantry
Wilson, R., private .... company I, 95th Ohio infantry
Rush, J., private .... company L, 95th Ohio infantry
Hammel, Sam., private .... 95th Ohio infantry
McLeary, L., private .... company B, 96th Ohio infantry
Poland, J. L., sergeant .... company B, 97th Ohio infantry
Cishard, T. R., private .... company B, 97th Ohio infantry
Johnson, S., private .... company B, 97th Ohio infantry
Stevens, W., private .... company C, 97th Ohio infantry
Wilner, R., private .... company C, 97th Ohio infantry
Hess, Alexander, private .... company D, 97th Ohio infantry

51

Watts, T. W., private...............company E, 97th Ohio infantry
Lakin, W. H., 2d lieutenant.........company H, 97th Ohio infantry
Emerson, J. G., private.............company I, 97th Ohio infantry
Cornwell, J , * sergeant............company A, 100th Ohio infantry
McCrory, L. W., private.............company A, 100th Ohio infantry
Flemming, J. A., * corporal.........company D, 100th Ohio infantry
King, A. W., corporal...............company D, 100th Ohio infantry
Davis, J., private..................company D, 100th Ohio infantry
Hill, G., private...................company D, 100th Ohio infantry
Lambert, V., * private..............company D, 100th Ohio infantry
Wheeler, W., private................company D, 100th Ohio infantry
Sterknell, E. B., private...........company E, 100th Ohio infantry
Hiller, R., † sergeant..............company F, 100th Ohio infantry
Wagner, J., corporal................company G, 100th Ohio infantry
Flegel, John, * corporal............company K, 100th Ohio infantry
Dunume, J., private.................company K, 100th Ohio infantry
Hofinal, A., * private..............company K, 100th Ohio infantry
Squire, E. J., 1st lieutenant.......company D, 101st Ohio infantry
Rohder, Jacob. private..............company H, 101st Ohio infantry
Faggott, H. A., private.............company I, 101st Ohio infantry
Dilling, A., private................company K, 101st Ohio infantry
Shaffer, J., private................company F, 101st Ohio infantry
Wade, B. F., sergeant...............company A, 102d Ohio infantry
Beanten, J., private................company A, 102d Ohio infantry
Crawford, E., private...............company A, 102d Ohio infantry
Fabra, D., private..................company A, 102d Ohio infantry
Gein, J , private...................company A, 102d Ohio infantry
McGinness, L., private..............company A, 102d Ohio infantry
Grand, J. Watt, private.............company A, 102d Ohio infantry
Haley, John, private................company A, 102d Ohio infantry
Hall, G. L., private................company A, 102d Ohio infantry
Hass, Geo., private.................company A, 102d Ohio infantry
Homer, Jacob, private...............company A, 102d Ohio infantry
Henderson, W., private..............company A, 102d Ohio infantry
Lee, W., private....................company A, 102d Ohio infantry
Merchand, L., private...............company A, 102d Ohio infantry
Mitchell, Jas., private.............company A, 102d Ohio infantry
Peckham, C. R., private.............company A, 102d Ohio infantry
Rose, J. S., private................company A, 102d Ohio infantry
Ross, Wm., private..................company A, 102d Ohio infantry
Shrader, John, private..............company A, 102d Ohio infantry
Stagle, E. K., private..............company A, 102d Ohio infantry
Stephens, S. S., private............company A, 102d Ohio infantry
Wallace, W. A., private.............company A, 102d Ohio infantry
Richard, R., sergeant...............company B, 102d Ohio infantry
Krebs, H., corporal.................company B, 102d Ohio infantry
Bahn, A., private...................company B, 102d Ohio infantry

* Killed.   † Scalded and died at Memphis.

McCrea, J., private............. .....company B, 102d Ohio infantry
Fisher, D., private...................company B, 102d Ohio infantry
Mercer, J. M., private..............company B, 102d Ohio infantry
Potter, S. R., private...............company B, 102d Ohio infantry
Spafford, H., private...............company B, 102d Ohio infantry
Stocker, S., private.................company B, 102d Ohio infantry
Webster, A., private................company B, 102d Ohio infantry
Wells, Jos., private..................company B, 102d Ohio infantry
Whissemore, A., private............company B, 102d Ohio infantry
Woods, M., private..... ....company B, 102d Ohio infantry
Heimberger, W. C., * sergeant......company C, 102d Ohio infantry
Wolton, P. L., sergeant.............company C, 102d Ohio infantry
Bierly, J., corporal.... ....company C, 102d Ohio infantry
Beal, Amos, private.................company C, 102d Ohio infantry
Flint, B., private.....................company C, 102d Ohio infantry
Oyster, Simon, private.............company C, 102d Ohio infantry
Simon, J., private...................company C, 102d Ohio infantry
Wheeler, D., private................company C, 102d Ohio infantry
Wisler, W., private..................company C, 102d Ohio infantry
Willis, W. W., private..............company C, 102d Ohio infantry
Hosts, J. B.,* sergeant.............company D, 102d Ohio infantry
Omeveg, G. H.,* sergeant..........company D, 102d Ohio infantry
Baker, John,* private...............company D, 102d Ohio infantry
Bringman, J. D., private...........company D, 102d Ohio infantry
Burt, J. H.,* private................company D, 102d Ohio infantry
Errick, W.,* private.................company D, 102d Ohio infantry
Grice, David,* private..............company D, 102d Ohio infantry
Horn, P. L., private................company I, 102d Ohio infantry
Keley, J. Mc.,† private.............company I, 102d Ohio infantry
Kochendeffer, J. H., private.......company D, 102d Ohio infantry
Sidle, H., private...................company D, 102d Ohio infantry
Smutz, G., private..................company I, 102d Ohio infantry
Strawbaugh, S.,* private...........company D, 102d Ohio infantry
Ulick, G. W., private...............company D, 102d Ohio infantry
Underwood, Jas., private..........company D, 102d Ohio infantry
Warmly, M., private...............company D, 102d Ohio infantry
Williams, J. T.,* private ....company D, 102d Ohio infantry
Drocliss, J., corporal..............company E, 102d Ohio infantry
Irons, Jacob, corporal.............company E, 102d Ohio infantry
Couter, E., private.................company E, 102d Ohio infantry
Graber, D., private.................company E, 102d Ohio infantry
Lockhart, W., private..............company E, 102d Ohio infantry
Stuff, Fred, private................company E, 102d Ohio infantry
Anderson, G., private.............company F, 102d Ohio infantry
Keeler, Wm., private..............company F, 102d Ohio infantry
Saunders, J., private..............company F, 102d Ohio infantry
Shepperly, G., private............company F, 102d Ohio infantry

* Killed.   † Died next day.

Shoup, C. W., private................company F, 102d Ohio infantry
Stine, D. G., private................company F, 102d Ohio infantry
Torbet, R., private..................company F, 102d Ohio infantry
Hites, Dan., sergeant................company G, 102d Ohio infantry
Johns, D. W., corporal...............company G, 102d Ohio infantry
Price, S. P., private................company G, 102d Ohio infantry
Huntsberger, J., corporal............company H, 102d Ohio infantry
Ball, H., private....................company H, 102d Ohio infantry
Baney, John, private.................company H, 102d Ohio infantry
Bardon, Otto, private................company H, 102d Ohio infantry
Brenizer, A., private................company H, 102d Ohio infantry
Brenizer, D., private................company H, 102d Ohio infantry
Christine, H., private...............company H, 102d Ohio infantry
Crowe, Wm., private..................company H, 102d Ohio infantry
Harrington, G., private..............company H, 102d Ohio infantry
Smith, C., private...................company H, 102d Ohio infantry
Tracy, W. L , private................company H, 102d Ohio infantry
Wells, Miles, private................company H, 102d Ohio infantry
Wynn, W. J., private.................company H, 102d Ohio infantry
Fast, W. N., sergeant................company K, 102d Ohio infantry
Sprinkle, M. H., sergeant............company K, 102d Ohio infantry
Fast, W. A., corporal................company K, 102d Ohio infantry
Burnside, R., private................company K, 102d Ohio infantry
Castle, Jas. L., private.............company K, 102d Ohio infantry
Hartman, J. F., private..............company K, 102d Ohio infantry
Leidig, R., private,.................company K, 102d Ohio infantry
Ogden, C. P., private................
Singer, J. J., private...............company K, 102d Ohio infantry
Steinmetz, G., private...............company K, 102d Ohio infantry
Depmer, A., private..................company A, 103d Ohio infantry
Shaw, D , private....................company D, 103d Ohio infantry
Jenet, J., private...................company H, 103d Ohio infantry
Smith, W. W., private................company B, 104th Ohio infantry
Patterson, S., private...............company F, 104th Ohio infantry
Winkleman, private...................company H, 104th Ohio infantry
Hallett, G. W., private..............company I, 104th Ohio infantry
Molton, D., private..................company I, 104th Ohio infantry
Smith, B. F., private................company A, 105th Ohio infantry
Joseph, M., private..................company E, 111th Ohio infantry
McCord, G. B., 1st lieutenant........company F, 111th Ohio infantry
Humbarger, S., private...............company H, 111th Ohio infantry
Swarm, John L., private..............company K, 111th Ohio infantry
Long, B., private....................company C, 114th Ohio infantry
Hake, S. T., captain.................company B, 115th Ohio infantry
Eadie, John, 1st lieutenant..........company C, 115th Ohio infantry
Boosley, sergeant....................company C, 115th Ohio infantry
Elay, Jno., sergeant.................company C, 115th Ohio infantry
Jones, Arthur, sergeant..............company C, 115th Ohio infantry

Way, Chas., W., sergeant............company C, 115th Ohio infantry
Deitrich, C. W., corporal............company C, 115th Ohio infantry
Eadie, J. W., corporal..............company C, 115th Ohio infantry
Eatinger, G. W., corporal. ....company C, 115th Ohio infantry
Everhart, J., corporal..............company C, 115th Ohio infantry
Stevens, C., corporal.... ....company C, 115th Ohio infantry
Richardson, H., corporal............company C, 115th Ohio infantry
Tyson, Chas., corporal.............company C, 115th Ohio infantry
Garrett, E. W., musician...........company C, 115th Ohio infantry
Blair, M. V. B., private...........company C, 115th Ohio infantry
Cochran, H., private...............company C, 115th Ohio infantry
Cook, J. C., private...............company C, 115th Ohio infantry
Cook, J. S., private...............company C, 115th Ohio infantry
Coady, T., private.................company C, 115th Ohio infantry
Cross, Geo., private...............company C, 115th Ohio infantrv
Dickerson, R., private.............company C, 115th Ohio infantry
Dolan, James, private..............company C, 115th Ohio infantry
Dusonberry, private................company C, 115th Ohio infantry
Doty, Nathan, private..............company C, 115th Ohio infantry
Ellers, Edward, private............company C, 115th Ohio infantry
Garrison, J. J., private...........company C, 115th Ohio infantry
Greenover, J., private.............company C, 115th Ohio infantry
Gulord, Rob't., private............company C, 115th Ohio infantry
Harris, G., private................company C, 115th Ohio infantry
Harris, Jno., private..............company C, 115th Ohio infantry
Hume, F. L., private...............company C, 115th Ohio infantry
Hurbert, Chas., private............company C, 115th Ohio infantry
King, Edward, private..............company C, 115th Ohio infantry
Maley, V. A., private..............company C, 115th Ohio infantry
Norton, W. H., private.............company C, 115th Ohio infantry
Post, C., private............ ....company C, 115th Ohio infantry
Price, W. D., private..............company C, 115th Ohio infantry
Smothers, W., private..............company C, 115th Ohio infantry
Stevens, W., private...............company C, 115th Ohio infantry
Stout, Chas., private..............company C, 115th Ohio infantry
Sysor, Jno., private...............company C, 115th Ohio infantry
Weaver, P. A., private.............company C, 115th Ohio infantry
Whitmore, Chas., private...........company C, 115th Ohio infantry
Whitmore, I., private..............company C, 115th Ohio infantry
Woods, Isaac, private..............company C, 115th Ohio infantry
Zimmerman, J., private.............company C, 115th Ohio infantry
Hendrick, A. M., private...........company D, 115th Ohio infantry
Laffater, A., private..............company D, 115th Ohio infantry
Shaffer, J. K., 2d lieutenant.......company F, 115th Ohio infantry
Rue, F., sergeant..................company F, 115th Ohio infantry
Smith, W. H., sergeant.............company F, 115th Ohio infantry
Clapsaddle, F. A., private.........company F, 115th Ohio infantry
Crul, B., private..................company F, 115th Ohio infantry

James, T. H., private............company F, 115th Ohio infantry
Roath, R. W., private............company F, 115th Ohio infantry
Spencer, F., private............company F, 115th Ohio infantry
Thomas, L. A., private............company F, 115th Ohio infantry
Togle, J., private............company F, 115th Ohio infantry
Thompson, E., sergeant............company G, 115th Ohio infantry
Alexander, P. H., corporal............company G, 115th Ohio infantry
Patterson, Jas., corporal............company G, 115th Ohio infantry
Callon, J. C., private............company G, 115th Ohio infantry
Cox, Robt., private............company G, 115th Ohio infantry
Dana, W., private............company G, 115th Ohio infantry
Daro, J. M., private............company G, 115th Ohio infantry
Davis, Wm., private............company G, 115th Ohio infantry
Evans, Thos , private............company G, 115th Ohio infantry
Knapps, C., private............company G, 115th Ohio infantry
Myers, D., private............company G, 115th Ohio infantry
Keney, O., private............company F, 116th Ohio infantry
Robinson, J., private............company A, 121st Ohio infantry
Wallace, H. B., private............company A, 124th Ohio infantry
McDaniel, G., private............company D, 124th Ohio infantry
Adams, Jno., private............company A, 125th Ohio infantry
Watters, S. M., private............company H, 125th Ohio infantry
Lugenbeal, D. W., private............company F, 135th Ohio infantry
Fest, J., * private............company C, 153d Ohio infantry
Van Emore, M. T., private............company C, 175th Ohio infantry
Hendricks, G. W., private............company C, 175th Ohio infantry
Myers, W., private............company D, 175th Ohio infantry
Payne, Jas., private............company D, 175th Ohio infantry
Carroll, W., private............company E, 175th Ohio infantry
Gray, T. J., private............company E, 175th Ohio infantry
Huason, private............company G, 175th Ohio infantry
Morris, Stacy, private............company G, 175th Ohio infantry
Kenard, A., private............company C, 183d Ohio infantry
Koland, P., private............company C, 183d Ohio infantry
Sugder, A., private............company C, 183d Ohio infantry
Miller, Jos., sergeant............company D, 183d Ohio infantry
Polar, G. W., corporal............company E, 183d Ohio infantry
Gillisman, J., private............company F, 183d Ohio infantry
Manie, Davis, private............company G, 183d Ohio infantry
Zephrisharg, Gustave, sergeant....company H, 183d Ohio infantry
Barner, Jno., private............company H, 183d Ohio infantry
Bumgardner, W. J., private........company K, 183d Ohio infantry
Oliver, Thos., private............company K, 183d Ohio infantry
Genthar, J., private .... 183d Ohio infantry
Wade, W. H., corporal............company K, 1st Ohio cavalry
Graham, G., private............company A, 2d Ohio cavalry
Allman, J., private............company A, 2d Ohio cavalry
Lockwood, D., private............company A, 2d Ohio cavalry

* Killed.

Peas, Jas., corporal....................company B, 2d Ohio cavalry
Russell, C. G., private................company G, 2d Ohio cavalry
Brown, A. C., private..................company I, 2d Ohio cavalry
Brunner, D., private...................company K, 2d Ohio cavalry
Haley, C. C., private..................company K, 2d Ohio cavalry
Donald, H., private....................company K, 3d Ohio cavalry
Erwin, J., private.....................company K, 3d Ohio cavalry
Gutton, W. N., private.................company K, 3d Ohio cavalry
Jessow, R., private....................company K, 3d Ohio cavalry
Pickens, I., private...................company K, 3d Ohio cavalry
Pouch, E., private.....................company K, 3d Ohio cavalry
Rome, F., private......................company K, 3d Ohio cavalry
Tidwell, C. B., private................company K, 3d Ohio cavalry
Torvell, H., private...................company K, 3d Ohio cavalry
Wagoner, J., private...................company K, 3d Ohio cavalry
Whiscar, private.......................company K, 3d Ohio cavalry
Green, C., private.....................company L, 3d Ohio cavalry
Lewis, D. C., 1st lieutenant...........company M, 3d Ohio cavalry
Kertsteller, D., private...............company M, 3d Ohio cavalry
McWethy, C. H., private................company M, 3d Ohio cavalry
Stoner, J. W., corporal................McLaughlin's squadron.
Horter, J., corporal...................McLaughlin's squadron.
Noland, Jos., private..................company H, 4th Ohio cavalry
Smith., W. H., sergeant................company K, 4th Ohio cavalry
Browne, B., private....................company L, 4th Ohio cavalry
Bonkey, N., sergeant...................   5th Ohio cavalry
Donnelly, M., private..................company K, 5th Ohio cavalry
McMann, M., private....................company I, 6th Ohio cavalry
Hanam, T., sergeant....................company A, 7th Ohio cavalry
Lascur, A. J., sergeant................company A, 7th Ohio cavalry
Baldwin, J. R., corporal...............company A, 7th Ohio cavalry
Gilfiss, W. F.,corporal................company A, 7th Ohio cavalry
McCluchy, corporal.....................company A, 7th Ohio cavalry
Baker, Wm., private....................company A, 7th Ohio cavalry
Bell, J. K., private...................company A, 7th Ohio cavalry
Botts, Thos., private..................company A, 7th Ohio cavalry
Brickett, J., private..................company A, 7th Ohio cavalry
Burbink, A., private...................company A, 7th Ohio cavalry
Cameron, B., private...................company A, 7th Ohio cavalry
Daona, J., private.....................company A, 7th Ohio cavalry
Dugan, W., private.....................company A, 7th Ohio cavalry
Drum, Chas., private...................company A, 7th Ohio cavalry
Fanning, A , private...................company A, 7th Ohio cavalry
Faulkner. J., private..................company A, 7th Ohio cavalry
Foltz, P.., private....................company A, 7th Ohio cavalry
Hill, G., private......................company A, 7th Ohio cavalry
Hoyt, J., private......................company A, 7th Ohio cavalry
McChollister, C., private..............company A, 7th Ohio cavalry

McDaniel, J., private........ ....company A, 7th Ohio cavalry
Morganthater, J., private...........company A, 7th Ohio cavalry
Orbey, F., private...................company A, 7th Ohio cavalry
Robb, R. D., private................company A, 7th Ohio cavalry
Shannard, T. W., private...........company A, 7th Ohio cavalry
Shecrick, S. A., private.............company A, 7th Ohio cavalry
Trenol, I., private....................company A, 7th Ohio cavalry
Woodward, T., private.............company A, 7th Ohio cavalry
Harr, R., private....................company B, 7th Ohio cavalry
Harrison, L. D., private............company B, 7th Ohio cavalry
Maxwell, J. J., private..............company B, 7th Ohio cavalry
Lenyshaw, C., private...............company D, 7th Ohio cavalry
Dickson, A. C., private.............company E, 7th Ohio cavalry
Rieble, W., private ....company E, 7th Ohio cavalry
Weights, A. W., private............company E, 7th Ohio cavalry
Starrett, J. H., corporal......... ...company F, 7th Ohio cavalry
Curley, J. J., private................company F, 7th Ohio cavalry
Sharp. J., private....................company G, 7th Ohio cavalry
Laffin, J., hospital steward.................................... cavalry
Shultz, E., private...................company A, 9th Ohio cavalry
Gram, W., private...................company C, 9th Ohio cavalry
Davis, M. J., sergeant...............company D, 9th Ohio cavalry
Jopp, Jos., corporal..................company D, 9th Ohio cavalry
Hanson, Thos., private.............company E, 9th Ohio cavalry
Certcher, J., private............... ....company F, 9th Ohio cavalry
Molten, W. P., private.............company F, 9th Ohio cavalry
Mankin, T., private...... ....company H, 9th Ohio cavalry
Heager, G., sergeant................company K, 9th Ohio cavalry
Brown, I., private...................company K, 9th Ohio cavalry
Kirker, W., private.................. company K, 9th Ohio cavalry
Wright, F., private..................company M, 9th Ohio cavalry
Taylor, C., private...................company A, 10th Ohio cavalry
Bader, P. H., sergeant..............company B, 10th Ohio cavalry
Jennings, J., private................company B, 10th Ohio cavalry
Morgan, John, private..............company B, 10th Ohio cavalry
Taylor, A., private..................company G, 10th Ohio cavalry
Burnett, J., private............... ..company M, 10th Ohio cavalry
Hunter, A. E.,* private.............company M, 10th Ohio cavalry
Hayner, E., private..................company A, 12th Ohio cavalry
Roberts, C, private.................company E, 12th Ohio cavalry
Roberts, C. A ....company E, 12th Ohio cavalry
Collins, P., corporal.................company K, 12th Ohio cavalry
Clancey, W. F., hospital steward.................. 20th Ohio cavalry
Long, G. M., corporal...............company E, 20th Ohio cavalry
Lawstead, H. P., private...........company E, 20th Ohio cavalry
Bothenbaugh, E., private..........company K, 20th Ohio cavalry
Coup, D., private....................company D, 28th Ohio cavalry

* Lost.

Rinehart, J., sergeant............................... 22d Ohio Battery
Kerns, L., private. ....company C, 1st Tennessee cavalry
Powell, John, private..................company A, 2d Tennessee cavalry
King, Geo. A., private.................company B, 2d Tennessee cavalry
Atchley, T.............................company C, 2d Tennessee cavalry
Meek, R., private......................company C, 2d Tennessee cavalry
Jack, M., private......................company F, 2d Tennessee cavalry
Knight, J., private....................company F, 2d Tennessee cavalry
Culp, A. J., private...................company G, 2d Tennessee cavalry
Lost, D. M., private... ....company G, 2d Tennessee cavalry
Patton, R. E., private.................company K, 3d Tennessee cavalry
Pilington, A., private.................company K, 3d Tennessee cavalry
Cowan, S. A., sergeant.................company A, 3d Tennessee cavalry
Franelin, J. R.,sergeant...............company A, 3d Tennessee cavalry
Rule, A. M., sergeant..................company A, 3d Tennessee cavalry
Bell, F. M., corporal..................company A, 3d Tennessee cavalry
Donnellson, D. D., corporal............company A, 3d Tennessee cavalry
Kidd, Alexander, corporal..............company A, 3d Tennessee cavalry
Rodgers, M. H., corporal...............company A, 3d Tennessee cavalry
Copeland, J., private..................company A, 3d Tennessee cavalry
Curtiss, J. T., private................company A, 3d Tennessee cavalry
Dunlape, S. P., private................company A, 3d Tennessee cavalry
Everett, Jas., private.................company A, 3d Tennessee cavalry
Farmer, A., private....................company A, 3d Tennessee cavalry
Farmer, E., private....................company A, 3d Tennessee cavalry
Farmer, J., private....................company A, 3d Tennessee cavalry
Finley, B. N., private ....company A, 3d Tennessee cavalry
Gamble, M., private....................company A, 3d Tennessee cavalry
Hasser, A., private....................company A, 3d Tennessee cavalry
Hasser, H., private....................company A, 3d Tennessee cavalry
Hausser, L., private...................company A, 3d Tennessee cavalry
Hedrick, D., private...................company A, 3d Tennessee cavalry
Jeffers, Wm , private..................company A, 3d Tennessee cavalry
Keeble, J. H., private.................company A, 3d Tennessee cavalry
Kemble, J. H., private.................company A, 3d Tennessee cavalry
Kidd, J. W., private...................company A, 3d Tennessee cavalry
Kidd, L. M., private............... ....company A, 3d Tennessee cavalry
Osulivan, R. T., private...............company A, 3d Tennessee cavalry
Patty, J. A., private..................company A, 3d Tennessee cavalry
Payne, J. P., private..................company A, 3d Tennessee cavalry
Phelps, John, private..................company A, 3d Tennessee cavalry
Phelps, Wm., private...................company A, 3d Tennessee cavalry
Plumons, T. J., private................company A, 3d Tennessee cavalry
Rale, B., private......................company A, 3d Tennessee cavalry
Russen, B., private....................company A, 3d Tennessee cavalry
Russell, N., private...................company A, 3d Tennessee cavalry
Splann, A., private....................company A, 3d Tennessee cavalry
Thompson, U., private..................company A, 3d Tennessee cavalry

Tipton, C., private_____company A, 3d Tennessee cavalry
Wilson, A., private_____company A, 3d Tennessee cavalry
Vineyard, W. T., private_____company A, 3d Tennessee cavalry
Carver, Wm., sergeant_____company B, 3d Tennessee cavalry
Conellson, J. B., sergeant_____company B, 3d Tennessee cavalry
Davis, G. C., sergeant_____company B, 3d Tennessee cavalry
Davis, J. A., sergeant_____company B, 3d Tennessee cavalry
Tipton, A., sergeant_____company B, 3d Tennessee cavalry
Leise, Adam, corporal _____company B, 3d Tennessee cavalry
McClanihan, D., corporal_____company B, 3d Tennessee cavalry
Millsap, J., corporal_____company B, 3d Tennessee cavalry
Bailey, W., private_____company B, 3d Tennessee cavalry
Brown, M. S., private_____company B, 3d Tennessee cavalry
Brown, T. M., private_____company B, 3d Tennessee cavalry
Byron, J. H., private_____company B, 3d Tennessee cavalry
Carver, J., private_____company B, 3d Tennessee cavalry
Ellenberry, J., private_____company B, 3d Tennessee cavalry
Finger, A., private _____company B, 3d Tennessee cavalry
Hand, John F., private_____company B, 3d Tennessee cavalry
Lackly, J. B , private_____company B, 5d Tennessee cavalry
Leak, Jas., private_____company B, 3d Tennessee cavalry
Milsap, W., private_____company B, 3d Tennessee cavalry
Pinkney, W. C., private_____company B, 3d Tennessee cavalry
Prayer, Jos., private_____company B, 3d Tennessee cavalry
Purger, Wm., private_____company B, 3d Tennessee cavalry
Rodgers, T. W., private_____company B, 3d Tennessee cavalry
Rolen, B. W., private_____company B, 3d Tennessee cavalry
Swaggerty, Wm. S., private_____company B, 3d Tennessee cavalry
Tipton, Jas., private_____company B, 3d Tennessee cavalry
Cortney, J. S., sergeant_____company C, 3d Tennessee cavalry
Dyer, S. A., sergeant_____company C, 3d Tennessee cavalry
Mattock, G., sergeant_____company C, 3d Tennessee cavalry
Wade, W. D., sergeant_____company C, 3d Tennessee cavalry
Brown, P. H., corporal_____company C, 5d Tennessee cavalry
Cortney, W. S., corporal_____company C, 3d Tennessee cavalry
Cox, Jesse, corporal_____company C, 3d Tennessee cavalry
Lutrell, W., corporal_____company C, 3d Tennessee cavalry
McPhail, D. M., corporal_____company C, 3d Tennessee cavalry
Shortz, J. W., corporal_____company C, 3d Tennessee cavalry
Varnell, A. P., corporal_____company C, 3d Tennessee cavalry
Wade, J. W., corporal_____company C, 3d Tennessee cavalry
Bishop, John, private_____company C, 3d Tennessee cavalry
Bishop, W., private_____company C, 3d Tennessee cavalry
Brandon, Jno., private_____company C, 3d Tennessee cavalry
Dickerson, J., private_____company C, 3d Tennessee cavalry
Golden, J., private_____company C, 3d Tennessee cavalry
Graham, L., private_____company C, 3d Tennessee cavalry
Hickman, B., private_____company C, 3d Tennessee cavalry

Hoback, G., private................company C, 3d Tennessee cavalry
Kennedy, G. W., private............company C, 3d Tennessee cavalry
Kinsha, G. S., private.. ....company C, 3d Tennessee cavalry
Mann, W. S., private...............company C, 3d Tennessee cavalry
McPhail, B., private...............company C, 3d Tennessee cavalry
Mills, J. F., private...............company C, 3d Tennessee cavalry
Myers, J., private.................company C, 3d Tennessee cavalry
Neilor, W. N., private.............company C, 3d Tennessee cavalry
Newman, G., private...............company C, 3d Tennessee cavalry
Palmer, W. N., private.............company C, 3d Tennessee cavalry
Rease, L., private.................company C, 3d Tennessee cavalry
Richter, H., private...............company C, 3d Tennessee cavalry
Riddle, J. R., private.............company C, 3d Tennessee cavalry
Robinson, Jas., private............ company C, 3d Tennessee cavalry
Ronimes, L., private...............company C, 3d Tennessee cavalry
Russell, O., private...............company C, 3d Tennessee cavalry
Scott, Jas., private...............company C, 3d Tennessee cavalry
Stroud, J. N., private.............company C, 3d Tennessee cavalry
Trobaugh, I., private..............company C, 3d Tennessee cavalry
Wood, J. E., private...............company C, 3d Tennessee cavalry
Wood, L., private..................company C, 3d Tennessee cavalry
Wood, Jno., private................company C, 3d Tennessee cavalry
Harin, W., sergeant................company D, 3d Tennessee cavalry
Hines, O. E., sergeant.............company D, 3d Tennessee cavalry
Hooper, J. H., sergeant...... ....company D, 3d Tennessee cavalry
Mansfield, W. S., sergeant......... ....company D, 3d Tennessee cavalry
Maxwell, G. W., sergeant...........company D, 3d Tennessee cavalry
Douglass, J. E., corporal...........company D, 3d Tennessee cavalry
Elsey, R. M., corporal..............company D, 3d Tennessee cavalry
Harris, Wm., corporal..............company D, 3d Tennessee cavalry
Nichols, D., corporal...............company D, 3d Tennessee cavalry
Strickley, M., corporal.............company D, 3d Tennessee cavalry
Wadell, S. M., corporal.............company D, 3d Tennessee cavalry
Demman, T., private...............company D, 3d Tennessee cavalry
Fergeson, J. H., private............company D, 3d Tennessee cavalry
Haffager, J. W., private............company D, 3d Tennessee cavlary
Henry, J. W., private..............company D, 3d Tennessee cavalry
Long, A., private..................company D, 3d Tennessee cavalry
Long, John, private............ .....company D, 3d Tennessee cavalry
Pierce, R. M., private ....company D, 3d Tennessee cavalry
Saylor, John, private ....company D, 3d Tennessee cavalry
Smith, W. D., private..............company D, 3d Tennessee cavalry
Kidd, James, sergeant..............company E, 3d Tennessee cavalry
Landers, D., sergeant..............company E, 3d Tennessee cavalry
Rice, John, sergeant...............company E, 3d Tennessee cavalry
Anderson, Jas., corporal............company E, 3d Tennessee cavalry
Griffin, H., corporal...............company E, 3d Tennessee cavalry
Johnson, J. M., corporal............company E, 3d Tennessee cavalry

Meinsel, corporal................company E, 3d Tennessee cavalry
Miller, J. W., corporal................company E, 3d Tennessee cavalry
Swaggerty, S., corporal................company E, 3d Tennessee cavalry
Way, M. V., corporal................company E, 3d Tennessee cavalry
Whittenberger, D. A., corporal.....company E, 3d Tennessee cavalry
Williams, S. H., corporal............company E, 3d Tennessee cavalry
Baker, W. A., corporal.... ....company E, 3d Tennessee cavalry
Basley, W. J., corporal................company E, 3d Tennessee cavalry
Bennett, E. M., corporal............company E, 3d Tennessee cavalry
Burnette, O. H., corporal............company E, 3d Tennessee cavalry
Crusoe, Wm., R., corporal..........company E, 3d Tennessee cavalry
Hamilton, R. N., corporal..........company E, 3d Tennessee cavalry
Henderson, J. C., corporal..........company E, 3d Tennessee cavalry
Hicks, J. H., corporal................company E, 3d Tennessee cavalry
Hines, Joseph, corporal..............company E, 3d Tennessee cavalry
Murphy, E. A., corporal............company E, 3d Tennessee cavalry
Murphy, J. M., corporal ....company E, 3d Tennessee cavalry
Ottinger, M., corporal................company E, 3d Tennessee cavalry
Simpson, I. H., corporal............company E, 3d Tennessee cavalry
Thomas, Marion, corporal..........company E, 3d Tennessee cavalry
Allen, F. J., sergeant................company F, 3d Tennessee cavalry
Bailey, R. M., sergeant ....company F, 3d Tennessee cavalry
Hamilton, H. C., * sergeant........company F, 3d Tennessee cavalry
Lee, E., sergeant......................company F, 3d Tennessee cavalry
Estes, J., corporal....................company F, 3d Tennessee cavalry
Bogert, C. H., private...............company F, 3d Tennessee cavalry
Bogert, S. F., private................company F, 3d Tennessee cavalry
Bookout, J. L., private..............company F, 3d Tennessee cavalry
Cochran, H., private.................company F, 3d Tennessee cavalry
Collins, J. R., private...............company F, 3d Tennessee cavalry
Conner, G. W., private.............company F, 3d Tennessee cavalry
Doherty, J. M., private.............company F, 3d Tennessee cavalry
Elliott, J. W., private †.............company F, 3d Tennessee cavalry
Fuller, Jas., private..................company F, 3d Tennessee cavalry
Furgerson, W. H., private..........company F, 3d Tennessee cavalry
Howell, E., private...................company F, 3d Tennessee cavalry
Jones, O. C., private.................company F, 3d Tennessee cavalry
Leonard, T. J., private..............company F, 3d Tennessee cavalry
Long, M. B., private.................company F, 3d Tennessee cavalry
Marr, B. L., private.................company F, 3d Tennessee cavalry
McClure, M. D., private............company F, 3d Tennessee cavalry
Milton, Wm., private...............company F, 3d Tennessee cavalry
Mussin, H. M., private ....company F. 3d Tennessee cavalry
Reed, R., private......................company F, 3d Tennessee cavalry
Smith, J. R., private.................company F, 3d Tennessee cavalry
Sprongle, G., private................company F, 3d Tennessee cavalry
Stone, W., private....................company F, 3d Tennessee cavalry

* Probably lost.   † Died next day.

Ursery, J. R., private..............company F, 3d Tennessee cavalry
Whiteman, R., private..............company F, 3d Tennessee cavalry
Williams, N. G., private............company F, 3d Tennessee cavalry
Beard, J. O., sergeant..............company G, 3d Tennessee cavalry
Turner, R., sergeant................company G, 3d Tennessee cavalry
Williams, D. M., corporal...........company G, 3d Tennessee cavalry
Williams, Jesse, corporal...........company G, 3d Tennessee cavalry
Baker, G., private. ....company G, 3d Tennessee cavalry
Baker, Jacob, private...............company G, 3d Tennessee cavalry
Baker, John, private................company G, 3d Tennessee cavalry
Brooks, Joseph, private. ....company G, 3d Tennessee cavalry
Cantrell, Jno., private... ....company G, 3d Tennessee cavalry
Campbell, N. J., private............company G, 3d Tennessee cavalry
Collins, J. H., private.............company G, 3d Tennessee cavalry
Cunningham, Jas., private..........company G, 3d Tennessee cavalry
Curtin, R. A., private..............company G, 3d Tennessee cavalry
Gross, A., private..................company G, 3d Tennessee cavalry
Hamilton, Jas., private.............company G, 3d Tennessee cavalry
Hudson, P., private.................company G, 3d Tennessee cavalry
Humbrick, Jno., private.............company G, 3d Tennessee cavalry
Johnson, W. R., private.............company G, 3d Tennessee cavalry
Lee, Jas., private..................company G, 3d Tennessee cavalry
McClauson, J. M., private...........company G, 3d Tennessee cavalry
Millard, L. R., private.............company G, 3d Tennessee cavalry
Mills, W., private..................company G, 3d Tennessee cavalry
Padyot, B., private.................company G, 3d Tennessee cavalry
Wylers, L., private.................company G, 3d Tennessee cavalry
Walker, D. B., private..............company G, 3d Tennessee cavalry
Brown, M. E., sergeant..............company H, 3d Tennessee cavalry
Evitt, W., sergeant.................company H, 3d Tennessee cavalry
Jones, J, W., sergeant..............company H, 3d Tennessee cavalry
Barnett, A., private................company H, 3d Tennessee cavalry
Cursick, D., private................company H, 3d Tennessee cavalry
Farmer, E., private.................company H, 3d Tennessee cavalry
Farmer, J. O., private....... ....company H, 3d Tennessee cavalry
Farrer, G., private.................company H, 3d Tennessee cavalry
Firrett, Wm., private........... ... ..company H, 3d Tennessee cavalry
Hickox, J. E., private..............company H, 3d Tennessee cavalry
Hessinger, H. P., private...........company H, 3d Tennessee cavalry
Johnson, A., private................company H, 3d Tennessee cavalry
Lopt, J. H., private................company H, 3d Tennessee cavalry
Massey, J. J., private..............company H, 3d Tennessee cavalry
DeAmond, H. H., sergeant...........company I, 3d Tennessee cavalry
Fowler, A., sergeant................company I, 3d Tennessee cavalry
Frazier, J., sergeant...............company I, 3d Tennessee cavalry
Howard, T. A., sergeant.............company I, 3d Tennessee cavalry
Linconfelter, H., sergeant..........company I, 3d Tennessee cavalry
Rhed, P., sergeant..................company I, 3d Tennessee cavalry

Murphy, Jno., corporal..............company I, 3d Tennessee cavalry
Russell, R. T., corporal..............company I, 3d Tennessee cavalry
Atchley, P. A., private......... .....company I, 3d Tennessee cavalry
Atsher, Wm., private................company I, 3d Tennessee cavalry
Bagart, M., private.. ....company I, 3d Tennessee cavalry
Bean, P., private....................company I, 3d Tennessee cavalry
Brock, J. A., private................company I, 3d Tennessee cavalry
Cooper, Rob't., private..............company I, 3d Tennessee cavalry
Crawford, H. P., private.............company I, 3d Tennessee cavalry
Dailey, John, private................company I, 3d Tennessee cavalry
Draper, D. S., private...............company I, 3d Tennessee cavalry
Dunlap, A. B., private..............c mpany I, 3d Tennessee cavalry
Ellison, Thos., private...............company I, 3d Tennessee cavalry
Evans, S. M., private................company I, 3d Tennessee cavalry
Gibson, D., private..................company I, 3d Tennessee cavalry
Hayden, D. A., private...............company I, 3d Tennessee cavalry
Hill, W. S., private..................company I, 3d Tennessee cavalry
Hines, Jas , private..................company I, 3d Tennessee cavalry
Hockney, L., private.................company I, 3d Tennessee cavalry
Johns, W., private...................company I, 3d Tennessee cavalry
Johnson, Jacob, private..............company I, 3d Tennessee cavalry
Kaywood, B. F., private.............company I, 3d Tennessee cavalry
Kirkpatrick, J. R., private...........company I, 3d Tennessee cavalry
Kirkpatrick, W. C., private.........company I, 3d Tennessee cavalry
Linconfelter, G. T., private..........company I, 3d Tennessee cavalry
Lindsay, J. R., private...............company I, 3d Tennessee cavalry
McKann, A., private.................company I, 3d Tennessee cavalry
McTeag, D., private.................company I, 3d Tennessee cavalry
Morrison, G. C., private....... .....company I, 3d Tennessee cavalry
Noe, Wm., private...................company I, 3d Tennessee cavalry
Rodgers, W. J., private..............company I, 3d Tennessee cavalry
Rodgers, J , private..................company I, 3d Tennessee cavalry
Romins, G. R., private.... ....company I, 3d Tennessee cavalry
Romins, S., private..................company I, 3d Tennessee cavalry
Scott, James, private................company I, 3d Tennessee cavalry
Simpson, A. A., private..............company I, 3d Tennessee cavalry
Simpson, J. G., private..............company I, 3d Tennessee cavalry
Stanley, M., private.................company I, 3d Tennessee cavalry
Stevens, Jno., private...............company I, 3d Tennessee cavalry
Sumney, Jas., private...............company I, 3d Tennessee cavalry
Thompson, R., 1st sergeant..........company K, 3d Tennessee cavalry
Wayland, L. A., sergeant............company K, 3d Tennessee cavalry
Caree, Jas., P., corporal.............company K, 3d Tennessee cavalry
Cash, H. W., corporal...............company K, 3d Tennessee cavalry
Rule, I., corporal....................company K, 3d Tennessee cavalry
Allen, David, private................company K, 3d Tennessee cavalry
Battles, I., private..................company K, 3d Tennessee cavalry
Battles, W. F., private..............company K, 3d Tennessee cavalry

Beggett, J. D., private............company K, 3d Tennessee cavalry
Blane, M., private................company K, 3d Tennessee cavalry
Chandler, B., private.............company K, 3d Tennessee cavalry
Davis, E., private................company K, 3d Tennessee cavalry
Davis, Wm., private...............company K, 3d Tennessee cavalry
Dearman, L., private..............company K, 3d Tennessee cavalry
Dearman, Sol., private............company K, 3d Tennessee cavalry
Finger, F., private...............company K, 3d Tennessee cavalry
Hodges, J. W., private............company K, 3d Tennessee cavalry
Kinneman, J. M., private..........company K, 3d Tennessee cavalry
Lansom., G. M., private...........company K, 3d Tennessee cavalry
Leak, Wm., private................company K, 3d Tennessee cavalry
McMurry, R. R., private...........company K, 3d Tennessee cavalry
Ramsey, M., private...............company K, 3d Tennessee cavalry
Reed, Wm., M., private............company K, 3d Tennessee cavalry
Rule, C., private.................company K, 3d Tennessee cavalry
Scroggs, Isaac, private...........company K, 3d Tennessee cavalry
Smith, J. P., private.............company K, 3d Tennessee cavalry
Williams, E., private.............company K, 3d Tennessee cavalry
Knight, J. D., sergeant...........company L, 3d Tennessee cavalry
Mansfield, Z. M., sergeant........company L, 3d Tennessee cavalry
Hurry, J., corporal...............company L, 3d Tennessee cavalry
Jenkins, S., corporal.............company L, 3d Tennessee cavalry
Lemon, L., corporal...............company L, 3d Tennessee cavalry
Montgomery, J. L., corporal.......company L, 3d Tennessee cavalry
Wiggins., N. C., corporal.........company L, 3d Tennessee cavalry
Hancock, W. B., private...........company L, 3d Tennessee cavalry
Hinchy, L. C., private............company L, 3d Tennessee cavalry
Renlan, Thos., private............company L, 3d Tennessee cavalry
Rodgers, Wm., private.............company L, 3d Tennessee cavalry
Robinson, H., private.............company M, 3d Tennessee cavalry
McDowell, Wm., lieutenant.........company A, 4th Tennessee cavalry
Station, Henry, sergeant..........company A, 4th Tennessee cavalry
Dickens, Newton, private..........company A, 4th Tennessee cavalry
Dronsgea, R., private.............company A, 4th Tennessee cavalry
Hastshan, R., private.............company A, 4th Tennessee cavalry
McMurry, W., private..............company A, 4th Tennessee cavalry
Odin, P. H., private..............company A, 4th Tennessee cavalry
Sumner, J. B., private............company A, 4th Tennessee cavalry
Develin, Jas., private............company C, 4th Tennessee cavalry
Norman, J., private...............company H, 4th Tennessee cavalry
Bayless, W., private..............company I, 4th Tennessee cavalry
Thomas, H., private...............company L, 4th Tennessee cavalry
Phelps, O., private...............company L, 5th Tennessee cavalry
Sheton, O. G., private............company E, 5th Tennessee cavalry
Gray, M. L., private..............company G, 6th Tennessee cavalry
Walberton, private................company G, 6th Tennessee cavalry
Derryburg, J. H., private.........company A, 7th Tennessee cavalry

Smith, J., private................company C, 7th Tennessee cavalry
Harover, John, private............company D, 7th Tennessee cavalry
Small, H. J., private......... ....company H, 7th Tennessee cavalry
Campbell, W., private..............company K, 7th Tennessee cavalry
Davenport, J. K., private...........company K, 7th Tennessee cavalry
Montgomery, C., private............company A, 8th Tennessee cavalry
Nevins, L , private...... ....company A, 8th Tennessee cavalry
Minsey, R., private................company B, 8th Tennessee cavalry
Husted, T. D., private.............company C, 11th Tennessee cavalry
White, James, corporal............company D, 11th Tennessee cavalry
Pierce. R., private................company C, 12th Tennessee cavalry
Brownley, J. B., private............company A, 2d Tennessee mt'd. inf.
Emenery, W., private.... ....company A, 2d Tennessee mt'd. inf.
Grier, J. A., private................company A, 2d Tennessee mt'd. inf.
Moffatt, Jas., private..............company C, 2d Tennessee mt'd. inf,
Rease, W., sergeant................company G, 2d Tennessee mt'd. inf.
Anderson, J. F., corporal..... ......company I, 3d Tennessee infantry
Ramsey, J., private...............company I, 3d Tennessee infantry
Foster, H. C., private..............company A, 1st Virginia cavalry
Manner, A., private................company A, 1st Virginia cavalry
Cruddu, W. A., private ....company D, 1st Virginia cavalry
McHenry, Jas., private.............company D, 1st Virginia cavalry
Smith, G. G., private...............company D, 1st Virginia cavalry
Stephens, A., private........ ......company D, 1st Virginia cavalry
Craig, Anthony, private....'........company C, 1st Virginia cavalry
Reeble, C., private................company G, 1st Virginia cavalry
Loy, Geo. C., private..............company I, 1st Virginia cavalry
Stafford, S. D. L., private..........company L, 3d Virginia cavalry
Woodyard, L., private.............company A, 4th Virginia cavalry
Stelle, J. N., private...... ....company C, 5th Virginia cavalry
Lyons, J. H., corporal..............company B, 6th Virginia cavalry
Lawless, E., private................company B, 6th Virginia cavalry
Match, John, private...............company K, 6th Virginia cavalry
Morris, Jas., private................company H, 6th Virginia cavalry
Talmadge, J., private..............company H, 6th Virginia cavalry
Wilson, T. P., private...... ....company H, 6th Virginia cavalry
Hall, J. F., sergeant....... ....company I, 6th Virginia cavalry
Johnson, H., sergeant..............company I, 6th Virginia cavalry
Parker, J. R., corporal.............company I, 6th Virginia cavalry
Tucker, G. W., corporal............company I, 6th Virginia cavalry
Dabney, G., private................company I, 6th Virginia cavalry
Jones, Stephen, private.............company I, 6th Virginia cavalry
Maury, C. R., private..............company I, 6th Virginia cavalry
McDaniel, J. W., private...........company I, 6th Virginia cavalry
McDowell, F. M., private..........company I, 6th Virginia cavalry
Oaley, W., private.................company I, 6th Virginia cavalry
Rhodes, A., private................company I, 6th Virginia cavalry
McEwen, Jas., captain.............company K, 6th Virginia cavalry

Burns, Pat, private................... company K, 6th Virginia cavalry
Elder, J. J., private.................... company K, 6th Virginia cavalry
Hughes, H., private.................... company K, 6th Virginia cavalry
Martin, J. H., private................. company K, 6th Virginia cavalry
McCubber, J. B., private............. company K, 6th Virginia cavalry
Bradley, G., private................... company A, 7th Virginia cavalry
Goodflashler, G. W., private........ company A, 7th Virginia cavalry
Cardeirlle, W. M., private.......... company C, 7th Virginia cavalry
Handorf, Jno., H., corporal......... company F, 7th Virginia cavalry
English, W., private.................. company F, 7th Virginia cavalry
Mass, Jas., private......... .... company F, 7th Virginia cavalry
Ragsdale, Robert, private........... company F, 7th Virginia cavalry
Riley, Jno., private.................... company F, 7th Virginia cavalry
Willhelm, C., private................. company F, 7th Virginia cavalry
Mallaby, M., private.................. company G, 7th Virginia cavalry
Creen, A. W., sergeant............... company L, 7th Virginia cavalry
McKnight, J., private................ company L, 7th Virginia cavalry
Scott, Thos., H., private.............. company L, 7th Virginia cavalry
Roberts, J. R., private................ company L, 7th Virginia cavalry
Mattlinger, J., private............... company F, 10th Virginia cavalry
Barett, J. T., 2d lieutenant........... company A, 12th Virginia cavalry
Monday, J., private................... company K, 12th Virginia cavalry
Gambol, H., private................... company B, 14th Virginia cavalry
Cornell, E., private................... company G, 14th Virginia cavalry
Bartlett, E. M., private.............. company C, 16th Virginia cavalry
Springer, S., private................. company E, 16th Virginia cavalry

Persons Known to have been on Board but Not Reported in the Official List.

Sanders, S. F................................company I, 137th Illinois
Frazee, Martin ....company C, 2d Indiana cavalry
Lee, Asa E...............................company A, 6th Indiana cavalry
Kline, Henry J.........................company G, 9th Indiana cavalry
Mayes, J. H.............................company C, 40th Indiana cavalry
Stewart, Geo. W....................company D, 40th Indiana infantry
Hazellaige, captain.................company K, 40th Indiana
Taylor, Joe., lieutenant.............124th Indiana infantry
May, John.............................137th Indiana cavalry
Williams................................1st Kentucky cavalry
Gambill, Henry.......................company B, 14th Kentucky infantry
Curnsitte, Elisha.....................company G, 14th Kentucky infantry
Hamlin, O. E..........................company E, 2d Michigan cavalry
Johnson, B. F.........................company A, 5th Michigan cavalry
Clarkson, Geo. A....................company H, 5th Michigan cavalry
Norton, Henry........................company B, 8th Michigan cavalry
White, Manly C......................company B, 8th Michigan cavalry
Kinney, John *.......................8th Michigan cavalry
Wendt, Wm..........................company L, 8th Michigan cavalry
Dunsmore, J. W....................company I, 1st Michigan E. and M.
Stevens, Joseph ....company E, 4th Michigan infantry
Hindes, Elias E......................company A, 18th Michigan infantry
Jones, A..............................company B, 18th Michigan infantry
Smith, O. W.........................company B, 13th Michigan infantry
Thayer, C............................company B, 18th Michigan infantry
Porter, W. G........................company C, 18th Michigan infantry
Larkey, Pat *........................company E, 18th Michigan infantry
Hohns, M.............................company F, 18th Michigan infantry
Aldrich, H. C., sergeant...........company G, 18th Michigan infantry
West, C. A............................company G, 18th Michigan infantry
Nicholas, C..........................company H, 18th Michigan infantry
Hampton, E..........................company I, 18th Michigan infantry
Upton, H. H.........................company I, 18th Michigan infantry
Hinds, T. J...........................company K, 18th Michigan infantry
Mann, Jas. H........................company K, 18th Michigan infantry
Metta, A. R. †......................company K, 18th Michigan infantry
Russell, Jas..........................company K, 18th Michigan infantry
Shettleroe, Isadore.................company K, 18th Michigan infantry
Stremp, Geo.........................company K, 18th Michigan infantry

* Lost.   † Killed.

Henks, T. W., captain.............. 4th Missouri cavalry
Brown, A. C......................company I, 2d Ohio infantry
Lewis, lieutenant....................3d Ohio cavalry
Barnes, Wm ....company H, 22d Ohio infantry
Kearns, John.......................company F, 40th Ohio infantry
Oxley, Stewart .... company I, 51st Ohio infantry
Gregory, W. W.................. ......company C, 55th Ohio infantry
Friesner, W. S......................company K, 58th Ohio infantry
Boor, Wm , private................company D, 64th Ohio infantry
Norris, Albert......................company A, 76th Ohio infantry
Davis, J. W., lieutenant............77th Ohio infantry
Yeisley, Wm........................company E, 102d Ohio infantry
Sheafer, I. N.......................company E, 115th Oh'o infantry
Zazier, J. P.......................company F, 115th Ohio infantry
Morgan, L. G.......................company D, 121st Ohio infantry
Falderman, Benj....................company K, 121st Ohio infantry
Fisher, Geo........................company K, 121st Ohio infantry
Gaston, G. M.......................company K, 121st Ohio infantry
Green, Seth........................company K, 121st Ohio infantry
Trent, Rob't A , sergeant...........company B, 1st Tennessee cavalry
Carver, Wm........................company B, 3d Tennessee cavalry
Hamilton, John.....................company F, 3d Tennessee cavalry
Hamilton, R. N....................company F, 3d Tennessee cavalry
Hodges, Wiley J. ....company F, 3d Tennessee cavalry
Jones, H. C., corporal...............company F, 3d Tennessee cavalry
Atchley, P. L.......................company K, 3d Tennessee cavalry
Pangle, Thos. ... .company K, 3d Tennessee cavalry
Elliott, J. W , captain................company F, 44th U. S. C. T.

Name, Company, Regiment, and Present Postoffice, as far as Known, of those Living.

Abadaska, C. W., company F, 18th Michigan infantry, Waldron, Mich.
Aldrich, H. C., * company G, 18th Michigan infantry.
Allen, Daniel, company K, 3d Tennessee cavalry, Allensville, Tenn.
Allison, Hiram, company G, 9th Indiana cavalry, Muncie, Ind.
Anderson, Geo., company F, 102d Ohio infantry, Seville, Ohio.
Anderson, James, company E, 3d Tennessee cavalry, Knoxville, Tenn.
Atchley, P. L., company K, 3d Tennessee cavalry, Trotter's Store, Tenn.
Atchley, Thos., company M, 3d Tennessee cavalry, Catlettsburgh, Tenn.
Baggett, J. D., Stell's Depot, Alabama.
Baker, Murry S., company D, 4th Michigan, Williamston, Mich.
Bardon, Otto, company H, 102d Ohio infantry, Wooster, Ohio.
Barker, Frank, company K, 2d Michigan cavalry, Brockway, Mich.
Barnes, Wm., company A, 63d Ohio infantry, Nelsonville, Ohio.
Battles, W. F., Slate, Alabama.
Bement, Geo., company F, 25th Michigan infantry, Adamsville, Mich.
Berry, C. D., company I, 20th Michigan infantry, Tekonsha, Mich.
Boor, Wm.. company D, 64th Ohio infantry, Sandusky, Ohio.
Bracken, Wm. D., company D, 88th United States Colored Troops infantry, Putnam, Ill.
Bradley, C. H., company M, 3d Ohio cavalry, Ohio.
Brady, Jas. K., company B, 64th Ohio infantry, Morral, Ohio.
Bringman, J., company D, 102d Ohio infantry, Enon Valley, Pa.
Brown, A. C., company I, 2d Ohio infantry, Canon City, Col.
Brown, Jas., company F, 3d Tennessee cavalry, Boyds Creek, Tenn.
Brummer, Michael, company C, 59th Ohio infantry, Georgetown, Ohio.
Byerly, W. J., company E, 3d Ohio infantry, Ebenezer, Tenn.
Carmack, Thos., company A, 64th Ohio infantry, Cleveland, Ohio.
Carver, Wm., company B, 3d Tennessee cavalry, 612 east 3d st, Maysville, Ky.
Cassel, Abraham, company B, 21st Ohio infantry, McComb, Ohio.
Cheff, S. D., company G, 6th Kentucky cavalry, Lebanon, Kan.
Christine, W. H., company H, 102d Ohio infantry, 319 east Spring st, Columbus, Ohio.
Clapsaddle, Frank, company F, 115th Ohio infantry, Marlboro, Ohio.
Clarkson, G. A., company H, 5th Michigan, Oakwood Park, Mich.
Clinger, G. M., company E, 16th Kentucky infantry, Maysville, Ky.
Cook, J. S., company C, 115th Ohio infantry, Kent, Ohio.
Cornell, A. W., company B, 18th Michigan infantry, Rome Center, Mich.
Conk, W. A., Lowe, Kansas.
Cowen, Samuel, company A, 3d Tennessee cavalry, Marysville, Tenn.

* Dead.

Crawford, Ezra, company A, 102d Ohio infantry, Shreve, Ohio.

Cranmer, A. O., company B, 64th Ohio infantry, Marion, Ohio.

Crisp, Wm., company D, 18th Michigan, Silver Creek, Neb.

Curtis, Jas., company A, 3d Tennessee cavalry, Marysville, Tenn.

Darrow, Marvin, 18th Michigan infantry, Blissfield, Mich.

Davis, B. G., company L, 7th Kentucky cavalry, Covington, Ky.

Davis, John, company D, 100th Ohio infantry, Defiance, Ohio.

Davis, John C., company B, 3d Tennessee cavalry, Knoxville, Tenn.

Davis, John G., company K, 65th Ohio infantry, New Baltimore, Ohio.

Dawson, Geo , Whitehall, Ill.

Day, R. E., Raymond City, Ill.

Deerman, L. A., company K, 3d Tennessee cavalry, Steels Depot, Ala.

Demoss, John, Warsaw, Ohio.

Douglass, James E., Trotters Store, Tenn.

Duesler, C. W., Donovan, Ill.

Dunlape, Samuel P., company B, 3d Tennessee cavalry, Farmington, Ark.

Dunsmore, J. W., company I, 1st Michigan Engineers and Mechanics, Harrison, Mich.

Eddleman, David, company I, 64th Ohio infantry, Canton, Ohio.

Elder, W. H., company H, 58th, Bremen, Ohio.

Elliott, J. W., company E, 10th Indiana infantry, and company F, 44th United States Colored Troops infantry, Arab, Ala.

Elliott, J. T., 2d lieutenant company C, 124th regiment Indiana Volunteer Infantry, 84 east Market street, Indianapolis, Ind.

Engle, John, company B, 21st, Bentonridge, Ohio.

Everhart, John, Akron, Ohio.

Everman, Nathan, company F, 40th Indiana infantry, Lebanon, Ind.

Falderman, B., company K, 102d Ohio infantry, Indianapolis, Ind.

Farmer, Elias, company A, 3d Tennessee cavalry, Marysville, Tenn.

Fast, W. A., Sedalia, Mo.

Fast, W. N., company K, 102d Ohio infantry, Napoleon, Ohio.

Fies, Wm., company B, 64th Ohio infantry, Marion, Ohio.

Fogle, John, company F, 115th Ohio infantry, Hays City, Kans.

Foglesang, N., company A, 18th Michigan infantry, Prattsville, Mich.

Frazee, Martin, company C, 2d Indiana cavalry, 1209 New Main street, Louisville, Ky.

Frederick, G. H., company D, 7th Indiana cavalry, Fort Wayne, Ind.

Furnia, S. D., Erie, Mich.

Friesner, W. S., company K, 58th Ohio infantry, Logan, Ohio.

Gambill, H., company B, 14th Kentucky infantry, Blaine, Ky.

Garber, Daniel, company E, 102d Ohio infantry, Butler, Ohio.

Gaston, Stephen M., company K, 9th Indiana cavalry, 523 Magnolia street, Sherman, Texas.

Gibson, David, company I, 3d Tennessee cavalry, Swuinill, Tenn.

Goodrich, W. N., company E, 18th Michigan infantry, Menominee, Mich.

Graham, John, Dayton, Ohio.

Greenfield, R. I., Ontario, Ohio.
Gregory, N. W., company C, 55th Ohio infantry, Lead City, South Dak.
Guard, John W., company K, 7th Indiana cavalry, Elwood, Ind.
Haines, S. C., company G, 40th Indiana infantry, Romney, Ind.
Hales, O. P., company G, 18th Michigan infantry, Mosherville, Mich.
Hamblin, O. E., company E, 2d Michigan cavalry, Pulaski, Mich.
Hamilton, R. N., company F, 3d Tennessee cavalry, Van Alstyne, Texas·
Hana, H. H., company G, 121st Indiana cavalry, Dayton, Ohio.
Harberth, C. H., company C, 115th Ohio infantry, Cleveland, Ohio.
Harmon, Daniel, company K, 18th Michigan infantry, Defiance, Ohio.
Harris, John, Cuyahoga Falls, Ohio.
Hatch, A. N., company F, 1st Michigan, Ellington, Mich.
Hawk, Marion, company D, 3d Ohio cavalry, Fremont, Ohio.
Helminger, J., company B, 50th Ohio infantry, New Sharon, Iowa
Hershey, M. B., company A, 29th Michigan infantry, Hillsdale, Mich.
Hill, Wm. S., company L, 3d Tennessee cavalry, Rockford, Tenn.
Hines, Joseph, company L, 3d Tennessee cavalry, Trundles X Roads,
    Tenn.
Hindes, E. E., company A, 18th Michigan infantry, Clayton, Mich.
Hinson, Thos., company E, 9th Ohio cavalry, Steubenville, Ohio.
Hodges, Wiley, company I, 3d Tennessee cavalry.
Horn, P. L., company I, 102d Ohio Infantry, Wooster, Ohio.
Horner, Ira B., company K, 65th Ohio infantry, Weston, Ohio.
Horner, Jacob, company A, 102d Ohio infantry, Nashville, Ohio.
Huffsey, John, 49th Ohio infantry, Tiffin, Ohio.
Huld, W. A., company A, 64th Ohio infantry, Armerdale, Kansas.
Hulit, Geo., 104th Ohio infantry, Kent, Ohio.
Humphrey, W. C., company B, 50th Ohio infantry, Middletown, Ohio.
James, John, Akron, Ohio.
James, John H., company F, 115th Ohio infantry, 707 North Howard
    street, Akron, Ohio.
Johnson, G. J., company A, 18th Michigan infantry, Medina, Mich.
Johnson, James M., company E, 3d Tennessee cavalry, Knoxville, Tenn.
Johnson, Lewis, company G, 9th Indiana cavalry, Cowan, Ind.
Johnston, B. F., company A, 5th Michigan cavalry, Almont, Mich.
Jones, Arthur A., company C, 115th Ohio infantry, Parkman, Ohio.
Jones, Dock, Shady Grove, Tenn.
Jones, J. W., company E, 18th Michigan infantry, Pennfield, N. Y.
Jones, H. C , company F, 3d Tennessee cavalry, Coytee, Tenn.
Karns, Nicholas, company B, 18th Ohio infantry, Plain City, Ohio.
Kennedy, E. J., company K, 64th Ohio infantry, Berea, Ohio.
Kibble, Pleasant, company H, 3d Tennessee cavalry, Marysville, Tenn.
Kidd, Alexander, company A, 3d Tennessee cavalry, Marysville, Tenn.
Kidd, L. M., company A, 3d Tennessee cavalry, Marysville, Tenn.
Kimberlin, J. H., McCordsville, Ind.
Kimmel, Rinaldo, * company E, 21st Ohio infantry.
King, A. W., company D, 100th Ohio infantry, Defiance, Ohio.

* Dead.

King, Geo. A., company B, 2d Tennessee cavalry, Tong, Blount county, Tenn.
Kinser, Hugh, company E, 50th Ohio infantry, Albion, Neb.
Kline, Henry J., company G, 9th Indiana cavalry, Mill Grove, Ind.
Kochenderfer, John H., company D, 102d Ohio infantry, Galion, Ohio.
Kurtz, John J., company F, 7th Ohio cavalry, Waggoner's Ripple, Ohio.
Lahue, C. J., company D, 13th Indiana cavalry, Great Bend, Kansas.
Landon, Simeon, company D, 64th Ohio infantry,
Langley, James, company K, 3d Tennessee cavalry, Shook's P. O., Tenn.
Leake, Adam, company A, 3d Tennessee cavalry, Knoxville, Tenn.
Lease, A. G., company B, 3d Tennessee cavalry, Union Grove, Ind.
Lee, Wesley, company A, 102d Ohio infantry, Winston, Mo.
Lee, A. E , company A, 71st Indiana cavalry, Tulare, Cal.
Lee, J. W., company A., 102d Ohio infantry, Memphis, Tenn.
Lesley, John, company K, 3d Tennessee cavalry, Carlock, Tenn.
Leisure, A. J., company A, 7th Ohio cavalry, Cincinnati, Ohio.
Lewis, John B., company K, 9th Indiana infantry, Gallatin, Mo.
Ligfetter, company I, 3d Tennessee cavalry, Rockford, Tenn.
Lingenfelter, Thos., Miser, Tenn.
Lingenfelter, H., Rockford, Tenn.
Linkenfelter, T , company A, 3d Tennessee cavalry, Marysville, Tenn.
Long, Robert, company D, 65th Ohio infantry, Cardington Ohio.
Love, Thos., gunboat Essex, Clayton, Mich.
Luganbeal, D. W., company F, 135th Ohio infantry, Perryton, Ohio.
Lyborger, P. A., company L, 2d Michigan cavalry, Adamsville, Mich.
Mackelroy, J.. Delaware, Ohio.
Madden, W. P., company I, 44th Ohio infantry, Xenia, Ohio.
Maes, Jotham, company D, 47th Ohio infantry, New Boston, Mich.
Mahoney, Jerry, company I, 2d Michigan cavalry.
Manier, Darius, LaCarne, Ohio.
Martin, Jesse, company D, 35th Indiana infantry, Mt. Pleasant, Ohio.
Mayes, J. H., company H, 40th Indiana infantry, Carson, Ind.
Maxman, Marshall, company A, 2d Michigan, Bay City Mich.
McClanahan, D. B., company B, 3d Tennessee cavalry, Marysville, Tenn.
McCord, G. B., company F, 111th Ohio infantry, Hanford, Cal.
McCrory, L. W., company A, 100th Ohio infantry, Mungen, Ohio.
McDaniel, G. M., 10th Indiana cavalry, Cincinnati, Ohio.
McFarland, W. A., company A, 42d Indiana infantry, Evansville, Ind.
McIntosh, E. W., company E, 14th Illinois infantry, Decatur, Ill.
McLeod, Daniel, company F, 18th Illinois infantry, 818 Market street, St. Louis, Mo.
McMurry, Bart, company B, 3d Tennessee cavalry, Marysville, Tenn.
McNeal, David, company H, 7th Michigan cavalry, Irving, Kansas.
Millsaps, James, company B, 3d Tennessee cavalry, Marysville, Tenn.
Millsaps, J. W., company B, 3d Tennessee cavalry, Marysville, Tenn.
Millsaps, Wm., company B, 3d Tennessee cavalry, Marysville, Tenn.
Moore, James, Dayton, Ohio.
Morgan, L. G., company B, 21st Ohio infantry, 119 Frazer street, Findlay, Ohio.

Moulton, Dallas, Brimfield, Ohio.

Mourning, A. J., company D, 11th Illinois cavalry, Toledo, Ohio.

Nevins, J. F., company F, 18th Michigan infantry, Frontier, Mich.

Nickerson, Henry, Circleville, Ohio.

Nihart, A., company G, 90th Ohio infantry, Bolivar, Mo.

Niles, A. J., Spring Creek, Kansas.

Nisley, C. M., company D, 40th Indiana, 36 Elizabeth street, LaFayette, Ind.

Norcutt, J. W., company D, 18th Michigan infantry, Campbell, Mich.

Norris, Albert, company A, 76th Ohio infantry, Union Station, Ohio.

Norris, J. B., company B, 51st Ohio infantry, Randolph, Neb.

Norton, J. E., company A, 5th Michigan cavalry, 62 Duffield street, Detroit, Mich.

Norton, Wm. H., company C, 115th Ohio infantry, Hudson, Ohio.

Oxley, Stewart, company I, 51st Ohio infantry, Burr Oak, Iowa.

Pangle, Thos., company K, 3d Tennessee cavalry, New Madrid, Mo.

Patterson, J. S., company F, 104th Ohio cavalry.

Peachin, Edward, cor. 4th and South streets, Lata, Ind.

Peacock, Wm. H., company G, 9th Indiana cavalry, Cowan, Ind.

Perkins, F. M., company E, 2d Michigan cavalry, Parkersburg, Iowa.

Phelps, J. M., company A, 3d Tennessee cavalry, Knoxville, Tenn.

Phillips, Wm.

Pickens, Saul, company A, 3d Tennessee cavalry, Knoxville, Tenn.

Porter, W. G., company C, 18th Michigan infantry, Weston, Mich.

Potter, W. Scott, company G, 54th Ohio infantry, Dayton, Ohio.

Poupard, Samuel, Vienna, Mich.

Prangle, J. R., company K, 3d Tennessee cavalry, New Madrid, Mo.

Prindle, R. M., Indianapolis, Ind.

Potter, S. R., company B, 102d Ohio infantry, Mansfield, Ohio.

Randebaugh, G. H., company K, 65th Ohio infantry, Lindsay, Ohio.

Ray, Christian, company F, 50th Ohio, Greenville, Ohio.

Ray, Patson, company I, 3d Tennessee cavalry, Knoxville, Tenn.

Rhodes, Abraham, company I, 6th Kentucky cavalry, Kellerton, Iowa.

Riley, Wm., Oakland, Ind.

Robinson, G. F., company C., 2d Michigan cavalry, Owosso, Mich.

Roselot, Peter F., company E, 50th Ohio infantry, Mowrystown, Ohio.

Ross, Wm., company A, 102d Ohio infantry, Big Prairie, Ohio.

Rule, C., company K, 3d Tennessee cavalry, New Knob Creek, Tenn.

Rule, Robert, company A, 3d Tennessee cavalry, Rockford, Tenn.

Rush, J. W., company L, 3d Ohio cavalry, Larned, Kansas.

Russell, Adam, company C, 3d Tennessee cavalry, Homestead, Kansas.

Russell, Calvin, company A, 3d Tennessee cavalry, Marysville, Tenn.

Russell, Nick, company A, 3d Tennessee cavalry, Marysville, Tenn.

Russell, O. C., company C, 3d Tennessee cavalry, Morgantown, Tenn.

Rutman, Adam, company F, 115th Ohio Volunteer infantry, Akron, Ohio.

Saffen, Jas., Carthage, Ohio.

Sanders, Dr. S. F., company I, 137th Illinois, Holdredge, Neb.

Sangley, James M., company K, 3d Tennessee cavalry, Shooles, Tenn.

Saunders, Ignatius, company F, 102d Ohio infantry, Auburndale, Ohio.

Sayer, S. K., Mt. Union, Iowa.

Sayler, John, Strawberry Plains, Tenn.

Schievesmyre, L., company A, 32d Indiana infantry, Fort Wayne, Ind.

Schmutz, G. L., company I, 102d Ohio infantry, Wooster, Ohio.

Seabury, C. G., company B, 8th Michigan cavalry, Coloma, Mich.

Sheaffer, I. N., company E, 115th Ohio infantry, Canton, Ohio.

Sharp, Thos., company F, 2d Wisconsin cavalry, Dunleith, W. Va.

Shaul, W. R., company E, 95th Ohio infantry, Cable, Ohio.

Shettleroe, Isadore, company K, 18th Michigan infantry, Toledo, Ohio.

Shettleroe, Samuel, Vienna, Mich.

Shields, Peyton, company D, 31st Ohio infantry, Mt. Gilead, Ohio.

Shoemaker, A., company E, 72d Ohio infantry, Carroll, Ohio.

Shummard, W. T., company A, 7th Ohio cavalry, Brazilton, Kansas.

Simpson, J. H , company I, 3d Tennessee cavalry, Knoxville, Tenn.

Slick, J. L., company A, 18th Michigan infantry, Lambertsville, Mich.

Smith, Com., company F, 8th Michigan infantry, Remus, Mich.

Smith, G. F., Jonesville, Mich.

Smith, Truman, company B, 8th Michigan cavalry, Grand Rapids, Mich.

Solenborger, G. W., company A, 58th Ohio infantry, Sugar Grove, Ohio.

Sumerville, Perry, company K, 41st Indiana cavalry, Brazil, Ind.

Sorgen, E., company G, 4th Ohio infantry, Kenton, Ohio.

Soulier, Samuel, company K, 18th Michigan infantry, Willow Lake, Dak.

Spafford, Harrison, company D, 102d Ohio infantry, Hayesville, Ohio.

Sprinkle, M. H., company K, 102d Ohio infantry, Eaton Rapids, Mich.

Squire, E. J , company D, 101st Ohio infantry, Monroeville, Ohio.

Stevens, Joseph, company B, 1st Michigan sharpshooters, East Buffalo, New York.

Stewart, G. W., company D, 40th Indiana infantry, Wellington, Kan.

Strasser, Louis, company K, 2d Michigan cavalry, Columbus, Ohio.

Stubberfield, S., company F, 18th Michigan infantry, Waldron, Mich.

Sutenbaker, L., company D, 8th Michigan cavalry, St. Charles, Mich.

Swaggarty, Vance, 3d Tennessee cavalry, Linton, Ind.

Swain, E. H., Muncie, Ind.

Taggart. H. A., Tiffin, Ohio.

Talentine, J., Ashland, Ohio.

Thayer, Wm., company C, 18th Michigan infantry, Fairfield, Mich.

Thomas, Marion, company E, 3d Tennessee cavalry, Marysville, Tenn.

Thompson, J. B., company H, 6th Kentucky cavalry, St. Mary's, Ky.

Thompson, Mart., company I, 3d Tennessee cavalry, Marysville, Tenn.

Thompson, J. W., Fishers Switch, Ind.

Thorn, Thos. J., La Fayette, Ind.

Thrasher, S. J., company G, 6th Kentucky cavalry, Browns X Roads, Ky.

Tift, H., Cuyahoga Falls, Ohio.

54

Tipton, C. C., company B, 3d Tennessee cavalry, Trundle's X Roads, Tenn.

Tracy, Wilson S., company H, 102d Ohio infantry, Fredericksburg, Ohio.

Trent, R. A., company B, 1st Tennessee cavalry, Mitchburg, Tenn.

Van Fleet, H. C., company I, 14th Ohio infantry, Moncloon, Ohio.

Van Nuys, Isaac, company D, 57th Indiana infantry, Bethel, Ind.

Van Scayce, J. W., company A, 64th Ohio infantry, Luray, Kan.

Van Vlack, Alonzo, company F, 18th Michigan infantry, Cambria, Mich.

Varnell, Albert, company I, 3d Tennessee cavalry, New Knob Ck, Tenn.

Vergin, John, New Britton, Ind.

Walker, J. L., company B, 50th Ohio infantry, Hamilton, Ohio.

Wallace, H. B., company A, 124th Ohio infantry, Brooklyn Village, Ohio.

Waltermier, J. J., company B, 57th Ohio infantry, Fostoria, Ohio.

Warner, W. C., company B, 9th Indiana cavalry, Wellington, Kan.

Watts, G. W., company E, 97th Ohio infantry, Sonora, Ohio.

Weicard, A. B., company K, 18th Michigan infantry, North Toledo, Ohio.

Wendt, Wm., company L, 8th Michigan cavalry, Capac, Mich.

Whetmore, Al., company C, 115th Ohio infantry, Cuyahoga Falls, Ohio.

White, Geo., company B, 8th Michigan cavalry, Cincinnati, Ohio.

White, Manly C., company B, 8th Michigan cavalry, Hartford, Mich.

Williams, N. S., company B, 5th Indiana cavalry, Chester, Ind.

Williams, W. H., company F, 18th Michigan infantry, Jonesville, Mich.

Wilson, R. S., company F, 95th Ohio infantry, Winfield, Kan.

Wismire, Abraham, Mifflin, Ohio.

Wood, Henry, company D, 18th Michigan infantry, Air Line Junction, Ohio.

Wright, Francis, company B, 18th Michigan infantry, Adrian, Mich.

Young, G. N., company A, 95th Ohio infantry, Evans, Col.

Zacharias, A. K., 7th Michigan infantry, Ypsilanti, Mich.

Zaizer, J. P., company F, 115th Ohio infantry, Canton, Ohio.

Zimmerman, J., Altamont, Ill.